THE NEW ETIQUETTE

THE NEW ETIQUETTE

Real Manners for Real People in Real Situations— An A-to-Z Guide

MARJABELLE YOUNG STEWART

ILLUSTRATIONS BY LAUREN JARRETT

ST. MARTIN'S PRESS, INC.

New York

Design by Claire B. Counihan

Library of Congress Cataloging in Publication Data

Stewart, Marjabelle Young.
   The new etiquette.

   1. Etiquette.   I. Title.
BJ1853.S874   1987   395   86-27884
ISBN 0-312-00164-9

First Edition

10   9   8   7   6   5   4   3   2   1

For Erin Marjabelle Anderson,
with love

Acknowledgments

I thank my good friend Marian Faux for her excellent writing skills and for making this manuscript a reality. I thank my editor, Barbara Anderson, for her invaluable assistance, enthusiasm, and careful attention to every detail and every word in this book. And a special thank-you to my agent, Dominick Abel, for his constant support, love, and encouragement.

Introduction

Manners, I have always firmly believed, are primarily a matter of treating others well, treating them, to paraphrase the Golden Rule, as you yourself would like to be treated. Every etiquette book I have ever written is predicated on this simple principle. This book is no exception. Beyond this basic principle, though, there are specific rules and guidelines that help you know how to treat others kindly. I have attempted to compile in this book all these guidelines and rules for gracious living.

I have further put these rules and guidelines into a format that is unusual for an etiquette book. This is, to my knowledge, the first such book of its kind—an encyclopedia of manners.

The idea for this book came out of my own reading and from talking to people about what they wanted and needed in a basic etiquette book. As I perused my own extensive library of etiquette books, I began to realize that many of them were not as useful as they might be. Information about wedding invitations, to take just one example, might be located in two or three different places. Another problem was the amount of information a person had to read to find the one nugget of information that he or she sought. Ten pages might be devoted to a dinner party, and buried somewhere in those pages was the position of the dessert fork. I have devoted just as many pages to dinner parties, but I have included a separate entry on forks. You need only look up "Fork," and go right to the subtitle "Dessert Fork" to learn exactly where a dessert fork goes.

As I traveled the country extensively, giving lectures and making television appearances, I always took time to talk to people about how they really lived, how they entertained, how they organized the ceremonial events in their lives, and about their local customs.

I learned two things talking to my readers. The first is that while people are hungry for a return to gracious living and eager to do what is right in most social situations, they are also bound by local custom and by the need for manners that are practical. It is fine for me to tell a bride that the proper way of seating wedding guests is to seat her relatives on one side and her groom's on another. But if fifty of her family members have come to the wedding because it is in her hometown and only five of his family are there, it becomes a practical as well as a tactful solution to seat people, regardless of the familial affiliation, on both sides of the sanctuary. I learned, therefore, and have chosen to write about practical, everyday manners—situations and events the way they are likely to happen as well as the way they ought to happen.

The second thing I learned is that people live fast-paced lives. They need an etiquette book that they can use conveniently and quickly. That was another reason I came up with the idea of an encyclopedia rather than just another straightforward book of manners.

In *The New Etiquette*, you can look up only the topic you want to read about, and you can read only about that topic, if you wish. Of course, the great lure of etiquette books is that they are fun simply to browse through, and I hope you find yourself reading one entry . . . and another . . . and still another. But the topics are all here—over five hundred of them—describing how to behave in every conceivable situation life is likely to present to you.

I have attempted to accomplish several things in writing this book. First, I have tried to shape it to modern lives. I am aware that etiquette relaxed enormously in the Sixties and has only recently begun a swing back to more formality. Frankly, some of the frippery that got lost in the Sixties deserves to stay lost. It was never important whether a man or a woman extended a hand first to greet someone. It does matter, however, that we are gracious enough to stand up to meet another person.

As for entertaining, much has changed here, too. While we are entertaining more graciously than ever before, we are not necessarily entertaining more formally. We are also much more public creatures than we were even a few years ago. We are as likely to plan a dinner in a restaurant with friends as to invite our friends into our home for dinner. I have taken this into account as I researched and wrote this book. I have, for example, dispensed with the finger bowl that used to appear at formal dinners but which is rarely encountered these days except at an ultraformal dinner, and I have discussed the hot towels that diners are often presented with in Japanese restaurants. In this and other instances, I have tried to give you, the reader, a range of options that suits the way you live today. I show you how to entertain formerly or informally, as you like, but always graciously.

I have also played down situations that the average person is unlikely to encounter. Few of us will ever, for example, be a guest on a Greek shipping magnate's yacht, and thus do not need to know how to dress and behave. Even fewer people these days use a family coat of arms. Of those who do, most generally know how to use it.

Next, I have tried to cover thoroughly the areas where new etiquette has developed—in new patterns of dating, the lives of single parents, and throughout the increasingly egalitarian world of business.

Finally, although this book is an encyclopedia, I have still tried to make its tone personal. I make some judgments, offer some guidance, and try to provide plenty of anecdotes and examples to show you what's really what in the world of manners and behavior.

I hope all my readers will subscribe to the theme that runs throughout this book, namely that a truly well-mannered person is someone who always behaves with kindness and love toward his fellow humans.

How to Use This Book

Although all the entries in this book are alphabetical, I did envision and write the book around several general categories of information. Knowing these categories will help you use the book. They are:

Ceremonies
Entertaining
Protocol
Family Manners
Business Manners
Single Life

Most of the business entries, for example, start with the word "Business." In a similar fashion, most of the single-life entries start with the word "Single."

Extensive cross-references have been provided for those times when you want to delve more deeply into a subject.

The vast majority of entries are short and to the point, encyclopedic, in other words, but some topics are too complex and pivotal to be treated in this brief fashion. Those topics,

marriage and children being but two, are, I feel, of such major importance that they deserve lengthier treatment. On these and other important subjects I have written what amount to short—and sometimes not so short—essays.

Most long entries have several subheads. Occasionally, a cross-reference will direct you not only to an entry but also to a subsection within the entry. The cross-reference reads:

SEE ALSO *Women's Titles (Mrs.)*

The word in parentheses is the subsection.

Every single entry is in alphabetical order.

Other than these few simple guidelines, there is nothing else the reader needs to know to take full advantage of this encyclopedia of etiquette. You simply open the book to the subject that you wish to explore and begin reading.

THE NEW ETIQUETTE

À la Carte

SEE ALSO *Table d'Hôte.*

An à la carte menu is one in which each item of food is priced and must be ordered separately. Often an à la carte entree is served with some other food, such as rice or a vegetable. Unless you are selective and order only a few courses, an à la carte meal is more expensive than a table d'hôte meal.

Abbreviations

SEE ALSO *Stationery; Titles; Wedding Invitation.*

As a general guideline, the use of abbreviations is restricted in the wording of formal invitations, and here it is restricted only by custom. By tradition, only "Mr.," "Mrs.," and "Ms." are used in abbreviated form on a formal invitation. ("Ms.," it should be noted for trivia watchers, can never be anything but abbreviated since, unlike "Mr.," which is a short form of Mister, or "Mrs.," a shortened form of Missus, it stands for nothing when used as a title.) All other words that are usually abbreviated—military titles, states, months, years, and so on—are spelled out on a formal invitation.

"Mr." and "Mrs." are virtually never seen spelled out. Whether or not to use any abbreviation under other circumstances is purely a matter of personal taste.

Abortion

SEE *Miscarriage, Abortion, and Stillbirth.*

Adoption

SEE ALSO *Baby; Baby Shower; Single Parent.*

The arrival of an adopted baby is always cause for celebration. The adoption of a child should never be kept secret. A child

3

could be deeply hurt if he or she learns from someone other than his parents, particularly, as so often happens, from other children's taunts, that he is adopted. The best way to assure a child that he is truly a loved family member is to tell him that he is adopted as soon as he is old enough to understand what this means. Other family members, friends, and even acquaintances also should be told about the adoption.

ANNOUNCEMENTS. Adoption announcements, worded similarly to birth announcements, are an excellent way to let people and relatives know about an adoption. The wording is similar to that on formal birth announcements:

> *Mr. and Mrs. William Smythson*
> *take pleasure in announcing*
> *the adoption of*
> *Kimberly Lynne*
> *born February 3, 1987*

Alternately, the wording might read "are happy to announce the adoption of . . ." Parents who adopt older children or children from other countries may also want to mention the child's age and/or country of birth. In later years, the child can look back at the announcement of his or her adoption and see that not only was he loved and desired but also that his heritage was accepted and a subject of pride.

Preprinted birth announcements can be used, but care must be taken that they are not misleading in any way. For example, don't buy birth announcements with a hospital scene or storks on them, and don't select a card with a baby on it when you are adopting an older child.

SHOWERS. The festivities that surround the adoption of a child should be exactly the same as those that surround the birth of a child. Just as showers are not given for expectant mothers until shortly before their delivery dates, it is safer not to give a shower for an adopted baby until it has either been adopted or until the parents are sure there will be no last-minute snags in the adoption proceedings.

ADOPTION PARTY. More appropriate for an older child is an adoption party, at which he is the guest of honor. This is an opportunity to meet the family, especially any children his age, and some neighborhood children. An adoption party could be planned along the same lines as a birthday party.

ADOPTION BY STEPPARENT. Occasionally a stepparent, usually a stepfather, will adopt the children of a spouse. This generally occurs after the family has been together for several years, so the children are not babies. Preprinted or specially printed announcements may be sent out, and if the child is old enough, a small family party to celebrate may be in order. This is a time when the child's feelings must be consulted and followed, though, since a child who has thought of his stepfather as his father may be confused over any kind of celebration, and a child who has ties to his biological father also may have feelings about celebrating his adoption by another parent.

After-Dinner Drinks

SEE ALSO *Brandy; Glasses; Sherry.*

Some hosts like to offer a particular kind of drink—a liqueur, brandy, or sweet wine—to cap off a meal. These drinks may be served with coffee after the dessert, either at the table or after the group has adjourned from the table and moved into the living room. They are, as a rule, offered only after the evening meal, as they are too heavy to be drunk at lunch.

The best-known after-dinner liqueurs are brandy, which is in a class by itself and will be discussed separately; crème de menthe; crème de cacao; Grand Marnier; Benedictine; Cointreau; Chartreuse; Cherry Heering; and Drambuie.

Another category of after-dinner drinks are the fine sweet wines: sherry, port, Madeira, Málaga, and Tokay.

Most hosts offer their guests a selection of after-dinner drinks. The sweet wines and liqueurs are excellent with or following fruit and cheese or other light desserts, while the brandies and cognacs complement a heavy dessert.

After-dinner wines and liqueurs are often stored and served from decanters; sherry and other fortified wines may be stored like this without loss of quality.

After-dinner drinks are usually served at room temperature. The wines are served in dessert wine glasses, which are usually smaller than other wine glasses and more ornate. They may be colored, cut, or etched glass.

Sherry is served in a small V-shaped glass. Cognacs and brandies are served in a brandy snifter, a clear glass with a large bowl and short stem that is designed so the beverage can be warmed by the holder's hands before drinking. The smallest glass, a liqueur glass, is suitable for any other liqueurs *(see Figure 1).*

The host or hostess offers after-dinner drinks and pours them. Seconds should be offered, but they should never be forced on anyone.

Unlike other beverages, which are meant to be drunk, after-dinner drinks are quite properly sipped and savored over a period of time.

Figure 1. After-dinner glasses: dessert wine glass (top left); sherry glass (top right); brandy snifter (bottom left); liqueur glass (bottom right)

Air Force

Commissioned Air Force officers are called by their titles and their surnames, as in "Captain Silver." After the initial greeting or introduction, an officer may be called "Captain."

Noncommissioned officers, those with the rank of Sergeant and below, are addressed as "Mr." or "Ms." (alternately "Miss" or "Mrs.").

Commissioned officers in the Air Force parallel the ranks of the Army, except during wartime, when the top Air Force officer is the General of the Air Force.

The color on the warrant officers' bands is sky-blue enamel. *(See Army.)*

Noncommissioned officers and other enlisted men wear sleeve insignia of blue with pale blue stripes and pierced stars. The ranks are as follows:

1. Chief Master Sergeant—2 chevrons above 6 arcs, star
2. Senior Master Sergeant—1 chevron above 6 arcs, star
3. Master Sergeant—6 arcs, star
4. Technical Sergeant—5 arcs, star
5. Staff Sergeant—4 arcs, star
6. Sergeant—3 stripes
7. Airman 1st Class—2 stripes
8. Airman 2nd Class—1 stripe
9. Airman—no insignia

Air Force Academy

SEE *Air Force; Military Wedding.*

Air Travel

Air travel is very casual, and because it is so fast, it is also impersonal.

Persons seated together do not necessarily greet each other when they sit down but often make some polite conversation during the meal or snack.

A person who is reading or otherwise occupied obviously does not wish to talk and should be left alone.

Meals will be served by a steward or stewardess. Airline personnel will also provide other amenities—liquor, which must be purchased these days, except in first class; blankets; pillows; aspirins or an antacid; or soft drinks or warm beverages. Airline personnel are not tipped.

Airline personnel should be treated with courtesy at all times. Never monopolize their attention. It is polite to thank the stewardesses and stewards who are nearby as you leave the plane.

Alimony

When one partner, usually the man, has been married before, he may be required to pay alimony and/or child support to his ex-spouse and children. This often causes resentment with the present spouse, particularly if the couple is struggling to care for a family of their own. Difficult as this situation is, the new spouse should avoid complaining about it. These complaints will not make the other family go away and will only add tension to their marriage. This is one of those seemingly small kindnesses that a spouse can show to a partner that, in fact, contribute in a very large way to the happiness the couple will enjoy.

Amateur Performance

SEE *Ballet.*

American Style of Eating

SEE *Fork.*

Annapolis

SEE *Military Wedding; Navy and Coast Guard.*

Anniversary

SEE ALSO *Anniversary Party.*

Most couples opt to celebrate their minor anniversaries privately, and have parties only for their major anniversaries, especially since an anniversary party obligates guests to bring a present. The most celebrated anniversaries are the first (usually celebrated by the couple alone), the tenth, the twenty-fifth (silver), the thirtieth, the fortieth, the fiftieth (golden), and the sixtieth.

Some couples go out to dinner; others plan a weekend away by themselves. Anniversary gifts are usually exchanged, although the kind of gift depends upon each couple's style in gift giving. Many couples give each other a joint gift. I hope all couples make this gift something that commemorates their year together: a piece of art, a special set of records, a stereo, something special they both want for their home. While I sympathize with the practice of buying practical gifts (washing machines, microwave ovens, and the like), I do not think gifts like this do much to keep romance in a marriage, and I urge all couples to make their anniversaries a romantic occasion and to give gifts that they both share equally and can look back on with fondness.

For anniversaries you also may select your gifts around the traditional motifs, although you are under no obligation to do this. They are:

Anniversary	Theme
First	Paper
Second	Cotton
Third	Leather
Fourth	Linen
Fifth	Wood
Sixth	Iron
Seventh	Copper
Eighth	Bronze
Ninth	Pottery
Tenth	Tin or aluminum
Eleventh	Steel
Twelfth	Silk
Thirteenth	Lace
Fourteenth	Ivory
Fifteenth	Crystal or glass

Twentieth	China
Twenty-fifth	Silver
Thirtieth	Pearl
Thirty-fifth	Coral or jade
Fortieth	Ruby
Forty-fifth	Sapphire
Fiftieth	Gold
Sixtieth	Diamond

Anniversary Party

SEE ALSO *Anniversary.*

Couples give their early-anniversary parties, and their families (i.e., their children or siblings) generally give their silver- and golden-anniversary parties. The longer the marriage, the greater the (public and ceremonial) fuss that is made over an anniversary.

WHEN. Anniversary parties are often given on the weekend nearest to the date of the anniversary, as a matter of convenience and to permit out-of-town guests to travel to the party.

INVITATIONS. Invitations may be issued in writing or by telephone. They may be especially printed for the occasion, or pre-printed ones may be used. If preprinted ones are used, select something simple, perhaps the all-purpose invitations where you fill in the pertinent data. Try to avoid cute or coy invitations, but this is not to say that an anniversary invitation cannot be unusual or special. One family I know has a charming custom of writing poems to celebrate important family occasions. They have these printed and send them as invitations.

A handwritten invitation might read:

Dear Betty,

We're having a silver wedding anniversary for my parents on Saturday, October 15, and I do hope you and Bob will be able to join us. The party will be at the club, and we're gathering around 9 P.M.

Best,
Suzanne

If you issue your own invitations, you may or may not want to mention the occasion in advance, but they might read:

Dear Sandra,

Bill and I are having a small dinner Saturday, the twentieth of June, at our home, and we would like you to be our guests. I do hope you can join us.

Love,
Joan

Those who know you well will realize it is an anniversary celebration, and the others will still be with you to celebrate, which is what friendship is all about.

If you send formal engraved or printed invitations, the wording should be as shown in Figure 2.

The children of
Sarah and Charles Wiggins, Sr.
request the pleasure of your company
at a dinner dance
in honor of
the fortieth anniversary
of the marriage of their parents
on Sunday, the first of August,
Nineteen hundred eighty-seven
at nine o'clock
Tipton Golf and Swim Club

Figure 2. Formal anniversary party invitation (printed or engraved)

Informals can also be used for invitations:

Sarah and Charles Wiggins, Sr.
Reception
In honour of their Silver Anniversary
August 1 at 5 P.M.
Tipton Golf and Swim Club

The invitation list for an anniversary party should include family members and close family friends, particularly anyone who attended the wedding. If the couple have remained close to their attendants, they should be invited, too. (Often, when attendants cannot make it to an anniversary party, a conference call is arranged during the party so the wedding party can reminisce for a few minutes. This makes a lovely gift.)

DECORATIONS. Anniversary parties often call for special decorations or themes. Much of what you do depends upon your taste and personal inclination. A wedding cake makes a nice centerpiece, and other gay touches, such as balloons, crêpe-paper streamers, ribbons, and bouquets, can be used to create a festive atmosphere. Silver and white are traditional colors for a twenty-fifth-anniversary party, and gold and white for a fiftieth.

RECEIVING LINE. The couple and their children or the hosts of their party may decide to form a receiving line to greet guests as they arrive. A very old couple should be seated near the entrance of the party to greet guests; they need not stand.

SEATING. Seating may be provided for all the guests, or at a reception (as opposed to a buffet or sit-down dinner), a special table might be set up for the guests of honor.

Seated with the couple might be their children, their siblings, and their wedding attendants.

FOOD AND BEVERAGES. Any kind of food that is appropriate to the time of day can be served at an anniversary party. Some parties are receptions or teas, and others are four-course, sit-down dinners. The only special food is a wedding cake (although this is hardly required) and champagne or some other beverage for the toasts.

TOASTS. The couple should be toasted at their wedding anniversary celebration much as they were at their wedding reception. If many years have passed, it may be more appropriate for a son or daughter to lead off the toasts and introduce the best man and any other attendants who wish to toast the couple again.

The toasts should be warm and loving. An anniversary is not the occasion to remind the couple that no one thought this marriage would last or that they have gone through some very rough years. The most sincere toast is often the simplest: "To Sarah and Charles—May they have thirty more years of happiness."

GIFTS. An invitation to an anniversary party does obligate the guests to bring gifts, unless the invitation specifies "No gifts please," in which case this request must be honored. (If you still want to give the couple a gift, call on them a few days before the anniversary to deliver a gift.) For silver and golden anniversaries, gifts of silver and gold are appropriate, except that after so many years of marriage, the couple may have little interest in acquiring more silver or even more household items of any kind. It is rude, however, to indicate anything like this on the invitation. Often, the family joins together to present the couple with one special present, such as a trip, a lovely piece of crystal, an art object, or even a donation to their favorite charity. When you accept the invitation, you can ask if anything like this is planned (and the family should let you know if you inquire) and then contribute to this.

Announcements

SEE *Adoption; Baby; Change-of-Address Announcements; Divorce; Engagement; Funeral; Graduation; Newspaper Announcement; Wedding Announcement.*

Annulment

An annulment, a declaration that a marriage is invalid and thus never legally existed, occurs rarely these days, but it is always a sad occasion. For Roman Catholics who arrange for a religious annulment, often granted in many cases long after they have remarried, the annulment is a religious formality and need not even be mentioned except to family members and close friends. Legal annulments, which occur for a variety of reasons, including fraud and misrep-

resentation, often occur before the bride and groom have lived together for any length of time.

No public announcement need be made of an annulment, although one may be printed in the newspaper. Often, the bride or her mother and someone in the groom's family write notes to those who attended the wedding informing them of the sad news. A bride is obligated to return wedding gifts when a marriage has been annulled within a few months of the wedding. Women whose marriages have been annulled always take back their maiden names.

Answering Service

SEE ALSO *Telephone Answering Machine.*

Answering services have become more common in the past few years, perhaps because so many people lead such busy lives. The best way to find an answering service is through word of mouth. Your primary concerns must be reliability and courtesy. You will, of course, want all your messages to be accurate and ungarbled, and you will also want your friends and acquaintances to feel comfortable calling your phone service.

If your messages are being garbled, you will find this out soon enough when your social life begins to disintegrate. You can check out the politeness factor by simply asking your friends how they are treated when they call.

Apartment Living

SEE ALSO *Co-op Board Interview.*

A cooperative or condominium is, generally speaking, more sociable than a rental apartment building, because there is a greater common bond among residents. As a matter of courtesy and practicality, residents should be slower about picking or pursuing quarrels with one another, since their relationship is long-standing.

Residents also should take care to pay all bills promptly and should be willing to serve on committees when asked to do so, if it is at all convenient.

In any kind of apartment building, staff should be tipped extra for added services, in addition to tips given at holiday time.

The degree of friendliness that develops among those who live in an apartment building is entirely up to the individuals. You should feel free to be as friendly as you like, no more and no less. In some buildings, the children get acquainted, and this leads to friendship among the parents. In other buildings, people become acquainted because they know each other through co-op or condo committees or boards. Sometimes common interests draw even renters together, and sometimes the tenants never really become acquainted with one another.

Apéritif

An apéritif is a category of drinks served whenever cocktails are, that is, before lunch, around 5 P.M., and before dinner. Apéritifs are milder than drinks made with hard liquor. Typical apéritifs are Campari; Dubonnet; dry and sweet vermouth; dry sherry; certain kinds of light white wine, such as Liebfraumilch; and rosé. Apéritifs taken straight are served in a short tumbler (or sherry glass for sherry), with or without ice, based on the person's preference. Some apéritifs are mixed, usually with water or soda, and served in a tall glass over ice. Another example of a mixed apéritif is sangria.

Apéritifs are the perfect foil for appetizers, which are often spicy or salty and thus designed to whet the appetite. They may also be served without food.

Apology

An apology is necessary whenever you have done something to offend someone. If, for example, you bump into someone, an apology—"I'm so sorry"—is called for. If you pass in front of someone, for example, when entering a row of a theater, an apology is not called for, but saying "Excuse me" is. If you have not done something to offend someone, do not apologize. The person who apologizes too much is obsequious.

SPOKEN. Small, momentary offenses can be put right with an on-the-spot apology. If you start to introduce someone but forget his name, for example, simply say that you are sorry and consider the matter finished. If you have not recognized an acquaintance immediately because you are not wearing your glasses, that too calls for a quick, on-the-spot apology. These are examples of small offenses that are quickly dealt with.

WRITTEN. Some major offenses are most tactfully handled with a written apology. If you break something at someone's home, for example, send along a note of apology with the replacement, even though you will have apologized in person on the spot. If you misbehave at someone's party and cause a scene, a note of apology is definitely in order, especially if you ever hope to be invited again.

Appetizer

SEE ALSO *Food Courses.*

An appetizer, also variously known as an hors d'oeuvre or canapé, is a first course or, alternately, a cocktail food. The sole aim of an appetizer is to whet the appetite. Because of this, appetizers are often highly seasoned or salty. Salted (or these days, unsalted) nuts are the easiest and always correct no-fuss appetizer.

When an appetizer is the first course at a sit-down dinner, it need not be a finger food. It might, for example, be a small meat- or vegetable-stuffed pastry, a small serving of marinated vegetables, cold meat or fish, or a pasta dish. Almost any food can be adapted as an appetizer if it is served in small portions.

Apart from choosing an appetizer, one must also decide whether to serve it hot or cold. The French believe that all meals should start with a hot course, but some wonderful cold appetizers exist, and it would be a shame not to serve them on occasion. I tend to think that a warm appetizer is always a good start to a winter meal, and that cold appetizers are excellent starters for a summer meal.

When appetizers are served as cocktail food, they must be foods that can easily be eaten with the fingers. Unless they are the only food that will be served, appetizers should be offered in limited quantities so diners will not ruin their appetites for the later courses.

Applause

SEE *Ballet; Movies; Opera; Theater.*

Apple

SEE *Fruit.*

Army

Commissioned Army officers are called by their titles and their surnames, as in "Captain Silver." After the initial greeting or introduction, an officer may be called "Captain."

Noncommissioned officers, those with the rank of Sergeant and below, are addressed socially as "Mr." or "Ms." (alternately "Miss" or "Mrs."). Noncommissioned officers wear Army green insignia with yellow chevrons, arcs, and emblems.

The ranks are as follows:

Commissioned Officers
1. General of the Army (wartime rank only)—5 silver stars
2. General—4 silver stars
3. Lieutenant General—3 silver stars
4. Major General—2 silver stars
5. Brigadier General—1 silver star
6. Colonel—silver eagle
7. Lieutenant Colonel—silver oak leaf
8. Major—gold oak leaf
9. Captain—2 silver bars
10. First Lieutenant—1 silver bar
11. Second Lieutenant—1 gold bar

Warrant Officers
12. Chief Warrant Officer (W-4)—silver bar with 3 brown enamel bands
13. Chief Warrant Officer (W-3)—silver bar with 2 brown enamel bands
14. Chief Warrant Officer (W-2)—gold bar with 3 brown enamel bands
15. Warrant Officer (W-1)—gold bar with 2 brown enamel bands

Noncommissioned Officers and Other Enlisted Men
16. Sergeant Major—3 chevrons above 3 arcs, a star in the center
17. First Sergeant—3 chevrons above 3 arcs, a lozenge in the center
    and
    Master Sergeant—3 chevrons above 3 arcs
18. Platoon Sergeant or Sergeant First Class—3 chevrons above 2 arcs
    and
    Specialist Seven—3 arcs above an eagle device
19. Staff Sergeant—3 chevrons above 1 arc
    and
    Specialist Six—2 arcs above an eagle device
20. Sergeant—3 chevrons
    and
    Specialist Five—1 arc above an eagle device
21. Corporal—2 chevrons
    and
    Specialist Four—an eagle device, no arcs
22. Private First Class—1 chevron above 1 arc
23. Private E-2—1 chevron
24. Private E-1—no insignia

Art Gallery

SEE *Museum.*

Artichokes

This is definitely a finger food, one of the best there is. Pull off the leaves, dip in the sauce (usually lemon and butter melted together), and scrape the leaves through your teeth. Discard leaves on the plate or side dish or bowl that is usually provided. When most of the leaves have been removed, use your knife to cut away the remaining leaves and the choke. Use a fork and knife to eat the remaining artichoke heart.

Ashtrays

Ashtrays, not trays at all, but small dishes designed to hold the residue from cigarettes and cigars, used to be found in abundance.

No well-dressed house, in fact, was without one or more on every table. Ashtrays today are symbolic of the struggle between smokers and nonsmokers. What this means, more often than not, is that if an ashtray is not readily accessible, then smoking is not particularly invited and is possibly not even permitted. You may ask, but do not be surprised if the answer is no.

Don't assume that just any small dish is an ashtray. Always check with the hostess before appropriating what appears to be an ashtray.

When ashtrays are present, the only polite method of smoking is to use one. Never, ever, even in a public place, drop ashes on a floor. If you are smoking in public and don't have access to an ashtray, improvise, using a small paper cup, a napkin—anything will do rather than leaving your ashes in inappropriate places.

Avocado

SEE *Fruit.*

Baby

SEE ALSO *Adoption; Shower; Single Parents.*

BIRTH ANNOUNCEMENTS. Close family and friends will hear of the birth by the day after or as soon as the parents feel like telephoning them the good news. Other relatives and friends will learn of the birth when announcements are sent. Birth announcements do not obligate the recipient to send a gift, so they can be sent to anyone who would be interested in the news—family members, who will want the keepsake; old friends; current, new friends; and co-workers.

Either preprinted birth announcements or specially printed announcements are acceptable, with the latter being a bit more formal.

If you buy the preprinted announcements, the most popular and least expensive kind of announcement, you will need only to fill in the blanks, such as the baby's name, birth date, weight, and parents' names. When buying preprinted cards, avoid anything that is coy or overly cute (unless, of course, this is to your taste). Also fashionable in some circles these days is to avoid anything that is overtly sexist, i.e., that suggests there is some special joy in the sex of this baby as opposed to having a healthy baby of either sex.

The most charming birth announcements are, I think, the traditional ones *(see Figure 3)*, which incorporate a printed announcement and a small card with the baby's name. These cards are printed or engraved on white or off-white paper, and the two cards are attached with a small satin ribbon, which may be pink for a girl and blue for a boy. These days, the colors are less likely to be sex-coded, and pastel yel-

Mr. and Mrs. William Smythson
take pleasure in announcing
the adoption of
Kimberly Lynne
born February 3, 1987

Figure 3. Traditional birth announcement

low and green ribbons are enjoying great vogue. Stationers and department-store stationery stores will also have a variety of styles and colors for preprinted announcements.

Announcements for twins (or more) are worded similarly to the traditional announcement:

> John and Maryann Andrews
> are proud to announce
> the births of
> their daughter   and   their son
> Jaimie,   Michael,
> born April 12, 1987

Figure 4. Traditional birth announcement for twins

NAMES. Naming customs vary with religious and ethnic background so much that any examination of names here must be cursory; many books on names exist, and parents can consult them for more information.

Roman Catholic children must be given the name of a saint; it can be either their first or middle name. Roman Catholic sons of Hispanic origin are often named Jesus.

Jewish children usually are not named exactly the same name as a relative, but they may be named after a deceased relative, that is, the first initial of the relative's name is used and another, often similar name is chosen. For obvious reasons, Jewish children are rarely named Mary or John, although Jonathan is a frequently used Jewish name.

Many couples choose to name their sons after their fathers or some other relative. If the boy is named for his father, the father becomes "Sr." and the son becomes "Jr."

for as long as they are both living. A boy who is named for a grandfather or some other relative is "the second" (II), "the third" (III), and so on. This designation is also used occasionally for sons.

Girls are rarely named after their mothers, but if they are, "Jr." is not used.

In choosing a name, care should be taken that it is dignified enough to carry through life. Many a child named "Moonbeam" or "Blue Bird" during the freewheeling Sixties has by now grown old enough to rue his parents' choice of a name. If you don't like nicknames, do not give your child a name that can be readily converted to one. Before naming a child, write out his initials to be sure they do not spell something (RAT or PIG) that will lead to a silly nickname or forever after prohibit the use of the monogram.

If you choose a name that applies to both sexes, be sure you choose the appropriate spelling. Marion, Lynn, and Francis are masculine, and Marian, Lynne, and Frances are feminine. Think twice before hanging a decidedly masculine name (Michael or Glen) on a girl, or a feminine name on a boy (Michel, Bonnie).

CALLING ON NEW PARENTS. Immediate family members will call at the hospital, as will close friends. People also call on new parents during the first few weeks to meet the baby and deliver a gift. Telephone before you visit to be sure mother and baby feel like company, and don't stay too long (despite the protests) when you do visit. A new mother—or at least a first-time mother—is likely to be running on adrenaline, and she will love the attention, but she also may be tired and may need some uninterrupted time to herself.

If you live at a distance and receive a birth announcement, send a congratulatory note as soon as you hear the news.

GIFTS. New babies start out life with lots of presents, or at least many do. A birth announcement does not obligate anyone to send a gift, but people close enough to receive one are usually also close enough to want to give the baby a present. A lovely custom is to take both the new baby and any older sibling a present when you call on the new parents. The present for the older child can be quite modest, and this second gift is usually reserved only for very small children who are not quite old enough to understand why the new baby is getting all the attention.

Clothes are welcome gifts (buy at least a one-year-old-size unless the mother has specifically told you she needs newborn clothes), as are toys and small baby furniture and appliances. A baby gift is usually given in the first few months, if not weeks, of a newborn's life.

Bachelor Dinner

A bridegroom may give or be given a bachelor dinner several days before his wedding. On no account should the party be held the night before his wedding since this could be a major factor in his health on the day of his wedding. The party is often held in a private room of a restaurant or it may be held at a club. It is traditionally considered the groom's farewell fling with single life. Such parties are attended by his best man and ushers and his close friends.

When drinks are served (champagne is appropriate), the bridegroom toasts his bride. Custom used to dictate that the glasses used for this toast be thrown into a fireplace. This is rarely done today because (1) few restaurants are equipped with fireplaces and (2) few restaurants will tolerate the shattering of their glasses. Occasionally a restaurant may provide inexpensive glasses that may be used for this purpose. Any glassware that is broken without the restaurant's approval should, of course, be paid for by the host.

Bacon

If crisp, you may eat bacon with your fingers. (You may, in fact, find there is no other way to eat it.) If not, cut it and eat it with a knife and fork.

Baked Potato

Steady the potato with your hand and use your knife to slit it open. Use your fingers to push the slit open wider so the steam escapes. Press open, and eat with your fork. When you have eaten the pulp, you may use your knife and fork to cut the skin into bite-sized pieces and eat them.

Ballet

A ballet crowd usually dresses a little more casually than an opera or theater crowd, although gala and benefit nights can be dressy.

Be sure to arrive on time (indeed, many companies will not admit late arrivals until an appropriate break in the program).

In theory, applause is held until the end of an act or a ballet, whichever comes first, but in practice the audience is often so enthusiastic that it often bursts into applause spontaneously after a particularly spectacular section of dancing. These bursts of spontaneous enthusiasm are obviously a compliment to the dancers, but they can also be a hindrance if the appreciation goes on so long that it interferes with the dancers hearing the music and continuing the dance. Participate in the spontaneity by all means, but keep it short.

A newcomer to the ballet who is unsure whether or not a dance has ended (the dancers also pause and sometimes even take bows at the end of a particularly strenuous stretch of dancing) should wait until the bows begin before applauding or take a cue from others in the audience.

BALLET RECITALS. Compassion dictates the usual critical judgments be suspended at a ballet recital, and for that matter at any amateur performance. After all, you're there because you know someone, and because you know that someone you should give your wholehearted support regardless of the quality of the performance, particularly where children and young adults are involved.

Banana

SEE *Fruit.*

Banns

SEE ALSO *Engagement.*

The banns are the spoken or published announcement of an intended marriage. They are traditionally issued several weeks in a row. Banns are still issued orally by the Roman Catholic Church and some Anglican churches. An engaged couple may want to be present when their banns are announced to accept congratulations from the congregation.

Baptism

SEE *Christian Birth Ceremonies.*

Bar or Bat Mitzvah

SEE ALSO *Invitation.*

A Jewish ceremony, called a bar mitzvah for a boy and a bat mitzvah for a girl, is held when the child is thirteen years of age. It includes a religious service and a celebration. It is traditionally held on the first Sabbath after the child's birthday, but if this is not possible it may be held on another Sabbath. A bar or bat mitzvah is the culmination of several years of religious studies. The service is typically held in a synagogue, and there is usually a kiddish, or reception with wine and sweet breads, afterward.

Anyone in the congregation may attend. Occasionally luncheon may be served in the synagogue for family and friends. Whereas Protestant and Roman Catholic children are often confirmed in a group, usually only one child's bar or bat mitzvah is held at a time, but this is not always the case.

The larger, invitation-only celebration that follows is held after the Sabbath, usually on Saturday night or Sunday afternoon or evening. Family and friends of the child and the parents are invited. A buffet or sit-down meal is served, and there may be dancing afterward, often to live music. A bar mitzvah celebration resembles a wedding reception more than anything else.

During the synagogue service, the boy wears a white shirt and tie and dark suit, and the girl wears a pretty dress, something similar to but a little dressier than what she would wear to regular Sabbath services. She may or may not wear a hat and gloves, depending upon current styles; neither is required. Non-Jewish and Jewish male guests wear yarmulkes, which are provided especially for the occasion.

At the party held later, the boy wears a dark suit, sometimes black tie, depending upon the degree of formality, and the girl wears a party dress.

Guests wear clothes appropriate for a religious service to the synagogue service. Depending upon the degree of formality of the party, they may wear street clothes or black tie (men) and evening dresses (women). Black tie should be noted on the invitation.

The party is often held at a hotel or restaurant. The parents greet their guests as they arrive. Often the bar or bat mitzvah child receives with them, although if very many people are invited, this may be heavy duty for a thirteen-year-old. All the guests should speak with the guest of honor at some point during the evening, to offer their congratulations.

The bar or bat mitzvah child typically receives gifts of a permanent nature, such as a pen, cuff links, radio, or books. Money, stocks, or bonds are also acceptable presents. Religious gifts, such as a prayer shawl or kiddish cup, are usually given by the parents and grandparents.

Presents may be opened at some point during the evening or they may be opened later. When money is given, it is sealed in a white envelope with a card of congratulations and given to the youngster. Thank-you notes, of course, must be sent afterward for all presents.

Printed invitations, which are typically sent for a bar mitzvah, may follow the traditional wording of any formal invitation and are printed in black ink on white or off-white stock, or they may be less formal, that is, printed on colored stock and with more casual wording. This less formal version of a formal invitation is popular for bar and bat mitzvahs. In fact, since bar and bat mitzvahs are not bound by the more traditional etiquette of weddings, there is much more leeway in planning all aspects of the celebration. For example, the large party may have a theme.

Barbecue

SEE ALSO *Outdoor Entertaining.*

A barbecue, or cookout as it is called in some parts of the country, is a kind of picnic where the main attraction is food cooked over an outdoor grill. The menu can be as simple or as elaborate as you like. Hot dogs and hamburgers may be grilled, or you can cook a roast beef or roast suckling pig. The side dishes are the usual picnic fare: cold salads, corn on the cob, and other vegetable dishes. Wine, beer, and soft drinks are the best beverages.

The guest list can be as simple as a family picnic or a huge party for a hundred or more, depending upon your facilities for entertaining and your lifestyle.

By tradition, the task—or honor, depending upon your point of view—of doing the outdoor cooking usually falls on the host's shoulders. There is no reason, though, that a hostess, even a single one, can not be the chef at a barbecue.

A barbecue is a delightful and easy way to entertain, when the weather permits. Invitations are usually telephoned, and they may be issued at the last minute. A rain date can be scheduled if the weather fails to cooperate.

Everything should be kept simple for a barbecue, which is, after all, a kind of picnic. Paper or plastic plates are acceptable, as are paper or plastic glasses. Plastic eating utensils can be used, but I find these very unpleasant myself. I prefer metal flatware, even the most battered, aged set that has been relegated to outdoor entertaining.

Bath Linens

SEE ALSO *Linen Monogram.*

Brides no longer have a hope chest full of household goods, mostly linens, that they have been collecting since childhood. Instead, most women, or couples, receive the things they need to establish a household when they marry. As these things wear out, they must be replaced.

Try always to buy the best-quality linens you can afford. While linens are not indestructible, if purchased carefully, they will last for many years, and they do contribute greatly to your comfort while you use them. Although good-quality linens will wear longer and feel better to the touch than bargain-basement linens, this is not to say that you should not look for bargain prices. Many couples wait for the semiannual linen sales to replenish their supply.

The essentials for a well-equipped bathroom, to serve two people, are:

6 bath towels
6 hand towels
6 washcloths
8 small guest towels
2 bath mats

These quantities must be multiplied if there are more family members or more bathrooms.

Bathroom Etiquette

What is expected of anyone using a bathroom is really very simple, and can be summed up in two words: cleanliness and consideration.

Always leave any bathroom as clean, if not cleaner, than you found it. This applies to the family bathroom, a friend's bathroom, or a public restroom. For the sake of sanitation, if you use a cloth guest towel, do not refold it so that someone else will mistake it for unused. Instead, leave it unfolded. Do not use the host's personal towels unless no guest towels have been left out and you have no alternative.

An age-old question of consideration revolves around whether men should put the toilet seat down after using the toilet. I think they should. Consideration also consists of shutting off faucets tightly so they do not drip, telling the hostess when toilet paper or additional towels are needed, and not snooping in the medicine chest.

Attendants in public bathrooms are tipped fifty cents, more if they provide some special service.

Bed Linens

SEE ALSO *Linen Monogram.*

Brides no longer have a hope chest full of household goods, mostly linens, that they have been collecting since childhood. Instead, most women, or couples, receive the things they need to establish a household when they marry. As these things wear out they must be replaced.

Try always to buy the best-quality linens you can afford. While linens are not indestructible, if purchased carefully, they do last for many years, and they do contribute greatly to your comfort while you use them. Good-quality linens will wear longer and feel better to the touch than will bargain-basement linens. This is not to say that you should not look for a low price. Many smart shoppers wait for the semiannual linen sales to replenish their supply.

Your basic bedroom linen needs are:

3 sets of sheets for the master bed and each family bed (1 set consists of a bottom fitted or flat sheet, a top sheet, and 2 pillowcases, more pillowcases if more pillows are used)
2 sets of sheets for guest bed
2 heavy blankets or 1 comforter or 1 electric blanket per bed
1 bedspread or cover per bed
1 mattress pad per bed
Optional: 2 blanket covers per bed

Blanket covers are light covers, made of cotton, seersucker, or silk, that stay on the bed when the bedspread is removed at night. Ostensibly they are used to help keep blankets clean, but they are, in fact, primarily decorative. Many women choose to dispense with them entirely.

If blanket covers are not used, more practical blankets—in bright or dark colors that do not show dirt so easily—are preferred.

If a comforter is preferred to blankets, the investment in a down comforter is well worth the extra money. Synthetic comforters are less warm and do not hug the body the way down does. Buy the best down comforter you can afford—it is an investment that will give five to ten years service, depending upon the amount of use.

The best comforters are made of real goose down and not feathers and down combined. Comforter covers (also called duvet covers) can be purchased to protect a comforter. A minimum of two and preferably three per bed is needed.

Sheets come in various size to fit different-sized beds, but the sizes are standardized.

Kind of Bed	Standard Sheet Size (In Inches)
King	108 × 120
Queen	90 × 120
Full (double)	90 × 108
Twin (single)	72 × 108

Pillowcases come in either standard, which fits most pillows on a twin- or double-sized bed, or king.

The most practical sheets are those that require no ironing, and the best material is percale, or a combination of percale and a synthetic fabric. Muslin sheets, which will not wear as well as percale and are not as soft but are less costly, may be a practical choice.

The more closely woven a sheet is, the longer it will wear, and the softer it will be to the touch. The weave is noted on the label of sheets as the "thread count per inch." A 200-thread-count-per-inch is excellent quality, will be soft, and will wear well.

Beer

Beer is the perfect accompaniment to certain kinds of meals. Indian, Mexican, and picnic food all taste great with beer.

Serve beer in beer glasses *(see Figure 5)* or, on very informal occasions, in the can or bottle. Usually men are willing—and even prefer—to drink beer out of the can or bottle, while women tend to prefer a glass.

You need not offer a variety of beers, but simply may serve your favorite brand.

Figure 5. Beer glasses: pilsner (left); stein (right)

Belching

Occasionally what one ate for dinner reacts in one's stomach, causing one to burp or belch, both terms being synonymous for the same embarrassing biological function.

Burying a belch can cause great physical discomfort, so I cannot in good faith recommend this course of action. One should, however, squelch a belch as much as possible, cover one's mouth with one's napkin and/or hand, and always excuse oneself immediately after the deed is done.

Best Man

SEE *Wedding Attendants.*

Birth Announcement

SEE *Adoption; Baby; Newspaper Announcement.*

Black

SEE ALSO *Hispanic.*

To be called "Black" is the preference of most persons of Negro ancestry. To persist in calling them "Negro" or "colored" is to risk giving offense, and is indeed probably a subtle form of racism. People have every right to be called what they wish, and polite and kind persons abide by those wishes.

Black Tie

SEE *Men's Formal Wear.*

Blind Date

Some people find blind dates unbearably awkward, and others enjoy them. (Some blind dates, admittedly, *are* unbearably awkward, while others are quite enjoyable.)

Behavior on a blind date should be no different than that on any other date. Even if you know at first glance that this person is all wrong for you, kindness dictates that you behave graciously. After all, it is not your date's fault that the two of you are a mismatch. The ultimate in rude behavior is to ditch a blind date in the middle of an evening or even to avoid spending time with your date. You accepted the invitation to go on this date, and you have no choice but to be kind to the person even if he or she has five heads and bright orange eyes.

What you need not do—and what is actually unkind—is to pretend that this is someone you want to see again. At the end of the evening, if the person expresses an interest in seeing you again, consider this one of those occasions when a white lie is needed to let someone off gently. Say you are very busy, you are going to be traveling a lot, or that you are recuperating from a broken heart and do not think you can handle a relationship right now—anything that lets the other person know he or she will not be seeing you again. Even if the person does not ask about seeing you again, do not end the evening with a false promise to call. If your date persists, you may be forced to be a little franker and simply say, "I can tell you're a fine person, but I don't think we're right for each other."

Blowing One's Nose

Blowing one's nose is an awkward task at best, but one that cannot—at least in polite company—be neglected. The only method is to be as unobtrusive as possible.

When dining with others, if possible,

excuse yourself and leave the table if you must blow your nose; otherwise, turn your head away from the other diners. Always use a tissue or handkerchief, never the table napkin.

Blueberry

SEE *Fruit.*

Boating

SEE *Sailing, Yachting, Boating.*

Borrowing

"Neither a borrower nor a lender be" is one of the best pieces of advice ever given, but far too few of us heed it, and besides, it is almost impossible to live in a family or with anyone else for very long without eventually borrowing something. Borrowing should not, however, become a habit. Even those who appear to be generous lenders resent it when someone constantly borrows from them.

The most basic rule of borrowing is never to borrow something without first asking permission.

When you do borrow something, it must always be returned in the same or better condition than you got it. For example, if someone lends you a blouse that was not freshly pressed, you are obliged to have it cleaned or laundered and pressed before returning it. If a borrowed item breaks while you are using it, it must be repaired before it is returned. If a borrowed item cannot be repaired, it must be replaced with something of identical or comparable value.

Boss-Employee Relations

The most important professional relationship you must develop—and you must develop it in every single job you ever have— is with your boss. And make no mistake about it, *you* must be the one to nurture and develop the relationship. A boss has the power to hire and fire and does not have to mend his or her ways to fit the attitudes and values of employees. You, on the other hand, have to make an extra effort to work with the boss or be prepared to end up on the street.

Peter F. Drucker, a fountain of wisdom on boss-employee relations, has pointed out in his books that overrating a superior carries no stigma. You win an ally and show loyalty to someone whom you respect. Underrating a boss, on the other hand, can be insulting if he or she is sensitive enough to notice, and can eventually result in your being unable to work together.

UNDERSTANDING YOUR BOSS. Perhaps the best way to begin to understand your boss is to realize that he or she is human, has weaknesses and strengths, and may from time to time be beset with the same financial and personal problems that plague the rest of us.

Realize, too, that you are on this person's team. A boss does not owe an employee anything, whereas an employee owes his or her job to a boss. Therefore, your task is to fit into the boss's working habits, time schedule, and plans and goals for the future.

The rules of etiquette for getting along with a boss are fairly simple. First decide whether you have a reader or a listener. Since a large part of your time must be spent communicating with your boss, it is important to find the best way to do so right off the bat. Readers prefer to get their information in written form—via memos and reports. Try always to give them something to read before going in to talk to them.

Listeners, usually persons who issue statements such as "My door is always open" and "I always want to talk to you if there is any kind of problem," prefer that you come in directly and chat. They may even find a written communication slightly cold.

Still, appearances can be deceptive. A boss may have read a management book recently that advocated being more accessible to employees when, in fact, he or she still personally prefers little contact and lots of memos and reports. Look under the surface before you type a boss. A boss who says the door is always open but then proceeds to issue two written memos a day is not a boss who truly wants to chat with employees any more than is absolutely necessary. A boss who expresses a desire always to be available to talk with employees but is always rushing off to do something else does not really want this kind of contact. Stick with written memos when you have this kind of boss.

Another important guideline in getting along with a boss is never to confuse or surprise him or her. In other words, never make your boss appear stupid. The best way to avoid this is to keep a boss abreast of your work—the work you are currently handling, as well as the projects that you are going to tackle later and why you have put them off. If a problem arises that is your responsibility, make it known to the boss and discuss your plans for dealing with it.

Along with keeping a boss informed and helping him or her to manage time, always go to the boss's office prepared. You need not have every fact or detail on hand—to do so even could make you appear a bit too detail-oriented—but always be prepared to discuss the topic at hand.

Excuses for projects that have gone awry or work that simply has not been done on time can really hurt you. If you sense that you are going to need extra help with a project, discuss this with your boss long before the deadline approaches. If you will require an extension, this, too, should be worked out in advance rather than at the last minute.

Finally, if a boss has promised to do something for you, remind him or her politely if necessary. Give the boss a chance to do what he or she promises.

Never threaten a boss. A lot of ego is involved in being an executive. The higher one climbs, the less involved one is with actual products and the more involved one is with intangible products, such as the talents and skills of other persons.

It is hard for an up-and-coming employee with some ego involvement of his or her own not to threaten the boss. Yet business survival demands that you not threaten the person you work for. Many employees, especially executives, could use a course in nonassertiveness training, and some management programs are now offering seminars on this very subject. Assertiveness, which may also be somewhat necessary in the competitive work world, too often looks like arrogance or presumptuousness to the boss or to a conservative, old-school member of the board. Nonassertiveness, on the other hand, is a recognition of the fact that there are situations when a restrained style works best.

Remember that your boss usually will have more information than you will about the company and may or may not be able to share this information with you, and that keeping a relaxed attitude when you sense that you are confronting this situation will do a lot to keep you out of trouble. If your boss suddenly insists that a project be done a certain way, acquiesce.

There are several good nonassertiveness techniques to keep in mind when dealing with a boss. First, remember empathic listening. Give a boss time to tell you about his other plans and objectives rather than always pushing yours.

Second, develop the skill of delivering facts to your boss in a noncritical way. Occasionally you may be asked to do some research on a touchy project—closing out part of the boss's domain, for example. This is not the time to assert yourself. Instead, just give the boss the facts and let him or her worry about their interpretation. To come up with a finding that makes the boss unhappy, even if you do so innocently, may be threatening.

Third, learn the act of selective passivity. You will do better to remain aloof from some issues. If your boss has been ordered from above to cut back on managers because the company had a bad year, and you have some dynamic new management techniques that could save the situation, this is still not the time to mention them. Again, it just threatens a boss who is losing some power. Try to remain aloof from the situation, as far as your boss is concerned.

If you want to challenge your boss, and there is no reason not to do this occasionally, do it privately. Prepare your argument in advance and make sure it is well thought out. Public power plays with a boss are invariably seen as a threat to the boss's power base, and a smart boss won't let anyone get away with that very many times.

DEALING WITH A BOSS WHO ERRS. Sometimes your superior will make an embarrassing blunder, and you, as the subordinate trying your hardest to advance your career and the boss's, will find that you must react. There are three things you can do tactfully when this happens. First, you can ignore the error if it is minor enough. Second, you can defend it. Do this by pointing out the wisdom of your boss's decision. Pointing out the long-term value of the boss's decision is an especially good tactic. Few persons will remember the mistake when the future finally arrives and the decision has been proven right or wrong, and few people know what will happen in the future anyway, so who can say whether your boss has erred or not if you put the mistake in this light?

Finally, if you feel strongly about a boss's error, you can privately and tactfully express your views to the boss. If you feel that the error could harm your career, express your dissatisfaction in a memo for the boss's eyes only—and keep a copy for future reference.

COMPLAINING ABOUT A COLLEAGUE. It is an archaic philosophy to think that you cannot go to a boss to complain if someone with whom you work is not doing his or her job properly, but there is an etiquette to complaining. First, you must know what you can legitimately complain about. As one executive noted, "You can only lose face if you go in to complain because the secretarial pool doesn't get your letters out fast enough." Then, too, it is wiser not to complain about anyone on a level higher than you; it may threaten your boss, who will undoubtedly have his or her own peer loyalties.

Most bosses advise that a person go first to the colleague who is not doing his or her job satisfactorily. Since you still need to work with this person, it is more tactful to try to work things out with him or her before going to the boss. If this fails and you feel you have to go to your boss, you can do it, but as one man noted, "You can complain, but you have to couch the complaint in diplomatic terms. For instance, if you need to work with that colleague, you almost have to go to your boss and suggest another method of getting the job done, one that takes the burden off the person who is not carrying his load. You can't ever go in and bad-mouth a colleague. You really can't gossip, either. You mostly have to go in and describe the work situation to the boss—often without using names—and hope that he gets the message."

Most executives do get the message.

They know when they have someone working for them who is not pulling his or her weight, and they take a complaint from a colleague, however subtly it may be worded, as a sign that the time has come for action.

UNDERSTANDING YOUR EMPLOYEE. The other side of the coin occurs when you, the boss, have responsibility for a number of people. It is sometimes harder, just because of the power that goes along with being the boss, to treat employees in a nonassertive, gracious manner. Yet doing so can lower employee defenses, improve interpersonal relationships, and motivate young executives—in short, it can make everyone on your team pull that much harder for you, and this is what management is all about.

A good manager of others needs to remember to use the same nonassertiveness techniques that he or she used or uses with his own boss, plus a few other techniques. The art of procrastination has some benefits when you are motivating others, for example. Let employees work out their interpersonal squabbles. As long as no one is getting hurt, let an employee work out a project on his or her own time. Mature adults generally work well by themselves. They don't need a mother hen clucking over them every minute, nor should a boss assume that he or she has a captive audience whenever an employee comes looking for advice or a suggestion. If possible, help someone seeking advice to think through the problem and to find his or her own solution. Above all, when giving advice, avoid the tendency to expound. The boss who constantly expounds on various subjects to his or her employees often knows little about what truly goes on in the office and thus has little control over the persons he or she manages.

GIVING CRITICISM. One of the functions of being a boss is to critically evaluate the work of your employees. People work well only when they think they are good at what they do, and to undermine confidence is also to undermine the company, so criticism always should be couched in the most tactful terms. One way to do this is to minimize your authority when giving criticism. Let an employee know that you want to talk about his or her work and ask the person to prepare any notes or thoughts he or she may have. Evaluative sessions should always be a two-way street. If possible, get out from behind your desk when giving criticism and sit in a chair beside the employee or across a table. Let the employee begin. Ask, "How do you think things are going? Do you have any specific problems?"

Focus on just one or two issues and save anything else for another meeting.

Listen very carefully to any complaints an employee has, and avoid giving the impression that you are biding your time until he or she gets done speaking so you can get down to the real business at hand: criticism. When you do get down to specific areas that could be improved, it is important to phrase comments in plain but tactful language. Wrap up a critical session by soliciting the employee's goals for the future, by outlining his or her accomplishments, and by discussing what he or she will be doing on current projects. Reassure employees that you value their work and always try to

end the session by complimenting an employee on a strong point.

ACCEPTING CRITICISM. No one loves to hear criticism, but everyone wants reinforcement for a job well done. In most companies, one comes with the other, or at least you cannot escape hearing an evaluation of your work. How you respond to criticism depends in part on the personality of the person giving it and on your relationship with him or her. Never laugh off criticism—always treat it very seriously. Ask for specific examples of situations you have handled poorly. Ask for your boss's ideas on how you might better handle yourself.

When the session is drawing to a close, tell your boss that you appreciate his or her honesty and suggestions. Thank the boss for giving you such a fair report if, in fact, you got one.

Should you find yourself constantly subjected to what you feel is unfair criticism, it may be time to look for another job. You may need a lower-key job or a better boss. In either case, accept the criticism graciously while you work your way to another job or department. Don't give a former boss a chance to tell a prospective boss that you don't take criticism well.

ACCEPTING PUBLIC CRITICISM. Criticism should be given privately. Offering public criticism is invariably an underhanded power play. If someone suggests a truly rotten idea, it will fall of its own accord without another person's cynical prompting. Avoid such demeaning actions.

Should you find yourself being criticized publicly, stay calm—and stay polite. Attention, fairly or not, has been focused on you, and everyone will be watching to see how you handle the situation. Say as little as possible and treat the person who offers the criticism civilly. You could say something vague such as "You may be right," or you could offer to discuss the matter later.

Bouquet

SEE *Centerpiece; Flowers; Funeral; Wedding.*

Boutonnière

SEE ALSO *Wedding.*

Boutonnières, or lapel flowers worn by men, were once very popular for everyday wear. Now they are mostly worn on special occasions, such as a man's wedding day or at a formal dance. Traditional flowers for a boutonnière are the carnation, lily of the valley, or a rose, although any flower small enough to be worn on a lapel is acceptable.

Bowl

A bowl *(see Figure 6)* is an all-purpose dish that is used for such things as cereal, fruit, soup, ice cream, and pasta, to name but a few of the possibilities. A bowl is usually brought to the table with food in it so you will know from looking which utensil you

Figure 6. All-purpose bowl

must use. Either a fork or a spoon is used depending upon what is served. Obviously foods such as cereal and ice cream are not eaten with a fork. A knife is never used when eating from a bowl.

A bowl is placed on a plate in the center of the place setting. It may rest on a serving plate that will be removed with it.

Bowling

Individual alleys and leagues have rules regarding play, but some basic rules of courtesy are observed everywhere.

Do not bowl when someone in the lane next to you is bowling. If two bowlers step up to their lanes at the same time, the one on the right takes precedence.

Do not do anything to distract anyone who is preparing to bowl.

Do not ask to use someone's equipment.

Report your score promptly to the scorekeeper.

Brandy

SEE ALSO *After-Dinner Drink; Glasses.*

Brandy is served after dinner, usually with coffee. Brandy may be stored in and served from a decanter, but it would be a travesty to serve a fine old brandy from anything other than its original bottle.

Brandy is drunk from a brandy snifter, a glass that is designed to let the drinker warm the brandy with his hands as he drinks it *(see Figure 7)*. Occasionally a brandy glass will be first warmed by an inferior brandy, which is then poured out before the older, finer brandy is poured into it, but it is pretentious to do this with anything less than a genuinely precious brandy. The ritual of serving drinks should always be kept to the minimum.

Figure 7. Brandy snifters

Bread-and-Butter Note

SEE ALSO *Thank-You Note.*

These thank-you notes are required whenever you have accepted someone's hospitality overnight or whenever someone has done a special favor for you.

A bread-and-butter note can be short—even three or four lines will do—and it should be handwritten. A printed card is not acceptable.

Bread-and-butter notes require no response from the recipient.

A bread-and-butter note might read:

Dear Janice,

It was so kind of you to lend me your umbrella, which I'm now returning. It saved the day for me. See you soon.

Love,
Marilyn

Bread-and-Butter Plate

SEE *Dishes.*

Breakage

SEE *Apology.*

Bridal Registry

As soon as a woman knows she is going to be married, she—possibly accompanied by her fiancé—may go to her local department store or a specialty housewares store and register her gift preferences. Then when people ask her what she would like for a wedding gift, she or her mother can tell them where she is registered.

Most stores are very accommodating about bridal registries. They will, for example, gladly help an out-of-town guest who calls in by suggesting gifts the bride wants and has not yet received.

No one need feel obligated to choose a gift from among those that are registered, but if you want to give a practical gift, such as a small appliance, or send the couple some china or silver, it is smart to check with the bridal registry of the store (or stores) where the couple are registered to see if this is something they need or have possibly already been given.

Today, fortunately, most of the taboos against a woman marrying a second time have broken down, and the bride who is marrying again may have any kind of wedding she chooses.

As a rule, though, the woman who marries again does not register her gift preferences. There are, however, two exceptions to this guideline. One is the wedding of the bride who is not inviting the same friends to her second wedding as to her first because she has moved or has mostly new friends. The second is the wedding of the groom who has never been married before and who has many friends who would appreciate the guidance of knowing what the couple would like or might need. In the first instance, the bride can register and mention this to "new" friends who ask her what she would like. When relatives and old friends who were at her first wedding and who gave her a gift ask what she needs or wants, she should graciously tell them that one wedding gift is enough. If they persist, she may mention the registry. Many of these people, of course, will still want to give a gift. Few of us are not delighted when a friend or relative finds happiness the second or even the third time around!

Bride

SEE ALSO *Remarriage of Divorced Persons; Second Wedding; Wedding; Wedding Expenses; Wedding Reception; Widow (Remarriage).*

The bride's responsibilities are to plan her wedding and to look her loveliest on her wedding day. She should understand that although this is her wedding, her mother is also the hostess, and that the guest list may comprise several generations. As a result, some compromise on both sides may be required.

Increasingly these days, especially with an older couple, both of whom work, the couple give their own wedding. If the bride and groom give the wedding, the bride may, depending upon the circumstances, be the hostess at her own wedding. I say under certain circumstances, because the mere fact of the bride's issuing her own wedding invitations or paying for all or part of her wedding does not necessarily put her in the role of hostess at her own wedding, particularly if she prefers to relinquish this role to her mother. On the one hand, a young bride who shares expenses with her parents or who even pays entirely for her wedding might not necessarily become the hostess at her own wedding; that role could still fall to her mother. On the other hand, an older, independent bride or a woman who had been married previously might well—and quite naturally—assume the mantle of hostess at her own wedding, even if she did not pay for it, and no one would raise an eyebrow.

Sometimes these are delicate matters and must be negotiated within the family. If the bride and groom are paying for the wedding, but the bride sees that her mother would still very much like to be the hostess, then the tactful thing for her to do is to share some of her hostessing duties with her mother. This could be viewed partly as an act of generosity on the bride's part, and partly as an act of convenience, since few brides will want to shoulder totally the responsibilities of being hostesses on their wedding day.

If the bride is acting as hostess at her own wedding, the rules change slightly. She and the groom, for example, are quite likely to feel they should greet their guests as they arrive, although the bride who wishes to make her appearance as she comes down the aisle always has the prerogative of foregoing this hostessing duty. The bride and groom who give their own wedding must either stay until their guests have left or ask someone to take over as host and hostess for them, in the event that they must leave early.

I have watched mothers and brides stretch their relationship almost to the breaking point over the plans for a wedding, and have often thought how unnecessary it all is if only both sides would see the other's position and compromise a little. In one instance, I watched a bride stubbornly demand a rock band even though well over half the guest list consisted of older relatives and her parents' friends. I also have watched a mother chew her fingernails to the quick because her daughter insisted on a wedding dress that the mother found too revealing. In each instance, both women should have stepped back, the bride perhaps in the first case to consider her mother's position as hostess, and the mother perhaps in the second case to acquiesce to her daughter's taste, even though it was not her own.

Although the bride may not realize it when she is in the midst of planning her wedding and is even enjoying all the hectic activity, she also has some responsibilities to herself and to her future husband. She should try to balance her schedule so that the couple still have some quiet times together and she is not utterly exhausted when her wedding day arrives. To do this, she may have to relinquish some of her responsibility to her mother or to someone else.

DRESS. One of the bride's most enjoyable tasks and major preoccupations is to choose the clothes she'll wear for her wedding. If she has the money, she also may choose a trousseau, but many brides today, especially those who work, need only fill in with a couple of outfits for their new life.

Her wedding dress will depend upon the degree of formality and the time of day.

For a formal wedding, the bride wears a long and often elaborate dress with a traditional veil and headpiece. Her dress usually has a train.

At a semiformal wedding, the bride wears a long dress, although it may be less elaborate (and less expensive) than the dress for a formal wedding. It usually does not have a train, but it may. She wears a veil if she chooses to do so.

At an informal wedding the bride wears a pretty dress or suit in a shade of white or a color that flatters her.

Depending upon the bride's coloring, her "white" dress may be white, off-white, ivory, or a very pale pastel. The material varies with the season, but may be satin, taffeta, moiré, velvet (winter only), or (in summer) organza, batiste, piqué, or cotton. Year-round fabrics include silk, peau de soie, lace, and chiffon.

For many years, it was considered scandalous for a second- (or third-) time bride to wear a white dress, let alone a white *wedding* dress. Today's brides, being the independent women that they are, usually please themselves, and more than a few walk down the aisle a second time in a traditional white wedding dress and veil. If you want to do this, particularly if you did not have the dress of your dreams at your first wedding or if your groom wants to see you in a traditional wedding dress and veil, then I think you may do so even though you have been married before.

As far as I am concerned, women were denied the right to celebrate a second wedding only as punishment for having been divorced, and these are just the kind of pointless etiquette rules I would like to see ignored. After all, no one is hurt if a woman opts to wear a white wedding dress when she has been married before, and besides, more than a small element of hypocrisy exists in many first-time brides wearing the traditional white dress that represents virginal purity. I think every bride, no matter how many times she has been married, should wear the dress of her dreams.

For the remarrying bride who does want to go the traditional route, try to choose a white, off-white, or pastel dress and a hat that is becoming but not overtly bridish.

Older brides, women who reach forty or so and have never married, and women who have been widowed, do usually forego the traditional wedding dress and veil simply because it is a costume most suited to younger women. Even so, this is not a hard and fast rule, and the birde has great leeway today in choosing what she will wear on her wedding day.

RING. The bride chooses and buys the groom's wedding ring. This is something they should do together; he should choose a wedding ring within her financial means that reflects his taste.

GIFT FOR THE GROOM. In addition to the ring, the bride often gives the groom a wedding present. Suitable presents are a wedding portrait of her in a silver frame, a piece of jewelry for him, something of leather (a briefcase or datebook), a print, some rare wines if he's a collector, or a rare book or something related to his personal interests.

BRIDESMAIDS' LUNCH. The bride often gives a lunch or supper for her attendants a few days before the wedding. She may schedule this on the same night as the groom's bachelor party if she chooses. At the lunch, she gives her attendants their gifts. Occasionally, a friend of the family or a favorite aunt gives her this party.

Bridegroom

SEE ALSO *Wedding; Wedding Expenses; Wedding Trip.*

The groom has fewer responsibilities, in a sense, than does the bride, but his responsibilities are growing as the times become more liberated, and many men are taking a more active role in planning their weddings. Certainly an older couple or a couple who have been living together are likely to give their own wedding, in which case the groom is often very actively involved. The groom may do anything from ordering the cake or liquor, planning the meal, to meeting with the florist. Increasingly these days it is the bride and her husband-to-be who plan the wedding together rather than the bride and her mother.

If the groom is the host at his wedding, then his responsibilities increase proportionately. Even if his bride is not present, he should greet guests as they arrive. He should also circulate throughout the reception as he would at any party he gives and must remain until his guests have departed. If he must leave early, he should designate someone—his father or best man or the bride's father—to take over his duties as host.

Even when the wedding is planned by the bride and her mother, the groom chooses his own attendants, arranges for them and himself to be properly dressed, and arranges the honeymoon. He also often helps the bride set up their household.

DRESS. The dress of the groom and his attendants is determined by the degree of formality of the wedding. Briefly, for a very formal evening wedding, he and his attendants wear white tie; for a formal daytime wedding, they wear gray cutaways and striped trousers with the traditional accessories. For a semiformal evening wedding, the men wear black tie, and for an informal wedding, they wear dark suits or dark blazers. If his attendants are servicemen, they wear their uniforms: dress uniforms if the wedding is formal; regular uniforms if the wedding is informal.

RINGS. The groom buys the bride an engagement ring, if they decide to get one, and her wedding ring. The engagement ring is always optional; a wedding ring is required for the marriage to take place. Her engagement ring should be within his means; he may wish to visit the jeweler in advance and choose several rings for his fiancée to look at when they return together.

A bride and groom usually buy their wedding rings together. They may be matching rings, or each person may choose whatever pleases him or her.

GIFT FOR THE BRIDE. The groom buys his bride a wedding gift—usually a piece of jewelry or some item that she can keep forever.

GIFTS TO HIS ATTENDANTS. Like the bride, the groom is expected to give his attendants gifts to thank them for serving him. The gifts are traditionally something of lasting value: cufflinks, studs, a small memento box, a keyring, letter opener, or some other small gift of sentimental value.

The gifts may be presented at the rehearsal dinner, the bachelor dinner *(see separate listing)*, or the day of the wedding.

Bridesmaid

SEE *Wedding Attendant.*

Bridesmaids' Lunch

SEE *Bride.*

Briefcase

A briefcase is a status symbol. Since status symbols vary from business to business, the particular kind of briefcase that confers status will also vary, depending upon the business you are in. Canvas bags are popular with some reporters; leather photography cases with people in advertising, film, and video; conservative leather cases with lawyers, and so on. The trick is to figure out what invests you with status in your profession, and then to buy exactly that kind of briefcase.

Among high-ranking executives of either sex, there is only one status briefcase: the classic envelope, very thin and made of the best leather money can buy. It may be either black or brown.

Any briefcase should be made of good materials regardless of its style. If it is canvas, it should be sturdy canvas, and the trim should be good, probably leather and brass. A leather briefcase should be made of good-quality leather.

WOMEN AND BRIEFCASES. Professional women often try to choose briefcases that preserve their femininity while also managing to look businesslike, no small trick and one that leaves many women with no choice but to carry a tote. Many briefcases are suitable for either men or women, but executive women thus far have avoided the somber, heavier, hard-sided styles that some men carry.

Since most women need both a briefcase and a purse, it is smart planning to keep personal things in your purse and business things in your briefcase. Don't let yourself be embarrassed like one young female Turk I know who settled on a briefcase alone, only to have her makeup come tumbling out all over a conference table when she was making an important presentation.

Purses used for business should be of good leather and in conservative colors such as beige, brown, gray, navy, or black.

Bris, Brit, Brith Milah, Pidyon Haben, Naming Ceremony

SEE *Jewish Birth Ceremonies.*

Buffet Dinner

SEE ALSO *Dinner Party; Serving Food.*

A buffet dinner is an attractive alternative to serving a sit-down dinner. A small apartment or dining room can accommodate more persons buffet-style than when everyone must sit down. At a buffet meal, food is displayed on one central table, and the dinner guests walk by it to serve themselves.

Buffet dinners may be either sit-down or stand-up. At a sit-down dinner, a buffet table is used for serving the food, but the diners then retire to another table (or tables) where places have been set. At a stand-up buffet dinner, the food is set out on a serving table, and diners help themselves. They then stand to eat the food, although a considerate host has a few small tables and trays set up for those who cannot manage to eat this way, the elderly, a parent who is tending a small child.

At a sit-down buffet, any type of food may be served, but when guests are expected to stand and eat, they must be served food they can handle. Basically, this means fork foods, anything that does not require cutting with a knife. Stews; foods wrapped in very light, flaky pastry; and most pasta dishes are excellent for this. Vegetables and other side dishes should also be prepared in bite-sized pieces.

SERVICE TABLE. The table for serving a buffet must be arranged in a way that is most convenient for the diners. Usually this means that they first pick up their utensils, which are wrapped in napkins, then go to the main dish, and finally to the side dishes. The table is then either cleared for dessert, or dessert and coffee are served from a side table.

There are two usual approaches to a buffet table. One is to have all the diners go through one line, moving from one end of the table to the other, and the other is to have two lines moving from either end of the table. If you have room, you can also have two serving tables set up, and that will make things move more quickly. Figures 8 and 9 show the two alternate ways of arranging a buffet table.

Burping

SEE *Belching.*

Bus Travel

A certain camaraderie often develops among those on a bus tour. It is important, however, when there is a tour guide to

Figure 8. Buffet table for large party. Guests serve themselves from either end of table.

A. Dinner plates, utensils, and napkins
B. Main dish
C. Alternate main dish
D. Vegetable
E. Second vegetable
F. Salad
G. Bread
H. Dessert plates, forks, and napkins
I. Water pitchers and glasses
J. Wine bottles and glasses

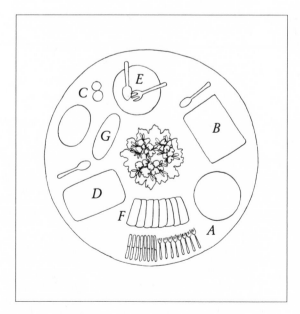

Figure 9. Buffet table for small party
A. Dinner plates, utensils, and napkins
B. Main entree
C. Salt and pepper
D. Side dishes
E. Salad bowl
F. Napkins
G. Bread

Following dinner, the buffet table can be cleared and reset with dessert plates and utensils, dessert, coffee cups and saucers, coffee pot, sugar bowl and cream pitcher.

listen to or, at the minimum, not disrupt his or her discourse. Tour guides are often tipped. One to two dollars is sufficient for a short trip, more for a longer trip. For a longer trip, a guide may be given a small gift instead. Liquor or candy are excellent presents.

When traveling cross-country by bus, you may or may not wish to chat with other passengers. A passenger who settles in to watch the scenery or read a book is signaling that he or she does not wish to be disturbed and therefore should be left alone.

You will have to carry your baggage yourself on a bus trip, so it is best to travel light.

When the bus stops for a meal or lay-over, always be in your seat at departure time, or you will hold up everyone else or be left behind, more often the latter.

Business

SEE *Briefcase; Business Appointment; Business Card; Business Club; Business Condolence Note; Business Dress; Business Entertaining; Business Entertaining at Home; Business Friendship; Business Gift; Business Introduction; Business Lunch; Business Stationery; Business Telephone; Business Writing Style; Client Relations; Firing; Hiring; Job Interview; New Job; Office*

BUSINESS (con'd)

Assistant; Office Decor; Office Gossip; Office Guest; Office Life; Office Love Affair; Old-Boy Ties; Professional Membership; Resignation; Sex in the Office.

Business Appointment

A business appointment should be honored as strictly as any other appointment, perhaps more so since a great deal may be at stake.

Whenever possible, to save time and look efficient, always make a firm appointment rather than a casual one that will require several more phone calls to firm up. Most executives make their own appointments. If you absolutely cannot work this way, say something like, "My secretary, who is very efficient, keeps my appointment calendar, so let me switch you to her to set up a firm date." Then stay on the line until your secretary answers.

If an appointment is made for a date fairly far in the future, it is a good idea to confirm it the morning of the appointment. Some executives routinely confirm all business appointments. It is acceptable for your secretary or assistant to do the confirming; he or she will undoubtedly call the secretary of the person with whom you have an appointment.

When you must cancel an appointment,

do so as soon as you know you cannot keep it. If the appointment was important, call in person to offer your explanation and to reschedule. Otherwise, your secretary or assistant may call for you, but he or she should be tipped off to sound apologetic in your behalf.

On the day and appointed hour of the appointment, arrive on time, even a little early if possible. The days are gone when the more powerful person tested the less powerful person by keeping him cooling his heels for a business appointment. Someone who cannot manage to be punctual is not likely to impress others with his executive skills.

If at the last minute you cannot keep an appointment, have your secretary or assistant call or, if necessary, go in person to the place where you were scheduled to meet to explain what has happened. You should then call to offer your personal apology and to reschedule.

Business Card

Almost everyone can use a business card of some kind. They provide people with something concrete to remember you by.

In some offices, you will be provided with business cards and will have little to say about their design. When you do have some control over the kind of business card you have, opt for something conservative and tasteful.

Choose a good, heavy stock in a white, off-white, or beige color, engraved or printed in black, gray, or brown ink.

Brightly colored inks should be avoided, as should unusual or flamboyant designs. A business card should contain your name (spelled correctly, of course), title, business address, and business telephone. A standard layout is shown in Figure 10.

Eugene Wolf
Comptroller
Early Enterprises, Inc.

189 West Skyline Drive
Manville, Kentucky 90876
Telephone: 746-465-9865

Figure 10. Standard business card

Be sure to include your ZIP and area codes. A personal or home phone number is rarely seen on business cards, but when it is, be sure to differentiate between the two:

Office: 756/857-6500
Home: 756/756-8345

SELF-EMPLOYED PERSON'S CARDS. If you work for yourself, it is even more important to have a nicely designed business card. It is not a good idea to put a logo or any other symbol on a business card. Corporations pay advertising agencies thousands of dollars to develop logos for them, and unless you can pay someone to develop an equally sophisticated logo, it is better to forgo the logo entirely. When in doubt, it is better to opt for a slightly more conservative business card over something unusual or highly designed. The only exception to this is in certain commercial arts, where a business card might be considered a sample of one's work.

Self-employed persons are often unsure as to whether or not to include their titles, and there are times when it is best not to. I somehow think I would only laugh if I were handed a card that said "Samantha Simon, Author" or "Will Ferguson, Artist." One writer I know who worked in the business sector did find she needed a title, so she settled on "Writing Consultant," and that seemed to work very well. Also, you can always assign yourself the title of "President" or "Director" when it is your own business. Some cards, though, do read better with a name and no title. A good rule of thumb is to include only as much information as you need to identify yourself properly and be of use to those persons who will be given your card.

PROFESSIONALS' CARDS. Most physicians and some lawyers list a specialty on their card. When professional titles are included, they go on a separate line after the name:

Anna Boardman, M.D.
Internist

Business Club

SEE ALSO *Private Club.*

While few clubs are, strictly speaking, for business only, some clubs are used almost entirely for business entertaining. Either a company will take out a corporate membership or individuals will obtain individual memberships that their companies pay for.

Business Condolence Note

A condolence note from one business acquaintance to another is the only kind of condolence note that may be typed. It may be written on your personal business stationery or a company letterhead. It should be written on the company letterhead if you are representing the company. If someone is a personal friend whom you happen to know through work, it is kinder and more personal to send a handwritten note on your personal stationery.

Most of the time, with a business acquaintance, you will not have known the person who died but will only know the survivor, so the condolence of necessity will be more impersonal. The note may be very brief; it is the thought that counts in circumstances like these. A sample note follows:

Dear John,

I was so sorry to read about your father's death in this morning's paper. I can imagine what a shock it must be to you to lose him so unexpectedly. Please accept my deepest sympathies and convey my condolences to your mother and others in your family.

Sincerely,

Sally

Note that you simply sign your name and do not use a title. You may sign your surname, too, if this will be necessary for the recipient to identify you.

Business Dress

Wherever you work, you will—if you take the time to look—observe similarities in the way people dress. Factory workers all wear blue jeans and workshirts. In one office, casual pants and even jeans may be acceptable dress, while in another, these clothes would be totally unacceptable. All offices have an official or more often an "unofficial" uniform, and to not wear it is to risk being seen as different, an outsider. In order to fit in, and, more important, to be seen as promotable, you need to dress for work very much like everyone else in your office or profession.

Dressing like everyone else does not mean there is no room for individuality. In some fields, that of high fashion, for example, or the tony art world, a unique look in an employee is much admired and is even to some extent required. But for all the individuality, there is still the uniform; sometimes in fact the individuality is the uniform. The man who showed up for a job interview dressed in wash pants and a worn denim jacket would not be a good prospective employee, nor would the woman who showed up in a conservative, blue twill three-piece suit with a prissy bowtie at her neck.

Most office dress codes are of the "unofficial" variety. Successful people always crack the code, however, for their particular office or profession and dress appropriately.

DRESS IN BUSINESS. The most rigid standards for dress are in the world of business—at banks, brokerage houses, law firms, and the like.

Women. In the past decade or so, as women have entered the executive ranks in many companies, a lot of people's time and attention has been taken up with telling women how to dress appropriately for work. A man named John Molloy, author of the phenomenally successful book *Dress for Success,* even came up with a uniform for women executives: a three-piece suit sewn in men's suiting material, a bowed scarf made of soft silk at the neck, and black or navy shoes—preferably pumps. One young lawyer I talked with told me her firm was so conservative she could not even wear T-strap pumps; they had to be absolutely plain.

The few older women who have made it to the executive ranks and who have spent their entire careers being warned away from looking like men, have never taken to the look and have stayed with their tried-and-true silk dresses and jackets.

Gradually the mousy look has fallen out of favor, and the "dress for success" suit is now worn only by very young lawyers and up-and-coming secretaries. Other successful women in business have adopted a softer, yet still businesslike wardrobe: silk dresses, sometimes plain and sometimes in small prints, with jackets; dresses that stand by themselves; and suits of feminine fabrics that are worn not with Oxford cloth shirts but with soft blouses.

Any basic color shoes may be worn, although most woman still lean toward a fairly classic cut, and neutral hose are favored over colored hose. Purses should be similarly tailored and of good leather. A good leather briefcase should coordinate with everything; it need not match.

Except in very cold climates and in certain businesses, fur coats are not appropriate office garb. Gloves may be leather or knitted and, like hats, are chosen for comfort and protection from the cold rather than as part of a fashionable outfit.

Jewelry is kept to the minimum and is conservative—a watch, a ring or two, and possibly earrings.

The above is the look for executive women, and of course any woman who is aspiring to the executive ranks should adopt a similar look.

Those women who work in business but are not executives will also want to build a professional wardrobe. In fact, just about the only difference between how a woman executive dresses and how her assistant or secretary dresses is the amount of money that each spends on her wardrobe. The executive woman can afford to spend more money on her clothes, and she does.

Regardless of one's business, most other office uniforms emanate from this one. Brighter colors may be acceptable; pants may be worn on occasion—the look changes but only slightly, especially for professional women.

There are some unacceptable ways to dress for any office. Generally taboo are:

- miniskirts
- odd-colored high boots
- any but the most conservative jewelry
- outlandish hairstyles or colors
- turbans or hats, other than those worn to protect one from the elements
- anything see-through
- anything low-cut
- anything tight
- anything too loose and flowing, too robelike

Men. Men's dress varies less than women's, especially for work. If anything, perhaps especially on the executive level, men are more conformist than women.

The basic uniform for a man is the tailored, well-cut suit. Whether it is three-piece or two depends upon the business. Bankers, stockbrokers, and lawyers favor the three-piece suit; most other occupations go with a two-piece suit. The suit may be custom-tailored or off the rack, but it should be fitted properly.

A man's suit is fitted properly when it hangs well. The jacket should lie flat on the back of the neck. The collar should not stand away from the shirt collar, and the back of the jacket should not wrinkle either vertically or horizontally when you are standing normally.

The vents on a man's jacket are there to ensure ease of movement. Two vents are considered sporty; one is conservative; and no vents are elegant but can only be worn by a very slim, trim man. The sleeves should be smoothly sewn in, with no wrinkles or puckers where they are joined to the body of the suit. Make sure you can move your arms freely. The length of the jacket can be made a little shorter or longer to accommodate an individual body line, but a good way to test length is to curl your fingers, with your arms hanging straight, around the bottom edge of the jacket. If the bottom edge of the jacket fits exactly into the curve of your fingers, that is the right length. Always wear the same kind of shirt you will wear under a suit when you try one on. The sleeves of the jacket should be long enough so that about one-half inch of the shirt shows. On most men, this means that the jacket comes to the middle of the wristbone.

Vests should fit smoothly, too, with no wrinkles or puckers. Check the armholes to make sure they do not gap.

Pants should hang straight, without bagging, when you are standing up straight. Make sure they are not fit too tightly. The belt loops should be neatly sewn in. A major mistake in fitting pants is to get the length wrong. Uncuffed pants should just barely break over the tops of your shoes. In the back, they should touch the tops of the heel of your shoes.

When a suit is being fitted, it is a good idea to wear the same shoes you will wear with the suit.

You will get longer wear out of a suit if you avoid fads when buying it. Cuffed pants and double-breasted suits look great when they are in style and passé when they are not.

A man's business suit may be gray, dark blue, charcoal, or black. Certain shades of brown also may be acceptable. The fabric may be solid, pin-striped, chalk-striped, or a very muted plaid. Beige, khaki, and seersucker are popular summer fabrics. Of all these possibilities, though, the suit that most clearly bespeaks power is the solid dark blue, well-tailored suit. All men of all body types are flattered by this color. It has none of the somber qualities of the black color family, and none of the rakishness of some pin-striped and plaid fabrics, however muted they may be. No man can go wrong with a couple of these in his wardrobe.

Shirts should be bought to go with suits and not the other way around. The standard man's business shirt is cotton or a cotton and polyester blend, dull finish, flat weave. White, pastels, and pin stripes are most acceptable in the conservative businesses; in the less conservative ones, dark-and light-colored plaids may be acceptable. In conservative businesses, the shirt should always be a lighter color than the suit. Shirts worn under business suits should always be long-sleeved.

Ties should be coordinated with shirts and suits. A tie should fit. By that I mean that it should come to the tip of the belt. Most ties are 55 to 56 inches long. If this does not suit your frame, consider ordering custom-made ties.

Silk is the best material for ties, and silk and polyester also works well. Wool challis is fine if it is not too bulky. Tie material must be thin enough to make a smooth knot. Cotton ties are often worn in the summer.

Ties may be printed, solid, or striped, but the pattern should be muted. The best all-round tie is a muted paisley.

Bowties are still considered a bit eccentric.

Black and brown are the best bets for shoes, and laced or wing-tip shoes are favored by most conservative businessmen, although loafers have also become acceptable. A loafer, if worn, should be very conservative with no flashy hardware or logos. Choose a belt the same color as your shoes, and be sure to wear socks that match your shoes.

Men's jewelry should be conservative. Most businessmen wear only a watch, and despite the wonders of watch technology, most opt for the old-fashioned kind. A gold band (read: fourteen-karat) has the most status if you can afford one; otherwise, opt for a plain leather band.

The men's coat with the most cachet is the trench, modeled along Burberry lines, although a good look-alike will suffice when you cannot afford the real thing. The other choices are a reefer in a small herringbone or a plain fabric or a camel-hair coat.

GROOMING. As important as how well dressed you are is your personal grooming. Not being flawlessly groomed will really count against you.

Shoes should always be polished, and they should be reheeled regularly—before they look as if they need it. Women should carry an extra pair of hose in case they get a run in the ones they are wearing.

Nails and hands should be immaculate at all times, and your hair should also be squeaky clean. Conservative haircuts should be favored by men and women in business. A beard or mustache may be taboo for men in some businesses, more acceptable in others.

Given the pressure that all of us encounter from time to time at work, a good deodorant is usually a necessity, as may be a mouthwash.

These are the kinds of things, as the ad used to say, that no one will tell you about, but they will definitely keep you from being executive material.

Business Entertaining

SEE ALSO *Business Entertaining at Home; Business Introduction; Business Lunch; Office Guest.*

BUSINESS PREMISES. Increasing numbers of businesses are set up to entertian in their own offices. This form of business entertaining, usually a breakfast or lunch, and occasionally a dinner, offers one great advantage, and that is that your customer or client is close to the product. Another advantage to entertaining on the premises is the amount of control you can exercise over the client. The customer who would not necessarily visit you for a plant tour may be much more interested when a good meal is thrown in. And he can hardly say no anyway once he is sitting in your corporate dining room. It is no wonder that some corporations have even gone to great lengths to hire top-notch chefs, whose job is to provide excellent meals for executives and their guests.

Any executive who entertains on the premises of his business must think of himself as the host, whether or not he is the president of the company. This means that guests should be greeted personally upon arrival and escorted around.

If drinks are usually served, they may be offered, although this is a decision that should be made based on your relationship with the visitor and the nature of the business being conducted. Often drinks are not served in a corporate dining room.

If a menu has been preselected, the meal service simply begins; if the guest can order for himself or herself, a menu is presented. As is the case with other business meals, it is considered polite to talk business over initial drinks or at the end of the meal but not throughout the meal, unless, of course, everyone has agreed to discuss business throughout.

There are less elaborate and expensive ways to entertain on premises than to hire a full-time chef and set up a dining room. An on-premises party can be an excellent way to entertain during sales conference or introduce a new line or product. Caterers can be hired on a one-shot basis, for large parties, small parties, or even lunches.

In some businesses, a party is expected on certain occasions—to celebrate a merger or other big business deal, to celebrate the completion of a major project. If clients are present, the value of these functions can hardly be overestimated, and even when the functions are exclusively for employees, they are the kind of perk that pays off in a certain kind of dividend—happier employees.

OFF THE PREMISES. Business entertaining may also be done in any other appropriate place—over dinner in a restaurant, at the theater, at a private club, even on a yacht. Under such purely social circumstances, business is often not discussed, and the event is used primarily to cement relations.

Whoever does the inviting is the host and pays for everything. Since the function is a business-related expense and the cost is not coming out of the host's pocket, the guest merely accepts what comes his way graciously and does not offer to pay.

CONVENTION ENTERTAINING. Conventions provide an excellent opportunity for developing new business and building up established ties. The atmosphere is usually more that of a party than any kind of business meeting, and hotels offer amenities that facilitate entertaining large or small numbers of persons.

Since the sexual atmosphere at many conventions is also rather partylike, a woman may want to exercise some caution about the circumstances under which she entertains, particularly in those situations where she is representing her company. If she feels it necessary (meaning, if there will be any question of propriety), she should not hesitate to schedule any entertainment for which she is responsible for public places—restaurants, suites, meeting rooms—rather than her hotel room, unless, of course, that room is a suite that includes a living room.

Business Entertaining at Home

STAFF AND COLLEAGUES. Whether or not you socialize outside work with your staff depends upon your management style and how much socializing goes on in the company. In some companies, everyone goes home at night, and co-workers would not think of seeing each other after hours. In other companies, the camaraderie of work extends into everyone's social life, and there is a lot of after-hours partying. Try to observe which kind of company yours is, and play along with it to some extent. On the one hand, you won't want to rock the boat by constantly extending dinner and party invitations to co-workers who would prefer to keep their private and professional lives separate. On the other hand, do not fail to entertain your staff and colleagues on occasion if that is what is expected of you.

Even if yours is an office that does little entertaining, it is still gracious to entertain your staff and possibly your colleagues at least once a year. Some people include their office staff whenever they entertain a large group. I think this is a good idea; mixing in co-workers with others makes for a more interesting party. If the party is all co-workers, you will have a tendency to talk about work, and your spouses are likely to feel left out, if not bored.

Alternately or in addition to this, if it seems appropriate, you might invite individuals on your staff and colleagues to dine with you at home every once in a while. This is an excellent way to develop some important friendships.

THE BOSS. An employer always takes the initiative in inviting his subordinates to his home. Once a subordinate has been invited, he can and should return the invitation. Several weeks, if not months, may elapse between invitations unless the boss and subordinate are personal friends, and the dinner invitations are personal rather than business.

A long-standing tradition exists of pulling out all the stops when entertaining the boss. People use their best china and silver, serve great wine, and prepare excellent food. But in these days of casual entertaining, this is not necessarily the case. Fortunately, since the boss invites you to dinner first, you can see how he likes to entertain and plan your return entertainment along the same lines.

If your boss invites you to a cookout and spends much of the evening talking about how much he enjoys casual entertaining, inviting him to a formal, four-course dinner might not be the best way to entertain him. Take a cue and serve a more casual dinner on your best pottery rather than your best china. Anything else may be viewed as putting on airs, and it is never a good idea to look as if you live better than the boss.

In this country, spouses are always invited together to someone's home. If the person is unmarried, you may invite him to bring a guest or not, as he chooses.

Wives used to extend all social invitations. Even if a man was the employee, his wife called the boss's wife to invite them to dinner. Today, when many women have their own careers, invitations are extended more casually. A man can ask his boss and the boss's spouse to dinner; the boss may stop by an employee's desk to say, "My wife [or husband] and I would like to have you come to dinner next Saturday, if you're free then." Being unmarried is no excuse not to return an invitation, either, although it may provide you with an excuse for inviting someone to dine with you in a restaurant rather than serving dinner in your home.

CLIENTS. You may choose to entertain clients in your home. Entertaining a client in your home for dinner is akin to having the boss for dinner. It should be something of a special occasion, but you need not serve a formal dinner if that is not your style of entertaining.

While the talk may inevitably get around to business, an invitation to your home, unlike an invitation to a restaurant, is purely social, and you, as host, should not be the one to bring up business talk.

Business Friendship

WITH PEERS. While you may form some genuine friendships at work, you should always, at least initially, exercise caution. Underlying most peer relationships is a strain of competition that will exist for as long as you are colleagues. If you become friends, it will also be an element of the friendship, something that must be dealt with from time to time.

You are wise to recognize the limits of a business friendship and refrain from becoming overly involved in a colleague's professional or personal life. If that person's career takes a bad turn, or he or she becomes bent on self-destruction, you may have to dissociate yourself as a means of self-preservation.

This is not to say that you should not be loyal to those who are friends and also to those with whom you have formed alliances. Earning a reputation as someone who cannot be counted on for loyalty only means that you will always be an outsider at work. Loyalty, it is safe to say, is the primary trait that co-workers value in one another. But it need not be blind loyalty of a type that could hurt your own career, and the best way to regulate this is to maintain some distance in your professional friendships.

There are often several levels of socializing in any office, and it is up to you to decide how much participation is comfortable for you. Some level of participation is probably necessary to avoid appearing snobbish or aloof. Many business friendships consist of camaraderie at work, an occasional lunch or a few drinks after work, and never go any further than that. Even if you are not enamored of your colleagues, it is a good idea to join in these activities on occasion.

In some offices, workers see even more of one another—socializing on weekends, exchanging dinners, planning family outings. If you are not interested in this level of socializing, you can probably get away with keeping your distance as long as you make a few token gestures. Some workers who do not want to socialize after hours plan an annual party, to which they invite their co-workers. Others join in only rarely, but do participate a few times a year. And it always helps to show a healthy interest in the activities. Ask who won the baseball game or how the bowling team is doing. Finally, always refuse invitations regretfully.

WITH CLIENTS. Friendships with business clients have always been part of conducting business. To the extent that they are part of conducting business, a certain, shall we say professional, distance is always part of these friendships. This is not to say that a client should not be entertained well, confided in (about everything but business), and treasured as any other friend would be, but rather that some professional distance, at least in matters of company business, where confidentiality and discretion are called for, is required.

One executive I know who counts several clients among his close frineds noted to me that they are all ex-clients, or clients whom he knows from his previous professional incarnations. Without a bit of rancor, he recalled, "You never know when someone is really your friend if you've got a business relationship with him. It's when one of you changes jobs or suppliers that the real friendship can get underway, assuming, that is, that it was there all the time."

Business Gift

SEE ALSO *International Business Manners.*

STAFF. It is appropriate and much appreciated to give a secretary and other staff members a gift at least once a year; in some offices the custom is to give gifts even more often—for birthdays and other special occasions. Secretaries usually receive a Christmas gift, and the tradition is growing to celebrate Secretaries' Day, either with a gift, flowers, or lunch. These gifts generally come out of your own pocket, although in some companies, they may be put on an expense account.

Gift giving is generally done more and on a more lavish level in small offices, where only one or two persons are involved. If you have a large staff, obviously you will not be expected to compensate all of them with personal gifts.

On the one hand, gifts to a small staff should be personal. Your secretary does not want a new stapler or pencil holder, regardless of how elegantly designed or expensive it may be. On the other hand, the gift must not be too personal, particularly if a member of one sex is giving a gift to a member of another sex. There is too much room to misread the intentions of an overly personal present.

Suitable presents are theater tickets, a gift certificate to a favorite restaurant or gourmet food shop, small accessories such as costume jewelry, a scarf, or a purse, a datebook, a paperweight.

THE BOSS. Whether or not to give a boss a gift at holiday time or his or her birthday can be a difficult decision. It is helpful if an occasion for the boss to give you a present has come up first, so that he can set the tone. If you are not that lucky, give him something modest, if you feel like it, or to be strictly polite, wait for him to give you a present first.

An employee never is obliged to give a boss as lavish a gift as a boss may give employees. No apologies need be offered: Just give him what you can afford, regardless of how modest it is, and how lavish his gift to you is.

A gift to a boss, like the gifts he gives you, should not be of a highly personal nature, although clothing accessories such as ties or suspenders are sometimes acceptable if you know the boss's taste, and if personal gifts fit in with the general style of office life in your office.

COLLEAGUES. Apart from the occasional office grab bag, if colleagues exchange gifts, in most offices it is because they have become friends. If you are good enough friends with someone to exchange gifts, you will know it and will be eagerly looking for a suitable present. If you suspect that someone is going to give you a gift whom you had not intended to give one to, buy a small, token present to have on hand for the gift exchange, should it occur.

CLIENTS. SEE ALSO INTERNATIONAL BUSINESS. Business gifts to clients may reflect the businesslike nature of your relationship.

On one level are gifts that are blatant advertising but completely acceptable: calendars, datebooks, pencils, and pens. On another level are the gifts that you give to a client with whom you have an ongoing and somewhat personal relationship: wine and liquor, more expensive datebooks, desk accessories, and food baskets. Although the IRS limits the deductibility of business gifts, the sky is sometimes the limit for a good client.

If the client is not personally known, the gift should be fairly impersonal, however expensive it is. If the client is known personally, a gift may cater to his personal tastes: sports equipment, a case of wine, theater tickets.

THANK-YOUS. When a gift is presented in person, opening the gift in front of the giver and thanking him personally is enough, especially if the gift is small and intended as an advertisement. When the present has obviously been especially selected to match your taste and/or interests, or when it obviously has invovled a great deal of expense or time on someone's part, a written thank-you note, which may be typed on your business stationery, is a gracious touch.

Business Introduction

SEE ALSO *Office Guest.*

Business introductions are very much like all other introductions, that is, introduce a lower-ranking person to a high-ranking person ("Jack, I'd like to introduce Sean, my assistant. Sean, this is Jack Riley, who gave us zillions of dollars in business last year"), a younger person to an older person ("Jim, I'd like you to meet my assistant, Shelly Martin. Shelly, this is Jim Woods, the company's past CEO"), and a woman to a man, except when the man is clearly higher-ranking. In most offices, this means almost everyone is presented to your boss. Your secretary, even if she is a woman, and most of your office staff are presented to most guests to your office, executives, and your peer colleagues ("John, have you met Suzanne, my secretary?"). If you were to introduce your secretary or female assistant socially, though—say, at an office party or a chance meeting outside the office—the situation would be reversed, and as a woman, men would be presented to her. A woman of a certain age who has worked for you for a long time might, with a few exceptions (the president of the company, the chairman of the board), have people presented to her instead of the other way around ("Mrs. Johnson, I'd like you to meet Mr. Riley, our new client"). As is always the case with manners, follow your instincts with regard to when to break the rules.

In an office and in this nonsexist era, anyone who is introduced to another person should stand to shake hands. An executive can stand behind his desk and reach across it to shake hands; more gracious still is to come out from behind it to greet someone for the first time.

A secretary who goes out to the reception area on behalf of her boss to greet a visitor does not offer to shake hands, but should be prepared to if a hand is extended.

Perhaps in no other realm of modern life is a firm handshake more important than in business. Friends can and will overlook a limp handshake; a competitor is likely to size you up as a wimp and be that much tougher on you in your business dealings.

A firm handshake should be just that: firm, but not bone-crunching. Put your five fingers around the hand you are shaking, squeeze it lightly, and pump it several times. Do not, especially in a business situation, use both hands; this is a bit too personal. Do not pump more than three or four times; even once or twice will do.

When shaking hands, always look the person directly in the eye. Americans do not generally hold eye contact for very long, but an evasive look is considered sneaky, and no one wants to give that impression in a business situation.

It no longer matters whether a man or a woman first extends a hand. Whenever you greet visitors to your office, be prepared, as the host, to extend your hand first.

Business Lunch

SEE ALSO *Business Entertaining*.

The most celebrated type of business entertainment is the ritual known as the business lunch. It serves many purposes, from simply getting to know a client or customer better to brainstorming over an exciting new deal to wooing new business to keeping employees satisfied. Business lunches are also typically used to interview prospective employees. They are used as celebrations, to honor an employee who's gotten a raise or promotion. Some bosses have used the business lunch to fire, but this is the height of bad manners, to say nothing about what it does to the digestive system.

Business lunches are most often set up by telephone. Unlike other social engagements, where a firm invitation is offered and a definite acceptance or rejection is the response, business lunches are often negotiated. Presumably both parties have a vested interest in sitting down together, either over lunch or at the conference table, and they will work to come up with a suitable time and place. The time is often left open until the day of the lunch so that everyone involved can work around their daily schedules.

Local custom also plays a role in dictating the time of the lunch, and unless the host clearly outranks his guest, it is a courtesy to let the guest name the hour. Some companies encourage their employees to lunch between noon and 1 P.M.; others do not object to late lunches. In some communities, noon is the businessperson's lunch hour; in other cities, such as New York, San Francisco, and Chicago, 12:30, 1, and even 1:30 P.M. are not unusual lunching hours.

PLAYING THE HOST. Whoever does the asking—initiates the lunch, in other words—is the host. He or she chooses the restaurant and in so doing sets the tone for the entire lunch. Many persons whose careers are heavily vested in the work they do over lunch have made themselves regulars at one particular restaurant, and they enjoy the cachet of having their own table, to say nothing of the extra attention from the staff.

Many smart business lunchers establish themselves as regulars at three or four restaurants, so they choose among them, depending on the personality of the client and the circumstances of the lunch. A luncheon spot should be chosen with great care. On the one hand, if a prospective client works for a company known for its austerity, and you are courting their business, it will not do to wine and dine him at a lavish, expensive restaurant; in fact, it might well be your undoing. On the other hand, if a client has had a long relationship with your firm and has given you a great deal of business, a lavish, expensive lunch may be more appropriate. Personalities matter too in choosing a lunch restaurant. A businessman who used to play linebacker for a pro team will not be comfortable in a restaurant that has a "ladies club" or tearoom atmosphere, but that kind of restaurant may be perfect for the client who has started her own cosmetics line.

Always make reservations for a business lunch, even if the restaurant does not require them. Making reservations is one way to ingratiate yourself and become a regular. When you call for reservations, say, "This is Maria Sims from ABC Advertising. I'd like to have lunch in your restaurant next Wednesday, and could I have that table in the window, please?" The maître d'hôtel will know you after a few calls like that.

In fact, several things will have been accomplished through your call. You have identified yourself with some authority, as a person who might well be worthy of attention. You have begun to establish

which table is "yours," having previously scouted the restaurant to see which table, in fact, you would like to be seated at. You will also have alerted the restaurant staff that you are planning a special lunch. After a few such calls (accompanied by lavish lunches at which you tip well), do not be surprised if you are greeted by name, asked if you want to sit at "your table," and attended by everyone in the restaurant.

There are a couple of other ways to ingratiate yourself with the headwaiter. You can tip him. He should be tipped after the meal, but many regular business lunchers say that a tip beforehand does wonders for the service, particularly if you are a stranger to the restaurant. The tip should be anywhere from two to ten dollars depending upon the community and the kind of restaurant. If you do tip the maître d'hôtel, do so discreetly. Most maître d's have some pride and a few even have some integrity. Making a public display of the pre-lunch tip can backfire because he may then feel awkward giving you the best table and letting the other customers see how easily he can be paid off. No headwaiter will turn down a pre-lunch tip slipped discreetly into the palm of his hand.

As the host at a business lunch, plan to arrive a few minutes before your guests. You can wait for them in the bar, at the entrance, or at your table.

It is your prerogative to arrange the seating at the table any way you like, and while there is no such person as a guest of honor at a business lunch, obviously the most powerful person will be accorded the best seat and will probably sit next to you.

As the host or hostess, it is your job to watch over things just as you would in your own home. You ask to see menus, offer wine to your guests, ask the waiter to correct something. If you have eaten in the restaurant before, you may make suggestions to your guests. If you do these things, the waiter will catch on that you are the host or hostess and will put the check at your place. Of course, it is your job to sign it.

Most business entertainment is paid for with a credit card. This is particularly useful to women, since they do not have to use money. Not many men these days have trouble letting a woman pay for their meal, particularly when the occasion is business, but using plastic makes the whole process that much smoother.

Your guest may offer to pay, or even to put down the tip if you are fumbling for change; do not accept.

WHEN YOU ARE THE GUEST. When you are invited to a business lunch, you are the guest. You need only sit back and enjoy yourself. The good host will take care of everything as unobtrusively as possible. Do not argue over the check. Do thank your host, although profuse thanks are out of place since everyone knows this lunch is tax-deductible and that its purpose is to conduct business.

DISCUSSING BUSINESS. The price of this seemingly free ride is that you do discuss business at some point during the meal. A smart host, without seeming overeager, should bring up business before his guest gets impatient and does so. It does not do to appear frivolous at a business lunch, particularly when lunching with someone whose business you are soliciting.

Some persons prefer to discuss business early on, over drinks, so that the more serious business—and pleasure—of eating is not diluted. Others like to discuss business at the end of the meal, although the risk here is that the other person will have to leave before you have accomplished whatever you set out to accomplish. Most people do not discuss business during the meal, unless both have agreed to do so.

WOMEN AND BUSINESS LUNCHES. SEE ALSO INTERNATIONAL BUSINESS. If the lunch involves a man and a woman, care should be taken to emphasize the business relationship. Unless the woman is very Old School, do not help her with her coat or hold out her chair for her or do anything you would not do for a male colleague. Do not sit next to her, as opposed to across from her, unless that is the same seating arrangement you would want with a male colleague. Women, take note: Do not expect social amenities; you cannot have it both ways, and it is better to opt for the power in business situations. Social amenities due you as a "lady" only compromise your power at a business lunch.

When a woman entertains a man at a business lunch, she pays. When the check arrives, she reaches for it, looks it over, takes out a piece of plastic, and puts it on the table. No words need even be exchanged. If she would be expected to pay if she were a man, she should expect—and be permitted—to pay without comment.

ENDING THE LUNCH. Either person may end a business lunch because either person may have an afternoon appointment that must be kept.

Business Stationery

SEE ALSO *Business Card.*

There are two kinds of business stationery, that supplied to you by your company and meant to be used whenever you are representing them in any kind of official capacity, and that supplied to you by yourself and meant to be used in your personal endeavors, such as freelance work or job hunting.

The first rule of using business stationery is never to use the letterhead of the company you work for to conduct your own "personal" business. A common mistake people make is to job-hunt using their present company's letterhead. You will not, as you may hope, impress a prospective employer with the importance of your current employer; you will only look like a petty thief.

There are times when you may choose to use your own personal letterhead even though you are representing your company. If a client who is also a good business friend, for example, is promoted, you might send a note on your own personal stationery. The advantage of using your own paper is that the letter takes on a more personal tone than it does when written on the company letterhead. Similarly a note of condolence might be written on your personal letterhead. These are, admittedly, close shots to call, and in either situation you could just as easily use the company letterhead. In fact, if the client is important enough to the company, you might even find yourself in a little hot water for *not*

using the company letterhead. As long as you know when not to use the company letterhead—for your personal business—you will develop a sixth sense for those times when using your personal business stationery is a gracious touch.

You have little or no control over the kind of writing paper that is supplied by your company, and must use whatever you are provided with, but you do fortunately have control over your personal business stationery. The first—the only—rule of thumb is to make sure it is tasteful. With a few exceptions, most notably people in the arts, it will be more successful if it is also on the conservative side.

Standard-sized business stationery is 8½ by 11 inches, although it may be slightly smaller, 7½ by 10 inches. If it is larger, it will not fit a standard typewriter, and all business correspondence should be typed.

The paper should be white or off-white, possibly gray or beige. Buy the best bond you can afford, certainly no less than sub 20 in weight. If you plan to use the paper to look for a job, white or off-white is highly recommended because it will still look good when it is photocopied. Beiges, grays, and other darker shades tend to look dirty when photocopied.

Business stationery should be printed with your name, address, telephone, and telex number, if applicable. Professional titles are acceptable on personal business stationery only in some professions; lawyers and physicians usually include them on their letterheads and cards. Those with academic degrees may include them if they are applicable, but remember that a string of so-so degrees may impress less than one very solid degree. If you plan to use the stationery to job-hunt, do not include a title or company name.

Unless you are incorporated, your stationery should not include any kind of logo or monogram. The simplest stationery is the most effective. Commercial artists and other suppliers can "design" stationery, perhaps with two colors of ink or a line to separate the various elements, but this should be done tastefully.

Engraving is the most expensive printing process, but if you can afford to use it, do so, for it is beautiful. Many inexpensive printers have a process that duplicates the raised letters in engraving, and this is acceptable, as is any high-quality photographic printing.

A variety of type styles is available, and any good stationer can suggest several that are suitable for business stationery. Some typefaces are even popular with certain professions—one face is commonly used by lawyers, for example.

The most acceptable color ink is black; brown, gray, and navy are runners-up. If you use a corporate logo, and if a commercial artist has designed the letterhead, other color inks may be used. You cannot go wrong sticking with conservative stationery on white paper and black ink.

Some people like their stationery and business cards to match, but this is not necessary.

Who needs personal business stationery? Everyone. The housewife who occasionally writes to merchants and others about household business matters needs business stationery. The young graduate who is looking for a job needs a smart-looking letterhead on which to write his letters. For that matter, anyone who is or will be looking for a job needs a personal letterhead.

The seasoned executive who stays in touch with business contacts via brief notes may want to use personal business stationery. In short, all of us have some business to conduct at one time or another, and that is when business stationery should be used.

Business Telephone

For some reason, the more highly placed the executive, the fewer gyrations one usually has to go through to get to him or her on the telephone.

WHEN CALLS MUST BE SCREENED. If you must have your secretary screen your calls, make sure that they are screened in a considerate, friendly fashion. She or he should be instructed to sound unrushed and organized. He or she had better, in fact, be unrushed and organized or you will get a lot of garbled messages. The secretary should never give the impression that you are in your office and unwilling to take the call. Asking "May I say who is calling?" and then announcing that you are out is an excellent way to give this impression. Instead, the secretary should say you are out before asking who is calling. Alternately, she can be honest and say you cannot take a call right now, but only before asking who is calling.

When the caller is asked to identify himself or herself, it should be done graciously: "May I tell Ms. Smyth who is calling, please?"

Unless absolutely necessary, do not let a secretary ask what the caller's business is with you.

ANSWERING CALLS. The best way to answer a business call is to pick up the phone and say, "This is Frank Jones." If your call has gone through a switchboard or a secretary, you may simply say hello.

Busy executives may think they can talk on the phone and do other things at the same time, but your lack of attentiveness will show, so grant your caller the same courtesy you would like to receive. Listen attentively, do not interrupt, do not shuffle papers on your desk, do not take interruptions (except necessary ones) from your staff.

Occasionally you will get a pesky call from someone who does not stop talking. A gracious way to end such a call is to say, "Herb, I really don't want to take any more of your time, so I'll say goodbye."

PLACING CALLS. Many companies ask executives to place their own calls since it is a waste of a secretary's time to have very much of her day taken up with calling people for someone who is perfectly capable of placing his own calls. It is also inconsiderate of the person whom you are calling to make him or her wait on the line while your secretary gets you. The solution: Whenever possible, place your own calls. The only exception is the President of the United States, whose calls are always placed for him, but that is mostly so people will have time to collect themselves before saying, "Hello, Mr. President."

To save time for everyone, always identify yourself immediately. Say, "Hello, this is Tom Jones calling. Is Jack Summerton there?" When Jack answers, identify yourself again, just in case his secretary did not inform him who was calling.

If you find yourself up against a tough,

"doorkeeper" secretary, the best strategy is to try to win him or her over. Fighting this misguided soul simply will not be worth the effort. Start right off by identifying yourself, and you avoid round one. When asked to identify your business, do so in a concrete enough way so as to satisfy the doorkeeper's curiosity and in so vague a way as to preserve some shred of dignity. With a little bit of courtesy, you will find that you can even win the doorkeeper as an ally and get all sorts of information from him or her.

Business calls are, for the most part, about business, so do not take up your own or other's valuable time during the workday with lengthy nonbusiness calls.

Business Travel

When you travel for business, less depends upon your personal style than on the style of your company. In some companies, employees travel first class; others expect their employees to pinch pennies. You must do whatever conforms to company policy.

Many employees who travel for business find themselves doing some entertaining. This, too, will depend on company policy. If your company wants you to entertain lavishly, then four-star restaurants are in order; if not, look for something more low-key.

WORKING WHILE TRAVELING. Plane travel during the week is geared to business persons, so if you plan to use your transportation time to catch up on office work or professional reading, quietly mention this fact to the ticket agent when you book your ticket or when you check in. If possible, you will be given a quiet seat away from any children who are traveling.

Once you begin working, most persons—stewards and seatmates—will out of courtesy avoid interrupting you. If the person who sits next to you does not realize you are working (or thinking), or as is so often the case, does not think this is reason enough to leave you alone, and persists in trying to make conversation with you, simply mention that you would like to talk but have a lot of work to do. This is rarely a problem these days, when so many people are sophisticated travelers.

WOMEN. Even in the short amount of time women have been traveling for business, some new etiquette has sprung up to help them. Women, for example, have to worry about security when they stay alone in hotels and motels. When checking in, try to list your name with a first initial only on the register.

If the person at the front desk calls out your room number when he gives the key to the bellhop, quietly request another room since anyone who is loitering in the lobby could have heard the number. Let the bellhop show you to your room, though; this is safer than roaming the halls of a strange hotel by yourself.

A woman traveling on business is still, unfortunately, subject to more public scrutiny than a man is. In some hotels, she is not particularly welcome to dine alone in the hotel dining room. She will arouse disapproval if she entertains or even has business meetings in her room, particularly at night. When you entertain or hold meetings with several people, ask about using a meet-

ing room of the hotel or renting a suite. When meeting with only one or two persons, use the coffee shop or the lobby at quiet times.

Another problem some women have reported when traveling alone on business is that some men think they are "lonely," i.e., sexually available simply because they are alone. Most women learn to reject the open and back-handed invitations tactfully. If tact does not work, a strong no always does. If a woman traveling on business assumes her most professional manner at all times, she should have few problems because of her sex.

Business Writing Style

SEE ALSO *Business Stationery.*

The archaic style of business writing that included such flowery phrases as "I beg to enclose," "Please find enclosed," "Yours of the second," and "I beg to advise you" is definitely passé. Not yet passé although it ought to be is the telegraphic style that includes such phrases as: "Received letter of December 1. Will advise no later than one week."

The best business writing consists of plain, ungarbled English. Do not use a long, multisyllabic word where a simpler one will do. Do not write five words where one will do. Do not write several sentences where one will do, and do not write several paragraphs where one will do. There is something about a blank piece of paper that makes most people think they must fill it up, even if they fill it only with trivia. Trivia has no place in the world of business. Here is an example of an acceptably written business letter, one that says no more or no less than is required to conduct the business at hand:

Dear Mr. Samuels,

I received your letter last week. I need a couple of days to respond to your proposal, and I'll try to get back to you next week.

Sincerely,
George Elwood

The same clear writing that works well in business correspondence is also the best style to use in writing reports and memos.

Here is a brief list of outdated business expressions along with some contemporary replacement phrases:

To Be Avoided	Substitute Instead
I beg to enclose	I enclose
Please find enclosed	I enclose
Will send same	I shall send you
Yours of the second	Your letter of July 2
Hoping to hear from you	I hope to hear from you
Thanking you	Thank you
And oblige me	Please tell me
Beg to advise	I think
In reply I would say	My answer to that is

Good business writing must be well organized. That means you should carefully think through anything before you write, possibly even outlining your main ideas for a major report or memo. Do not go off on tangents. Most letters, memos, and reports are written about one or at most two or three topics; make sure you stick to them as you write.

Above all else, business writing today is low-key. Highly inflammatory or emotional language is not used to persuade others to your point of view. If you are angry about something, wait until you cool down before committing your thoughts to writing.

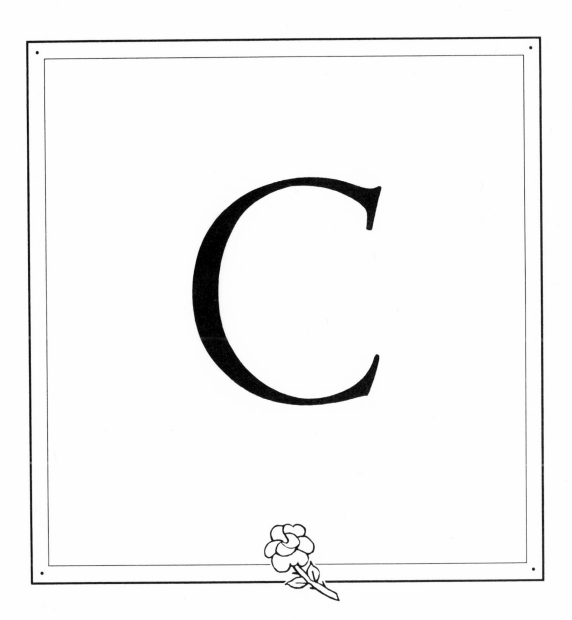

Cafeteria

The rules for going through a cafeteria line are much like those for any other line: Wait your turn, and don't crowd out others. If there is a lull, as often happens in a cafeteria line, it is acceptable to skip ahead of others.

Extend the same courtesy to those waiting on you in a cafeteria that you would to those providing table service.

No tipping is required in a cafeteria except when special services are provided at the table.

Cake Cutting

SEE *Cakes*.

A helpful if minor social skill involves knowing how to cut a cake that will serve a fairly large group.

A sheet cake can be cut in one stroke across one of its shorter sides. That piece can then be subdivided into smaller serving pieces. Each piece should be at least three by three inches in size.

A small round cake should be cut first into quarters, and then into smaller individual servings.

Trickiest of all are wedding cakes, which are usually designed in tiers. By tradition, the bride and groom cut only the first piece (from the bottom tier), which they share, and then someone else—a professional caterer—takes over to cut the rest of the cake. If you do this yourself, start by removing the tiers. The top tier, which is about the size of a small cake, is sometimes saved and frozen for the bride and groom to enjoy at a later date. After all tiers are removed, begin to cut individual slices from the bottom tier. Work in concentric rings, as shown in Figure 11. As more pieces are needed, use the remaining tiers.

Figure 11. Cutting a wedding cake

1. Bride and groom cut two slices from bottom layer.

2. Top tier is removed and saved for bride and groom.

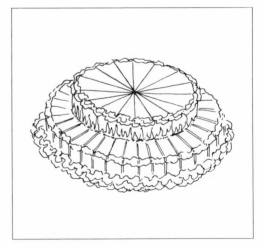

3. After middle tier(s) has been removed, cut each layer as shown, beginning with the bottom tier.

Cakes

SEE *Cake Cutting.*

Cakes are often served on festive occasions—birthdays, anniversaries, showers. Certainly they are featured at weddings, where the most elaborate cakes are seen.

A celebration cake can be homemade or bought from a bakery. Depending upon the skill of the baker, a special design may be worked out. At minimum, the cake usually bears some sort of message for the guest of honor: "Happy Birthday," "Good Wishes," "Congratulations." It should also be made in flavors to please the guest of honor. Even wedding cakes no longer need be the traditional white cake.

Calls

SEE ALSO *Condolences.*

Formal calls are now virtually a thing of the past except in the military services and diplomatic corps, but a few occasions exist when a less formal call is expected and/or welcomed.

CONDOLENCE CALL. A close friend of a family will, immediately upon hearing of the death of a close relative of the friend, call at the home of the bereaved to offer comfort and assistance. The first few callers are often delegated such tasks as notifying other friends and relatives, shopping, and cooking.

All other friends and acquaintances can pay a more formal call at the funeral home. Family members may or may not be present when this call is made, but the caller always signs the register so the family knows who has called.

CONVALESCING-FRIEND CALL. It is obligatory and kind-spirited to call on any friend who is ill enough to be in a hospital or undergoing a long recuperation at home. Depending upon how quickly the friend tires, plan to spend anywhere from five or ten minutes up to an hour. The purpose of the call is to help your friend while away the long hours and to determine whether or not you can be of any assistance. It's pleasant to arrive with a small gift that will amuse the invalid—light reading, flowers, a funny gadget.

When calling on an ill friend, never tell them how poorly they look. If you are shocked at a friend's appearance, hide your feelings as much as possible.

Do touch an ill friend, taking care to do so gently so he is not hurt in any way. People in our culture, particularly where health is the rule rather than the exception, sometimes are afraid of seriously ill persons. This results in the ill person's not being touched when this is often the best medicine in the world. Do touch with care, though, as seriously ill persons are also often physically tender. Save the bear hugs for healthier days, and never sit on the bed of an ill person without first asking if that will be comfortable for them.

MILITARY CALL. Above a certain level, members of the military and the diplomatic corps formally call on their superiors when they report to duty at a new post. Both the services and the diplomatic corps have printed materials that supply details on the protocol of making these calls.

NEW-NEIGHBOR CALL. In most urban and suburban communities, old neighbors call on new neighbors to welcome them to the neighborhood. In some parts of the country, particularly the Midwest and the South, the caller takes a dish of food—either a dessert or a casserole of some sort. This simple custom permits the new neighbors to return the call, ostensibly to return the dish.

The initial call is often unannounced, although it is traditionally made around the cocktail hour, when the family should be home and together. In some parts of the country, where people simply do not drop in on each other unannounced, a phone call can be used to set up the visit.

NEW-PARENTS CALL. Although the obligation to entertain would seem to place an excessive burden on new parents, just the opposite is true: They are usually so excited to show off their new offspring that adrenaline gets them through the many rounds of visitors.

Family and close friends will call on mother and baby in the hospital. Otherwise, it is a kindness to give the new mother a few days to settle in at home.

Calls to new parents should not be made unannounced. Telephone the parents and ask if it is convenient to visit at such-and-such a time.

Camp

SEE ALSO *College and University Life.*

A child's behavior at camp is much like that at any private boarding school. The child who does not borrow, is not excessively noisy, respects others' privacy, and does not leave a mess behind him wherever he goes will have little trouble earning the respect and popularity of his peers.

When food is sent from home, it is helpful to send enough so the child can share with his or her friends.

Canada

Canadians are much like citizens of the United States, except that they are not citizens of the United States. One need not be apprehensive about a visit to Canada, expecting a radically different terrain, but neither is it polite to lump Canadians in with their neighbors to the south. Canada has its own culture, literature, languages, customs, and foods, and these differences should be respected and enjoyed when visiting or entertaining Canadian visitors. Finally, visitors from the United States should remember that Canadians are also North Americans, an appellation we often arrogantly claim only for ourselves.

Canapé

SEE *Appetizer.*

Canceled Wedding

A change in wedding plans may arise for any of several reasons, the most important being that either the bride or groom has some serious doubts about proceeding on the charted course.

A wedding need not be, but may be postponed when there has been a death in the immediate family. Alternately, depending upon the feelings of those involved, it may be scaled down.

As soon as plans for a wedding change, everyone who has been invited or hired to work on the wedding should be notified. If invitations have been sent, they must be recalled. If time permits, handwritten or printed announcements may be sent. If not, invitations may be recalled by telegram or telephone. Persons other than the bride and her mother may be enlisted to help, and, in fact, they may find it more comfortable to let others make these awkward calls.

If the wedding has been canceled, a formal printed announcement should read:

> Mr. and Mrs. George Anson
> announce that the marriage of
> their daughter
> Mary Lynn
> to Sandor Herman
> will not take place

This is all you need say, and all you are required to say. Most persons who have called off a wedding do not feel like explaining what has happened to everyone. Those who are close to you can hear the story when you feel like talking, but the rest of the world requires nothing more than this official explanation.

When a wedding is canceled, all wedding and engagement presents must be returned. This task falls on the woman's shoulders since gifts are sent to her prior to the wedding. Only presents that have been monogrammed need not be returned. Since people will already have been notified of the canceled wedding, only the briefest note need accompany the returned gift:

> Dear Sarah,
>
> I am returning the lovely towels that you were kind enough to send me. Hope all is well with you.
>
> Best,
> Jeanne

If a wedding is postponed and no future date is set, the announcement should read:

> Mr. and Mrs. George Anson
> regret that
> the invitations to their daughter's wedding
> on Saturday, the first of August,
> must be recalled

This announcement may also be used if there has been a death in the family, and a large wedding is being scaled down. The announcement may even have this additional line: "(regret that) owing to a death in the family." In this sad instance, the invitations are recalled, and the wedding is quietly held with just the immediate family present at a later date. Announcements are sent later. Wedding gifts must be returned under the circumstances, but those who know the couple will either write immediately, insisting that the wedding gift be kept, or will send one if they have not already, upon receiving the announcement that the wedding has taken place.

If a wedding has been postponed but will take place at a later date, even a considerably later date, wedding gifts may be kept. It would be too inconvenient to send them back only to have people return them a few months later.

When a wedding date is changed, and the invitations have not been mailed, if there is time, a card announcing the change may be printed and enclosed. It should read: "The wedding date has been changed to the sixth of August."

If there is not time to order printed cards, the bride, her mother, and several helpers may telephone or send notes.

It is also acceptable to cross out one date on an engraved or printed invitation and neatly write in the new date in black ink.

When an engagement is broken, a woman also must return the engagement ring and any other valuable gifts (especially heirloom jewelry) that her ex-fiancé or his family may have given her.

If a wedding cannot take place because the groom has died, the woman may keep the engagement ring and any gifts she has received, although it would be a kindness for her to offer to return any heirloom jewelry.

Candles

SEE ALSO *Centerpiece.*

Too often candles are reserved only for formal or romantic dinners, yet candlelight is so lovely that it should not be saved only for special occasions. I urge everyone—newlyweds, couples who have been married for years, families—to make candlelight if not a regular part of their dining habit, then at least not something totally foreign. Candles may be used on any table as decoration, but they may only properly be lighted after dark. A candlelit lunch makes no sense.

On a table, candles should be placed either above or below eye level. Looking directly into the flame is unpleasant.

Candy

SEE ALSO *Host/Hostess Gift.*

AS HOSTESS GIFT. Candy used to be more of a traditional hostess gift than it is today, but with the attention that is currently being paid to health and fitness, fewer hostesses than ever before are pleased to receive such a calorie-laden gift. Still, on occasion, it's a pleasant departure from flowers.

FOR GUESTS. When candy is available in dishes in the presence of guests, they are free to take a piece. A tactful way to tackle the candy dish is to say, "Oh, this looks delicious. You don't mind if I take a small sample?"

Car Travel

There are few rules for traveling in a car, and all have to do with making sure that the comfort of fellow passengers is not infringed upon. Smokers should ask if anyone minds before lighting up. If there is no objection, they should still smoke with extreme discretion, since even a small amount of smoke can make a small, enclosed space uncomfortable. Make sure an open window doesn't blow excessive amounts of air or ash on others.

Finally, when sharing a car with others, front-seat riders should offer to switch off with back-seat riders every now and then.

Card Games

SEE ALSO *Card Party.*

Never play with players who are better than you, or at least never play with them without acknowledging the level of your playing ability. When playing for money, never play harder or viciously because money is at stake, and never play for more money than you can afford to lose.

At the table, keep your cards in plain sight at all times. And keep them close to your chest. If another player's cards are out where you can see them, you may say, "Chest (or breast) your cards, please."

Follow the local rules. Some bridge players play certain conventions such as a "short club," while others do not. Make inquiries before playing with strangers to be sure you understand the informal rules of the game.

Be quiet if the play is serious, and be willing to chat if the game seems friendly.

Avoid making any annoying noises during play—tapping your fingers, clucking, whistling, humming, or scratching.

Be a graceful loser, and be modest when you win. After all, however much skill is involved, cards are also based on the luck of the draw.

Card Party

SEE ALSO *Card Games.*

Those invited to a card party should not only play the particular kind of card game, but also should all play on the same level. It is unfair to everyone to throw an amateur in with experts, and vice versa.

The hostess provides the tables, cards, and refreshments during the afternoon or evening. The latter varies depending upon whether both sexes or only one sex is playing and the expectations of the group. If all women are playing, more elaborate food may be the order of the day; men are often easily satisfied with chips and dip or hearty sandwiches. If couples meet regularly for a card game, a buffet dinner may be expected.

Whether or not alcoholic beverages are served also varies with the group, but something to drink should be provided throughout the party.

Carving

Meat and poultry may be carved at the table or in the kitchen. If the joint or bird is carved at the table, the portions are transferred to individual plates. If it is carved in the kitchen, the meat or poultry is arranged on a serving platter and passed at the table.

An old saw states that it is the man's job to do the carving, yet in reality few men have the vaguest notion of what they are supposed to do with a whole bird when it is put in front of them. There is no reason that this task should fall on any particular person's shoulders. Either a man or a woman—or a child who happens to be particularly adept—may assume this responsibility.

Caterer

A caterer is a person hired to prepare the food at a party. There is a caterer to meet every need. Some specialize in coming into your home and will prepare dinner for two or four persons. Others' stock-in-trade is handling large parties; a caterer is the ideal choice for preparing a wedding or an anniversary party.

A caterer may work only in his kitchen or on his own premises, or he may be willing to come in and prepare food in your kitchen. He also may supervise the waiters and other help needed for the party. Some caterers are what is known as "full service," that is, they will provide servers (waiters or waitresses, bartenders, etc.) and sometimes even dishes and flatware, etc., as well as the food. The most limited kind of caterer, often a small operation, is the person who will cook the food, period. Most caterers fall somewhere in between being a full-service operation and a one-person food show.

When a caterer does provide full service, you may still request the kind of service you prefer. For example, if the caterer prefers to serve hors d'oeuvres on trays on a table and let guests help themselves, and you prefer to have them passed on trays, you should make your wishes known. Depending upon what you request, you may pay more for doing things your way, but it is your choice.

A caterer may charge a flat fee, but the price is more likely to be based on a per-person charge. The hostess is usually required to supply the caterer with an estimate of the number of expected guests 48 hours or so before the party. Many caterers may add on a service charge. If none is added, tip 15 to 20 percent, just as you would in a restaurant.

The best way to choose a caterer is through personal recommendation, or, better yet, because you have eaten his food and seen him manage a party and liked what you saw.

Caviar

If you are lucky enough to be served this luxury item, here's how to eat it: Put a *small* portion on your plate, along with toast and garnishes. Spread the caviar on the toast, top with lemon juice and/or garnishes (but note that superb caviar needs no garnish), and eat in several bites. Pray that there are seconds.

Cats

SEE *Pet*.

Centerpiece

SEE ALSO *Candles.*

This decoration is placed on the dining table for festive occasions, such as Thanksgiving, Christmas, and for dinner parties.

The traditional centerpiece is candles and flowers. Less traditional and often stunning centerpieces can be concocted of anything that is available—a piece of driftwood, a bowl of brightly colored balls or any other ornaments, fresh vegetables, a single flower at each place setting—whatever catches your eye and appeals to you. Candles, too, need not always be paced in the center of the table or paired; scatter them all over the table or put them at individual place settings, or deck the table with an array of unmatched candlesticks. You are limited only by your imagination.

Only one guideline need be followed when planning a centerpiece: Make sure it does not obstruct the view of anyone at the table. Neither candles nor the actual centerpiece should be high enough to block people's views of one another across the table. Candles, in particular, should not be at eye level, as this causes discomfort.

Champagne

SEE ALSO *Wine.*

A myth exists that champagne is the one alcoholic beverage that goes with every course of food. This is not exactly correct. Even a very dry champagne is not strong enough to stand up to most roasts or even to a heavy soup.

Champagne is best served with the appetizers, and, of course, it is the traditional beverage for toasting and celebrations. It is also lovely with dessert.

True champagne comes only from the region of the same name in France, but American vintners have begun to make some excellent domestic champagnes, which are less expensive than most good French champagnes. Dry champagnes always cost more than sweeter ones, and they are the best. Always buy the best champagne you can afford, and if you must stint on cost, ask your wine merchant to steer you toward a good (read: dry) brand. Don't waste your money on pink champagne or mixed breeds that are really nothing but sparkling wines.

Champagne is served in one of two kinds of glasses: the tulip glass, which is tall and slender, and the wide-mouthed "champagne" glass (*see Figure 12*). Great battles rage over which is the best glass. I say the

Figure 12. Champagne glasses: tulip shaped (left); wide-mouthed (right)

best glass is the one you happen to own. Above all, champagne should be served in stemmed glassware, not in plastic glasses.

When uncorking a bottle of champagne, always take care to point the bottle away from people's faces, as the popping cork is dangerous. But don't go to the length, as some do, of uncorking the champagne in the kitchen or somewhere where your guests are deprived of the festive popping of the cork.

Change-of-Address Announcements

People who move often want to send a change-of-address announcement to friends and acquaintances. There are several ways to do this.

First, and most graciously, short notes announcing your new address may be sent on your informal stationery *(see Figure 13)*. The notes can be brief and simple since it is obvious that you will be writing many of them:

Moved!

New address: 112 West Tenth Street
New York, N.Y. 10001

New telephone: 212-865-8665

Figure 13. Change-of-address announcement handwritten on informal stationery

Similarly, you may have postcards printed announcing your new address. It is gracious but hardly necessary to write a personal message on them.

Finally, you can buy custom or preprinted change-of-address cards in a stationery store and have them printed or fill them in yourself.

To save your social life from a lot of confusion, send change-of-address cards as soon as you know you are moving.

Change-of-Name Cards

Not so rarely today does someone decide to change his or her name. Women probably do this more often than men, as they return to their maiden names after divorce or change them when they remarry. If you send a formal announcement, it should read:

Maria Staff
wishes to announce
that her name has been legally changed
to
Maria Dell

A less formal way to let people know is to mention the news on your holiday greeting cards.

Chapel Wedding

SEE *Bride; Groom; Wedding; Wedding Reception.*

A chapel wedding is essentially the same as a church wedding but on a smaller, more intimate scale. If the guest list is so small that the guests will not begin to fill up a main sanctuary, consider having the wedding in the chapel. A processional can be easily dispensed with in a chapel wedding. If it is, the bride and groom simply walk out from a small side room to the altar with the clergyperson. Since chapels are small in scale, less money can be spent on floral arrangements; too many or too elaborate flowers will overwhelm the small space of a chapel.

Charity

Charitable contributions may be made with money or time. Of the two, the latter is sometimes the more difficult to give. A commitment to help organize some charitable activity or to donate a certain amount of money should always be honored. If you cannot afford either the money or the time, scale down your giving or refuse entirely, but do not make a commitment that you will have difficulty honoring. I am told that many people who pledge money during telethons and other drives to raise funds fail to make good on their pledges, and I find this indescribably ill-mannered and inconsiderate.

Charitable contributions are often excellent gifts to make in the name of someone who seems to have everything. If possible, find out what the person's favorite charity is, and donate to it. If not, donate to a charity you think he or she would like. The charity will send a card announcing that a donation has been given by you in honor of your friend.

Increasingly often, families are requesting that charitable donations be made in lieu of sending flowers to someone's funeral. Such a request should always be honored.

Checkroom

Checkrooms are typically encountered in restaurants. A man usually checks his coat. A woman may check her coat if she wishes, but more often drapes it over the back of her chair. Most checkrooms will not assume responsibility for a fur coat. Persons of either sex should check bulky packages and briefcases, so they do not take up space at the table. Packages may not be put on the table. Women never check their purses and may not put them on the table, but keep them near them.

If the checking service is free, tip the attendant a dollar or so. If there is a charge, add 50 to 75 cents as a tip.

Cherry

SEE *Fruit*.

Chewing Gum

Chewing gum is crass; that is the bottom line. If you must chew, try to confine your activity to the privacy of your own home.

Never, never chew gum (or anything else) while talking on the phone. If you must chew in public, don't crack the gum or chew it noisily. Mothers who supply chewing gum to their children do them a great disfavor, for if the habit is never acquired, it never has to be broken.

Chicken

At picnics and informal family dinners, chicken may be eaten with one's fingers. It is more polite to use a fork and knife on other occasions. When a quarter or half chicken is served, it is acceptable to cut it into pieces if your dinner knife is sharp enough to handle the job.

Use your hostess as a guide. If she picks up the chicken and eats it with her fingers, you may, too. If she does not eat it this way, best to stick with the fork and knife.

Children

SEE *Adoption; Baby; Children and Manners; Children and Strangers; Children's Allowances; Children's Party; Forms of Address—Spoken; Single Parent; Teenagers and Manners; Telephone Manners.*

Children and Manners

SEE ALSO *Children and Strangers; Children's Party; Forms of Address—Spoken; Playground; Teenagers and Manners; Telephone Manners.*

Nowhere is example a better teacher than when small children are being taught manners. They are so pliant, and they love to mimic their elders. Even before your child is old enough to understand what manners are, you can show him many things about how people treat one another through your own actions toward others. A child who hears his parents being harsh to those who work for them or wait on them, who sees his parents ignoring people who need assistance, or pushing or shoving others, soon begins to think that these are acceptable forms of behavior. When a child sees his parents treat others with dignity and respect, his manners may require some polishing as he grows up, but the foundation will have been laid.

COURTESY OWED A SMALL CHILD. In addition to learning how to treat others, children must also be treated well themselves if they are to develop gracious manners. Parents most often think in terms of how they can teach their child to behave toward others and only rarely stop to think of the courtesy that even a small child is owed.

Here are the basic courtesies that any child is owed:

- Do not talk down. Children may not think or act like adults, but they do know when they are being condescended to, and they do not like it.
- Do not discuss your child in his presence. Discussing a child as if he were not in the room, when, in fact, he is standing right there, is a serious indignity. It does not matter whether you are relating something complimentary or not; it is still rude behavior.
- Do not speak babytalk. Apart from the fact that speech experts have determined that babytalk only confuses a child, the child may think this is an acceptable way to speak. And there are few things more ridiculous than an adult speaking jibberish.
- Do not use vulgar language. In today's media-oriented world, with standards at what must be an all-time low, he will learn vulgar language soon enough. There is nothing cute about a two-year-old using obscene expressions that he does not understand.
- Do not, if you can possibly avoid doing so, discipline your child in public. Obviously a reprimand will occasionally be necessary, but a full dressing down or a spanking should be done privately.

WITH COMPANY. A visitor is always a special occasion for a small child, and parents can take advantage of this to begin to discuss "company" manners with their children. Before a guest arrives, sit down and talk with your child about what is expected of him. Describe how you would like to introduce him to your friend. Practice the introduction so you can coach your child on standing still, shaking hands, and rising to meet someone.

Also helpful is to remind the child that this is "Mommy's (Daddy's) friend" and that you would like some uninterrupted time to visit. Discuss how important it is to say "please" and "thank you" around other people.

When a visitor is around, a small child may become shy or rowdy. A few gentle reminders of your earlier talk should suffice to put him more at ease.

After your guest has left, praise the things that your child did right. With very little children, under the age of four or five, I let the things that went wrong slip by. They can be mentioned again in the next pre-visitor talk.

As your child gets older, expect and ask for more from him in the way of manners, both with company and with the family. Teach your child to answer the telephone politely *(see Telephone Manners)*. Teach him to greet guests, and when he is old enough, to invite them in and offer to take their wraps. If you are having a party, and your child wants to be present, allow him to do so for a short time. If he is old enough to help out, assigning him some small task is excellent experience because it gives him a definite and fairly defined way to behave around others. One word of warning, though: Small children are not attractive, cute, precocious, or anything else when serving alcoholic drinks. Reserve this assignment for an adult.

IN PUBLIC. Along with learning how to behave in front of company, it is necessary for a small child to learn that different behavior may be expected of him in public than at home. Pointing, commenting on others' appearances, loudness, and other similar, offensive forms of behavior should be reigned in the minute they occur.

Parents also have a responsibility not to let their children take over in a public place. I recently witnessed an interesting situation with a three-year-old who was dining out with her parents. While the parents drank their coffee, the child was permitted to roam around the restaurant. She went from table to table carrying on what were admittedly rather charming conversations with the other diners. The first time she visited my table, I found her enchanting. The second and the third time, as she interrupted me, I became a little annoyed. I cannot help but think that there were other persons in that restaurant, far less tolerant than I, who were far more annoyed.

The lesson here is that parents should not assume that the entire world thinks their child is adorable or that other adults want to carry on a conversation with their child. If your child receives some attention from a stranger in a public place, you may smile and encourage your child to respond, but to send your child out to seek attention is inconsiderate of those around you.

AT HOME. Children must also learn, from an early age, that as family members, they have certain social obligations. Home should never be a place where the rules of good behavior are suspended; it is far too hard on everyone who must live in such close quarters over a long period of time. Therefore, you should expect your child's table manners to be as good with the family as they are with company. Teach your child to wash his hands before dinner, and give the dinner call a few minutes early so he has time to do so.

Emphasize that consideration toward others and neatness are the keys to getting along harmoniously in a home. A child should learn that there are times when he cannot play a stereo or the television loudly, that the bathroom is communal, and that rooms that are messed up must be picked up. Insist that your child keep his room neat, especially if he shares it with a sibling.

If your child is assigned chores, make sure he accomplishes them. I think all chores should be in keeping with a child's capabilities, but I do think they are an excellent way to teach cooperation and discipline.

DRESS. Children should be dressed appropriately to their age group. This means they should wear what others in their peer group are wearing. There is no need to dress a child more expensively than his peers. If he cannot be dressed as expensively, he can still be dressed similarly.

Children should not be dressed to look like little adults. Few things are sadder than seeing a child, stiffly overdressed, attending a party with other children, all of whom are in jeans and casual clothes.

Monograms and clothes with your child's name embroidered or printed on them are not a good idea. They make it too easy for a stranger to strike up a conversation with your child.

MONEY AND STATUS. If you are obsessed with money and status, your child will be too, even if you never discuss these things directly with him. And while this is obnoxious in an adult, it is pathetic in a child, who does not even understand his snobbery. Few values will be so helpful to your child in getting along with others as instilling the sense that all people are equal. As he grows older, he will, of course, learn otherwise, but there is no reason for a small child to know that his father and mother have more money than his friends' parents or that his family has some special status.

Children and Strangers

SEE ALSO *Children and Manners.*

Of all the contradictory things we must teach our children, the fear of strangers is the worst. We strive to teach them to be friendly, respectful, and outgoing, to treat all people equally, and then we tell them that there are certain adults whom they must not treat in this way.

From a young age, children must be warned about strangers who might seek to harm them. Public playgrounds or other public places are unfortunately often good places to teach a child about this. If you and your child are approached by a stranger toward whom you do not wish to be friendly, and you brush off the person, your child will have some questions and that is probably the time to introduce the subject of "bad" strangers.

Be direct in your discussion without giving your child explicit sexual details, that is, unless he asks. Tell him that there are some "bad" people around who might hurt him, and that he must be careful with strangers who try to befriend him. While reminding him that he is to be nice to people, reinforce the idea that this does not mean strangers. Do not tell him the person is sick or angry. Parents get "sick" and "angry" on occasions and this concept may be confusing to a small child. Simply describe the person as "bad." That is a kind of concrete abstraction that even a three-year-old can assimilate.

There is no need to teach your child to fear every stranger or every poor demented soul whom he encounters. If you do see a homeless person or an obviously harmless but mentally ill person, explain to your child that this person probably is "sick" and means him no harm.

Children's Allowances

SEE ALSO *Family Finances.*

Children need to be taught a sense of responsibility about money, and one of the best ways they can learn is through observation of how their parents handle money. If their parents spend money carefully, they will learn to do this almost by osmosis. If their parents are stingy about money, the children will be, too. If the parents are spendthrifts, then their children will grow up thinking this is acceptable behavior.

Beyond observations about money, children can also learn about it by being given a regular allowance. A child's allowance, which should increase with his age, should be based on what the parents can afford to give and what other children receive as allowances.

When discussing an allowance with your child, you should figure out together what he is to buy out of his allowance and what, if anything, he is to do to earn it. Very young children may not be able to do much to earn their allowances, but when children are older, they can be assigned household chores.

When children enter their teens, their financial needs seem to escalate astronomically. This is a good time to review the child's allowance. In an attempt to meet the teen's growing need for money, many parents pay their teens a regular allowance and then let them earn additional spending money by doing extra chores or errands.

No parent does his child a service by providing him with more money than his peers have. When children go out together, they always go Dutch treat. Because of this, children are much better off having about the same amount of money to spend as their peers do.

Giving a child an allowance is an excellent way to teach him that money is not in unlimited supply. Children, like adults, need to learn to say, "I'm sorry, I can't afford to do that this week." It is a rare family that does not have some money pressures, and there should be no embarrassment in acknowledging that you cannot afford something or that because of your budget you prefer to spend your money one way and not another.

Children's Party

SEE ALSO *Teen Party.*

Even very small children love parties, and come to expect one, if not on every birthday, then on some birthdays. A children's party is simple to organize and carry out.

UNDER-SIX SET. Children under six usually have an attention span no longer than two to two and a half hours at a party. Children's birthday parties are usually held in the afternoon; a weekend afternoon means that more parents will be around to help out. Ask some to stay and help you handle the group.

The most cordial way to entertain is to invite your child's entire class, if possible. If this is not possible, try to invite nonschool friends and only a few school friends. The point is to avoid giving the appearance of excluding only a few classmates.

Invitations may be written or telephoned. They should state an hour for the party to begin and one for it to end. That will let parents who do not stay know when to pick up their children.

Food can be very simple. Pizza, sandwiches, popcorn, and other snack foods will be a big hit. Ice cream and birthday cake, of course, are the pièce de résistance.

Children under the age of six have short attention spans, so any entertainment is probably best kept simple. Renting a movie to play on the home video machine is all the entertainment children in this age group require. Another form of entertainment, of course, are the traditional party games like

Pin the Tail on the Donkey. Most libraries have books of children's party games.

The agenda is fairly simple for the under-six set: As soon as everyone has arrived, begin the entertainment. It is a good idea to schedule more active games first and then conclude with some calmer ones. After the games it is time to open the presents, an activity that all the children enjoy, although none more than the birthday child. At this age, it is nice and sometimes expected that favors will be provided for the young guests.

After the gifts have been opened, everyone sits down to refreshments, which are capped off with a birthday cake and ice cream.

And shortly after that, almost all adults present hope that parents begin to arrive to collect their own children, and the party is over.

OVER-SIX SET. In this age group parties last three to four hours. Invitations should state a beginning and ending time for the party. Birthday parties for this age group are either held in the afternoon or early evening. Sometimes an outing, such as a movie or play, is planned. By the time children are ten or eleven, they are old enough to enjoy a planned, special activity.

All children in this age group appreciate some form of entertainment—a clown or a magician—as well as party games.

Decorations are also worth the effort for older children. Balloons and crêpe-paper streamers are the traditional birthday decorations.

The favored foods are pizza, sandwiches, fried chicken, and other picnic and/or "junk" food. Popcorn is always popular.

If entertainment is planned, it should begin shortly after everyone has arrived.

After the entertainment, the birthday child may open gifts. By the time children are over six, they can open their presents one by one and should be gracious about thanking their friends. Party favors for guests are still a good idea at this age. Suitable ones are candy or some small toy or gadget.

After the gifts are opened, the food should be served. Older children can also handle free time on a limited basis, where they simply play with toys and socialize among themselves. This usually concludes the party.

Children's Table Manners

SEE ALSO *Belching; Business Lunch; Doggy Bag; Eggcup; Elbows; Food Stuck in Teeth; Fork; Knife; Passing Food; Plates; Ramekin or Individual Casserole; Relishes; Restaurant; Salt and Pepper; Soup; Spoon; Table Manners; Toothpick.*

Teaching a child under the age of three or four table manners is a nearly impossible task, and the best—the only—solution for adults who want and need a quiet—or a company—meal is to feed the children early so they do not eat with the adults. At informal family meals, the custom today is to include the children, even if they are still in highchairs. Without passing judgment, I would only suggest that many parents impose undue hardships on themselves by not feeding their children early and enjoying a quiet meal together sans children.

WHEN TO BEGIN. Most children are too young to understand manners and what they really mean much before age four or five. For example, children naturally eat with their mouths open. It may be hard to correct a child of this habit until he or she is old enough to understand *why* it isn't an acceptable way to eat. Trying to explain this to anyone under the age of five is something you may as well spare yourself. Unless your child is especially well coordinated and socially mature for his age, don't make any formal attempts to teach table manners until he or she is around four or five. In fact, as much as possible, avoid correcting your child's table manners before this. Just accept the way your child eats. That way, table manners will not have been turned into an issue before you start to teach them formally.

A child of five or six, on the other hand, is not only old enough to grasp what you are talking about, but also will enjoy working toward various goals that you can set up for him as you discuss table manners.

I break the teaching of table manners into four steps. This gives a small child something to work for, look forward to, and the small steps make learning easier than it would be if you expected the child to grasp everything all at once. Here are the steps you can use at home:

Step 1. Discuss the possibility of learning table manners with your child. If the child has not been eating with you, point out that this is a step toward being able to eat with the adults. Discuss how he learned to share his belongings and to say "thank you" and "please." Tell him that the same good feelings he gets from doing these things can happen when he uses good table manners. Then make a date with your child for a few days later for an intimate lunch or dinner *à deux,* during which you will begin to show him what table manners are all about.

Finally, explain all the other steps to your child so he will have things to look forward to. Depending upon your child's personality, you might even make a chart (maybe in the shape of a rocket?) with various levels of achievement. Silver or gold stars could be pasted down on the chart as the child successfully shows off his table manners during the various steps I suggest.

Step 2. Prepare a dinner or lunch for you and your child. You are the only adult at this meal. Its purpose is to explain table manners to your child step by step.

This meal should be planned in several courses so you can teach your child how to use several eating utensils in one sitting. But, and this is important, it should consist of your child's favorite foods. For example, if you decide to have a soup course and your child loves alphabet-chicken soup, then that is what you should serve. If canned spaghetti is his favorite entree, then the meal should include canned spaghetti. This is to avoid having food become an issue at the meal.

You must also use your best crystal, china, and silver. Never mind that your china has never before seen the likes of canned soup and spaghetti. It will survive the shock. Put on soft music, and dress up a little more than usual. This is a very special meal. Use a bread-and-butter plate, if you like. Definitely plan on a soup bowl or cup and a separate salad plate. Skip wine glasses and use a milk glass or water tumbler.

Call your child to the table. Washing the hands before eating is necessary for most people, especially little people, so you might begin by asking your child to wash his hands and meet you at the table. Explain to your child that he should wait for everyone to arrive at the table before sitting down. You might say, "Children usually wait for adults to sit down first or begin to sit down before they take their seats. Men also let women sit down first and sometimes even pull their chairs out for them." (Show your child how to do this as you talk.)

Talk about how to sit at the table: Sit back in your chair but never so far that you risk tipping over. Keep your hands in your lap.

If you regularly say grace in your home, this is the next step. If you don't, you might explain to your child what it is and when he might encounter it. Your child will feel more secure about table manners if you reassure him that he can always look to the hostess for what to do. Explain that he can look at her to see whether or not grace will be said before he puts his napkin in his lap.

Picking up your napkin, say, "Right after grace, you put your napkin in your lap. Simply pick it up and open it about halfway and put it across your lap. You use it to wipe your mouth—very gently—especially before you take a drink.

"If you leave the table during the meal, put the napkin at the side of your plate. That's also where you put it at the end of the meal. Don't refold it perfectly, and don't wad it up or crush it into a ball, especially if it's a paper napkin."

Next, serve the soup course. Then say: "Let's start with soup. I will pick up this spoon. You see it is the one at the very right of the place setting. I hold the spoon in my right hand like this." Help your child hold the soup spoon correctly.

"Then I dip the spoon into the soup, moving it away from me, getting the top portion that is already cooling off. Don't stir the soup or blow on it to cool it.

"When I'm done, I put the spoon in the soup bowl if it is large and flat. If the soup was served in a small cup, I rest the spoon on the plate underneath it.

"Only take small spoonfuls of soup, because you never want to slurp it while you eat."

Now introduce your child to the bread-and-butter plate. Say: "Right above your plate is the bread-and-butter plate. See, it has a special knife resting on it. I would like to show you how to break a piece of bread in half or in quarters and butter it as you eat it. When you are served a roll or a piece of bread, you break off a small piece and butter it. Then, after you have eaten this, you may break off and butter another small piece." As you say this, break off a piece of bread and show your child how to butter it.

Remind your child never to place a piece of bread in the palm of the hand or on the table to butter it. A bread-and-butter plate may be difficult for a small child to reach. If so, he can either move the plate closer to him or butter and break bread over his dinner plate, whichever he prefers and whichever the table setting permits.

The entree is served next. Introduce it by saying: "Here's our main course. Here are the knife and fork you use to eat these foods. Here's how to hold them." Several minutes will be required to introduce your child to the proper ways to hold a knife and fork. Have patience, and don't expect the child to do this with much finesse right away. Lots of practice is required to do this.

Then say: "Your fork is used to hold the meat that you wish to cut, like this, and the knife does the cutting. Don't stab the meat or tear at it." Decide whether you want your child to eat Continental or American style, and teach that method only. Show the child where to put his knife (American style) or how to hold it (Continental style) while conveying the food on the fork to his mouth.

Then say: "Don't eat too fast or cut big bites. You also cut only one piece of meat or of any other food at a time." Let the child practice a few bites before introducing the vegetables.

Next introduce the vegetables, saying: "When you want to eat your vegetables or other foods that do not need cutting with a knife, here's how to do it. Put the fork in your right hand like a shovel and scoop up the food. Be very careful not to pile more food on your fork than you can eat in one bite. Don't stop to talk when your fork is filled with food, leaving the food to dangle in midair. Never use your fork or knife to play with your food, and never mix the food together on your plate. If you can't cut a food with your fork like this"—show child how to cut with fork—"it's okay to use your knife the way you did with the meat." Show the child what to do with his silver when resting and when finished eating.

Explain that flatware should never be rested half on and half off the plate. When the child has finished with the main course, clear away the dishes and bring in the salad.

Children may find it easier to eat salad if the plate is in the center of the place setting. There is nothing wrong with making these accommodations for a small child. Once he has mastered basic manners and achieved some self-confidence in using them, small details like buttering bread over the bread-and-butter plate and leaving the salad plate to the left of the dinner plate can easily be explained. Then say: "This is your salad fork. You hold it the same way as the dinner fork." Show the child how to hold the fork again. "Bring the food up to your mouth, and lean slightly over your plate as you put the food in your mouth. Don't circle the plate with your left hand or lean on the table in any way."

Use the salad course to explain further the fine points of eating with a knife and fork. If the child is not familiar with salt and pepper shakers or pepper mills, show him how to use them.

Since attention may be waning at this point, keep your explanation about dessert as simple as possible. You will also win points by serving a favorite dessert. To introduce dessert, say: "When eating dessert, you may use a spoon and a fork if necessary. Cakes and pies are usually eaten with just a fork, and ice cream and other similar foods are eaten with a spoon. When you have finished, put them in the finish position just as you did with your dinner knife and fork. Putting a knife and fork or spoon in this position means that you have finished eating. When we go to a restaurant, it will be a signal to the waiter that he can take your plate away."

Finally, give the child pointers on ending the meal graciously: "When the meal is over, the hostess will put her napkin back on the table. At home, I am the hostess. You do the same thing. Everyone then stands up. Men often help women by pulling out their chairs for them. To do this, stand directly behind a woman's chair and pull it out far enough so she can get away from the table.

"If you ever have to leave the table before the meal is over, excuse yourself. Children are often excused from the table before adults, since they don't sit around and drink coffee the way adults do. When you are a guest at someone's house, you wait until the hostess says you may be excused."

Step 3. Prepare a formal dinner for your child and his other parent or some other honored adult guest. The goal of the first meal, as far as your child is concerned, is to prepare to show off the newly learned table manners at this meal. The goal of this step is actually to show them off.

Step 4. Take your child to dinner in a nice restaurant. You need not opt for the most expensive restaurant in town, but do choose one where the service is especially good. If possible (this depends upon your child's age and attention span), reward your child right after this meal with something special. You could combine the meal with a movie or children's play, or plan a trip to a special soda fountain for dessert. Or your next stop might be a toy store, where your child can choose a new toy or book.

These are the four simple steps to teaching your child table manners of which you and he can be proud. They are designed to catch up both of you in the spirit of things and, especially, to make your child want to learn good manners.

Chinese Restaurant

SEE ALSO *Chopsticks; Doggy Bags.*

Chinese restaurants offer a unique and enjoyable dining experience. Most can accommodate large groups. If you would like to order a special banquet, most Chinese restaurants can also accommodate this on only a few days' notice.

The best way to eat Chinese food, whether there are two or ten of you, is communally. Most Chinese restaurants are not geared to serving food in individual portions, that is, a meat dish and vegetable dish on one plate. Instead, they serve large helpings that are meant to be shared.

Some Chinese dishes taste very hot to the average Western palate. If this bothers you, you can usually order the seasoning done to taste: mild, medium, or hot.

The Chinese invented doggy bags, only they went one better and came up with well-designed little white cartons that hold leftover food. (In ancient China, it was an insult to the host to leave a banquet without taking some food.) If there are leftovers, by all means ask to take it home.

Depending upon how westernized their clientele is, some Chinese restaurants put forks on the tables, while others use chopsticks. If you are not comfortable using chopsticks, you may always ask for a fork. And vice versa, of course.

Choking

When someone chokes on a piece of food, he is not only unable to breathe, but also unable to talk. Therefore the universal sign that one is in trouble with a piece of food is to move the hand or fingers across the throat. Never let someone who is choking leave the table or go off by himself, as he is in need of immediate assistance to survive.

The Heimlich Maneuver should be applied to any person who is choking or who is even suspected of choking on a piece of food:

1. Make the victim stand if possible. Stand behind him and quickly wrap your arm around his waist. Make a fist with one hand, pressing the thumb against the choking person's body in the place where the ribcage forms a V. Grasp the fist tightly with the other hand.
2. With a quick upward thrust, jab your fist into the person's abdomen. Repeat until the piece of lodged food flies out.

Note: When dining alone, the Heimlich Maneuver may be performed on yourself by pressing your body against a chair or kitchen sink. The object of this procedure is to force the piece of food physically up and out of your windpipe by forcing a burst of air up from the lungs.

Chopsticks

These are the eating utensils of the Oriental world. In many cities, non-Orientals have adapted the use of chopsticks when eating Oriental food. Learning to eat with them does take a little practice, and that is best done at home.

To use chopsticks, hold them by the large end and eat with the narrow end. Follow the directions in Figure 14.

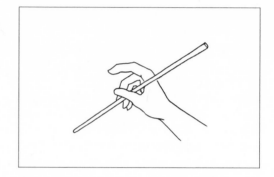

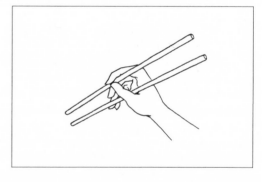

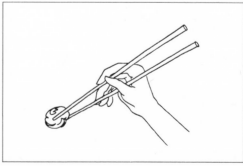

Figure 14. The correct way to use chopsticks

Christening

SEE *Christian Birth Ceremonies.*

Christian Birth Ceremonies

PROTESTANT. Protestant christenings vary with the denomination (some require godparents and others don't; some christen in the first few months after birth and others wait for several years; some require that the ceremony be held in the church and others encourage home services). Parents should consult with their clergyperson for specific guidelines.

A baby is dressed in white, as is an older girl, but a boy older than two or three more often wears a navy jacket and gray shorts or pants.

Protestant christenings are often part of the church service (this is especially true in the Presbyterian Church) or they are held just before or after it. A reception is usually scheduled in the parents' home for close family and friends. Since most christenings take place in the morning or early afternoon, "tea" food or a light lunch is served, and dessert is a christening cake. Invitations are issued by telephone or handwritten notes, and guests who have not already given a baby gift may bring their gifts to the party.

ROMAN CATHOLIC. In the Roman Catholic Church, babies are baptized in the church as soon after birth as is possible, almost always within one month. A reception is held afterward, usually in the parents' home.

Close family and friends are invited, and invitations may be issued by phone or handwritten note. Guests who have not yet given the baby a present usually bring a gift for the infant.

The baby wears a white christening dress or outfit, which may be elaborately embroidered and trimmed with fine lace (especially if it is a family heirloom) or may be a simpler white outfit.

Godparents, who must be Roman Catholic, are required. They stand with the parents at the alter during the ceremony. (Catholics also may not be godparents for persons of other faiths.) If the godparents cannot be present, proxies may stand in for them. The godparents usually give the baby a lasting present—a sterling mug, rattle, or spoon—or they may give a bond or stock or contribute to a trust fund. If they cannot afford so expensive a gift, they may give something more modest.

Catholic christenings are usually held on Sunday afternoon, and a reception takes place in the church or at the parents' home. Light refreshments with punch are typical fare, and a white christening cake is traditional. Wine and other alcoholic beverages may be served, depending upon the family's drinking habits.

HOME CEREMONY. When a home ceremony is planned, the clergyperson will usually provide some guidance about setting up a small altar. Generally, a white cloth covers a table large enough to hold a Bible and a small font of baptismal water.

DONATION. The parents usually give a small donation to the church at the time of the baptism since no fee is charged.

Christian Mourning Customs

SEE ALSO *Jewish Mourning Customs.*

Most religions have a period of formal, public mourning. Christians mourn before the funeral, when the family gathers at the home of one family member and also often during prescheduled hours at the funeral homes to receive callers. Very close friends telephone and often go immediately to the home of the bereaved upon learning of the death of a loved one. This is so they can offer any assistance that may be needed, such as telephoning friends and family, shopping, or making other arrangements. Others may call at the home or more usually at the funeral home.

If the family is not at the funeral home, the caller should sign the register and pay last respects to the deceased if he or she wishes to. If the family is there, the caller should stay long enough to offer condolences personally. Family members are often preoccupied with one another at a time like this, but friends' condolences nonetheless are a great consolation.

Funeral arrangements are announced in newspapers. A friend or acquaintance may attend a funeral, unless the newspaper notice indicates that it is private, in which case only invited guests are expected to attend. Generally only invited guests and the family attend the gravesite service, which is brief.

Flowers are usually sent, unless the family has requested that donations be made to charity instead. The family's wishes should be respected. Flowers should be addressed to "The funeral of John Smith" at such-and-such a funeral home. Often several friends or groups of relatives ("The Smith Cousins," for example) arrange together to send a spray of flowers.

Handwritten thank-you notes must be written in response to all flowers and condolence notes. The preprinted cards supplied by funeral homes may be used to respond to preprinted cards, or, if necessary, they may be used to respond to a handwritten note, provided a personal message is also written to them.

Christmas Cards

These holiday greeting cards have become so much a part of our lives that, in part, they have lost much of their religious symbolism and now serve as an annual letter-writing fête for friends who do not keep in touch any other way. I realize that they provoke no small degree of antagonism and, I suppose, guilt, particularly among those who do not send them. Let me put your minds at ease: No one is obligated to send Christmas cards, and if they are not your style, by all means do not send them, and also do not feel guilty about receiving them.

For those of you who do participate in this enjoyable custom, there are only a few guidelines to follow.

WHEN TO SEND. Christmas cards can be sent any time within the three-week period before Christmas. It is the post office's heaviest period of business, as they are fond of reminding us, so as good citizens we should mail them as early as possible. Some people have begun sending New Year's cards, or have simply stopped bothering to get their Christmas cards mailed before Christmas. That is acceptable, too, provided the cards sent late do not carry a specific Christmas message.

TO WHOM. There are no limits to whom you may send Christmas greetings, since the recipients are under no obligation to send you one back. Some people send them to every acquaintance, every business colleague, every client, persons who have done them special favors during the year—basically, to everyone they know. Other people send only to good friends. Still others tell me they limit their Christmas-card list to out-of-town friends.

Christmas cards may be sent to non-Christians, provided some tact is exercised *(see next section)*, and to those in mourning. Select a solemn rather than a frivolous card for a friend who has recently lost a loved one.

STYLES OF CARDS. Christmas cards, as noted, have taken on a decidedly ecumenical nature, in contrast to the days when most cards carried a religious theme. You may send religious cards if you choose, but it is insensitive to send a Christian religious message to non-Christian friends. Try to find a card that does not have the traditional symbols of Christmas such as Christmas trees, Santa Claus, etc. Cards that carry a message of peace or love usually can be sent to anyone.

SIGNING. If you have a very large Christmas-card list, you may have your name printed or engraved on the cards, but I always find this practice a little cold among friends. Business cards are another matter; printed or engraved cards are entirely acceptable. A good compromise, I think, is to also write in your first name or even your initial above your printed name, especially if you are sending a card that contains your full printed name to a good friend. If the cards will go only to close friends, then first names only can be printed on them; if they will go to persons who may not immediately recognize who "Mary" or "John" is, then your full name must be printed on the cards.

A family card should have everyone's name on it: mother, father (in no special order), and each child. It is coy to sign pet's names.

A Christmas card is the only communication where you can sign your spouse's name (and children's names) for him or her. If you add a brief note on the card, however, sign your name only. If your spouse adds a line or two, he can sign his name, but you can—and often should—send best wishes and love on behalf of your spouse.

CHRISTMAS LETTERS. Some people—alas—also go to the trouble of preparing preprinted or copied letters that describe, often in far too great detail, the events and activities of the family throughout the past year. I do not dislike these letters across the board, but I must admit that I find some of them overly detailed (I'm sorry your pet turtle died last July, but think it might not be important enough to mention in a Christmas letter many months later). Another disadvantage is that if the sender has had less than sterling year, they can be chronicles of doom in a season that is meant to be joyous. Finally, some of them take on a note of braggadocio—mostly, from what I can see, about minutiae—that I find difficult to bear ("Susie was voted best dissector in her biology class and placed first in the spelling bee"). I also object to the mass-market element in receiving a printed "personal" letter. Now, having said all that, I do think they have their time and place, if you must. If you gave birth to quadruplets this year, and really have not had time to write anyone, this might be your year to send a Christmas letter. If you can write a witty one, if you can manage to convey the impression that you are sending this to your closest ten friends and not your closest hundred acquaintances, and if you can manage to separate out the trivia from the major events in your life, then I think you can get away with one of these letters. All others, stay away, or better yet, write a personal note on the Christmas card.

Chuppah

A chuppah (pronounced hŭppă) is a wedding canopy used in Orthodox and Conservative Jewish ceremonies. Reform Jews may or may not be married under a chuppah, according to the guidelines of their particular congregation or their personal choice.

The chuppah is usually white. It may be decorated with flowers or embroidered. Occasionally a prayer shawl is used as a chuppah. The wedding party, including the parents of the couple, stand under or around the chuppah during the ceremony. Another meaningful custom is to ask siblings or friends to hold the four poles of the chuppah during the ceremony.

The chuppah is believed to have originated during the Middle Ages, when the custom was to marry outdoors, often at night, so the marriage would be blessed with as many children as the stars in the sky. Some say the chuppah symbolizes the home.

Tradition holds that a woman is considered married from the moment she steps under the chuppah even though the ceremony has not yet taken place.

Church

SEE *Religious Services.*

Church Wedding

SEE *Chapel Wedding; Sanctuary Wedding.*

Circumcision

SEE *Jewish Birth Ceremonies.*

Civil Wedding

A civil wedding ceremony, that is, one held in City Hall or in a judge's chambers, may be the choice of a couple who do not wish to be married in a religious ceremony, or it may be a necessity because they cannot be married in a religious ceremony (either because one or both of the couple are divorced or because they are marrying out of their faith).

Such ceremonies are usually quite simple. The couple are typically accompanied only by two witnesses, although if the wedding is in a judge's chambers, there may be room for the immediate family. Street clothes are worn, and the bride carries a small bouquet if she chooses.

Being married in a civil ceremony does not mean that a couple cannot have a large and lavish reception if they choose, nor does it necessarily mean that they cannot be married later in a religious ceremony.

Clambake

A New England specialty, clambakes are a special kind of beach picnic. The menu is always the same: steamed clams, lobsters, corn on the cob, and other regional specialties. The seafood is often caught right before it is cooked. A clambake is a messy but particularly gratifying meal for those who appreciate the fresh seafood. Because of the messiness, old clothes are usually worn to a clambake.

Clams

SEE ALSO *Clambake; Fork.*

BAKED. Use an oyster fork to eat clams baked in the shell. They must be eaten in one bite, as it is impossible to cut them.

ON THE HALF SHELL. Eat the clam with an oyster fork, and then, if you like, pick up the clam shell and drink the liquid from it.

STEAMED. Use your hands to pry open the clam shell. If it does not open easily, discard the clam, as it probably is no good. Reach inside and use your fingers to remove the clam. Eat it with your fingers. Steamed clams are served only at clambakes, picnics, and on other informal occasions.

Class Ring

SEE ALSO *Club Jewelry; Jewelry.*

Class rings are not usually worn by anyone older than twenty-two. There are other, more subtle ways to announce your background, if it is important to you to do so.

Clergy—Forms of Address

SEE ALSO *Forms of Address—Written.*

PROTESTANT. There are many different forms of correct address among Protestants as, indeed, there are many sects, and most people simply follow local usage or the custom of their congregation. Protestants generally use the title "Reverend" in addressing all clergypersons, unless the clergyperson has a doctorate, in which case "Doctor" may be preferred. "Reverend" or "The Reverend" is not, however, ever used alone. Say "Reverend Flowers," not just "Reverend."

When making introductions, in general, present others to a clergyperson as a sign of respect.

Letters to clergy who are called Reverend So-and-So are addressed to "The Reverend Smith." In the letter, he or she is referred to as "Reverend Smith," just as if you were talking in person.

ROMAN CATHOLIC. People are always presented to high-church dignitaries, the Pope, and cardinals. Anyone who is a bishop or higher is addressed as "Your Holiness," "Your Eminence," or "Your Excellency." Roman Catholics curtsy and kiss the rings of high-church officials; others may bow slightly and shake hands if a hand is offered. *(See Dignitaries—Addressing Correspondence.)*

Nuns' forms of address vary with the order. Some use "Mother" and others use "Sister," combined with a first or last name. The head of the order may be addressed as "Mother Superior," "Reverend Mother," or "Mother," depending upon the order.

These same titles are also used when addressing correspondence to nuns.

Priests are addressed as "Father" when they are ordained, as "Brother" when they are not yet priests or will not become priests but are members of a religious community.

JEWISH. Clergypersons, regardless of sex, are addressed as "Rabbi Cohen" or simply "Rabbi."

The cantor is called by his name. "Cantor" is not used by itself as a form of address.

Clergyperson

SEE *Chapel Wedding; Clergy—Forms of Address; Forms of Address—Written; Rectory Wedding; Sanctuary Wedding; Wedding Expenses.*

Client Relations

SEE ALSO *Business Entertaining; Business Entertaining at Home; Business Friendship; Business Gift.*

The tone for client relations will be set in large part by the company for which you work. Some companies maintain a fairly distant, "we're all business" posture, while others go out of their way to cultivate clients in a more obviously friendly way.

Whichever route you find yourself taking, keep one thing in mind: However chummy you become with a client, this is still basically a business friendship. Even during social encounters you still represent your company, and this person is still a client—someone with whom you presently do business and someone with whom you hope to continue doing business in the future. It will not do to discuss company secrets, plans, disappointments, and so on. In short, keep your distance and stay loyal to your company; do not take this person into your confidence about company matters that do not concern him—or worse, that do concern him. You could easily end up telling him something that will make him take his business elsewhere.

This warning having been given, there is still no reason not to see a client socially, if that suits both of you. Some social entertaining will have business overtones, while other occasions for getting together with a client will be purely social. The ground rules, of course, always apply, regardless of what you are doing or how chummy you become with one another.

Club Jewelry

SEE ALSO *Class Ring; Jewelry.*

Those of you for whom college meant little else other than joining the right club, fraternity, or sorority may be surprised to learn that club-related jewelry is simply not worn in the workplace. Phi Beta Kappa keys are occasionally worn, mostly in the world of academia, but even they are considered too precious for everyday wear. Upon acquaintance with you, people can learn what clubs you belonged to, as well as what honors you have earned. Such information should be imparted in the course of everyday conversation in a subtle way. It should not be announced in so unsubtle a way as to wear it on your person.

Coasters

These small pads are placed under drinks to protect the table. Coasters are not needed under wineglasses, but are needed under other glasses. A hostess or host should feel free to slip one under a guest's drink.

Cocktail Buffet

SEE *Cocktail Party.*

Cocktail Party

A cocktail party is a relatively easy, inexpensive way to entertain almost any number of people. Unfortunately, the ease with which cocktail parties are given has made many hostesses think of them as a sort of throwaway entertainment as opposed to an event that needs care, attention, and a personal touch.

INVITATIONS. If fewer than ten or fifteen people are invited, invitations are usually telephoned. If the group is larger, written invitations are sent. I recommend specially printed ones if the occasion warrants it or, if it does not, the preprinted ones with blanks to fill in the date and time.

Cocktail parties usually start between 5 and 6 P.M. It is appropriate to put a time for the party to end on the invitation so late arrivals know what hour will be too late.

Cocktails parties end around 8 or 8:30 P.M., because it is assumed that guests will go on to dinner.

Regardless of what the invitation says, cocktail parties do not begin promptly at the stated time. Guests start arriving about one-half hour after the appointed time. Nor do they end at the stated time, but it is still smart to state a time, and the hostess who does not want the party to go on all night will take some steps to prevent this. The best way to wind down a cocktail party, of course, is to close the bar. Slowing down food service, or stopping it altogether, also works.

Usually no formal response is required to an invitation to a cocktail party, but if the host is a friend, it is kind to let him or her know whether or not you will be attending.

Obviously any number from one to several hundred can be invited for cocktails. But a word of caution is in order here: This does mean that the guest list should be prepared indiscriminately or designed simply to pay back persons for having entertained you. Even a large cocktail party will be livelier as a result of having a compatible, carefully thought-out guest list.

BEVERAGES. Plan to serve a wide range of alcoholic and soft drinks. It is better to have too much on hand than to run out. Count on each guest having three drinks. A quart of liquor will provide approximately 21 drinks, if 1½ ounces of liquor are used for each drink. A bottle of wine will provide about six to seven drinks, depending upon the size of the wineglasses.

Wine should be offered in addition to mixed drinks, but where only wine may be acceptable at a lunch or dinner, a wider range of alcoholic and nonalcoholic beverages must be provided at a cocktail party. Soft drinks should include colas, soda and mineral water, and fruit juices.

Drinks may be served from plastic glasses, especially if the crowd is large, but glass ones are much preferred. Paper napkins and coaster are acceptable at most cocktail parties. Be sure to have lots of coasters on hand to protect your furniture, and lots of paper napkins because these are needed for your guests' comfort as they stand around holding cold drinks.

Drinks come and go in popularity, and you are safest serving the old standbys rather than currently fashionable drinks. Whiskey and scotch are considered winter drinks and gin and vodka are the basis of most summer drinks. You should have whiskey, scotch, gin, and vodka on hand, though, regardless of the time of year.

FOOD. Two kinds of food are served at cocktail parties: finger food and buffet food. Finger food is anything that is completely edible and can be eaten with the fingers. It should not be very large or sticky or anything that cannot be eaten with one hand while holding a drink with another.

Buffet food is served at a buffet cocktail party. You need not provide a multicourse meal, but the food at a buffet cocktail party should be substantial enough so guests do not need a meal afterward. Theme food—for example, Mexican, Polynesian, or Chinese—works well at this kind of buffet. Large roasts and accompanying salads and side dishes also work well. This is never a sit-down dinner, so the food must be something guests can handle standing up or sitting in chairs with no table. The acid test for stand-up buffet food is whether it can be eaten with only a fork; if it can be, it is acceptable to serve. A cold buffet can be served in warm weather; warm or cold foods are welcome during cold weather.

If a cocktail party will include a buffet dinner, this should be specified on the invitation, and the party may be held at a later hour.

SERVICE. SEE ALSO SINGLES' CO-HOST. If the party is small, a hostess or host can serve the guests alone; as soon as the group expands to 20 or more, outside help is usually needed. One bartender can serve every 20 to 30 persons, and if food is passed, one waiter is usually needed for every 15 to 20 persons.

If a buffet meal is served, no one may be needed to oversee the food service if the guests can help themselves, but the hostess or caterer will have to refill dishes. If more than 25 to 30 people are invited, outside help will be needed to serve the dinner.

A cocktail dinner is always served at buffet tables. With the possible exception of appetizers, food is never passed at this type of party. At a regular cocktail party, the food may be passed on trays or served from a table. To avoid congestion, one table is set up for the bar and another separate table or tables are used for the food.

Drink service is similar. A bartender can serve drinks from a table set up as a bar, or they can be premixed and passed on trays. The latter method is by far the more complicated, and many more drinks than may be used must be prepared. An alternate method is to have one or more bartenders mixing drinks and one or more waiters taking drink orders from guests and serving them. Still another method is to pass wine and champagne on trays, and let the guests

who want mixed drinks go to the bartender.

LOGISTICS. Whether your home is large or small, some planning must usually be done to accommodate a group the size of most cocktail parties.

Bathrooms should be set up for guests, with hand towels and individual soaps, if possible.

Coats always look messy piled in sight of guests, but they may be put on a bed or in some room out of sight. If there is room to set up coat racks, consider using them.

A cocktail party, as well as a cocktail buffet, is a stand-up party; seating need not be provided for guests. People will mix more readily if they are forced to stand, and a slight overcrowding will even help get the party in full swing.

THE PROBLEM GUEST. One of the more unpleasant side effects of planning a party at which alcoholic beverages are featured is that occasionally a guest overindulges. The host or hostess should be alert to this.

If the inebriated guest insults another guest (less rare than one would imagine), the hostess or host must try to smooth things over and certainly should get the offending soul away into another room.

If a guest becomes ill, he must be attended by the host or hostess or someone designated by him or her.

If a guest becomes too inebriated to drive, the host and hostess should consider themselves directly responsible and should take action to ensure that this person does not drive. Arrangements should be made for another guest to take the ailing person home or a cab should be called—anything rather than letting an ill or drunken friend get behind the wheel of a car.

Coffee

SEE ALSO *Tea.*

SERVING. Coffee is served either with dessert or as the last course, in which case it is usually offered with after-dinner liqueurs of one sort or another. It can be served at the table, or everyone can adjourn to the greater comfort of the living room to sip their coffee and liqueurs.

Coffee used to be a much more elaborate ritual than it is today, with men and women going their separate ways for this course, mostly so the men could enjoy their after-dinner cigars. In the past few decades men and women have more commonly taken their coffee together, and smokers have lit up at the table after everyone was done eating. Because of the hardening of positions between smokers and nonsmokers, one hostess I know has taken to separating her guests once again during coffee, but this time she separates smokers and nonsmokers.

Today, many hosts also offer tea, both herbal and regular, as well as coffee. And although decaffeinated coffee used to be too awful to consider serving to company, there are now some excellent decaffeinated coffees that are quite acceptable to serve to guests. These are ones that come in the bean and are brewed. It is never acceptable to serve any kind of instant, powdered coffee to guests. More and more often these days,

guests take advantage of the opportunity to drink a decaffeinated brew late at night.

Coffee should be offered with cream or milk and sugar. Put these out on a tray so that guests may help themselves.

DRINKING. Coffee poses no problem when it is served in a cup and saucer, as it always should be a formal dinner, but for casual dinners, coffee is more and more often these days served in a mug. These are excellent containers, but they occasionally pose a problem as to what to do with the coffee spoon. A coffee spoon should never be placed directly on the table, certainly not on a good tablecloth or placemat. It may be placed on a butter plate or even a serving plate if one is available, but most hostesses clear the bread-and-butter plate before serving dessert. If the hostess fails to provide something, a guest can ask her for a small plate to hold the coffee spoons. She will be grateful to be reminded and have her tablecloth spared from a possible stain.

When coffee is served in a cup and saucer, the spoon rests on the saucer. When coffee is served at the table, except at the most formal dinners, it is okay to put the cup and saucer in the middle of your place setting. At a formal dinner, it should be left to the right of the plate.

Another problem occurs when coffee spills over onto the saucer. In a good restaurant or someone's home, this can be remedied by asking for a clean saucer. In the average coffee shop, where asking for a clean saucer would bring sighs from most waiters and waitresses, it is acceptable to slip a paper napkin under the cup to soak up the coffee. On no account are you expected to suffer through dripping coffee while drinking.

ESPRESSO. This strong, excellently flavored coffee is sometimes served at the end of a dinner. Those who love coffee but turn down offers of espresso late at night because they think it will keep them awake might be interested to learn that the espresso coffee bean, being riper than other beans, actually contains less caffeine. I can't vouch for the strength of the espresso brew that any one hostess will make, though. Espresso is served in small cups and saucers called demitasse cups. Regularly brewed, strong coffee may also be served in these cups; they are an excellent way to sip coffee in small quantity.

Espresso is drunk with a lemon twist and sugar. The twist, which may be served in a small bowl or put on individual saucers, is twisted to release its essence and dropped into the demitasse cup. Small desmitasse spoons are required to stir in the sugar. Milk and cream are never added to espresso. Anise-flavored liqueur is sometimes added to the coffee.

Coffee, either espresso or regular, is the one course that it is perfectly acceptable to decline.

Cohabitation

A couple who live together are committed to each other, but the commitment is not the same as the commitment of marriage, and neither is the etiquette. Not too many years ago, a couple who cohabited tried to keep their living arrangements a secret, and society, when it did not moralize, collaborated in ignoring the relationship. Now that living together before marriage has become so widespread and is therefore more accepted socially, some guidelines have emerged for handling the various situations that arise when man and woman share not only their emotional lives but also their households.

ANNOUNCING YOUR LIVING ARRANGEMENTS. While cohabitation may be more accepted these days, no one sends engraved announcements. Some discretion is still called for. In some families, relatives have trouble dealing with couples who live together openly, and in some communities, there exists an aura of disapproval that can make life difficult. In both situations, varying degrees of discretion are called for, if only because this makes life easier for the cohabiting couple. Living under the disapproval of an entire community of one's entire family is difficult indeed and, where possible, I think that couples should protect themselves from this censure.

I do feel, though, that two adults should not hide their living arrangements from either set of parents, of if they are an older couple, from their own grown children. (Amusingly, when the tables are turned many children who thought nothing of setting up housekeeping with someone to whom they were not married put up a fuss when their own parents do the same thing.) Your family may not approve, but telling them avoids a lot of awkward moments such as what to do with your partner's clothes or where to sleep when they come to visit. It is always wiser to tell your immediate family, even if they will disapprove.

The immediate family—parents and children—would be wise to keep any misgivings to themselves. Expressing disapproval is likely to accomplish nothing other than to strain the familial relationship even further. For most people conhabitation is a serious step in a relationship and often leads to marriage. Expressing disapproval of a child's (or a parent's) choice of a mate often does lasting damage to the parent-child relationship.

TELLING SMALL CHILDREN. Small children, of course, must be handled entirely differently from adult children. Their lives stand to be much more upset by the change in living arrangements. Your decision to live with someone will create as much upheaval in their lives as if you had decided to remarry, and perhaps more, since you have not, in fact, remarried but have chosen another course.

If possible, have your partner move in with you so your children do not have their lives upset any more than is necesssary. Obviously, you will have known your partner for some time before taking this important step, so your children will also know him or her. They still may be surprised and upset when the move takes place.

Depending upon the situation, they also may have to fend off a few questions from curious outsiders—that is, relatives, acquaintances, neighbors, teachers, and so on. It is your responsibility to arm your children with the appropriate responses to handle these situations tactfully and gracefully. When people ask them who the strange man or woman is who is living with their mother or father, teach them to say, simply, "That is David Jones. He lives with us."

Your children should continue to call your live-in partner by his name and should probably not be encouraged, even for appearances' sake, to call her or him "Mom" or "Dad." This person is not their biological parent, nor even a stepparent, and until he or she is, their emotional lives should not be cluttered or confused in this fashion.

Your new living arrangements will undoubtedly prompt some tough questions from your children similar to those you heard when you divorced. They may want to know if this relationship is permanent. You should answer as honestly as you can, all the while reassuring them that you love them, that their other biological parent loves them, and that your partner loves them. Usually, at the heart of such questions is not any real concern about your relationship with your partner, but rather, a concern over whether you might stop loving them at some point. This is the real issue you should attempt to address in such conversations.

Other relatives who are not closely involved in your life have no reason to be told about your living arrangements, particularly if they are of a generation that has not come to accept such arrangements and will be unnecessarily upset by the news. Most of the time, you need not lie; you simply need not go out of your way to clarify things. I have observed a great deal of mutual collusion in these matters. Your Great-Aunt Minnie, who has always adored you but disapproves of the fact that you are living with someone, will go to great lengths to ignore any evidence of the relationship.

Friends, of course, should be told, so they will know where to find you. Acquaintances are another matter, especially if you happen to live in a community where you are likely to encounter disapproval. With acquaintances and business associates, some discretion may be necessary until you figure out who approves and who does not.

Inform others only when they need to know. In a large city, the mailman need not be given notice; simply add a new name to the mailbox. In a small town, you may have to tell the postman that "Jim Riley will be getting mail at this address." A landlord or doorman may need to be informed. Neighbors need not be told unless you are friendly with them. Your child's teachers need not be told, but you may have to discuss this with them if the new living arrangement appears to be affecting your child's schoolwork.

SETTING UP HOUSEKEEPING. In any close relationship, you must, on the one hand, share for the relationship to be successful. On the other hand, this is not a legal relationship in the sense that marriage is. Never mind that some big palimony suits have established some rights for live-in partners: You will be better off protecting your rights right from the start rather than after the fact.

Most cohabiting couples develop some arrangement to share household expenses. Many open a joint bank account. It is also smart to maintain separate accounts. A smart couple also obtains legal advice about any major joint purchases they plan to make.

WHAT STAYS SEPARATE. Not only should some of your finances stay separate, but so will some of your relationships. When a couple marries, they have no choice but to start forging relationships as a couple because the world views them as a couple, a single unit. One cannot politely invite only one partner of a married couple to any social event. Even an old friend who is eager to dine alone with his old buddy must, out of politeness, extend the dinner invitation to his friend and his friend's wife. He can hope that his friend (or his friend's wife) will say, "Oh, let's make this a boy's night out," but he cannot properly suggest it. If anything, the married man or women who wishes to maintain some separate friendships, something of which I heartily approve, must take the initiative.

This same situation exists, but not nearly to the same degree, when a couple live together. Friends and family have the freedom to keep some distance if they wish. They are—and should be—cordial and even genuinely friendly to your partner, but they are under no obligation to make the friendship mutual. They may not even wish to make it completely mutual, knowing that if the relationship does not end in marriage, they will then not have to go though the painful process of taking sides and choosing between two friends, as so often happens when a couple divorce. In a sense this works to your advantage, too, since many living-together relationships do not end in marriage. I always encourage a couple who live together to maintain these separate ties so that if the relationship ends, they will not have so much difficulty picking up their old social lives again.

ENTERTAINING AND BEING ENTERTAINED. Despite the healthy separation that does exist, your family and friends should treat you as a couple socially. A cohabiting couple receives joint invitations just as a married couple does. Whenever an activity is planned that involves couples, the couple who live together should be invited together. A woman, for example, may invite a friend who lives with a man to dinner alone, if it will be just the two of them, but if she is inviting the woman to a dinner party involving couples, she must invite the woman's partner. Invitations to family events—weddings, christenings, holiday dinners—must also be issued jointly.

The couple who live together also entertain jointly. When they have a party, the invitations are issued in both their names, and they both function as host and hostess.

BUSINESS ENTERTAINING. Sometimes questions arise regarding your live-in partner and business entertaining. Theoretically, a live-in partner should accompany you anywhere that spouses are welcome. Practically, this may not always be possible, particularly if you work for a company or employer that is a bit stuffy about cohabitation. For example, at many office Christman parties, workers are encouraged to bring spouses but not dates. If your boss knows you live with someone and handles this knowledge well, then you are probably safe in bringing your partner. (You also may want to ask first.) But if your boss and colleagues do not know about your living arrangements because some unerring sixth sense has told you this knowledge about your intimate life would not help your career aspirations, then you would do better to skip bringing your partner. (And under the circumstances, your partner should be understanding about this.)

As for business entertainment that you initiate, such as taking a client out to din-

ner, there is no reason that you may not bring a "date" along, especially if the client is bringing a date or his or her spouse. Again, some discretion may be called for about announcing your exact living arrangements. Many business dinners are designed for the conduct of business, and spouses, live-in partners, and dates are not necessarily welcomed, nor would they find the evening particularly scintillating.

TRAVEL. Unmarried couples traveling together have become so common an occurrence that few hotel or motel clerks are surprised when an unmarried couple register under their own names. Furthermore, so many married women use their own names that it is difficult to tell from a hotel register which couple is married and which is cohabiting.

There are some parts of the world, though, where extreme discretion is called for. Muslims strongly disapprove of premarital sex, and in some Arab countries, couples who are caught together are subject to extreme punishment and even death. If you are planning to travel to this part of the world, you should consult with your travel agent about the degree of discretion that will be required and about whether you can safely travel together at all, even if you register in different rooms. Outside the major cities in conservative Roman Catholic countries such as Spain and Portugal, cohabiting couples may not be particularly welcome if they want to share a room.

Elsewhere in the world, you may simply travel under your own names and share a room or you may pose as a married couple, whichever is more comfortable for you.

PARENTAL VISITS. Even if your parents have managed to accept your living arrangements, they still may have difficulty visiting you in your shared home or having you visit as a couple in theirs.

Your parents have a right to adhere to their own moral values in their home, and if they are uncomfortable with you sharing a room with someone who is not your spouse, you should accept this and be polite, if not gracious, about it. Either sleep in separate rooms or register in a nearby hotel or motel. If you do the latter, try to do it without incident. Say something such as: "I think we'll be more comfortable staying at the inn, but as soon as we're settled in, we'll be over to spend the day with you."

The situation is reversed when your parents visit your home. They know, of course, that you share a bed, and should not expect you to change your living arrangements for them. If they cannot handle this situation, they, too, may opt to stay in a hotel.

If your parents do decide to stay with you, and you know they are uncomfortable, remember that a little discretion can go a long way to ease the situation. For example, they need not actually see you in bed with your partner, nor do the two of you need to take a twenty-minute shower together in the morning.

WHAT TO CALL YOUR PARTNER. To show how accepted cohabitation has become, the most frequent question I hear about the etiquette of cohabiting is what to call a live-in partner. A lot of silly answers have been proposed, including the Census Bureau's official designation of a live-in partner as a POSSLQ, or "Person of the Opposite Sex Sharing Living Quarters." I am delighted to report that I have yet to hear anyone say by way of introduction, "I'd like you to meet John, my POSSLQ."

I would love to come up with a term that covers the situation, but, frankly, the solution, as I see it, is to say nothing. When introducing your partner, say simply, "I'd like you to meet John" or "I'd like you to meet Mary." If you want to add more, say, "John is the man I live with." That is all you need to say. And anything else—my "lover," my "live-in partner"—is awkward.

ADDRESSING MAIL TO AN UNMARRIED COUPLE. If you know both partners, address mail to them under both their names:

> Ms. Samantha White
> Mr. Jon Billingham

If you are sending an invitation and only know one partner but you know he or she lives with someone, you can either make an attempt to learn the person's name or simply address the invitation to your friend "and guest."

If you know the partner's name, however, this is not an acceptable way to address an invitation, any more than it would be acceptable to invite a married couple in this manner. Little signs of disapproval like this are merely rude.

Friends and family who do not personally know the partner may send mail to the person they know separately. It is cordial to send greetings to the other partner if you know of his existence even if you have never met him.

College and University Life

ADMISSION INTERVIEW. Unlike a private or preparatory school interview, where parents are encouraged to attend, youngsters are expected to go into their college interviews alone. The interview may be scheduled when a representative of the school visits the city where the prospective student lives, or when the student, usually accompanied by his parents, pays a visit to the campus.

Good school clothes should be worn to an interview. Jeans are not acceptable, but there is no need to wear overly dressy clothes either.

Parents can help their child prepare by reviewing the college catalogue with him to make sure that he understands the school's entrance requirements and by helping him to formulate in his own mind some good reasons why he would like to attend this school. If there are problem areas, for example, the student was not particularly proficient in one subject, some coaching may be needed to help the child emphasize his strengths while acknowledging his weaknesses.

DORMITORY LIFE. Living in a dorm is like living in a large extended family. One must be tuned into the sensitivities, needs, and wants of others, and must respect them.

The student who shares his room must tolerate his roommate's foibles while downplaying his own. He should not borrow from others without their permission, and even then, he should keep borrowing to the minimum. The constant borrower is never very popular.

Noise is often a problem in a dormitory, and it should always be kept to the minimum during study hours or during any other restricted hours.

Students using the public rooms of a dormitory should take care to leave them clean so that others may enjoy them. Candy bar wrappers, potato chip bags, and soft-drink bottles should all be cleared off study tables and thrown in the garbage when leaving the room. Take special care to clean up after yourself in the bathroom or shower, leaving these places in good condition for the next person who uses them.

It is important to respect others' privacy. Knock on any closed door, even the room you share with a roommate, before entering. Do not interrupt someone who is studying, reading, or otherwise absorbed in an activity. Never go through another person's personal belongings. Do not eavesdrop either on conversations or telephone calls.

While it would be useless to tell a student to avoid cliques entirely, since we all like to have our own special group of friends, students should avoid excluding others where possible. A student may, for example, go out for a beer or to the movies with two or three friends, but if he is having a small party in his dorm room, and someone who is not part of his special group walks by or is reading in the room next door, it is only basic courtesy to ask that person to join in the fun.

Also helpful is to know how to assert yourself graciously when someone does infringe on your life in an inconsiderate way. For the first time in your life, perhaps, your parents will not be around to settle a "sibling" dispute, so you must attempt to handle the situation as fairly as possible on your own. When someone is doing something you do not like or find unfair—leaving the bathroom sink a mess, entering your room without knocking—first of all be upfront about what you do not like. Do not hint at what is wrong or get angry at the person without telling him why you are angry. Second, once you have told the person what makes you unhappy, do not harp on it. Assume that the person will make an attempt to straighten himself out. Finally, if possible, use a little humor or discuss what is offending you in a light tone. To someone who is entering your room without knocking, you might joke: "Listen, I'm having a torrid love affair with my biology book. If you walk in unannounced, you might see something that embarrasses you."

A messy roommate can sometimes be jollied out of his bad habits. You might say, for example, "Jack, I can't remember what the furniture looks like in this room. Do you think we could pare down the mess a little?"

A roommate or suitemate who makes too much noise could be handled similarly. With a smile, say, "I know you like to think you're the only survivor on this planet, but we have just arrived from another world, and noise hurts our ears. So can you turn it down a little, puh-leeze?" Your comments are light, yet direct enough so the offending person should get the point.

When other students do intrude in your life more than you would like, you may have to do something. Whatever you do, try to do it tactfully, at least initially.

A more serious problem, of course, is when you are pressured to drink or use drugs. In a situation like this, you can often still use humor to get off the hook. Just laugh and say, "Sorry, my doctor says that stuff will

interfere with my pacemaker" or "My doctor says I can only take that under prescription." If you can produce a light-hearted refusal, and if you do not preach to others, you can usually say no to just about anything without repercussions.

Commuter Transportation

Commuter transportation is unlike other forms of transportation in that any acquaintances struck up are likely to be more enduring than those established on other forms of transportation. There is nothing wrong with speaking to, and occasionally sharing a cup of coffee with, a fellow commuter. If a real friendship develops, that is an added bonus.

Anyone who cherishes solitude, though, probably should maintain a reserve with regard to commuter acquaintances, because these casual friendships have a way of taking on patterns of regularity.

Regular commuters can also be territorial, with the result that you will find yourself feeling uncomfortable if you invade their turf. It is sometimes impossible to know whether or not you are taking someone's seat when you ride a surburban train the first time, but if you do see that regulars have their seats, it is kinder to find a seat elsewhere so they can sit together.

The first time you ride, there are some obvious seats to avoid. The seats at either end of a train car, the ones that face each other, are often the "property" of card players. Also, if two people get on who would obviously like to sit together and are unable to do so, and if you could help their cause by giving up your seat, you will win some friends by this favor. This applies only if there is another seat you can transfer to, though. You are never obligated as a paying customer to give up your seat to stand under these circumstances.

Many commuter trains have some sort of food service. If you use it, clean up after yourself. Actually, you should take care to do this even if you bring on your own food.

Other annoying habits that should be avoided for the comfort of your fellow passengers are painting your nails or applying makeup (the scents are too heavy, especially on the A.M. commute), eating noisily, leaning against others in a crowded car, playing a radio or television, or even talking loudly enough to annoy others. These rules apply, of course, to all forms of transportation that are shared with others.

The etiquette of commuter riding is much like that of any other form of public transportation. Although there are usually enough seats to go around, especially if the ride is long, seats should still be surrendered to the elderly, infirm, and pregnant.

Companion

SEE ALSO *Nurse.*

Companions are often hired to care for the elderly. Persons hired in this capacity, unlike nurses, often have little or no job training. They must possess certain personal traits, though, namely an ability to handle their charges with gentleness, tact, and patience.

When interviewing for the position of companion, explain the job thoroughly and make no attempt to conceal the situation, whatever it may be. If the old person has a serious memory loss, is cantankerous, or even has a major medical problem such as incontinency, for example, do not hide this fact. Always portray the job as realistically as possible and carefully outline what will be expected of the companion, since responsibilities vary greatly from job to job. Finally, discuss whether you prefer a uniform (supplied by you) or street clothes.

A companion's basic responsibilities are to accompany the charge outdoors and to be near at hand at home, as well as to provide whatever basic care is needed to make the charge comfortable.

A live-in companion should have his or her own room and a reasonable amount of time off. Most expect two, not necessarily consecutive, days off per week. A companion also should be free whenever his charge is otherwise occupied—napping or visiting.

Condiments

Condiments such as catsup, mustard, mayonnaise, and chutneys, as well as relishes like baby carrots, olives, and nuts should be served on a plate or in a small bowl, never in the jar in which they were purchased.

At a very informal meal or a picnic, catsup, hot sauce, or Tabasco may be served in its original bottle. Mustard in a decorative container may be served right from the jar; otherwise mustard should be served in a small mustard dish.

The guidelines for eating condiments vary with the formality of the meal and the type of food being eaten. At a formal meal, it is politest to take a small portion of catsup, mustard, or mayonnaise on your plate with the serving utensil and then to use your own knife to transfer it to a sandwich. Except for a sandwich, catsup, mustard, mayonnaise, or relish should never, even at a casual meal, be poured directly on food. Pour out a small amount on your plate and dip the food into it as you eat.

Condolence Note

SEE ALSO *Business Condolence Note; Christian Mourning Customs; Condolences; Jewish Mourning Customs.*

There is one occasion when only a personal, handwritten note will do. It is when a friend has lost someone close to him. At such times, a printed sympathy card simply does not have the personal touch that a handwritten note does.

A condolence note need be only a few lines. If you knew the departed, try to recall some memory associated with him. Tell your friend how sorry you are over his or her loss. If you didn't know the departed, focus the note on your friend's feelings and loss. Here is a note that one might write to a close friend:

> Dear Sally,
>
> I was so sorry to hear about your mother's death. I'll always have such a lovely memory of that call we paid on her last summer. Even though she was ill then, she took such pains to entertain us elegantly, and she looked so elegant herself. Remember how beautiful she looked in that blue dress?
>
> I know the weeks and months ahead will be difficult for you, and I want you to know that I am here for you—whatever you need. You know you have my deepest sympathy, and if there is anything I can do, please let me know.
>
> Love,
> Janie

To a less close friend or an acquaintance, you may write something a little more formal:

> Dear Jeanette,
>
> I just heard about the loss of your mother. I've often heard you speak of her, and I know how very much she meant to you. I just wanted to let you know that you have my deepest sympathy, and that I'm thinking of you. If there is anything I can do for you, don't hesitate to call.
>
> Love,
> Maria

I am not a person who believes that a tumultuous relationship should be covered over at the time of death, so I feel that condolence notes should be honest. This is sometimes the only way to offer real comfort to a friend. They should, of course, always offer support to the living. For example:

> *Dear John,*
>
> *I just learned of the death of your father, rather belatedly, I fear, because I was away at the time of your loss. I know you two had your ups and downs over the years, but I also know you can take comfort in the fact that you were a good son to him.*
>
> *Please know you have my deepest sympathies over this loss, and if there is anything I can do for you, just call.*
>
> *Regards,*
> *Henry*

A condolence note should be written as soon as you hear about someone's loss. Obviously, you would not write one a year a more after a death, but several months after a death is not too late to offer your sympathies.

Most correctly, condolence notes should be written on plain white paper in black or navy ink, but if you have personal stationery that is not gay or frivolous (no funny drawings, please, at this time), you may be use it.

Condolence notes should be answered with a handwritten thank-you note.

Condolences

SEE ALSO *Business Condolence Note; Christian Mourning Customs; Condolence Note; Funeral; Jewish Mourning Customs; Mourning.*

Condolences are the kind words of sympathy that are offered to someone who has lost a loved one. Too often, people avoid talking to the recently bereaved, perhaps because they feel awkward about what to say. Keep in mind, though, that even the simplest words—"I'm so sorry" will suffice—offer great comfort to someone who has suffered a loss. You need say very little, even with a dear friend; a hug will suffice.

Condolences can be offered when and wherever you see a friend—at work, on the street, certainly at the funeral service or at a call paid on the family.

At a formal wake or when paying a call at the family's home, the mourners usually take over once you have offered your sympathy. Often, they will feel like discussing the departed, and you can either join in with your own reminiscences or simply listen.

Formal condolence calls for Protestants and Catholics are paid in the two or three days before the funeral. Close friends and relatives call at the funeral home and sometimes at home as well. Less close friends and acquaintances call at the funeral home, where they sign the guest register and talk with any members of the family who happen to be there. If no members of the family are there, they may sign the register and depart.

Among Jews, condolence calls do not begin until after the funeral, when the observant family sits shiva for anywhere from three to seven days (excluding the Sabbath).

If you cannot call in person, a handwritten condolence note may substitute, and even if you call, a note is appropriate.

Confirmation

SEE ALSO *Bar and Bat Mitzvah; First Communion.*

Depending upon the religion, Protestant and Roman Catholic children are confirmed sometime between the ages of eleven and fifteen. The children have usually devoted several months to religious training in preparation for the ceremony.

Only Reform Jews are sometimes confirmed. Orthodox and Conservative Jews celebrate a bar or bat mitzvah at age thirteen as do many Reform Jews.

Family and close friends often attend the confirmation service, and a reception may be held afterward in the church parlor for all the new communicants. Many families also choose to celebrate privately at home or in a restaurant with a brunch, lunch, dinner, or tea. A white cake is often served for dessert.

Boys wear white shirts, ties, and dark suits. Girls wear suits or dresses, the same kind they would wear to a regular religious service or possibly something a little dressier. A hat and gloves may be worn; whether

they are depends more on fashion than religious requirements. If a head covering is required, the child will be informed of this in communicants' classes. Unlike First Communion dresses, which are always white, a teenager will obviously wear a more sophisticated dress, but her age should be kept in mind, and she should not wear anything too sophisticated. Black, for example, is not an appropriate color to wear for a confirmation ceremony.

Guests invited to either the church ceremony or the party should wear dressy clothes such as they would wear to any church service.

Parents, godparents, and others who are close to the child may give a present; others need not unless they are invited to a private celebration. Any religious gift is appropriate, as are jewelry, small leather goods, books, and other lasting gifts. Frivolous gifts are not given to celebrate a confirmation. It is appropriate to offer congratulations to a new communicant.

Congratulations

ORAL. Congratulations are words of praise offered to friends and acquaintances whenever the occasion merits it. The most obvious times when congratulations are called for are announcement of an engagement, birth of a child, promotion, or any other good fortune. Congratulations are also offered at weddings, graduations, confirmations, bar or bat mitzvahs, and other ceremonial occasions. They are in order when a friend's book is published, when a friend wins a sporting event or anything else he or she has worked for.

BACK-HANDED CONGRATULATIONS. Too often, someone who is feeling envious of another's accomplishment manages to offer only weak or back-handed congratulations. Some people simply cannot enjoy others' good fortune, while other may be well-meaning most of the time but on this occasion cannot control their envy. And sometimes, to be honest, it is difficult to offer congratulations—such as when you were working hard for a promotion and someone less qualified was brought in from the outside to do the job. If you think you will have trouble congratulating someone, either save the congratulations for a time when you are feeling more upbeat or keep them very simple. You can never go wrong saying simply "Congratulations" or "That's great." You can sometimes go wrong with anything more.

TO A BRIDE. You can virtually never err in offering well-meant congratulations to a friend or acquaintance who has achieved something or come upon some bit of good fortune. Well, almost never. There are those sticky souls who still maintain that a woman should never be congratulated on her "good luck" in landing a man—when she becomes engaged or is married, for example. Instead, one offers the woman "Best wishes." I think this notion is archaic, and congratulations should be offered whenever the spirit moves and the occasion requires. If you find it awkward or tiresome to remember to say "Best wishes" to a woman simply because she is a woman, then offer your congratulations and never worry about it again.

WRITTEN. Although correspondence is suffering a sad decline, few gestures are more gracious than written congratulations. Such notes need not be long. For example, to a friend who recently was promoted, you might write:

> Dear Emily,
>
> I read about your promotion in the company newsletter. Nice going! I couldn't be happier for you—and, of course, the powers-that-be are lucky to have you in this position.
>
> All best,
> Carol

A new or prospective member of the family might be welcomed this way:

> Dear Julia,
>
> As you undoubtedly know, you have stolen the heart of my favorite nephew. But I can't say that I'm anything but delighted. Welcome to the family.
>
> Love,
> Aunt Betsy

Here is yet another example:

> Dear John and Mary,
>
> Eleanor and I feel very comfortable that you both will be at the helm of B'nai Brith next year and want to offer you our congratulations—and our assistance. Do let us know if we can do anything to help.
>
> Best,
> Burke

NONCONGRATULATORY NOTES. Although I just said that few gestures are more gracious than a congratulatory note, I can think of one: a noncongratulatory note. Sometimes a note to the person who didn't get the promotion, who broke an engagement, or who otherwise lost something important is just the right touch, too. For example:

> *Dear Cissie,*
>
> *I felt so bad when I learned of your miscarriage. I know there is little I can say to comfort you, but I want to know how very sorry I am and that I'm thinking of you.*
>
> *Love,*
> *Janice*

Or you might write:

> *Dear Jerry,*
>
> *Your mother told me how unhappy you were not to be admitted to Yale. I was so sorry to hear about your disappointment. The only consolation I can offer is to tell you that these things sometimes turn out for the best. I hope you will put your all into life at Michigan. I know you will be a success anywhere.*
>
> *Love,*
> *Uncle George*

RESPONSES TO CONGRATULATIONS. Acknowledge congratulations by saying "Thank you," "How kind of you to mention it," or something to this effect. Personal letters of congratulation call for a handwritten thank-you note. In business correspondence, congratulatory letters and thank-you notes are typed. Preprinted cards need not be acknowledged this way unless you want to respond.

Consommé Cup and Saucer

SEE ALSO *Soup.*

A consommé cup, which rests on a consommé saucer, is used for clear soups (*see Figure 15*). It is a small bowl with handles. While it is proper to drink the soup, far more persons eat consommé with a spoon. A consommé spoon, which is small and round, is used with a consommé cup, or a regular soup spoon may be used. If the cup is very dainty, as it is with some chinas, a teaspoon may be more suitable.

Figure 15. Consommé cup and saucer

Continental Style of Eating

SEE *Fork.*

Convention

On the one hand, conventions have a kind of party atmosphere that sometimes gets people in trouble when they act on their impulses. On the other hand, no one likes a dullard, and conventions are often the time when you get to know your colleagues better, mostly by tippling a few with them, dining with them, and participating in all the other extracurricular activities that are part and parcel of a convention.

Despite all this, when attending a convention, it is important to keep in mind that you not only represent your company or business, but also that you must face your co-workers after the convention.

Is is an unfair world, but women still have to exercise more caution than men, not because they are less likely to be able to hold their liquor or more prone to sexual indiscretions, but because their indiscretions will hurt them more than a man's will hurt him. A woman would do better not to hold a business meeting in her room, for example, even with a colleague.

Certainly, anyone whose boss is in attendance should affect something of a businesslike posture during a convention. Mostly this means not being seen on the dance floor at 3 A.M. when there is a 9 A.M. seminar the next morning, and not being seen ordering the third cognac after dinner.

The name of the game at a convention, if you are serious about your career, is to remain above suspicion, while still, of course, sneaking in a fair amount of fun.

Conversation

Conversation is an art, and some would say, a lost art at that. But we are not concerned here with scaling the heights of elegant discourse since no one can teach another that social skill. Instead this discussion will encompass some of the more usual ins and outs of everyday conversation.

SMALL TALK. Small talk is the conversation one must often make with virtual strangers and casual acquaintances with whom one comes into contact on various kinds of social occasions.

Two tricks will help to erase the panic that besets many people at the thought of having to make polite small talk with a stranger. The first is to be well informed. This can be accomplished by reading at least one daily newspaper or a weekly news magazine. Before going to an event where small talk will be expected, try to have in mind several books, films, or television shows of current interest, and bring up these topics during the first conversational lull. Unless the other person is a total lout, he or she will be grateful to you for filling the silence and will quickly follow your lead.

The second trick is to ask a person about himself. Most people are flattered to talk about themselves, and once this process has been put into motion, one need only sit back and listen. Some of the world's great conversationalists have insisted that what they really are is great listeners.

EYE AND BODY CONTACT. This varies around the world. In some cultures, for example, it is a sign of disrespect to look directly at a person who is speaking to you; in other parts of the world, it is a sign of disrespect not to look someone directly in the eye.

Body contact varies, too. Americans mostly look each other in the eye when they converse, with frequent breaks to scan the room. A too-steady gaze is unnerving. Americans also give each other a couple of feet of breathing room when possible, unlike for example, Arabs, who stand very close to one another when they talk. When traveling, you needn't take on the customs of those you are visiting, but you should be aware of them so you won't feel uncomfortable.

RUDE QUESTIONS. Occasionally a stranger will ask a question that is none of his or her business, such as how much did you pay for something or some other intimate detail that you don't wish to reveal. Ann Landers long ago suggested an excellent response, which is to ask the person why he wants to know that about you. A tactful way to not respond to such questions is to brush them off ("I don't remember what I paid for this coat" or in response to what you paid for a house, for example, "Too much, I can assure you"). If the person persists with his rudeness, he deserves a rude answer, and the more direct it is, the sooner he or she will get the message that this is information you don't intend to reveal. Try saying, "I really don't want to discuss that" or "I can't answer that question."

TACTLESS COMMENTS. I'm convinced that about fifty percent of people who make tactless comments regret them the moment they say them, and the other fifty percent don't know they've said something tactless. If you're offended, you can treat a tactless comment the same way you treat rude questions, for example, by saying, "Why would you say a thing like that!" If you can find it in your heart to let the comment go by, though, the kindest thing to do is to ignore a tactless comment.

CORRECTIONS. Correcting someone's grammar or mispronunciation it its own brand of tactlessness, and is rude to boot. The only exception to this rule is when the offender is one's own child.

BORES. No one likes to listen to bores, but in this case, the afflicted do not know they are afflicted, and some tact is required to extricate oneself from the situation without hurting any feelings. At a big party, the easiest way to do this is to excuse yourself on grounds that a drink must be freshened, a plate filled, or an old friend greeted. At a small party or a dinner party total escape may be unavoidable, but one can spend more time talking with the more interesting dinner partner or start a conversation that involves several persons instead of just two.

The easiest bores to avoid are those encountered in public places—on planes or waiting in line at the grocery store. Simply tune out. Nod briefly once or twice and then look away. You are under no obligation to have a conversation with a stranger who has invaded your privacy with no encouragement from you.

Co-op Board Interview

SEE ALSO *Apartment Living*.

Persons who buy shares in a co-op or condominium apartment usually must be approved by an admissions board. An interview is held to determine the prospective owner's suitability.

Prior to meeting with the board, prospective members have submitted personal and business letters of recommendation. The persons who write these letters should be carefully chosen for the kind of information they can impart. The co-op board will be most interested in a prospective tenant's ability to carry the financial load, and the letters should emphasize this as much as possible. The letters are intended to make you look like an upright, responsible citizen who always pays his bills.

When asking someone to write a letter, it is acceptable and helpful to suggest the kinds of things that you would like to have emphasized. For example, if one letter were written by a relatively new acquaintance with whom one had some financial dealings, and another by an old friend, it might be helpful to suggest to the new friend that she emphasize the financial dealings and to the old friend that he mention the longevity of the relationship.

The interview itself is in some ways more trying than a job interview, in large part because far more personal questions way be asked. One childless couple I know was turned down by a co-op board after they declined to discuss what they could do about day care were they to have a child.

It is helpful to prepare for the interview by talking with friends who have been through a similar one. If there are any problem areas, a couple should discuss them in advance and possibly even decide which one of them will attempt to answer the tough questions.

Such interviews are often held in the evening in the apartment of someone presently living in the co-op. The interviewers are quite likely to be in casual dress, but the person being interviewed should wear work clothes or something comparable to what would be worn to a job interview.

Corn on the Cob

You will never encounter this at a formal dinner, but on the occasion when corn is served, here is how to eat it. Use both hands on either end of the cob to hold it. Butter and salt only a few rows at a time. A larger ear may be broken into smaller pieces, but be forewarned that this is difficult to do with a hot ear of corn. You may eat straight across or around the ear, whichever suits you.

Corsage

Less expensive than bouquets, corsages vary in price depending upon the flowers chosen. Not all flowers work well in a corsage. Some flowers, such as daisies and large lilies, simply would not make an attractive corsage, while other flowers, such as carnations, camellias, gardenias, roses, and orchids, seem made for these small arrangements.

A corsage should be chosen to match or complement a woman's dress; if its color is not known, white flowers are always safe.

Wrist corsages, which adorned the arms of highly sophisticated women during the Twenties and Thirties, are generally considered the province of teenagers these days. Corsages are generally worn on a dress or coat, or they may be pinned to a purse. They also may be worn in the hair. When pinned to a dress or a coat, the corsage usually goes on the woman's right shoulder (so the flowers will not be crushed when she dances), but there is no reason they could not be worn anywhere on a dress—at the neckline or waist—where they work especially well.

The florist always sends a special pin that is used to hold the flowers in place. Corsages are always worn with the stems down, the way flowers grow naturally.

The occasions when corsages are called for are not very many these days, but it is my hope that corsages will experience a revival any day now. They are such a lovely touch. No woman can look anything but special wearing fresh flowers. Today, teen girls expect to receive corsages from their dates before formal dances and proms. Brides—some but not all—still wear them on their going away outfits. Unfortunately, many brides are unwilling to be so clearly labeled, since a corsage on a sparkling young woman, accompanied by an equally happy young man, is an undeniable tipoff that these are honeymooners. Corsages are worn by mothers of the bride and groom, and the thoughtful bride also has flowers made up into corsages for her and her groom's grandmothers. Corsages also make a lovely present on any other occasion, such as an anniversary, a bar or bat mitzvah, or even for no occasion at all other than a night on the town.

When a woman receives a corsage as a gift, she is expected to wear it, even if it clashes with her dress—an unlikely occurence.

Romantic myth holds that the man who gives a woman a corsage should pin it to her dress. Few men are comfortable doing this, and even fewer women, I suspect, are comfortable having them do this.

If you are given a corsage, you may pin it to your dress or purse yourself. If there is another woman in the room she may offer to help if she sees that you need help.

Coughing

If you have to cough, you have to cough, but there's a way to do it politely. Cover your mouth, if possible with a handkerchief or tissue. Turn away from those around you. And when you're done coughing, apologize.

If a serious coughing fit seizes you, leave the room so others will not be disturbed. At a live performance, you can usually stand at the back of the theater until a break in the action offers an opportunity to return to your seat without disturbing others.

If you are a frequent cougher, you may find it helpful to carry cough lozenges or hard candy to soothe your throat. Never, however, unwrap candy or a cough drop, or otherwise rustle paper, during a live performance. Leave the room or wait for intermission.

Cousin

Everybody knows what a sibling is and who his siblings are. No one gets confused about his parents. The confusion that does arise in families almost entirely revolves around cousins. To help clear up the confusion, keep in mind that cousin relationships are defined across generations. You are first cousin to your aunts' and uncles' children because you are in the same generation. Or to put it another way, the children of siblings are first cousins.

The children of first cousins, who also go across a generation, are second cousins to each other, and so on down, or rather across, the family tree.

Then we get to the cousins who are "removed," which by the way, has always reminded me of the "begats" in the Old Testament. Your first cousin's child is your first cousin, once removed. Your second cousin's child is your second cousin, once removed. And so on.

Crab

HARD SHELL. *(See Figure 16.)* Remove the legs with your fingers and suck the crabmeat (gently and quietly) out of them. Use a fork to get at the rest of the meat and dip it in the sauce. Spear the body with your knife and cut out the meat gently in sections. You can eat the tomalley or the roe (female only) with a fork.

SOFT SHELL. The whole crab is edible. Cut up with knife and fork.

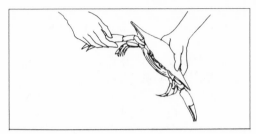

1. *Remove the legs with your fingers. Pull out meat with a fork or quietly suck it out.*

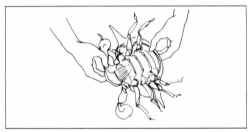

2. *Remove undershell with an oyster fork and eat the meat.*

3. *Pull meat out or away from hard outershell.*

4. *Pick out remaining meat and eat with fork or fingers.*

Figure 16. How to eat a hard-shelled crab

Crackers

SERVING. At home, crackers should always be served in a bowl or on a plate without their wrappers. In a restaurant, they may be served in small packages, as oyster crackers are, or in individual wrappers.

WITH SOUP. Unless you are under the age of two (presumably too young to read this) or home alone with an awful case of the flu or a cold, never break crackers into small pieces and put them directly in soup. Never dunk them, either. Eat them along with the soup. Oyster crackers are the only crackers that may properly be sprinkled over soup, and the only soup they are served with is clam chowder.

WITH CHEESE. Serve unsalted crackers with cheese. They complement the cheese and are a more sensible accompaniment since most cheeses have a high salt content.

Cremation

SEE ALSO *Christian Mourning Customs; Jewish Mourning Customs.*

People whose religions and personal beliefs permit it sometimes choose to be cremated. A funeral service may be held first, but more often the body is cremated and a memorial service is scheduled at a later date for family and friends. If there is any ceremony at the cremation, usually only the immediate family attends. The family may,

if they choose to do so, accompany the body to the crematorium.

The ashes are given to the family, who may dispose of them as they please. Most families place them in an urn, bury them, or scatter them over a site that was particularly beloved by the person who died. Others have them buried by the crematorium in common ground.

Cup and Saucer

SEE *Dishes.*

Curtsy

SEE ALSO *Papal Audience.*

The issue of whether or not an American curtsies to royalty, or, for that matter, whether or not a non-Catholic curtsies to a cardinal or the Pope had all but resolved itself in the somewhat unmannered Sixties: Americans curtsied to no one. Recently, though, curtsying seems to have made something of a comeback, in part because an American diplomat's wife chose to curtsy to the Prince of Wales when she met him in an official capacity. This caused a minor flurry, pleasing some and offending others.

For the record, Americans, democrats with a small *d*, do not curtsy before royalty, nor need a non-Catholic do so before a cardinal or a pope. You may do so, of course, but you need never feel obligated to do so.

If you wish to show respect in a less traditional manner, bow slightly. This is a lovely gesture that can be used whenever you meet anyone. One of its advantages is that it permits men and women to use the same kind of greeting.

In some parts of the country, very young children (under the age of four) are still sometimes taught to curtsy when they meet adults.

Custard Cup

Custards are meant to be eaten in the cup in which they are served *(see Figure 17)*. A custard dessert is usually brought in and placed on the service plate, or it is brought in on a service plate.

To eat its contents, steady the cup, if necesssary, with one hand and use a spoon to eat the custard with the other. When resting between bites and when you are finished, rest the spoon on the service plate, never on the tablecloth, and never leave it in the custard cup.

Figure 17. Custard cup

Cutting In

SEE *Dancing*.

Dance

SEE ALSO *Debutante Ball.*

Unlike a ball, which is usually given in a public place and sponsored by a charity or some other organization, private individuals give dances. A dance may be given to celebrate a debutante's coming of age, an anniversary, a party—any festive occasion, actually. A dance may be held in one's home or at a club or restaurant.

INVITATIONS. Invitations can be simple or elaborate. For a white-tie dance, printed or engraved invitations are sent; for black-tie and less casual dances, invitations may be written on personal stationery or pre-printed invitations.

Invitations should include the date, time, name of host and hostess, whether a response is requested, and some idea of the dress. If the dance is black tie, that should be noted. Similarly, if dress is casual, it, too, should be noted. Invitations should be sent about three weeks before the dance.

Most dances begin late, around 9 or 10 P.M., and last until 12:30 or 1 A.M., sometimes even later. Because of the late hours, almost without exception, dances are held on weekends, usually on Saturday night.

As a rule, people do not begin arriving until thirty minutes to one hour after the appointed time.

DANCE FLOOR. A suitable place to dance is, of course, the most important aspect of this kind of party. If a home has a good nonslippery tile or wood floor, that can be used. Furniture should be cleared away so guests will have room to dance. A patio or poolside can also provide an excellent dance floor, but it must be lit well enough so guest can see to dance.

MUSIC. After a dance floor, the most important element of a dance is the music. It is even worthwhile to stint on decorations to provide a good group of musicians. The most elaborate dances feature a full orchestra, but a good dance can be held with far fewer musicians, even a good pianist. Live musicians are most festive, but taped music could also be used.

FOOD AND DRINK. Since most dances are held at night, the usual menu is a light supper served around 11 P.M. It can be either a hot or a cold buffet.

Beverages can consist of anything from an open bar to a champagne, wine, or liquor punch.

DECORATIONS. Decorations can be elaborate and related to a theme for the party or they can be so simple as to be almost nonexistent. Particularly for a dance held in a small space, decorations may only get in the way, and should be used sparingly. Given a choice between providing good music and elaborate decorations, I would opt for the music; it goes to the heart of the matter.

DRESS. At a white-tie affair, the men wear tails, and at a black-tie affair, they wear tuxedos. At any other kind of dance, unless the invitation specifically states casual dress, men usually wear dark suits and white shirts.

Women wear long evening dresses to white-tie affairs. They often wear long gloves, but this is a decision that depends in part on the style of the dress. At a black-tie event, women may wear either long or short evening dresses or cocktail dresses, depending upon the current fashion. Long gloves are not appropriately worn with anything but a long ballgown (except as a matter of individual style), and gloves are optional anyway. At other than black-tie affairs, women may wear cocktail clothes, a dressy street dress—almost anything but a tailored suit.

Dancing

Dancing is an absolutely delightful social custom, something that people of all ages and skills can enjoy. In fact, if you do not know how to dance and often have occasion to, a course in ballroom dancing is an excellent investment that will more than repay you, not only in improved dancing skills but also in greater self-confidence.

It has generally been the prerogative of the man to ask the woman to dance, but young people today often do not make these distinctions, and I don't think they are so important anymore either. Sometimes a shy man is dying to dance and will only do so when a woman takes the initiative to invite him. There is certainly nothing wrong with this, nor should there be anything awkward about it.

FOR WOMEN. A woman need not dance with everyone who invites her, but she must take care not to hurt anyone's feelings. If she declines to dance with a man, she must give a polite excuse, such as she is tired and needs to sit out this dance. She must not then turn around and accept an invitation to dance with someone else. Of course, a man also has a right to refuse a woman's invitation to dance.

FOR MEN. A man is expected to dance with his wife, the hostess at a party, and any women sitting near him at his table at a social function. If he is the host, his obligation to dance is more expansive, and he should try to dance with as many of his guests as possible.

He should avoid leaving a woman alone

when he goes off to dance, though. After dancing with a woman, a man should walk her back to her table, or at minimum, should escort her off the dance floor.

THE DANCE POSITION. The classic position for ballroom dancing begins with a couple standing face to face. The man places his right arm around her waist, holding her firmly without clutching. With his left hand, he holds her right hand. The woman's right hand rests on his right shoulder.

You may talk with someone when you dance with him or her, or you may simply enjoy the moment.

With the newer dances, men and women do not so much dance together as they dance around each other. The only advice I can think of with this kind of dancing is not to dance too far away from your partner, lest you lose him or her.

CUTTING IN. The custom of cutting in has fallen on bad times, and people these days mostly dance with their escorts. To cut in, tap the man on the shoulder and say, "May I?" A couple cannot refuse to let someone cut in on them. If possible, do not cut in on a couple who have just begun dancing or who have danced only a few bars since they were last cut in on.

Dating

SEE ALSO. *Blind Date; Teen Dance; Teen Social Life.*

Dating is courtship, make no mistake about it. It is a series of social encounters that permit a man and a woman to become well enough acquainted with each other to determine whether or not they wish to marry. It is fashionable in some circles to pretend that dating is something less than courtship, but this is a naive point of view, one that eventually confuses all the parties involved in a dating relationship.

Except for young women in certain Hispanic cultures, dating is an unchaperoned activity these days. A dating couple has great discretion in how they conduct themselves.

ACCEPTING/REFUSING. Even for an experienced dater, the act of asking someone with whom you aspire to have a romantic relationship for a date is an ego-wrenching experience. The gracious recipient of an invitation understands this and reacts accordingly, by either accepting or refusing an invitation as soon as possible, preferably at the moment the invitation is tendered. If you cannot reply immediately, then let the person know as soon as possible. It is cruel to keep someone dangling, especially when the delay is a stalling tactic against telling someone you do not want to go out with him or her.

A gracious acceptance is enthusiastic: "I'd love to go the movies with you Friday night." A refusal should be equally gracious, especially if you hope to receive another invitation. If possible, indicate why you cannot accept: "I'm sorry, but I've already made other plans and can't go to the movies with you Friday. I'd love to do it another time." In other words, make it clear that another invitation is welcome. The invitee, female or male, might also suggest another day: "I can't go out with you Friday, but what about a movie Sunday evening? I'm free then. Are you?"

If you receive an invitation from someone whom you do not wish to go out with, it is sometimes kinder to send out some signals to that effect rather than leading the person on. Start by saying no, very politely, and possibly offering some polite excuse. Some people do not read subtle messages, though, and you may have to escalate the signals. When someone repeatedly asks you out despite your offering no encouragement, make your excuses a little curter: "No, I can't go out that night. Thank you for asking me, though."

ASKING. Never be coy about asking for a date. Don't say, "So, would you like to go out with me sometime?" Even worse is, "Do you like to go to the movies?" A woman who loves movies but does not want to go out with you will not consider this an invitation, and a woman who hates movies but wants to go out with you will be frustrated. Far better is the specific, direct invitation: "Would you like to have dinner and go a movie with me Friday night?"

Responsibility for asking for dates used to fall entirely on the shoulders of men, while women passively waited for invitations. Today, although women still take the initiative less often than men do, there is no reason that a woman cannot ask out a man. She should, of course, expect to pay for the evening when she does. And she should realize that she may be rebuffed. Just as men have been laying their egos on the line for years and occasionally getting knocked down by uninterested women, so, too, must women expect to find the occasional man who is not interested or is otherwise engaged.

BEHAVIOR DURING DATES. A date should be like any other occasion when you get together with a friend, but it is not. Much more of your ego is on the line, particularly if you have any romantic interest in developing a relationship. And even if you do not know whether that is a goal or not, the pressure is still on to make a good impression and please the other person. Despite this, behaving much as you would on any other social occasion can do a lot to set the tone of the evening and make it enjoyable. Your goal should be to put your date at ease so you can get to know him or her better.

As the "guest" on a date, try to participate enthusiastically in whatever is planned for the evening, although you, of course, also have a voice in the planning. The person who does the inviting is technically the host, but you should both help plan the evening, with few exceptions. If you have already seen a movie, for example, speak up, or if you ate Chinese food last night and your date is suggesting it again tonight, say you would rather eat somewhere else.

ENDING THE DATE. When you are both adults, you have a certain leeway about how and under what circumstances you end a date. Either of you, at the end of the evening, can suggest that it is time to go home. There is usually a crucial moment when a woman must decide whether to invite a man into her apartment for a few minutes, and when a man can hope that a woman will accept his invitation to stay longer than a few minutes. When a woman invites a man into her home or accepts an invitation into his, she is usually opening herself up for an invitation to sex. She need not accept, but she should realize that she has, in accepting or offering the invitation to extend the date, left the door open to this. A woman who is not ready to put the relationship on this level may want to send a clear message by saying good night at the door.

FIRST DATES. First dates can be awkward, and they can also be wonderful as you discover a potential partner for a relationship. There is basically nothing to set them apart from other dates, and your behavior should be the same regardless of whether you are on a first date or your seventy-second (and no longer counting) date.

DATE ACTIVITIES. What people do on dates depends upon where they are in a relationship with someone and how old they are. (Obviously, young teens will be restricted in acitivities, whereas adults are free to do just about anything they want to do.) Regardless of age, any couple's first few dates are generally more structured than later dates. You make plans in advance to go out to dinner and to a basketball game. After a couple have been dating for a while, "dates," if they can still be called that, become more casual, to the point where the couple may often agree to stay home and read or watch television together. Dates are also an excellent opportunity for a couple to pursue their individual interests and to introduce each other to them. One of the joys of friendship, after all, is to interest a friend in something new that he or she might not otherwise have done.

Death

SEE ALSO *Christian Mourning Customs; Condolence Note; Condolences; Donation; Flowers; Funeral; Jewish Mourning Customs; Obituary; Widow; Widower.*

When someone dies, three steps must be taken immediately: (1) notify the family members, (2) contact the deceased person's lawyer, and (3) call an undertaker. These three steps will set into motion the process of planning the funeral.

Family and friends are usually notified by telephone, but those living or visiting so far away that they will not be able to attend the funeral in any event are often notified by telegram or letter. If the next-of-kin do not feel up to the task, this and other tasks may be delegated to a close, sympathetic family friend.

The deceased person's lawyer is contacted so that he or she can inform the family of anything in a letter or a will regarding preferred burial arrangements. The deceased's wishes should be followed as closely as possible, but where they cannot be followed, no one need feel guilty or burdened.

The undertaker will assume responsibility for the funeral arrangements. These days, burial services are often held in a funeral home rather than at home or in a church or synagogue.

The undertaker will guide the family in making arrangements. He will, for example, arrange for newspaper notices of the death, work with the clergyperson and family members on the service, arrange for transportation to and from the cemetery.

These three steps kindly set into motion a process that carries a family through the numbing days following the loss of a beloved one. People, including close family and friends, will be there to support them and to guide them as they make the appropriate arrangements.

DEATH AND CHILDREN. Very young children do not understand death, and they will not derive any comfort from attending the funeral, nor will they be able to participate in the mourning of a loved one. Children of ten or eleven are old enough to understand, however, and may even benefit from participating in the mourning process. Children do not wear black as a sign of mourning. They wear their regular clothes, or white ones. For funeral services, they should be dressed in the kind of clothes they would wear to any religious service.

DEATH OF EX-SPOUSE. No one has a social obligation to attend the funeral of an ex-spouse, and, indeed, may not even feel like mourning. This is one of those times when you may do whatever your feelings dictate. You may, however, find that your presence at the funeral or memorial service will be a comfort to your children or your ex-in-laws if you have remained close. If there are still ties like this, you may call at the home or the funeral home and attend the services. Depending upon whether your ex-spouse has remarried, you may or may not be treated like a member of the family. Obviously, if he or she has a spouse, that person will be a chief mourner and you will be relegated to the position of close family friend. Even if an ex-spouse has not remarried, you are not a chief mourner, nor are you a widow or widower if you have been formally divorced. Naturally, at times like these where families are encountering new and fairly uncharted emotional territory, rules are written as we go along, and we must mostly count on our good instincts to carry us through.

RESPONSIBILITIES OF FAMILY MEMBERS. The immediate family's most important responsibility is to plan the funeral. Decisions are made by the widow and her children (or the widower and his children), and the children should defer to the living parent's wishes. If there is no widow or widower or children, siblings or any other close relative plan the services.

I am often asked about another matter, which is the extent to which the deceased's wishes regarding funeral arrangements must be respected. With all due respect to the dead, I think that funerals and mourning are intended to help the living, and that their needs come first. If someone did not like the idea of a large funeral while he was living, those wishes could and should be taken into account when planning a funeral; if the deceased expressed a desire to have no funeral, however, but the family feels it needs some ceremony, then I think they must serve their own needs first.

The extended family usually gathers in the days or hours before the funeral. Death, perhaps more than any other event in a family, draws it together. Family members should be especially kind to one another, and old grudges should be buried at least for the time being, if not permanently.

RESPONSIBILITIES OF FRIENDS. Close family friends, like relatives, will gather around the mourners to comfort them. You can go directly to someone's house when you receive news of the death, or you can telephone and find out what assistance you can give. Friends are often asked to pick up children at school or camp, call other friends, bring in food—or, more often, they are not specifically asked to bring in food, but this is one of the major things they just go ahead and do to help. A mourning family is in no condition to handle everyday household chores, and to the extent that you can just step in and provide food and run small errands, you will be of immeasurable help.

Even less-than-close friends and acquaintances can perform some kindnesses to those who have suffered a loss. If possible and appropriate, attend the funeral. It always means so much to the mourners. If you cannot attend, be sure to tell the person how sorry you were to hear of his or her loss. You can either telephone your condolences or send a condolence note. You should always offer condolences to the newly bereaved the first time you see him or her after the loss.

Condolences, by the way, do not require any particular verbal eloquence. Simply say, "I'm so sorry for your loss." The bereaved will reply "Thank you" and go on to say something about the loss or will change the subject.

Your obligations as a friend do not end when the funeral or period of formal mourning ends, either. Years ago, people were obligated to show their mourning to the world in how they dressed and conducted their social lives, and perhaps this was too much, but today things may be over with a bit too quickly. The funeral and the few intense days of mourning that surround it are all that most people have. When this is over, they are still walking wounded, but everyone expects them to have resumed their normal lives. This is when people who have suffered a loss need most to know that their friends are there for them. Call a friend a week after the funeral just to find out how she or he is doing; ask him to join in a low-key social outing, particularly if the mourner is a widow or widower. Widows and widowers especially feel—and are—abandoned after the death of their partners. Don't force the person to resume a social life he or she isn't ready for, but do help him get out—if only for a walk or to run routine errands. Even a month or so later, send some flowers with a card that reads "Just thinking about you." Such little kindnesses will mean so much to those who need them.

Debutante Ball

Debutante balls, on the wane for a while, are enjoying a resurgence in popularity, although they have changed somewhat in form. Young ladies of eighteen to twenty or so used to be presented at elaborate private balls, given by their parents or grandparents. Today's debuts are more likely to be group efforts sponsored by various charitable organizations. Parents who wish to have a daughter presented are expected to make a sizable donation to the charity. They are usually invited to make a donation; it is not acceptable to offer to do so except under the most discreet circumstances.

Entree to these affairs is not achieved overnight. A minimum of several years of charitable work, and not exclusively with the charity that sponsors the debutante ball, either, is often required to be assured that one's daughter will receive the cherished invitation to be presented. Those who work regularly for charities; make donations to the proper, i.e., social, charities; and sit on (and chair) committees when asked to do so will usually find themselves in good standing when the invitations are issued for debutante balls.

Depending upon the ball at which she is being presented, a debutante may be given some guidelines regarding her dress. All the young women may be asked to wear white or pastel dresses, for example. White is the traditional color for debutantes, but these days, colors and dresses in every degree of sophistication are worn, according to the young woman's personal taste. A young woman choosing her coming-out dress should keep in mind that this is a *rite de pasage* from a more innocent, protected period of her life into a more sophisticated, adult period and should perhaps make some attempt to dress accordingly.

At many debutante balls, the young ladies each choose two men to escort them. These men are chosen from among their personal friends and schoolmates.

The social practices regarding escorts vary with the city and the ball. In some communities, the girl's parents may escort her to the ball; in others, both or one of her escorts may accompany her to and from the ball. These days with so many young people paired off at such young ages, a girl may prefer only one escort, who will be her regular steady. A young man who is asked to be an official escort does not bring another date to a dance. Her escorts send flowers.

The order of events for the evening, including the receiving line, is usually determined by the charity, and a young woman and her parents are told what will be expected of them. At a private debutante dance or tea, a receiving line, made up of the hostess and the debutante, should be organized to greet guests as they arrive.

Private debuts these days tend to be either very elaborate parties given by parents who can well afford to lavish thousands of dollars on their daughter or they are more modest afternoon teas. A tea is obviously the least expensive form of entertainment, as punch and sandwiches may be all that is served. At an evening dance, a supper is served around 11 P.M. Friends of the parents, as well as friends of the young lady, are invited, and even though the guest of honor is a minor, alcoholic beverages are served to the adults. A nonalcoholic punch is provided for the minors.

FLOWERS. Flowers are the quintessential decoration for a debut. In addition to the planned decorations, bouquets may arrive from well-wishers and the young lady's dates will send her flowers. If she has two escorts, she may pin one corsage to her shoulder and attach another to her purse. If she cannot comfortably wear both flowers, she should wear only one.

PRESENTS. Debutantes receive presents from close friends and family. Her parents often give her a special piece of jewelry. Others close to her—grandparents or godparents—may choose to give her a gift to remember her special day by.

THANK-YOUS. The debutante must send thank-you notes to everyone who has given her a present. She does not send them to her escorts, who were honored enough by escorting her, unless, of course, one of them has given her a present other than flowers.

Dentist

SEE *Doctor*.

Dessert and Coffee

In some parts of the country, it is acceptable to ask people over for dessert and coffee without feeding them a meal. In other parts of the country (I suspect where people must drive great distances to visit one another), people are rarely invited just for dessert.

Often a dessert party is planned around some event, a television special or a special movie that has been rented for the VCR. People with small children who cannot easily accommodate their schedules to dinner parties find that asking friends over for dessert provides an excellent way to stay in touch.

If only dessert is served, it must be something special—a beautiful cake or pie, or a more elaborate dessert. Some hostesses serve several desserts. A nice touch is to serve everything as elegantly as possible, using china, silver, and cloth napkins. Set the table with your best tablecloth, and put a pretty bouquet on it.

Diction

Diction may be a word you have not heard since grammar school. It refers to the choice of words one makes. Using the wrong word at the wrong time or, for that matter, at the right time, can hurt or even be downright hilarious. A business acquaintance who frequently overextended her vocabulary without first checking definitions once admitted to having had a highly erotic evening when in fact she meant to say she had enjoyed a highly *exotic* evening. The laugh, unfortunately, was at her expense.

Although there seems to be no reason for many of the distinctions in usage and pronunciation of certain words, knowing how to use words correctly is the mark of an educated person. It is also the mark of a promotable person.

Good English is available to everyone. You may have learned it later than someone whose parents corrected every word, but there is simply no reason not to catch up. The following list consists of words that are frequently misused, to the social detriment of the user.

all the farther When this means "I am going," say, "This is as far as I am going," not "This is all the farther I'm going."

allow and *allow me* This means, "Permit me," not "I allowed as how he was right," an expression that should be banished by a well-intentioned speaker.

an invite The word is "invitation," and nothing else will do.

anywheres, somewheres It seems like such a little thing to attach an "s" to these words, and it is part of the everyday dialect in some cities. Still, try to say "anywhere" and "somewhere."

aunt The broad "a" pronunciation is used on the East Coast, and some persons from other areas of the country may feel illiterate not using this pronunciation; however, the short "a," as in "ant," is perfectly acceptable and nothing to apologize for. Say whatever is comfortable for you.

between and *among* "Between" refers to an exchange involving two persons; if there are three or more persons, use "among."

between you and I People who are trying hard to sound literate often use this expression; the correct one is "between you and me."

bad, badly Adverbs, which generally take an "ly" ending, are another example of overdoing it in the name of literacy. The correct answer to "How do you feel?" is "I feel bad." "Feel," a copulative verb, is the equivalent of "am" and takes an adjective. On the other hand, someone does "perform badly." Adverbs can cause problems, but you will do well if you remember to avoid such awkward and pompous expressions as "importantly" and "firstly."

can't hardly This is a double negative; say "I can hardly."

chaise longue You may never have a chance to show this one off, but to do so correctly will show that you know your way around. This is the proper term for what many people call "chaise lounge." It is a kind of long chair on which one can semi-recline. The last word in this French term is pronounced "long." Never shorten this to "chaise," which only means "chair" in French.

Chinamen and other racial epithets A chinaman is someone in the business of selling fine china; it is never a proper reference to someone from China. A literate (and compassionate) person does well to avoid ethnic slurs of any kind. Among other things, it is just good business: even if you think you can identify ethnic gestures or names, it never pays to risk offending someone.

congratulate Do not pronounce this "congradulate." Do not shorten the word in any way unless you are among old high-school buddies and talking about old slang expressions.

consensus This means "agreement of opinion," so it's incorrect to add "of opinion" when you use the word.

dias The platform you stand or sit on at a banquet; pronounce it with a long "a" sound: "da-is," not "di-as."

dialogue Help fight fancy English. Why use this when the word "talk" will do just as well?

egoism, egotism An egoist is someone who tends to see things in terms of how they affect him or her; an egotist is someone who cannot stop talking about himself or herself.

either Either an "e" or an "i" pronunciation is fine.

end result A result *is* the end. Use one or the other.

federal, national "Federal" refers to the government of the United States; "national" conveys a sense of the spirit or patriotism that the citizens feel for their homeland.

fine, splendid, excellent Do not say "finely," "splendidly," or "excellently," when talking about how you feel. Also see *bad*.

folks Avoid using this term to describe your family. "Folk" is correctly used to refer to a people, a nation.

fifth Be careful to sound all the letters.

gent This and other cute nicknames or terms such as "dearie," "honey," "tootsie," "hubby," "little woman," and "girls" (when referring to women) should be avoided; they make most literate persons wince, as well they should.

give me, get me, let me Be sure to pronounce these as two separate words, not as "gimme" or "lemme."

guesstimate This word seems to be worming its way into the language. For the time being, use "estimate" or "guess," depending upon which one you mean.

graduate The verb form should be used as follows: "He was graduated from," or "He graduated from," but not, "He graduated."

high class and other similar expressions Try to avoid saying someone is high class, well-to-do, or wealthy. They are rich. Even if they are not rich, they may be of high quality, but not of high class. Such expressions suggest that you have a sense of inferiority and lack contact with the rich.

hopefully In most sentences "hopefully" is not correctly used, and you can test this by trying to find the word it modifies. Consider: "Hopefully the sales deficit can be made up in the third quarter." Now see who is hopeful. The sales deficit? Whenever you have the urge to use "hopefully," bite your tongue and instead say, "I hope," which is correct.

house, home This pair is a lot like "national" and "federal." A house is the building. A home is the spiritual place. The correct answer to the question "Where are you?" is "At home," but you are physically in your house.

itch, scratch An itch is the sensation that calls for the act of scratching.

kudos This always takes a singular verb. There is no such thing as a kudo.

lady, woman These are two words that have taken on new significance in the wake of the feminist movement. They seem to be reversing their meanings, with "lady" now being used disparagingly: "Look, lady, that's your problem." Women today—particularly women seeking equality with men in the professional sphere—frequently resent being referred to as girls, as well they should, since their colleagues would not be overjoyed to be referred to as boys. "Ladies" seems to offend less, but men and women who want to show respect for their colleagues will try to use the word "women." Also see *person.*

leave, let Do not confuse these two words. You leave a room. When someone is detaining you, you may want them to let you go. Do not say, "Leave me go."

lend, borrow You lend something to a friend or acquaintance. They have borrowed something from you.

like This may be the most abused word of our time. It is not a conjunction, as in, "It is cloudy today like it was last Wednesday." Instead say, "It is cloudy today just as it was last Wednesday." Also, if you are describing examples, do not say, "The products are similar to those of our competitors, like the XYZ Co. and Plank Corporation." Instead, say, "The products are similar to those of our competitors, such as the XYZ Co. and the Plank Corporation."

manufacture Pronounce the "*u*" distinctly

and do not slip into "man*a*facture."

myself This has come into common usage as a substitute for the correct form of "me" or "I." Just say "I am fine" rather than "I myself am fine," and "as for me" rather than "as for myself."

neither See *either*. This word always goes with "nor," not "or."

off Never use this in place of "from." "I got it off of *(from)* Jane" is illiterate.

pardon me This is a rude expression, indicating that you have been offended. Instead say, "Excuse me" or "I beg your pardon."

person Terms such as salesperson and chairperson have gained wide usage today, despite their seeming awkwardness. Few women object, and many men and women are now using the terms with ease. There is really no etiquette on this subject, except that each person should do what is comfortable for him or her and, more important, for those to whom the terms will be applied.

personal friend Just the word "friend" will suffice. Friends are always personal.

the reason why, the reason is because "Reason" means "why" and "because"; therefore, say, "The reason is that . . ."

restroom, bathroom Restroom is generally used to refer to public bathrooms, at work, in hotels, and anywhere outside the home; bathroom is used at home.

second Be sure to pronounce the "d."

sore This is how you feel when something hurts. It is not a substitute for "angry."

strength Pronounce every letter, taking special care not to omit the "g."

tomato See *aunt*, and stick to saying tomato the way you learned to in the old neighborhood.

you know This has filtered into the language to an incredible degree; and while there is nothing grammatically wrong with it, it irritates a lot of persons who were born before it came into common usage.

yeah The same thing applies here. You take your chances when you use this word in the business world; it is a sign of sloppy thinking.

Dinner

SEE *Bachelor Dinner; Barbecue; Buffet; Business Lunch; Dinner Party.*

Dinner Party

SEE ALSO *Brunch; Buffet Dinner; Guest List; Host/Hostess Gift; Lunch.*

The rigidly formal dinner, with proscribed rules concerning even minute details of service, has become mostly an event of the past, largely because so few of us have the requisites to give such a dinner, namely, a staff of full-time servants, fine china, sterling, and crystal, and the space to entertain on so grand a scale. As a result, I think of a "formal" dinner party as any dinner for which the hostess and host have made an effort to set the most elegant possible table and to put the most delicious possible food before their guests. Beyond even today's "formal" dinner party, I hasten to add, is a wide range of entertaining, including the last-minute casual supper with friends. It is up to you to choose from among the following suggestions those that are best suited to your personal style of entertaining.

INVITATIONS. You may invite people by telephone (the most common method), by preprinted invitation in which you have filled in the time and date, or by printed or engraved formal invitation. The latter is pretentious, unless the occasion warrants it—you are entertaining a head-of-state, for example. Engraved invitations for dinner are rarely used today except at the State Department and the White House. Engraved formal invitations should be mailed about three weeks in advance (see *Invitations*). For an informal dinner, invitations may be issued anywhere from a week or a few days to a few hours in advance ("We're having lasagne tonight. Why don't you bundle up the kids and come over and join us?").

The advantage to telephoning invitations is that the response is immediate. If someone must decline the invitation, you can invite someone else. Fortunately, though, the days when a hostess insists on an equal number of men and women have passed except in the most formal of social circles, and most hostesses do not worry if they have less than a full table, unequal numbers, or even more of one sex than another.

The disadvantage of telephoning invitations is that people will not have a written reminder. I solve this problem by mailing reminder notes to those I have invited about ten days before the party.

A mailed invitation should be answered within a few days of its receipt. If an address is given, a written response is preferred; if a telephone number is listed on the invitation beside the R.S.V.P., call to respond. The latter is the most popular method of response. If you cannot reach a hostess and the time of the party is approaching, you may have to drop her a note even if she is expecting you to telephone.

Any but the most casual dinner invitation must be treated with great respect and should not be canceled at the last minute. No hostess or host wants to have to juggle a seating plan or worse, have an empty place at the table, or cook food that will not be eaten. Cancel only for an emergency.

DINNER HOUR. Regardless of how the invitation is issued, the hostess mentions a specific time when she extends the invitation. Most hostesses have a favorite dinner hour—usually somewhere between 7 and 8:30. Some hostesses like to schedule an earlier dinner hour during the week or on Sunday night; Saturday-night dinners are often held later.

MENU. SEE ALSO MENU PLANNING. Once the invitations have been issued, the next order of concern is the menu. Heavy, multi-course meals no longer have much appeal, and only at the most formal of dinner parties would a five-course meal be served. If five courses are served, they are: an appetizer; a first course of soup, pasta, or fish; an entree; a salad; and a dessert. Four is more usual: soup or a first course, an entree (served with vegetables and other side dishes), a salad (sometimes served with cheese), and a dessert.

At a formal dinner, I strongly favor serving salad after the entree and keeping it very plain—one or more lettuces and a good vinaigrette are all that is required. Salad is meant to cleanse the palate, and that is why it belongs after the two heaviest courses. Wine is not served with salad, and you may want to take a slightly longer break between the entree and the salad so your guests can finish their wine.

Dessert may be served with coffee or guests may retire after dessert to another room for coffee, whichever you prefer. Dessert also may consist of fruit and cheese rather than something sweet. If fruit and cheese are served, after-dinner mints are a nice touch for those who have a sweet tooth.

Both coffee and tea should be offered, and today guests are also offered a choice of caffeinated versus decaffeinated coffee, and tea drinkers are given the option of an herbal, decaffeinated tea *(see also Coffee and Tea)*.

TABLE. As important as the food is the table setting at a formal dinner party. It should be elegant and decorative. I like to think of a formally set table as a still-life painting *(see also Centerpiece and Candles)*.

A formally set table is also balanced. This means that each place setting is an equal distance from the others. All the silver is arranged identically at each place setting. The same number of glasses are at each setting. A table setting, formal or not, should also be convenient to those who will be using it. If the table is large, it may be necessary to put two bottles of wine on the table; salt and pepper shakers may be needed between each two diners, or you may use individual ones. Survey the table carefully to be sure your guests will be comfortable dining at it. Figure 18 shows the table set for a formal dinner.

Figure 18. Formal dinner party place setting

The components of the table setting will naturally vary depending upon the menu. A fish knife is used when fish is served; a soup spoon is required when soup is served, etc. Only glasses, dishes, and flatware that will actually be used during the course of the meal are put on the table.

SEATING. Seating arrangements are much less formal these days than they used to be. The general rule of thumb is that a female guest of honor sits to the right of the host, and a male guest of honor sits on the hostess's right. A guest of honor may be the oldest person at the table, a new acquaintance, an old friend, and so on.

In religious, military, and government and diplomatic circles, protocol is observed, and people are seated according to their rank and/or title. The rules for seating officials are stringently observed, and should protocol be required at a dinner you are giving, you may contact the Office of Protocol in Washington, D.C., for advice. Even if you do not move in diplomatic circles, you should be aware of the times when "rank" may matter in your seating arrangements. When your clergyman, mayor, local congressman, or an aged schoolteacher is visiting your home, for example, he or she has "rank" and should be accorded a seat of honor.

A great deal of fuss may be made about a guest of honor, with toasting and deference, or no attention may be paid other than the seating positions. You certainly will not want to announce in so many terms that so-and-so is in the honored seat because he is so old.

Husbands and wives may sit together, but many hostesses feel that splitting them up makes for a livelier evening. Hostesses used to take great pains to have only couples at their dinner table, and of course men and women always alternated in the seating arrangements. Few of us have such tidy social lives, and these days a smart hostess does not worry about balancing the number of men and women at her parties. It is, I know, still customary to alternate men and women, but I would not hesitate at a dinner party to put two women or two men together whom I thought would enjoy each other's company if the numbers were unbalanced.

A hostess may simply tell people where to sit when they gather around the table, or she may use place cards. (see also Place Cards).

GREETING GUESTS. Depending upon the community, guests may arrive punctually or up to fifteen minutes late for a dinner party. A guest who is any later should call the hostess to alert her and insist that she serve dinner without him.

As they arrive, guests are greeted at the door by both the host and hostess or by at least one of them. If someone else answers the door, the host and hostess should be nearby to greet their arriving guests. The cook should be sure to clear free time to greet arriving guests and to say goodbye to departing ones.

COCKTAILS. Drinks are usually offered to guests as they arrive. It is acceptable at a dinner party to offer a limited range of drinks ("We've got some martinis mixed or we can offer you scotch, gin, or wine"). Some hostesses like to offer only wine, on the theory that anything stronger dulls the palate. Both alcoholic and nonalcoholic beverages should be available during cocktail hour.

Anywhere from twenty minutes to an hour is usually allowed for cocktails. This is entirely up to the hostess.

When dinner is served, guests usually do not carry their drinks with them to the table. If the hostess encourages them to do so, they may, but a guest should not ask, nor should he assume that this will be acceptable. The hostess often wants to start serving the dinner wines as soon as her guests are seated. At a casual dinner, a guest may be sipping the same wine that is served with dinner, and the hostess should let him know whether she would like him to take his wineglass to the table.

LATE GUEST. If you will be more than fifteen minutes late, call the hostess. Encourage her to start without you, as her meal may be carefully timed. Whether she does start without you or not is another matter. She may feel free to do so or, if her menu permits, she may stretch the cocktail hour out a few minutes longer until you arrive. Since holding up dinner for very long for one person puts many others at a disadvantage, most hostesses opt to start dinner without the missing guest if he or she will be more than a few minutes late.

The guest who arrives late should quickly take his seat and join the other diners. No one stands to greet him as this would disrupt the dinner too much. The hostess may have to get up and serve him; the guest should not, at least at a formal dinner, offer to serve himself from the kitchen.

SERVING. The rules about the serving of a very formal dinner can be altered to suit the space and hostess's taste.

Very formal dinners are also based on the premise that a hostess has a full-time staff, maids to serve her guests, and a butler to stand by awaiting her every request. Few of us have such a staff, and many hostesses—the majority, in fact—have no steady household help. How, then, do you juggle the elegant, formal dinner?

Depending upon your experience and how complicated the food is, most hosts/hostesses can serve up to eight at dinner without help. Up to sixteen can be served by the hostess and one helper; more guests than that will require more outside help. If more than sixteen are invited, a minimum of two outside helpers will be required—one to help the hostess serve and another to handle the kitchen. When outside help is hired, it is up to the hostess to set standards for the kind of service she wants and expects. An experience caterer will have a trained staff, but a hostess should be able to add her personal touches.

The table should be set with all the flatware, glasses, and at least a service plate—and possibly the first course—when the guests sit down.

When guests come to the table, the water glasses should be filled. The candles should be lit. A centerpiece—flowers are the classical one—is in place.

Guests are served from the left, and dishes are removed from the right, unless this is inconvenient to diners. The hostess is always served last, and the female guest of honor is served first. If there is no guest of honor, women are served before men, or, if this is not convenient, the first plate should be passed to a woman, and people may then be served in order around the table.

At a formal dinner, a place setting always has a plate in place. The soup, for example, or any other first course is put down on a service plate, which remains when the first-course dishes are taken away. The service plate may be used for the entree.

Wine is poured after the guests sit down. With the exception of a sherry glass, which is removed with the soup bowl, wineglasses are left on the table during the meal.

If the hostess has help for the night, food can be passed formally on platters carried around to each guest. If she has no household help, she or the host may either carry the platters of food around to each guest or serve from the head of the table. Even when the entree is served from the head of the table, side dishes are often passed. If the host serves, he fills the hostess's plate last; if she serves, she serves the host last.

Alternately, food may be put on a sideboard or table so guests can help themselves. Since the dinner table looks its prettiest with plates on it, the plates may be put in place and guests can pick them up as they go to the buffet table.

SECONDS. Seconds are an interesting question at a formal dinner. If many courses are served, guests will be full without seconds, and often choose to pass on them in anticipation of what is to come. The hostess may offer them, but a guest may feel free to decline without giving any offense.

ENDING THE DINNER. When the meal is over, the dishes are cleared. They will also have been cleared between courses.

Between salad and dessert, crumbs are cleared off the table, and all dishes are removed.

Dishes should not be stacked as they are cleared, nor should food be scraped onto one plate. In short, do not treat food as garbage until it reaches the kitchen.

Guests may jump up to help the hostess as she clears, but she should not permit this. Note, though, that as marriages have become more egalitarian, the host and hostess have begun to divide the work more evenly. In many homes today, it is not unusual for the man to be the cook or, if the wife cooks, for the man to be the server and clearer. Men and women, quite literally, seem to co-host today, and I applaud this. Nowhere in this book have I intended, through the use of the word "hostess," to suggest that the role is restricted to the woman.

Finally, just as guests should not be permitted to help clear, they also should not be permitted to help clean up, except under the most casual of circumstances.

A host may need to rinse off a few dishes in the process of serving a complicated meal, but no one (except hired help) should start cleaning up or seriously washing dishes until the guests have gone home. To do so is to suggest to your guests that you have more important business than spending your time with them.

DEPARTURE. Guests should stay a minimum of one hour after a dinner party, and if the party is an amusing one, they may stay much longer. Anyone who must leave a dinner party early should do so quietly, as one person's departure can break up the party prematurely. When leaving, thank the hostess and host for having you as their guest. As a strict point of etiquette, you do not thank them for the food, but rather, for the pleasant evening, but if something was outstanding about the food, it is only gracious to mention how wonderful it was. The best compliments are specific ones ("That fruit tart was wonderful"). Don't linger over goodbyes, especially if you are among the first to leave, since you will be keeping the host and hostess from their other guests.

INFORMAL DINNER PARTY. Informal dinner parties are primarily variations on formal dinners, with the level of formality reduced to what suits you and your guests.

Food may be served family style, for example, or guests may be asked to keep their dinner forks for the next course. I think there are limits as to how casual a meal should be when guests are present. I know many people who are flattered and made comfortable by a family dinner, and there are times when down-home food is exactly what the doctor ordered for someone. But even when I am cooking simple fare, I always try to make the occasion somewhat special or festive. When a friend came to visit on his way home from a year of living in Asia, I knew meatloaf and baked potatoes would be the most appealing meal I could serve him since he had not had home-cooked American food in so long, but I also made sure my table looked beautiful and that there were fresh flowers on the table.

LUNCH. A formal or informal lunch is also a variation on a formal dinner party in terms of the way food is served. (See also Lunch.)

INFORMAL VS. FORMAL. Occasionally the somewhat touchy question arises of whether to serve a less formal dinner than you usually would to people who are put off by formal dining. On the one hand, a gracious hostess does nothing to make her guests uncomfortable; on the other hand, to lower one's standard of entertaining for some guests and not others is to condescend to the guests for whom the standards are lowered.

I do not believe in compromise in this area as long as your motives are above suspicion. If you like to serve several courses and use the right flatware for all of them, and your husband's second cousin is put off by this because she entertains far more casually, that is her problem, not yours. On the other hand, if you insist on serving her a five-course dinner on your finest china when you could just as easily serve lasagna and salad on your pottery, which you frequently use for company and which would make her feel more comfortable, then I would say you are pressing the point a little, and your pride may be getting in the way of your hospitality.

Similarly when friends come over with small children, you often have to adjust your standards a little. I do not recommend that the woman who has never owned and hopes never to own a plastic dish go out and buy a set to accommodate a two-year-old guest, but neither should she be expected to use her good china or a damask tablecloth.

Dinner Plates

SEE *Dishes*.

Dirty Dish or Flatware

When a dirty dish is encountered in a restaurant, it should be handed, without any fuss, to the waiter, who, in turn, without making any fuss, will replace it.

In someone's home, quietly mention the problem to the hostess. Say as little as possible so as not to let other guests know there is a problem.

Polite persons, either in a restaurant or in someone's home, do nothing to focus attention on situations like this.

Dishes

SEE ALSO *Bowl; Consommé Cup and Saucer; Custard Cup; Dishware; Eggcup; Ramekin or Individual Casserole; Soup Plate.*

It is safe to say that dishes, and by that I mostly mean plates, are the mainstay of any table setting since they are what the food is served on *(see Figure 19)*.

At a sit-down dinner, the plates are already on the table when the diners sit down *(see Figure 20)*.

At a buffet dinner, they are stacked near the food. The plates that comprise a place setting are the dinner plate, the salad plate, the bread-and-butter plate, possibly a service plate, and a cup and saucer.

DINNER/LUNCHEON PLATE. The entree, plus any vegetables, and the salad if there is no salad plate are eaten on the dinner plate. Dinner plates vary in size (an American dinner plate is larger than a European one, and a luncheon plate is smaller than a dinner plate). The dinner plate goes in the center of the place setting.

When serving food, take care not to overload a dinner plate. If necessary, take as much food as your plate can handle, eat some, and then try the remaining foods that did not fit on the plate on the first go-round.

When done, leave your plate where it is. It is rude to push a dinner plate away from your place setting. Why should you move your dirty dinner plate away from yourself and closer to another diner? In a restaurant, if you want the plate removed after you have finished eating, it is proper to ask the waiter to take it away.

SERVICE PLATE. Smaller than a dinner plate, a service plate goes on top of the dinner plate. An appetizer or soup bowl is then placed on the service plate, and both are removed when you finish eating. If neither of these courses has been served or ordered, the service plate is removed when the entree arrives. Service plates are frequently used in restaurants, particularly the better ones, and they should be used for formal dining. They are not necessary for casual or informal dining, but they are a nice touch. Service plates often double as luncheon plates.

SALAD PLATE. Smaller than a luncheon plate, the salad plate correctly goes to the left of the dinner plate, although these days, it is more and more often being placed

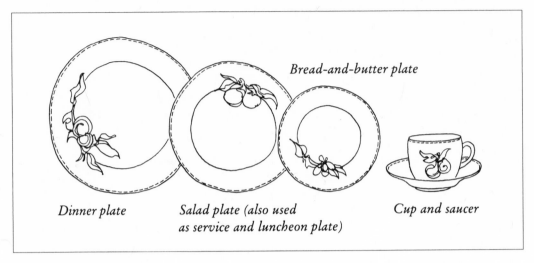

Dinner plate   Salad plate (also used   Cup and saucer
as service and luncheon plate)

Bread-and-butter plate

Figure 19.

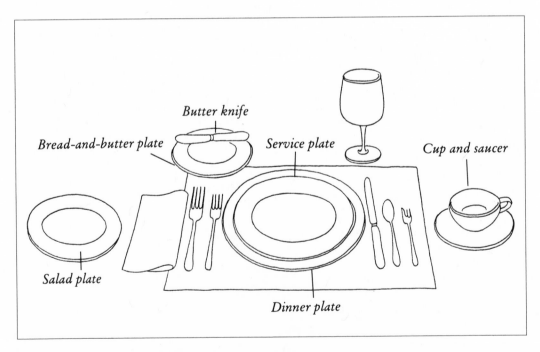

Butter knife

Bread-and-butter plate   Service plate   Cup and saucer

Salad plate

Dinner plate

Figure 20. Correct placement of dishes at a sit-down dinner

directly on the dinner or service plate. (If this occurs in a restaurant, you may move it off the service plate to the left if you plan to keep your salad and nibble on it throughout the meal or even eat it after your entree. If the salad plate is placed on a service plate in someone's home, leave it. You should never rearrange a hostess's place setting or tamper with her service.)

Salad may be served in bowls at casual family dinners and picnics. Alternately, at a casual dinner, the salad may be put directly on the dinner plate. The French almost always put the salad on their dinner plates after they have finished their entrees; most Americans are uncomfortable with this.

BREAD-AND-BUTTER PLATE. This plate goes above the fork and slightly to the left of the dinner plate. In addition to being used for bread and butter, this plate is the resting place for small finger foods such as radishes, celery, carrots, and olives, which are always politely put on a plate before they are eaten. (If there is no bread-and-butter plate, these foods may be put directly on the dinner plate.)

CUP AND SAUCER. These go directly to the right of the dinner plate. They may be placed there when the diners sit down, or, especially if space at the table is limited, they may be brought in when coffee and tea are served. Strictly speaking, the cup and saucer should be left where they are at a formal dinner; when the meal is more casual and the plates have been cleared, they can be moved into the center of the place setting.

DESSERT PLATE The dessert plate goes in the center of the place setting, after the dinner plate has been cleared. Dessert may be brought to the table on the dessert plate, or it may served at the table, in which case the plates are first put down in front of the person serving, who fills them and then passes them around to each diner. The dessert plate should be left where it is when dessert is finished.

Dishware

Dishes are made of china, earthenware, pottery, and plastic.

CHINA. China is fired at a very high temperature, and because of this, it is the toughest and most chip-resistant kind of dishware. It comes in a wide range of quality and prices. A good bone china should be translucent. When the china is held up to the light, and you put your hand behind it, you can see your hand behind it, you can see your hand through the plate.

China is available in an incredible array of patterns. The best and most expensive is handpainted, but there are also many lovely inexpensive chinas.

EARTHENWARE. This stoneware is a cross between china and pottery. It is opaque. Because earthenware is fired at a higher temperature than pottery, it is more chip-resistant. It is impossible to tell the difference between earthenware and pottery just by looking.

POTTERY. Pottery is the least chip-resistant of all the glassware. Both pottery and earthenware come in a variety of painted and plain patterns. These dishes are considered casual, but there are some very elegant designs in each kind of dishware.

CHOOSING A PATTERN. One set of casual dishes—well-chosen—can work for everyday family life and for casual entertaining.

China is not so versatile. Some patterns are very formal and would look out of place on a table set with stainless steel flatware and casual glasses. They cry out for fine sterling and crystal, all elegantly combined in a sparkling formal table setting.

The most formal china patterns are those trimmed with metal—gold, silver, or sometimes pewter. The rest of the plate usually has a solid color band, and the center is white or ivory. The darker the color and the wider the rim of the precious metal trim, the more formal the china—and the more formal the sterling or silverplate and crystal that must be selected to go with this kind of china.

Other china patterns, especially the painted geometric and flowered ones with plain (nonmetallic) rims, can be dressed up or down. They work with stainless or sterling, with elaborate cut-glasses and with perfectly plain ones.

Most china is sold in "open stock." This means it will be continuously produced and widely available on store shelves for as long as it is popular. When china is not in open stock, it may be necessary to special-order it, or it may not be possible to order it at all. Styles in china patterns do change, though, and a china pattern can be difficult to locate once it is no longer in open stock. China patterns do stay in open stock for a number of years, but styles in dishes change, and china does not stay in open stock as long as sterling does.

China is purchased by the place setting. A place setting consists of a dinner plate, a salad or service plate, a bread-and-butter plate, and a cup and saucer. Additional pieces, all-purpose bowls, soup plates, consommé cups and saucers, demitasse cups and saucers, and small, deep dishes used for serving fruit, ice cream, and other desserts, may be purchased in any number. Matching serving pieces can also be purchased.

Whether you want to order a complete, matching set of china is another matter. There is no reason that china must all match. Many women order the basic china place settings, and then choose or are given demitasse cups, luncheon plates, and dessert plates in other patterns. A lovely table can be set by mixing and matching patterns. The only guideline is that all the dishes for the same use should match. Keep in mind, though, that matching does not mean identical where dishware is concerned. A set of dessert plates might be identical, that is, they might all be the same shape and have the same rims, but the centers might each be painted with something slightly different.

CARE. It is best to stack dishes and hang cups, if possible. When storing china with metal trim, place protective felt pads between each plate. Gold and silver trim is not dishwasher safe. China dishes should always be handled with care. Far more damage is done by the person who puts them in the dishwasher than by the dishwasher.

Never use chipped or cracked dishes. They are unsightly and unsanitary.

NEEDS. The number of place settings needed depends upon the size of the family.

Since inexpensive dishes are often sold in six- or eight-place settings, many women buy a complete set of casual, everyday china. A couple would need a minimum of four place settings for everyday use. Eight to ten place settings is standard for entertaining.

If extras are purchased, extra service (salad or luncheon) plates are always useful, and extra cups and saucers, as well as extra consommé cups and saucers are needed. Since these pieces have handles, they break more easily than other pieces in a place setting.

Divorce

SEE ALSO *Forms of Address—Spoken; Names; Separation.*

A divorce is an extremely sad event in a person's life. For most it is a period that fraught with a sense of failure and isolation. It is a time when a person needs the understanding and support of his or her family and friends.

When a couple decides to get a divorce, they tell their families first, and then tell the friends whom they see regularly. No formal announcement is ever made of a divorce, and sending printed announcements or having a divorce party is the height of bad taste. Friends whom one does not see regularly may be told the news whenever one sees them next. Some people mention their divorces to faraway friends when they write their Christmas cards. While this is not exactly the most cheerful news to include in a Christmas card, it is sometimes simply the easiest and least painful way to make the announcement. No details need be given. Simply write: "Jack and I separated in July, and our divorce will be final soon. It was a rough time for both of us, as you might well imagine," or something to that effect.

It is better to tell what may be a white lie and express sadness over a divorce than to act happy, even if that is how you feel down deep. There are two reasons for this. The first is that for every spouse who is overjoyed to be free of marriage, there is often another one who is greatly saddened and disoriented by the breakup. The second, and admittedly less important, reason is that out of respect for the institution of marriage itself, which is held in great esteem by our society, one does not trample on the grave of late marriage.

Obviously your close friends will hear all the grisly details and will be there to help put you back together again, but you should be careful not to overburden even close friends. Accept the finality of the divorce even if it was not your idea. Work out whatever arrangements must be made to accomplish a clean and final separation. Then pick up the pieces and get on with your life. However supportive and loyal your friends are, you will try their patience if you spend all your time wallowing in bitterness and self-pity. You need not be pushed into dating until you feel ready, but do see your friends, make some new friends, take a class, pursue a hobby you never had time for when you were married.

NAME CHANGE. SEE ALSO TITLES. Only the woman's name is subject to change in a divorce. Most women decline to use any name that identifies them as a divorcee, preferring instead to take back their maiden names or use their forenames and their married name. Mrs. Robert Jones thus becomes Sally Jones or Sally Smith. She does not remain Mrs. Robert Jones because of the confusion that will result if her ex-husband remarries.

WEARING RINGS. Divorced persons usually do not wear their wedding rings, although a mother might continue to wear hers for her children's sake. A woman need not return her rings although it is kind to return an heirloom ring if she does not have children who will inherit it.

SOCIAL LIFE. A divorced person conducts his or her social life much as any other single person does. He goes out on dates if he feels like it, entertains friends, and has affairs.

TELLING THE CHILDREN. When a couple decides that they are going to get a divorce, they should discuss this with their children. It is almost impossible not to tell children that you no longer love your spouse (their other parent), but do not emphasize this too much. Children who go through the painful experience of learning that their parents no longer love each other often fear that their parents no longer love them either. If the fact that you no longer love your child's other parent can be avoided, do so; if not, explain to your child that the love between two adults is different from that between parent and child. Your child will need reassurance that the divorce does not mean that he is losing a parent, nor does it mean that his parents no longer love him.

Do everything you can to cooperate with your ex-spouse regarding custody arrangements, for your children's sake if not for yours. Your children are entitled to the attention of two parents, and you should help to make that possible.

RELATIONS WITH EX-IN-LAWS (SEE ALSO NAMES). If you have children, you will still probably see your ex-in-laws fairly regularly. If not, these relationships have a way of gradually lapsing. Your life will go more smoothly if you attempt to maintain a cordial relationship with your former in-laws.

Gradually, of course, they will become a smaller and smaller part of your life. If you are friends with them, there is no reason that you cannot remain on friendly terms, except that you will no longer see them with your ex-spouse. It is kinder not to take your problems with your ex-husband or wife (their child) to them; their loyalties are probably not that divided. Furthermore, although you may feel pain at your spouse's remarrying, if it occurs refrain from criticizing the new spouse around your ex-in-laws.

Since your children need grandparents as much as grandparents need children, it is vindictive to restrict your child's time with his grandparents because you are angry over your divorce.

Doctor

SEE ALSO *Titles.*

The academic title of doctor is not used socially except in university circles.

Physicians and dentists use "doctor" socially, although in these days of informality when people jump to first names a few minutes after they are introduced, many physicians do not bother.

Using the title "doctor" becomes more complicated with the increase in two-career couples. The couple who are both doctors can either be addressed as "Dr. and Dr. Jones," and alternately if they are married with two surnames: "Dr. Mary Jones" (first line); "Dr. John Jones" (second line). Or they can opt to be "Mr. and Mrs." socially.

Doggy Bags

Doggy bags, for those who are unacquainted with them, are small packages of leftover food that are taken home from a restaurant. The custom has honorable roots: In ancient China, guests were provided with white boxes of food to take away from a banquet. (This may explain why your waiter is likely to look downcast in your local Chinese restaurant if you decline to take home the leftovers.) People used to ask for a doggy bag only at a casual restaurant and never at a fancy restaurant, and that is still a good guideline, but at today's food prices, many people also feel free to accept a doggy bag whenever it is offered—and some fancy restaurants offer them these days.

Dogs

SEE ALSO *Pet.*

Some are pets and some are working dogs, and there is a difference in the way the two

are treated. A pet should be well trained so that it will not threaten or annoy those who come in contact with it. Owners should also be alert to those persons who are not comfortable for whatever reason around dogs and should keep an even more careful eye on a dog when it is around someone like this. A dog is not welcome everywhere. In most communities, they are not permitted in stores and restaurants and on public transportation.

A seeing-eye or hearing-ear dog is permitted to go anywhere its owner goes. Because these dogs are highly trained animals who have a serious job to perform, no one should interfere with them in any way, either by petting or talking to them.

Doors

HOLDING. Before feminism, it was a given that men hold doors open for women. Some women even stopped in front of doors they were perfectly capable of opening themselves and waited for the first available male to provide this service. In the age of humanism in which we now live, people open doors for one another regardless of their sex. Admittedly, if a survey were taken, it would probably reveal that far more women than men have doors held open for them, but today, a woman should not hesitate to hold a door for a man, especially when the man is burdened with packages or in some way needs her assistance. It goes without saying that everyone should go out of his or her way to open doors for the elderly, for women with small children, and for anyone else who seems in particular need of assistance.

ANSWERING. After you have knocked or rung the doorbell, you must wait for someone to answer the door. This might seem like an obvious thing to say, but in some communities the knock is considered the announcement, and the caller then feels free to walk in. At the risk of sounding cliché, this is the kind of familiarity that breeds contempt.

When someone answers the door, if you are not known, give your name and state your reason for calling. Do not assume you will be invited in, and never enter someone's home without a specific invitation to do so.

When no one responds to a door knock or doorbell, give up. It is rude to continue knocking (twice is enough) or to walk around to another door or peer in windows, unless you have reason to believe the person inside needs assistance. People have a right to be "not at home" even when they are in the house.

FRONT DOOR VS. BACK DOOR. In some parts of the country, the front door is for formal callers and occasions, and the back door is for family and close friends. People who use the back door often enter without knocking, but even a close friend or relative should exercise some caution. People dislike being startled in their own homes.

Double Date

There really are no specific rules for double dating except that four people, rather than just two, must juggle one another's interests. A double date can be a lovely way for four good friends to spend an evening. Often a couple who have arranged a blind date for two friends will join them in a double date.

Double Wedding

Double weddings are held when two sisters or sometimes two good friends decide to marry on the same day. A double wedding is basically the same as any other wedding. Each bride has her own processional and recessional. If there are two main aisles in the sanctuary, I think a joint recessional is ideal and also stunning to watch.

The processional, however, is never joint. Each bride is entitled to her special moment to walk down the aisle, and she is never expected to share that moment with anyone else. If there are two aisles, and I strongly advise that a double wedding be held in a sanctuary with two aisles, each bride can have her own aisle. If there is only one aisle, one bride and her wedding party go down the aisle, followed by the second bride and her wedding party (see Figure 21). If the brides have a joint wedding party, the bridesmaids go first, followed by the first bride, who is preceded by her honor attendant, and then followed by the second bride, who is, in turn, preceded by her honor attendant.

Because there seems to be no other fair way to decide these things, the oldest bride usually enjoys the privilege of going first in the processional. The younger sister (or cousin or friend) has the privilege of going first in the recessional if a joint one cannot be arranged (see Figure 22).

During the ceremony, no one stands in the center of the altar. Instead each wedding

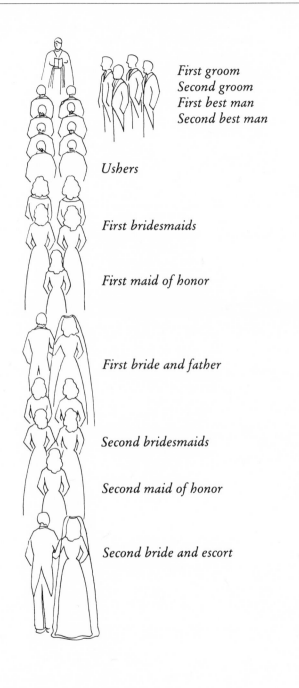

First groom
Second groom
First best man
Second best man

Ushers

First bridesmaids

First maid of honor

First bride and father

Second bridesmaids

Second maid of honor

Second bride and escort

Figure 21. Double wedding processional

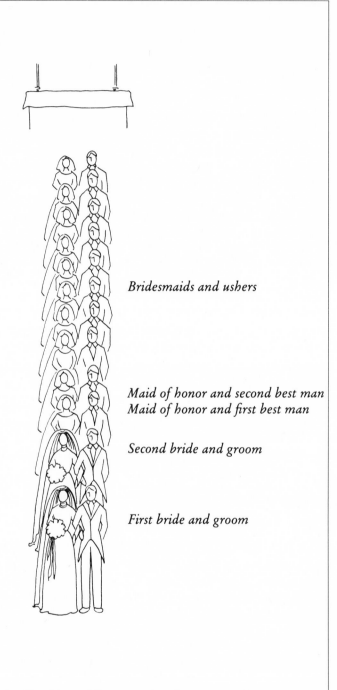

Bridesmaids and ushers

Maid of honor and second best man
Maid of honor and first best man

Second bride and groom

First bride and groom

Figure 22. Double wedding recessional

party stands off to one side. The clergyperson conducts the first ceremony (again, the eldest bride claims privilege here), and then moves across the altar to the other wedding party to conduct that ceremony.

There are, of course, alternate ways to arrange a double wedding. The brides could even draw straws to see who goes first and last. The couples could stand side by side at the altar with their wedding parties off to either side. I have only described the most usual way of organizing this unusual kind of wedding. Those who are involved may, and should, feel free to improvise.

The men in the wedding party dress similarly, that is, all are in black tie or all are in white tie, all are in white jackets, etc. The brides' attendants probably should be coordinated, at least in terms of color, so the wedding party does not look too confusing at the altar, but they need not be dressed identically. Neither need the brides, although they may wear identical or similar dresses if they want to.

Jews rarely have double weddings, because they do not believe the happiness of one child's wedding day should be diluted in any way.

Books on wedding etiquette and bridal consultants can provide detailed information on planning a double wedding, and the clergyperson will be invaluable in working out the specifics of the processionals and recessionals.

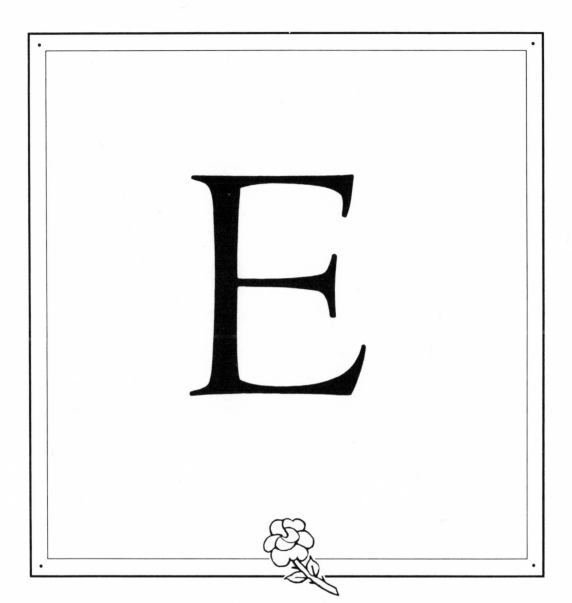

Ear Piercing

SEE ALSO *Jewelry.*

Young girls often want to have their ears pierced, and ear piercing has become so acceptable that there is, frankly, no reason not to let a child do so, provided she is old enough to appreciate that she is doing something permanent, if quite minor, to her body. I notice younger and younger girls with pierced ears, but I think it is advisable to wait until a child is at least in her early teens before permitting her to have her ears pierced. Prior to this age, little girls wear very little jewelry.

Pierced ears open the door to wearing all manner and kind of earrings. If huge, dangling earrings are all the rage, it may be impossible to prevent your child from looking like her peers most of the time, but on some occasions, when she dresses up and goes somewhere with you, for example, you may be able to persuade her to wear jewelry more suitable to her age—small gold studs, pearls, or small colored stones. Diamond studs are not appropriately worn by teenagers.

It has even become the custom on occasion for boys to pierce their ears. However dismayed parents may be over this prospect, they probably would do best to accept the deed once it is done rather than to create an ongoing harangue over it. This is a stage, and like other stages of life, one can hope that it, too, will pass. Remember that while pierced ears are permanent, the wearing of earrings is not.

In some cultures, most notably Hispanic, it is the custom to pierce little girl's ears shortly after they are born. This is sometimes done in the hospital. There is nothing wrong with piercing a baby girl's ears when it is the tradition in one's culture.

Eating Habits of Guests

SEE ALSO *Liquor.*

FOOD. People who choose to keep kosher or are Muslim or vegetarian have two options: They can decline invitations where they know nothing suitable to their diets

149

will be served, or they can accept the invitation and make the best of it. Making the best of it means possibly fortifying oneself with a light meal beforehand and eating whatever is served that can be eaten. It does not mean announcing one's restrictions to the hostess when the invitation is accepted. To do this is to request a special menu, and no hostess is expected to do this.

A sophisticated hostess, however, should be aware that some of her guests may have some dietary restrictions, and she may choose to take this into account, either by providing a substantial vegetarian dish, which is acceptable to almost everyone, or by serving fish, which may or may not be totally acceptable but will not offend as pork or beef might.

Savvy hostesses these days, even nonvegetarian ones, are not afraid to plan an all-vegetable meal. These are healthy, and there are many current delicious recipes for vegetable dishes. The time when a crown roast of lamb or a prime rib roast of beef had to serve as the centerpiece for a meal is long gone—fortunately for all of us.

Eating in Africa

This huge continent is a land of great diversity, and it is impossible to cover everything you are likely to encounter if you visit more than two or three countries. You will come across formal English service, manners, and eating customs in many places. You will also come across a community where communal dining from one pot is the rule, and your fingers are the eating utensils. In countries where the fingers are used to eat, often only one hand—usually your

right—goes into the pot. Watch your host carefully and follow his lead.

In some African countries, the guest starts first, and in others the host is expected to take the first bite. Again, you will probably be given some sign or gesture to help you understand what to do.

Eating in China

Chinese food is one of the world's three or four great cuisines, and should you be lucky enough to be invited to someone's home—where you will probably be served a special banquet meal—by all means accept immediately. You are in for a real treat. Chinese food, of which there are four main regional specialties, attempts to balance flavors, seasonings, and color combinations. It is truly a work of art and a gustatory delight.

Although Western-style linens show up fairly often these days at a traditional Chinese meal, you are more likely to confront a bare table. Bits of food are often spilled when they are lifted from the serving plate to the diner's plate, and, if the table is bare, no one minds. There are no napkins, but hot towels are passed around several times during a meal.

It is good manners to show reticence about entering the dining room. The host may even have to announce twice that dinner is served. A westerner can take his clues from other Chinese guests who are present, but just remember not to jump up and walk toward the dining room the minute the host suggests dinner. Further reticence is often shown over who enters the dining room first, and the confusion may mount as the host tries to get people to sit down where he designates. Eventually, though, everyone is seated, with the guests being given the choicest seats.

Before the meal, the host may say, "I apologize for this poor meal I am about to serve you." This, too, is good manners. His wife won't blanch a bit; in fact, she will smilingly nod her agreement. The guests protest, tell the host he's being modest, that he's well known for his fine food and hospitality.

The cold foods are on the table when you sit down. Guests at a Chinese meal serve themselves with the chopsticks that are in the serving dishes. When laying down your chopsticks, never cross them. This is considered bad manners, for the Chinese believe crossed chopsticks to be a sign of ill luck for the host.

The order of dishes at a Chinese meal—particularly a banquet—is fairly well established. First are the cold dishes. Then come stir-fried dishes or possibly a fairly heavy soup. The host may serve the soup as a gesture of hospitality. Chicken and fish dishes of varying elaboration may follow. The last major course is usually a whole fish. After that comes a light dessert, perhaps pudding or some tasty fruit. No one can eat much at a meal that may number eight to ten or more courses, but then, that's the whole point to Chinese hospitality. As each course is finished, the dishes will be set to one side. You may take seconds if you want to, but only a foolhardy soul stuffs himself early on at such a meal. It is polite, however, to take a little of everything.

No special ceremony surrounds the drinking of tea in China as it does in Japan. While you may be offered a mixed drink Western-style when you first arrive, you may also be offered a cup of tea as a sign of hospitality. Tea is also drunk throughout the meal, and a cup of tea concludes the meal.

The Chinese also drink their own wines, although to the Western palate, they may resemble liquors such as sherry or gin. Much drinking is indulged in throughout any meal where the company is convivial. Toasting is frequent. If your host offers you a toast, offer one back, praising his fine hospitality and outstanding food. You may even find youself playing the finger game, a popular Chinese mealtime custom. Two players—usually men—each throw out several fingers on one hand. Each player simultaneously—and not especially quietly—calls out his guess for the number of fingers the other person will throw out. The loser—which means the person who did not guess correctly—must drink up. Occasionally, he even turns his glass over to show that it has been emptied, although it is probably best not to do this until your host has done it first. The game can be played the other way round; that is, the winner drinks up. The point is the same: to drink. A lot. Play at your own risk.

At a Chinese meal, the guests begin eating. After guests have served themselves, the hosts fill their own plates. Don't mix foods together, as each dish has been carefully planned for its own unique flavors and colors. At the end of the meal, the host may again protest his poor food. Since most Chinese hosts are extremely hospitable and Chinese food is delicious, you will now be able to insist heartily that you have been well fed and that the hospitality offered you is surely the best in all China.

In conclusion, there is a charming way

that a Chinese host may choose to honor a guest. He selects a choice morsel from his own plate and transfers it to the plate of his guest. This is an honor for which there is no reciprocal gesture. You do not return the favor, however much your Western tit-for-tat mentality may make you feel like doing so.

Eating in Europe

Our current table manners are directly descended from the ones that our ancestors brought over from Europe, so you will have little to worry about traveling almost anywhere there. Virtually without exception, Europeans eat Continental style, but they are familiar with the way Americans like to change hands as they eat, so you will be comfortable eating American style.

If anything, you may observe that manners are slightly more decorous than you normally encounter in the United States. Table manners in the U.S. have become rather informal in recent years, and the same relaxation has not occurred everywhere in Europe. You may be surprised to find out that your elbow is not welcome anywhere on the table at any time during a meal.

Meals are served in courses more often in Europe than in the United States. Even a simple family meal of soup, stew, and salad may be served in three separate courses. Despite Americans' growing fondness for wine, more Europeans than Americans consider wine a necessity at meals. They also take great pride in it, and your host will be appreciative of any compliments you give him regarding his choice of wine.

Coffee or tea is also served as a last course, after dessert, throughout Europe. Often demitasse or espresso is served. This is a very strong, rich black coffee served in small cups. The Italians are great coffee drinkers; the French also drink coffee, and the British prefer a good cup of tea at the conclusion of a meal.

It is in Italy that you are most likely to encounter a variety of coffees. Espresso is the most popular. It is drunk black, with a twist of lemon rind or a little sugar, if that is your preference. Cappuccino is a rich coffee served with cream in it. You need add nothing to this and other similar coffees you may encounter in Italy and France.

The British drink a strong tea to which they normally add milk. Sugar may also be added, and they will be prepared to offer lemon if that is your preference.

Finally, in Europe and in many other cultures in the East and Mideast, a well-mannered person keeps both hands in sight of the other diners while eating.

Eating in India

You are apt to encounter a variety of eating customs and table manners in India. Curries and other similar foods are often served in one large dish; small side dishes filled with condiments surround it. In large cities, the dining customs are much like those found in the West. In people's homes, though, you may be expected to eat with your right hand, or, rather, fingers, primarily because the left hand is reserved for toilet functions. The Indians are also finicky about just how much of the fingers get used. Southerners often pile food into a banana leaf and use all of their fingers to eat—an act that is viewed with great disdain by northerners, who carefully train their children never to dirty any part of the finger below the first knuckle. Because the finger is the utensil of choice, northerner and southerner alike look with even greater disdain on anyone who does not wash his hands very carefully before eating. Be sure to do so at your host's house when dining with him. You excuse yourself to go wash your hands in someone's home; in a restaurant, a finger bowl may be passed. The meal concludes with dessert and perhaps coffee.

Eating in Japan

Slightly more ritual surrounds even a simple Japanese meal than a Chinese meal, although the table setting is similar to that in China. You will often sit on tatami mats on the floor at a low, bare table. Since Americans do not usually sit this way, you will find you have to shift positions during the meal. Do so with as little interruption of the meal as possible. Sit cross-legged or on your knees, whichever is comfortable for you. Napkins are not common, but, instead, *oshibori*—small, wrung-out towels—are used to clean your fingers between courses and sometimes before eating.

To begin the meal, make a light bow to your hosts after sitting down. The main guest always starts the meal, as etiquette dictates that others cannot begin eating first.

Your chopsticks will be in front of you.

They are used the same way as in China— or whatever way you have found that is easy for you.

Rice is the main food, and, as such, it is part of the ritual. It will also be covered. Use your left hand to uncover it and place the cover beside the bowl. Then use your right hand to uncover the soup, which is always on the right. Use both hands or one hand to put the empty rice bowl on the serving tray that will be offered to you. It will be filled with rice. Be sure to place the bowl back on the table—it is considered gauche to begin eating without first touching a bowl to the table, much as one does not take a small finger food in the United States and plop it in one's mouth without first putting it on the bread-and-butter plate or service plate. After you have returned the filled rice bowl to its position, you may pick up your chopsticks and begin eating.

Rice is usually the first food eaten, although this isn't a firm rule, and you may quite politely opt to dip into your soup first. A soup is the real test of a Japanese cook, and it is gracious to be very generous with your praise about the dish. Drink some of the soup first directly from the bowl and then eat some of it, using the large ladlelike spoon as you would any other soup spoon.

As other foods are passed or offered to you, use the serving chopsticks. If there are none, you may use your own chopsticks, but be sure to use the large ends that you won't eat with.

It is customary to hold all bowls in your hands as you eat. Hold them resting against your four fingers balanced against your thumb. Use your right hand to take up dishes on the right and your left hand to take up dishes on the left, although if it is awkward for you to eat with anything but the hand you normally use, then you may omit this small nicety.

After the rice and soup have been eaten, you may eat any of the other dishes served or on the table. These foods are usually alternated with a few bites of rice. Pickled foods and pickles are usually reserved until the end of the meal, when they serve the same purpose as the Western green salad— to clear the palate.

Seconds will be offered at most meals. To show that you want more rice, leave some rice in your bowl. If you have finished, a clean bowl will signal this. If you do take more rice, you are expected to finish it off. The trick to doing this is to ask for a small second—it's far preferable to leaving rice in the bowl when you are finished eating. Besides, in an old-fashioned Japanese home, your tea may be poured into your rice bowl. It is polite to lay down your chopsticks while being served.

Sake may be drunk throughout the meal. Hold the cup in your hands or hand while being served. Then take a small sip or at least move the sake cup to your lips before returning it to the table. It is more polite to accept sake even if you don't drink it than to turn it down.

Tea is served at the end of the meal. It is customary to dip your chopsticks lightly into the tea to cleanse them when you have finished eating. Replace them on the table or tray you are eating from and drink your tea, sipping it at a comfortable pace. After tea, replace the covers on the rice, soup, and other bowls you may have been served. Thank your host for the lovely meal and bow lightly once again.

Sushi, a Japanese specialty, is raw fish wrapped around rice. The fish and rice is often wrapped in seaweed. There are also vegetable and egg sushi varieties. Generally, in a Japanese restaurant, you order a platter of sushi. Sushi is also prepared and served at a sushi bar in many places. Sushi should be eaten with chopsticks, although under casual circumstances in an American restaurant, you can pick it up with your fingers. Eating sushi with a knife and fork causes it to fall apart and only makes it harder to eat.

Sashimi, usually served in a small bowl, is slices of raw fish over rice. It, too, is best eaten with chopsticks.

Eating in the Mideast

Eating customs and manners vary throughout the Mideast, depending upon which country you are visiting. Then, too, many Mideasterners have traveled extensively throughout the West and are familiar with Western ways of dining. You may not always eat Western style, however, when you are invited to dine with someone.

Egypt is the country where you are most apt to encounter familiar dining circumstances. When guests are present, a waiter is hired to help serve the foods, although at an informal family dinner, each person may serve himself. Men and women eat together, and, usually, no grace is said, although the meal may begin with a brief toast. Everyone starts eating at the same time. The meal concludes with coffee, which is served after dessert, Western style.

In other Arab states, an invitation to dinner does not necessarily mean that your wife accompanies you. Arabs do not introduce their wives to anyone except very close friends, but many Arabs are familiar with Western ways, so if a man and a woman are both invited to dinner, your host's wife will probably be present.

Food is either served communally or passed by a servant. It is polite to heap food on a guest's plate and politer still for the guest to eat as much of it as possible. The host takes the first bite, just as an Arab friend will often turn a corner or go through a door first—to confront any potential danger for a friend. The host also takes the first bite to show that he is eating the food with his guest, not merely giving it to him. The meal may begin with a short prayer, and it ends with coffee or tea.

If you visit someone's home almost anywhere throughout the Mideast, hospitality demands that you be fed. Particularly in rural areas, you risk offending a host if you refuse an offer of food. Your host will also appear unhappy if you do not eat heartily.

It is customary to thank your host for his food and hospitality but not so profusely as is the rule in the United States.

Eavesdropping

Eavesdroppers should remember the old adage: "He who eavesdrops often hears ill of himself." A polite person does not hear what he is not supposed to hear, namely, conversations that are not directed toward him or her.

Even when you are in someone's presence, there are times when a polite person must tune out other conversations. If someone receives a phone call in your presence, for example, although it may be impossible for you not to listen physically, you should still not listen socially. By this I mean that a polite person never comments on a phone conversation held in his presence that does not concern him. If the other person comments, feign disinterest, saying something such as, "Well, I couldn't help overhearing, but I really wasn't paying attention." If possible and necessary, occupy yourself with a bookshelf or some ornament in the room so you do not even give the appearance of listening.

Eggcup

Eggcups (see Figure 23) are used only for soft-boiled eggs. Leave the egg in the cup and, using a knife, crack it firmly (but not too firmly, lest egg fly everywhere) to break the shell. Lift off the top of the shell, place it on the service plate, and use a spoon to eat the egg out of the remaining shell. You will need to steady the eggcup with your left hand (your right if you are left-handed). Salt and pepper and butter may be added as you eat, to the egg in its shell.

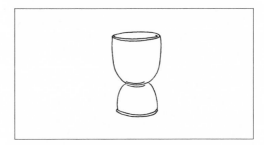

Figure 23. Eggcup

Elbows

Despite years of advice to the contrary, you may place your elbows on the table at all except the most formal dinners. Elbows are acceptable between courses and at the end of the meal, particularly when coffee is being served and conversation has intensified and/or relaxed.

Putting your elbows on the table does not give you carte blanche, however, to slouch. That always looks sloppy and should be avoided.

Elderly

SEE ALSO *Companion; Financial Aid to Elderly; Nurse; Wedding Family Members.*

Simply because they have lived a certain number of years, the elderly are entitled to certain small courtesies. Doors should be opened for them; seats should be provided; and when possible, other small courtesies, such as carrying a package or running an errand, should be extended to the aged.

I was gratified by a heartwarming courtesy I recently observed in friends. The friends in question had just finished lunching at a private ladies' club, and both were rushing to another appointment. As they crossed the lobby, an elderly lady with a walker moved slowly toward them. There was ample room to walk past her, but with beautiful instincts, both my friends stopped, stepped aside, and bowed and

smiled as the woman slowly made her way past them. That, I thought, is the respect that is due old age.

Unless there is absolute evidence to the contrary, the elderly should also be treated as if their intelligence were still intact. Old people do like to reminisce, and sometimes live in the past, but they should be indulged without being condescended to.

The elderly should always be consulted on decisions that affect their lives, and their opinions should be respected. Too often, we tend to treat the elderly as if they no longer had minds of their own when, in fact, if anything, they often have even more decided opinions than they held in their younger days.

Elevators

Elevator etiquette is one of the areas of behavior that thankfully has become more "human" in recent years. People used to crawl all over one another in elevators, mostly for purposes of ensuring that women would be permitted to enter and exit an elevator before men. As one can well imagine, this led to a great deal of physical juggling. Men also religiously removed their hats in elevators.

Admittedly, some old-school gentlemen do still yield to women, especially in an uncrowded elevator, and gracious women always thank the men who do this, but in today's crowded, frenetic world, most people leave and depart elevators based on physical convenience rather than sex.

It is perfectly acceptable today for men to wear their hats in elevators.

Elopement

A couple may decide to elope for any of several reasons. Sometimes the bride does not want her parents to assume the financial responsibility that a large wedding would entail, although these days when the bride so often works and may be able to pay for a lot of her wedding herself, this is a less and less common reason. Sometimes the couple have been married before, have had a big wedding, and they opt for a simple ceremony at city hall. Sometimes, and this is the least happy reason for an elopement, a couple elope because of parental disapproval of their marriage.

Too often, an elopement means running off to ciy hall and gathering up two strangers to serve as witnesses. But I would hope that no couple would permit themselves so antisocial a ceremony, even if their families do not approve of the match. Arrangements can always be made to be married in a judge's chambers and a couple of good friends can be taken along as witnesses. There is no reason that an elopement should not still be a celebration, however low-key, of the marriage.

Engagement

SEE ALSO *Engagement Gifts;*
Engagement Party; Engagement
Ring; Newspaper Announcement.

As soon as one person has proposed and the other accepted, they are officially engaged even though no one else yet knows of their plans to marry. The first persons to be told the good news are both sets of parents. Traditionally, the bride's parents have been informed first, because the groom asks for her hand in marriage. Practically speaking, few men formally ask for the hand of their beloved these days, mostly because few active, professional women like to be thought of as one of their father's possessions. And thanks to Alexander Graham Bell, parents may be told almost simultaneously. They may also be informed in a letter or in person, depending upon how far or near they live.

The engagement period is a busy one for most couples. Most engaged couples are immediately immersed in planning their wedding and their future lives together. And as the date of their wedding nears, they will be the guests of honor at several parties, as well as doing some entertaining for their wedding party and out-of-town guests.

LENGTH OF ENGAGEMENT. Most engagements last three to six months. That much time is required to plan a formal wedding. If more time is taken, tension and stress often begins to take its toll on the couple.

If one person is in the military, living outside the country, finishing graduate school, or is for some other reason unable to marry within a few months after becoming engaged, a couple often becomes engaged, but delays any formal announcement until six months or so before the wedding.

BEHAVIOR DURING ENGAGEMENT.
Once engaged, a couple do not date others,

but neither do they give up their other friendships. If a woman's fiancé lives out of town, she may, for example, go out to dinner or to a movie or concert with a male friend, provided, of course, that neither of them construes this as a "date."

An engaged couple may be totally involved with one another and with the life they are planning during this period, but they should realize that others still exist. Friends will want to hear about wedding plans, but only up to a point. The couple should know when to stop discussing their lives and listen to what is going on in other people's lives.

Public displays of affection are just as taboo for an engaged couple as for any other couple. Although people expect and tolerate a certain amount of cooing and billing, there is a limit to what is acceptable here, too.

PUBLIC ANNOUNCEMENT. An engagement may be announced publicly in newspapers by the bride's parents. The newspaper announcements may run in the bride's' and the groom's hometown newspapers, in which case the groom's mother helps the bride's mother with the announcements in her local papers, supplying information and even sending the announcement to the papers. Despite this, the actual wording of the invitations is such that the announcement is being made by the bride's parents.

It is never proper to send engraved or printed announcements of an engagement. An engagement also may be announced to close family and friends at a party or reception in honor of the couple. Sometimes the newspaper announcement is timed to the party, or the announcement may be withheld so the engagement is a surprise to those attending the party.

The only time an engagement is not announced formally or at a party is when there has been a recent death or serious illness in the immediate family. News is then allowed to filter down to relatives outside the immediate family and close friends.

RELATIONSHIP WITH EACH OTHER'S PARENTS. During the engagement, both partners continue calling each other's parents whatever they have been calling them—their first names or Mr. and Mrs. Smith. It is usually after the wedding that the parents-in-law and their new son- or daughter-in-law work out more intimate names. Usually, the parents bring up the subject of names. If they do not, the son- or daughter-in-law may take the initiative.

BROKEN ENGAGEMENT. When an engagement is broken, the bride-to-be returns the engagement ring, as well as any engagement presents of great monetary value that she has received. Her fiance also returns any valuable presents she has given him. Presents may be returned in person or through the mail. The mail is the more indirect route, but is often easier under the circumstances. A brief note of explanation must accompany all returned presents. It may simply say:

Dear Aunt Eleanor,

   I am afraid that I must return the lovely necklace you gave me as an engagement gift because Harry and I have decided to call off the wedding.

Love,
Jill

Engagement Gifts

SEE ALSO *Engagement Ring; Gift.*

BRIDE AND GROOM. The groom's engagement gift to his bride is usually her engagement ring. The bride, in turn, may choose to give the groom a gift, usually something of lasting value such as a watch, a key chain, cufflinks, a leather or silver desk accessory, a picture frame (usually of silver and usually containing a picture of her).

OTHER GIFTS. In some families and communities, the couple, or to be more accurate, the bride, are given engagement gifts from close friends and family members. It is acceptable to give a bride a personal engagement gift, such as lingerie or jewelry, but the trend today is to make the man a more active participant in the marriage plans, so many engagement gifts are something that can be used by the couple in their new life together.

RETURNING PRE-WEDDING GIFTS. If the engagement is broken, the bride should return all gifts of great monetary value that she has been given by the groom and his family. Heirlooms, in particular, should be returned.

THANK-YOU NOTES. Handwritten notes of thanks must be sent for all engagement presents. These may be written on the bride's personal stationery or her informal stationery. They may be printed with her name or monogram, but it must be her unmarried name. She cannot use her married name on stationery until she is married.

Engagement Party

An engagement party may be held by either set of parents, by the couple themselves, or by good friends or close relatives. Often the announcement of the engagement is kept secret until the party.

Within the bounds of good taste, any of a number of frivolous methods may be used of making the actual announcement. One couple I know whose courtship took place primarily at a Chinese restaurant held their engagement party there. The fortunes in the fortune cookies delivered the good news.

If formal invitations are sent, they invite people to a party "in honor of Mary Riley and Howard O'Connor." Most people will read between the lines, and they will further get the picture when they are greeted by the hostess and the engaged couple. The couple's names and the date of the party may be printed on napkins.

In any event, a toast is usually proposed in honor of the couple that leaves no doubts. The toast is made by the bride's father or, if he is not present, by her mother or another close relative or a family friend.

Engagement Ring

Although many things have changed in our society, so far, only the bride wears an engagement ring. Traditionally, the engagement ring is a gift from the groom to the bride, although the days when a man goes down on bended knee and surprises his beloved by presenting her with a small black velvet box containing a huge diamond ring are long gone. For one thing, most women want to be consulted about the style and size of a ring they will wear every day for the rest of their lives, and for another thing, many women want some say-so in the cost of the ring. After all, if the two of you are planning a lavish wedding and paying for it totally or partially yourselves, as so many two-career couples do these days, then the price of the engagement ring will be a matter of concern to both of you. Sometimes it is just a matter of how you want to spend your money. One bride I know was adamant about preferring the memories of a European honeymoon to an expensive stone. Another couple spent less on the engagement ring so they would have more in the new-house fund. You must do what pleases you.

Although the woman is consulted about the cost of the engagement ring, it is a gift from the man. Her funds are not used to buy it. If price is a subject of concern, as it is for most of us, the man can pay his jeweler a visit before he brings in his fiancée to try on rings. He and the jeweler can preselect some rings in his price range or their agreed-upon price range, which are then shown to his fiancée when they come in together. One woman I know departed from even this convention and made her own preselection of rings. She loved antique jewelry and knew a fair amount about it, whereas her fiancé not only knew nothing about it but also had little time or patience for shopping. So she went to her antique-jewelry dealer, after having first discussed with her fiancé what he would pay, and chose a selection of rings. He returned with her and they made the final selection together.

The diamond is the traditional engagement ring, but any stone is appropriate. Diamonds, particularly investment-quality ones, are expensive, and there are many other beautiful precious and semiprecious stones from which to choose. Some other precious stones, such as rubies and emeralds, are more expensive than diamonds, so it is a good idea to do some investigating before setting your heart on a particular stone.

Also keep in mind that your wedding ring will be worn with your engagement ring. They may be purchased as a matched set or separately, but they must look good together. When trying on engagement rings, also try on some wedding bands to see how they look with it.

Your fiancé may offer you an heirloom engagement or wedding ring. A ring that is an antique may look beautiful, but jewelry that is only one or two generations old often has a way of merely looking dated. If the ring you are offered is not suited to your taste, you can either turn it down tactfully (say you have always wanted a ring that was chosen just for you) or see whether you can have the stones reset. The stones are what is valuable about most engagement rings, so it is not blasphemy to suggest resetting them.

Finally, should something go wrong, causing the wedding to be called off, the woman is obliged to return the engagement ring. It is particularly important that she do so if it is a family heirloom.

Entertaining Style

Each of us has a unique style of entertaining that suits our personality. One person may delight in planning elaborate, theme-oriented parties; another may prefer intimate, elaborate dinners where the conversation is the main attraction. The secret of successful entertaining is not to take on a style that is burdensome and laborious, but to find one's one personal style—whatever it may be—and stick with it.

Escargot

When served in the shell, escargot (see Figure 24), as snails are called much of the time, are accompanied by a small tong. Pick up the tong and place it securely and carefully around the snail shell. Be careful; for some reason the tongs are always stiff and the shells are always slippery. Holding the tongs in one hand, use a seafood fork to remove the snail from its shell. It is acceptable to drink the juices from the shell after the snail has been eaten.

Figure 24. How to eat escargot, using tongs

When escargot is served on a plate (stuffed in a mushroom for example), eat them with a regular or a seafood fork.

Estimate

It is always acceptable to get an estimate for someone's services—a doctor, a contractor, a carpenter, a lawyer, a decorator—before buying them. If you feel it necessary, certain persons, those whose fees are likely to change as they work, may be asked to provide a written estimate. While one would discuss fees with a physician or a lawyer, professionals like this are not usually asked to provide a written estimate, nor could they easily do so.

While discussion of money on a social occasion is not always the best idea, discussion of money for business reasons is only smart.

Esquire

SEE ALSO *Titles.*

This is the traditional title of lawyers. It is acceptable to address a woman lawyer as "Mary Jones, Esquire," although it is usually abbreviated to "Esq." "Esquire" is not used socially in the way that "doctor" is.

Ethnic Insults.

SEE *Humor; Prejudice.*

Expense Accounts

SEE ALSO *Business Lunch*.

You might not think there would be any etiquette attached to an expense account, but there is. It is both bad manners and bad business to use an expense account for personal reasons and to announce, i.e., brag, to others about your misuse of one.

It is quite appropriate, when picking up the tab, to silence a customer's protests by saying, "Don't worry, it goes on my expense account." It is also acceptable, when you and a client are studying a menu, to say, "Order whatever you like. It's on ABC, Inc." These are not misuses of an expense account but are simply ways of making a customer feel at ease—and ways of wooing a customer.

Falsehood

SEE *Lying*.

Family Dinner

Family dinners can be dreadful or joyous occasions, and how they turn out has a lot to do with how they are planned.

I think a hostess should pay as much attention to seating her family as she does to seating her guests at a dinner party. Those who have little in common should not be put together, and those who have reason to get to know each other better should be. Husbands and wives may sit together or not, as the hostess chooses. At least one parent of a young child should be seated with him. If the children must sit at a separate table, pay attention to the teenager who has grown up enough to join the adults, and don't insult him by keeping him at the children's table.

And speaking of the children, they are often the ones who dread family dinners. If possible, something should be done to provide entertainment for them: a movie on the VCR, some games, even an outing supervised by local teens so the adults can have some uninterrupted time to sit and talk with one another. Everyone will be grateful.

Family dinners often revolve around traditional meals, and there is a tendency to serve the same food year after year. Consider experimenting with the menu a little. This need not be a radical departure from the foods people have come to love—and expect—but even an old favorite can be prepared in a slightly different way and a new side dish can be added to the menu every once in a while.

Although some compromises may have to be made in large families (paper napkins and mixed china and flatware, to name two of the more common ones), most hostesses use their best dishes and flatware for festive family dinners.

Guests at family dinners have some obligations, too. Unlike a formal dinner party, everyone should pitch in to help the hostess. Some hostesses may want others to bring some of the food, and some will prefer that assistance come in the form of serving the meal and cleaning up afterward. Family members with grudges should set them aside for the day, if only as a courtesy to the hostess. Finally, a very nice touch is to call the hostess a day or so later to thank her for the lovely dinner.

Family Finances

SEE ALSO *Children's Allowances.*

The family budget may not seem like the most likely topic for an etiquette book, but arguments, unreasonable behavior, and a great deal of unkindness over money has plagued many a marriage. There is rarely a more important time to be courteous to your partner than when the two of you are having a joust over finances.

WHEN BOTH PARTNERS WORK. These days the wife is likely to make a major contribution to the family income. But since many men are still touchy about looking successful, and since success is often measured (erroneously, I believe) in terms of earnings, some tact may be required if the wife earns a great deal of money, perhaps even more than her husband earns. The best approach, when this is a problem and when it is not, is to avoid discussion of one's personal finances. It is no one's business how a couple divide their family expenses or who brings in what income.

Some couples maintain separate checking accounts while others merge their money into one account. This, too, is no one's business.

Discussion of money matters, though, has become more acceptable socially than it used to be, and furthermore, we live in a groundbreaking era in which family life—not least the economic side of it—is being restructured. I can therefore imagine a situation where a young couple might talk frankly among their friends about various financial arrangements they have made, simply because each couple would have something constructive to learn from the conversation. Never initiate a conversation like this, however, without first testing the waters to see if your friends are open to this kind of discussion. If they are not, drop the subject immediately.

WHEN ONE PARTNER WORKS. When only one spouse works, it is usually the man, while the woman stays home to take care of the children. Particularly if the woman has worked, she may find it awkward suddenly not to be earning her own money. The sensitive husband does what he can to ease a wife through this period. Regardless of how a couple handles this matter, neither partner should ever have to wheedle or beg money from a spouse. Each spouse should have equal access to their money.

PAYING THE BILLS. While each partner should be knowledgeable enough to handle the bill-paying if necessary, there is usually one person who is better at it. It makes sense, therefore, for this person to pay the bills and balance the checkbook at the end of the month.

WE VS. I. When speaking of purchases, a couple usually says "we" if the purchase was made together or is for the household.

A husband would not say "I sold the house" when speaking of his and his wife's residence unless he was a complete clod and had indeed sold the house without her knowledge or permission.

It is appropriate when speaking of more personal purchases, however, to say "I" instead of "we."

GIFTS OF MONEY. Many parents are aware of the difficulties of putting together a household, and they occasionally try to help out their married children with a gift of money. While such gifts are often needed, they are not always welcome and can even be cause for resentment in the marriage, especially if they are not given the right way.

A husband may resent a check from his wife's parents because he thinks it implies that he does not earn enough. A wife may resent a check for a new car from her husband's parents when she wants to redecorate the living room. Presents of money should be presented jointly to a couple, not to one or the other, and no strings should be attached regarding how the money is spent. The wise parent will not even make a suggestion, unless he or she is very sure it is something the couple wants. Better to say, "I know you are just starting out and will want to buy things for your life together, so I want to give you some money." A wise parent never says, "I know you probably want to decorate your home, so let me give you something to help," when that, in fact, may be the parent's priority but not the young couple's.

CHILDREN AND FAMILY MONEY. Children do not need to know much about family finances, not because they should be protected from the realities of life, but because there are few things more obnoxious than a small child who knows he is rich.

If a family is poor, even a very young child will somehow sense this, and still need not be told a lot of details. If possible, a small child deserves some protection from the more overwhelming burdens of family poverty.

Family-Style Food Service

SEE *Food Service.*

Farewell

AMONG FRIENDS. Some friends kiss when saying goodbye even if they will see each other the next day. Some friends shake hands. Some friends merely wave. The mode of leave-taking seems to vary throughout the country. New Yorkers are notorious kissers. Bostonians like to shake hands. Midwesterners are wavers. You should feel free to do whatever is comfortable for you personally.

AT A SMALL PARTY. When leaving a small party, always seek out the host and hostess to thank them personally. It is kind to chat with them for a few minutes. When thanking them, try to mention something specific that made the evening a success: "The leg of lamb was just great. May I call you and get your butcher's name?" or "The dessert was simply out of this world" or "Your table looked stunning."

Take care, however, not to stretch out the farewells more than a minute or two so the host and hostess do not neglect their other guests. A twenty-minute farewell is not gracious; it is annoying. Once you decide to leave, do so rather quickly.

Timing is important, too, when leaving a party, since the first couple or person to leave often break up the party. Guests should stay at least an hour after dinner, and they may, of course, stay much longer. If you must leave much earlier than an hour, explain why to your host and hostess ("Harry has been fighting off the flu all week, and he really needs his rest" or "Our babysitter told us this is finals week, and she has to get home early").

As the evening grows old, keep an eye on the host and hostess, though, for signs of fatigue, and do not stay long after the first couple of stifled yawns. They aren't bored; they were busy all day cooking.

AT A LARGE PARTY. The host and hostess are often very busy at a large party, and may not be able to chat for any length of time with departing guests. Despite this, you must seek them out to say goodbye and thank them for what presumably was a lovely evening.

Farewell Party

A farewell party is often planned for someone who is moving to another community, leaving a job, or even going away, if not permanently, then for an extended period of time.

GIFTS. The person for whom the farewell party is held usually receives gifts from those who attend, or more often, one gift that everyone has contributed to. The gift should be appropriate to the occasion—that is, if a person is leaving to take a new job, a briefcase or other work-related gift would be ideal. A person or family moving to a new community might appreciate something for the new home.

WHOM TO INVITE. Anyone who is a close friend of the honored guest may be invited to a farewell party. Less-than-close friends should probably not be invited since a gift will be solicited.

INVITATIONS. These may be issued informally, in person or by telephone, or written invitations may be sent. Either way, the purpose of the party should be explained. One advantage of issuing invitations by telephone is that if a group gift is planned, whoever does the calling can make arrangements right then and there. If written invitations are sent, a phone call will still be necessary to discuss the present.

FOOD. A farewell party often resembles a shower. Lunch or dinner is served, and a cake is the usual dessert. Farewell parties among business associates are often held in restaurants.

RETURNING THE FAVOR. A farewell party is the only kind of party that need not be reciprocated—for the simple reason that the person is not around to do so. A thank-you present should be sent to the host and hostess, though.

Father of the Bride

SEE *Wedding Family Members*.

Fig, Date

SEE *Fruit*.

Financial Aid to the Elderly

Some family members, especially the elderly, may need financial assistance, and, when possible, others should help them out. The most tactful way to do this is to sit down and discuss the person's financial situation with him or her, and arrange to send a monthly amount to help out.

A check to help support someone should always be sent promptly as the person may count on it for living expenses. It is tactful not to do anything to remind the person of his or her dependence upon you, including asking how the money is being spent. Gifts of money that are necessary to someone's subsistence should always be given without strings attached and without infringing on the other person's dignity.

Finger Food

SEE ALSO *Buffet Dinner; Cocktail Party*.

Some foods are meant to be eaten with one's fingers, and because of this, finger foods are especially popular at cocktail parties and stand-up buffets, since you don't have to juggle a plate and eating utensils.

Certain foods are always finger foods—small sandwiches, fruit, small cakes and petit fours, cookies, candy—while others are finger foods only when the occasion dictates that they be. Chicken, for example, is not a finger food at a formal dinner, but it is at a stand-up buffet dinner or a picnic.

Note to party-givers: Never ask your guests to hold food in their fingers; always provide service plates that can be used to hold finger food.

Firing

At some point in your career, you may be in a position to fire others. There are a few rules of etiquette that anyone should follow to ease this awkward task.

1. Keep all transactions of this nature confidential. Nothing is more painful to everyone in an office than to know that someone is about to be fired. If you plan to dismiss someone for any reason, keep silent until you have told the person being dismissed. Afterward, discuss the matter as little as possible. You may need to reassure your staff or bolster morale if there are mass firings or layoffs, but there is never any reason to discuss the details of an individual case.

2. Do all firing yourself, in person. It is a courtesy to the person involved, a kind way to end a relationship.

3. When dismissing someone, show respect for his or her feelings and opinions. After all, the ability to take away someone's job is the ultimate sign of power; it is more potent than giving raises, benefits, and promotions, and it

can become an ego trip for you if you are not careful.

4. If possible, stretch the truth a little when firing someone for a minor offense—too many sick days, tardiness, long lunches—and let the person walk away with his or her ego intact. It is fine to tell the person what he or she has done wrong, but do not elaborate or talk at great length about the offenses.

5. Do not promise someone a recommendation that you will not be able to deliver. Mention, if asked, that the person might better seek a recommendation elsewhere. If at all possible, though, try to give someone a good recommendation, even if you have fired him or her. What you disliked may not offend another employer so badly. If you must say something unflattering, couch it tactfully and surrounded it with the person's good points.

First Communion

Roman Catholic children take communion for the first time when they are six or seven. (Other Christians usually take communion for the first time when they are confirmed.) First Communion is an occasion for community and family celebration. A reception is often held after the service in the church, and many families also plan a private party later at home. A white cake is usually served, along with punch and other beverages. Lunch, brunch, or dinner also may be served.

Those invited to share in a First Communion are the family, close family friends, and some friends of the celebrant.

Boys wear dark suits, white shirts, and ties; girls wear white dresses and white veils. Depending upon the congregation and community custom, a First Communion dress may be a simple street dress or a much more elaborate long, white dress that resembles a wedding dress. Girls cover their heads, again with anything from a simple piece of lace to an elaborate veil.

Gifts are given to the child who celebrates First Communion. Especially appropriate are those with religious connotations such as a cross, religious medal, or a prayerbook, but some jewelry or a special memento that is not religious may be given. Frivolous presents, including toys, are inappropriate.

First Lady

SEE ALSO *Forms of Address—Written; White House Invitation.*

The title First Lady, used to describe the wife of the President of the United States, is informal since the President's wife has no official title. Although she receives no pay and has no official position, First Ladies work very hard and have certainly earned the designation, official or not. The President's wife is referred to either as the First Lady or as Mrs. Washington, usually according to her instructions to her staff, but she is never directly addressed as the First Lady. In other words, no one ever introduces her saying, "First Lady, I'd like you to meet Elinor Jackson." The correct way to introduce the President's wife is to say, "Mrs. Washington, may I present . . ."

In correspondence, the First Lady is addressed as Mrs. George Washington or mail is sent to the President and Mrs. George Washington.

Place cards at formal dinners may be labeled "The First Lady."

Fish, Whole

Cut off the head. Make a slice with the fish knife along the center back. Lift one slice of the fish off to the side of the plate. Using a fish knife and fork, carefully lift off the spine, which will usually come away in one piece. Flake off the skin if you like. Use a fish fork and knife to pick up and eat small pieces of fish. The big bones will have been removed, but small ones may remain.

It is always appropriate when ordering fish in a restaurant to ask the waiter if it is a particularly bony kind of fish, but even fish that has been filleted will probably contain some small bones.

Flags

AMERICAN. The American flag is our primary national symbol, and it should be displayed with respect. Any American has the right to display the flag. It may be flown from sunrise to sunset. It may be flown after dark if it is part of a patriotic display and is well lit. The American flag should never be used as part of clothing or home decoration. It should never be used to cover anything,

with the exception of a coffin. It should never be used as advertising. Red, white, and blue bunting may be used but never the flag.

When the flag is displayed over a street, it should be hung with the blue field (the Union) facing north on a north-south street, and the Union facing east on an east-west street.

When displayed with one other flag, the American flag is always on the right. When displayed with two or more other flags, it is on the right or takes a center position in front of the other flags. The American flag is always hoisted before other flags and carried before other flags in a procession. Alternately, it is carried slightly higher than other flags.

International protocol forbids the flying of one national flag higher than another in peacetime, so the flag is usually displayed with other national flags on separate flagpoles of equal height.

When displayed in a house of worship, the American flag always goes to the right of the clergyperson. Other flags go to the clergyperson's left.

A flag may be flown on a powerboat that is under power and a sailboat that is under sail.

When the flag covers a casket, the Union is always at the top and over the left shoulder of the body. The flag is always removed before the casket is lowered into the grave, and while it is being carried, the flag never touches the ground.

The flag may be flown at half-mast by Presidential order as a sign of national mourning. When it is hoisted in the morning and taken down in the evening, it is always first taken to the top of the flagpole and then brought down to half-mast.

When displayed in any way, the flag

should never touch the ground or, if possible, other objects. It should always be handled with respect. It should never be wadded up but should be carefully folded into a triangle.

The flag should always be clean. A soiled or dirty flag should not be displayed.

When dirty, the flag may be washed or dry-cleaned, preferably dry-cleaned. It should not be hung on a line in a public place to dry.

When the flag passes by, Americans either stand in respectful silence, or they place their right hands over their hearts as it passes. Military personnel salute. When the Pledge of Allegiance is given, all present stand and face the flag. Civilians cover their hearts with their hands and stand attentively, repeating the pledge in unison. Hats are removed. Military personnel salute and continue to wear their hats.

When you are in another country and find yourself present at a flag ceremony, it is polite to stand attentively throughout it. A person never pledges or salutes a flag other than that of his or her own nation.

Flatware

SEE ALSO *Fork; Knife; Spoon; Table Manners.*

Like China, flatware is available in several types, and you must buy whatever suits your lifestyle. It is pretentious to choose sterling silver if you never do any formal entertaining, and it can be equally pretentious to reject sterling silver (many women inherit a set) when it is such a lovely heirloom.

STERLING. Sterling silver is not pure silver, as many people suppose, but is 92.5 percent silver and 7.5 percent copper. Pure silver flatware would be very soft and not very durable. As it is, sterling must be handled with care to maintain its beauty. With use, though, sterling silver acquires a patina, many tiny scratches that create a beautiful, polished glow that is highly desirable.

VERMEIL. This is gold-plated sterling. It is too ornate for anything but the most formal entertaining and is little used today.

SILVERPLATE. Silverplate is a base metal coated with silver. To wear well, silverplate must be heavy and of very good quality. Silverplate never wears as well as sterling, which is handed down through families for many generations.

Silverplate is available in as wide a range of patterns as sterling. When the price of sterling climbed rapidly in the late 1970s, many couples purchased silverplate instead of sterling silver.

STAINLESS STEEL. Like silverplate, the best stainless steel is the heaviest and most expensive. Stainless steel comes in a variety of styles, ranging from traditional patterns that resemble sterling patterns to some elegant, modern patterns. Stainless steel is very durable and does not need regular polishing the way silverplate and sterling do.

It comes in two finishes: dull and shiny.

CHOOSING A PATTERN. When choosing any kind of flatware, look for weight and balance. In other words, it should feel good in your hand and be easy to use. Some marvelous modern stainless steel patterns have been created, but they do not necessarily make eating any easier, and that, after all, is the only thing that we ask of eating utensils.

A flatware pattern should complement the dishes that are used with it, or since flatware is more lasting than most sets of dishes, it might be more accurate to say that dishes should complement flatware. The fact is, however, that most women choose dishes first and flatware second, or they choose them simultaneously. If your dishes are very formal and of a plain design, an elaborate or a plain sterling or silverplate will go well with them. When using a stark, modern pottery, choose an equally modern set of stainless to go with them. Some silversmiths are creating lovely, modern sets of sterling that also go well with modern pottery.

When choosing sterling or silverplate, keep in mind that you are buying an heirloom. It will last and probably will be handed down in your family. It is better, therefore, to opt for a classic pattern that has some longevity built into its design than to choose a more up-to-date pattern that may look dated in just a few years. Tried-and-true sterling and silverplate patterns have been around for several generations, and remain in open stock for a long time.

Flatware need not match, especially if it is old silver. A set of dinner forks and knives might be paired with a complementary but unmatched set of salad or dessert forks. The only guideline is that all the silver being used the same way should match, that is, all the salad forks should be alike, all the dinner forks should match, and so on.

Unmatched stainless steel does not work quite so successfully as sterling and silverplate, but a skilled artistic eye will be able to mix and match just about anything.

NEEDS. Sterling used to be bought, as was china, by the dozens of pieces, but today it is sold by the place setting. That is fortunate since few of us could afford to order silver by the dozen of pieces at today's prices.

A place setting consists of a dinner knife, a dinner fork, a salad fork, a teaspoon, and sometimes a soup spoon (see Figure 25). Additional pieces that may be ordered are demitasse spoons, oyster forks, steak knives, dessert spoons and forks, iced-tea spoons, and fish knives and forks. Serving pieces can also be ordered. Not all patterns come with all these extra pieces, or with all serving pieces, and this is something to check before selecting a pattern.

A couple needs at least four place settings of flatware, and depending upon their entertaining needs, most women try to acquire between eight and ten place settings of sterling or silverplate. Extra spoons are always needed, as they are the most used pieces and also seem to suffer the highest casualty rate, mostly, I suspect, by being thrown away accidentally. The next-most-needed extra item is the salad fork, which also doubles as a dessert fork and luncheon fork in most place settings. Many women order a service for eight with eight extra teaspoons and an equal number of extra salad forks.

CARE. Sterling silver, vermeil, and silverplate must be polished regularly with a good brand of silver polish, and, when not in use, should be stored in tarnish-proof bags. Silver can be used regularly,

Figure 25. Standard place setting

and only gets more beautiful with use, but it should not be left unstored for long periods of time since air pollution will take its toll. Most silver is dishwasher-proof, although old knives should be washed by hand, since they become loose with age.

Stainless is maintenance free, but after long use, it does benefit from being polished with a good metal polish. If stainless steel is not dried, it will waterspot.

MONOGRAMMING. The custom of having sterling monogrammed has mostly fallen out of fashion. Certainly no one who is giving a gift of flatware should have it monogrammed without first checking with the person to whom the gift will be given.

Flower Girl

SEE *Wedding Attendants.*

Flowers

SEE ALSO *Centerpiece; Corsage; Host/Hostess Gift; Wedding Flowers.*

FRESH. Thanks to air freight and huge "industrial" greenhouses, fresh flowers are much more available today than they were even a few years ago. Flowers such as tulips and snapdragons no longer have seasons, and no longer cost an arm and a leg.

I think everyone should consider budgeting a few dollars a week to purchase fresh flowers, or, at minimum, should buy some on special occasions. When I was younger and had to stretch my entertaining budget more, I was always willing to cook an inexpensive stew and use the few dollars I saved to buy a few posies to decorate my table.

The social etiquette of giving flowers has changed a lot, too. These days, for example, women need not wait for men to buy them flowers, and men should stop thinking of flowers as something only for special occasions or heavy courtship. There is no more romantic domestic touch than flowers, whether the vase if filled with a single bud or a lavish bouquet, or, as is often the case, something in between. And there is no reason that women cannot buy flowers for each other. When a friend has been promoted or even when a friend needs cheering up for one reason or another, I often send a small bouquet.

OCCASIONS THAT CALL FOR FLOWERS. There are occasions when flowers are not simply a nice touch but are called for.

Most religions permit and encourage flowers at funerals (see Jewish Funeral Customs for the most notable exception). When someone you know has suffered a loss, consider sending flowers to the funeral. An even more loving nice touch is to send flowers a few weeks after the funeral to your friend. It shows you are still thinking of him or her.

Flowers are the traditional gift to those in the hospital and shut-ins, perhaps because they bring a bit of the outdoors inside. Check, though, with the particular hospital before taking flowers: Some do not permit flowers at all because they carry bacteria, and others do not permit them as gifts to asthmatics and others with similar illnesses.

Flowers are perhaps the best host or hostess gift these days when dieting is the rage and candy is thus not always welcome. Take whatever your budget allows: A single bud is as lovely and desirable as a whole bouquet, and sometimes, as when you buy one flawless orchid, anything more than a single flower would be overkill.

The host or hostess who receives flowers need not use them as a centerpiece if there already is one (or even if there is not), but the flowers should be put in water and displayed somewhere where everyone can enjoy them.

Other times when flowers are a welcome gift are when a friend has been promoted or achieved some other honor or whenever congratulations are in order. And, as I mentioned earlier, flowers are also an excellent way to cheer up a friend who is, for whatever reason, feeling low. And sometimes it is nice to send flowers for no reason at all—except to express love.

ARTIFICIAL. Fake flowers have their place, but one must exercise caution in using them. A bouquet of silk flowers may be just the right decorative touch in a room, but the flowers must be of the very best quality, and never, never made of plastic.

CORSAGES. Corsages are given less rarely these days, perhaps because we have been living in a less-than-romantic age for the past few decades. Women mostly wear them on "ceremonial" occasions such as weddings, proms, and anniversaries. A corsage still makes a lovely accessory to a cocktail or evening dress, though, and a romantic soul who is inclined to send one to his lady should not hesitate to do so. For that matter, in these liberated days, a woman might consider sending a boutonnière to her favorite man.

If the color of the woman's dress is known, the flowers should be chosen to complement or match it. If it is not known, white flowers go with everything.

A corsage should always be worn with the stems down, the way flowers grow. It may be pinned to the shoulder or waist of a dress, worn on a coat, attached to a purse, or worn in the hair. Wrist corsages are pretty much the province of teenagers.

Food Allergies

At a small dinner party, the simplest approach for a person with food allergies is not to make a fuss and to place a small portion of the food on your plate. Usually, the hostess or host will not notice, or, if he notices, will not comment on your failure to eat one food. If pressed, you can then say that you have an allergy.

On no account does one mention allergies to the host or hostess when one is invited. To do so is tantamount to requesting that something special be prepared for just one person, and this is rude. There is one exception to this, and that is when allergies encompass several foods and are a major problem in planning what to eat. Even then, one can almost always eat something that is served.

Occasionally, a host or hostess must do something when a guest is not eating much of anything. I once had the experience of having prepared a very simple meal of pasta made with four cheeses, only to notice that one guest was not eating. When I asked what the problem was, I leanred that my guest was allergic to cheese. In this instance, something clearly had to be done, so I quickly whipped up an omelette to replace the pasta dish. All was well.

Food Courses

A meal is served in courses when each course of food is brought out and eaten separately. For example, soup is served, eaten, the dishes are then cleared, and the entree (or perhaps the salad) is brought out. The days of nine-course or even five- or six-course meals are long gone in our diet- and health-conscious society, and rarely does a formal meal today consist of more than four courses: a first course (which may be either an appetizer or a soup), an entree, a salad, and a dessert. Occasionally, at a very formal dinner, a first course and a soup will be served. Many families eat far more simply.

The first course is, quite predictably, served first. An appetizer may be served in the living room with drinks or at the table. The first course is often at each person's place when the guests sit down, but this is entirely a matter of personal choice. For example, if you happen to have a beautiful soup tureen, it would be a shame to have soup already on the table in bowls when your guests arrive at the table. It is far more interesting to serve the soup in your guests' persence and let them ogle your beautiful dish.

If soup follows the appetizer, it is served immediately. As soon as everyone has finished the appetizer, clear away the appetizer dishes and serve the soup. At a formal dinner, the fish course follows.

The entree is also served without much delay after the soup or fish has been finished. Vegetables and other side dishes are served with it.

I like to serve the salad after the entree,

although many people prefer to serve it at the start of the meal. I also let a little time elapse between the entree and the salad. If I have some last-minute work to do on dessert, I often do it while my guests chat and catch their breath between courses. If the salad is served last, the salad fork goes next to the plate; if it is served first, it goes on the outside.

The last course, dessert, caps off the meal. Before dessert is brought in, the table is cleared of serving dishes and crumbs are removed. In many homes, dessert is served at the table, and coffee is taken in another room—usually the living room—and sometimes dessert and coffee are taken together in the living room.

Strictly speaking, the last course is coffee and tea, although these beverages are often served with dessert.

Food Service

SEE *Barbecue; Buffet Dinner; Clambake; Cocktail Party; Dinner Party; Kaffeeklatsch; Lunch; Tailgate Picnic.*

Food Stuck in Teeth

In public, if food gets stuck in your teeth, it is not polite to use a toothpick at the table or to pick at the food with your finger. Also unattractive is to move your tongue around in your mouth trying to dislodge the food. If the food causes enough discomfort to need remedy, excuse yourself and go remove the food in private.

When the family is dining, the use of toothpicks may be permitted, but users should be discreet; it's never a pretty sight.

Foreign Menu Terms

The foreign terms that Americans are most likely to come into contact with are those found on menus in French restaurants. Here is a list of the most commonly used expressions:

agneau lamb
ail garlic
à la in the style of
amandine made with almonds; often used in preparing fish fillets
ananas pineapple
anchois anchovy
anglaise, à la cooked in either water or stock
artichauts artichokes
artichauts à la vinaigrette artichokes in olive oil and garlic
asperges asparagus
assiette anglaise assortment of cold cuts
aubergine eggplant
au jus in its own juice
au lait with milk
avocat avocado
baba au rhum cake soaked in rum after it has been baked
banane banana

basilic basil

béarnaise thick sauce made with shallots, tarragon, thyme, bay leaf, vinegar, white wine, and egg yolks, served with grilled or sautéed meat or grilled fish

béchamel sauce of milk thickened with butter and flour

beurre d'ail garlic butter

beurre noir brown butter served on eggs, fish, or vegetables

bière beer

biscuits cookies

bisque soup, usually made of puréed shellfish

blanquette de veau veal stewed in a cream sauce

boeuf beef

boeuf bourguignon braised beef prepared in the style of Burgundy (with small glazed onions, mushrooms, and red wine)

boeuf rôti roast beef

bombe glacée ice-cream dessert

bonbon candy

bonne femme, à la cooked with bacon, onions, potatoes, and a thick brown gravy

bordelaise brown sauce made with wine and bone marrow

boudin blood sausage

bouillabaisse fish chowder from French Riviera; made with fish, olive oil, tomatoes, and saffron with water or bouillon

bouilli boiled

braisée braised

brioche a kind of fancy French yeast roll

brochette a skewer; anything cooked on a skewer may be called a *brochette*

brocoli broccoli

brouillé scrambled

café glacé ice cream with coffee flavoring

calmar squid

canapé a small round of bread, topped with various spreads and used as an appetizer

canard duck

canard à l'orange duck in orange sauce

caneton duckling

câpres, sauce aux caper sauce, used most often on lamb

carbonnade à la flamande beef cooked with beer

carottes carrots

cassoulet stew made with white beans and pork

cervelles brains

champignons mushrooms

Châteaubriand cut of beef, grilled and served with vegetables cut in strips and with a *béarnaise* sauce

choix choice

choux de bruxelles Brussels sprouts

ciboulette chives

citron lemon

coeur d'artichauts artichoke hearts

compote de fruits stewed, mixed fruit (fresh or dried), served cold

consommé meat stock that has been enriched, concentrated, and clarified

coq au vin chicken in a red wine sauce with mushrooms, garlic, small onions, and diced pork

coquillages shellfish

coquille St-Jacques scallops

cornichon type of small pickle, served with pâté and other dishes

côte de boeuf grillé grilled beef rib

côte de veau veal chop

courgette zucchini

crabe crab

crème custard or cream

crème brûlée a rich dessert pudding made with vanilla and cream, which is lightly coated with sugar, placed under the broiler, and then cooled for two to three hours before serving

crème caramel custard with a burnt sugar flavor

crème Chantilly whipped cream

crêpes thin pancakes

crêpes Suzette thin dessert pancakes topped with a sauce made with curaçao and the juice of mandarin oranges, usually served flaming

crevettes shrimp

croissant crescent-shaped roll made with a puff pastry or yeast dough; most often served at breakfast

croque madame grilled chicken and cheese sandwich

croque monsieur grilled ham and cheese sandwich

croûtons bread that has been diced and sautéed in butter; used in soup and on salads

crudités raw vegetables served as an appetizer

cuisses de grenouilles frogs' legs

daube chunks of meat stewed with vegetables

demiglace a thick, brown sauce

demitasse strong, black coffee served in a small cup

diable, sauce à la spicy sauce of white wine, vinegar, shallots, and pepper

dinde turkey

dolmas stuffing wrapped in a grapevine leaf

duglère, à la with a cream sauce made with wine and tomatoes, served with fish

échalotte shallot

écrevisse crawfish

en croûte baked in a pastry crust

entrecôte translates as "between the ribs"; steak cut from between two ribs of beef, usually grilled or fried

entrecôte marchand de vin steak cooked with red wine and shallots

épinards spinach

escalopes de veau thin, boneless slices of veal

escalopes de veau cordon bleu thin slices of boneless veal stuffed with ham and cheese

escargot snails

farci stuffed

filet de boeuf tenderloin

filet mignon small, choice cut of beef prepared by grilling or sautéeing

flambé describes a dish that has been ignited after being doused in a liqueur

florentine, à la foods cooked in this style (usually eggs or fish) are put on spinach, covered with mornay sauce, and sprinkled with cheese

foie liver

foie gras the livers of fattened geese and ducks

fraises strawberries

framboises raspberries

frappé chilled

frites french fries

fromage cheese

fruits de mer seafood

garni garnished or decorated

gâteau cake

gigot d'agneau leg of lamb

glace ice cream

gratin, au prepared with a topping of toasted breadcrumbs; usually includes grated cheese

hareng herring

haricots beans

herbe herb

hollandaise sauce made with egg yolks and butter; served over vegetables and fish

homard lobster

hors d'oeuvres appetizers, hot or cold

huîtres oysters

jambon fumé smoked ham

jardinière, à la fresh vegetables, served with roast, stewed, or braised meat and poultry

julienne meat or vegetables cut into thin strips

lait milk

laitue lettuce

lapin rabbit

légumes vegetables

lyonnaise prepared with onions

macédoine fruit or vegetables, diced and then mixed

madeleine spongecake made from flour, butter, eggs, and sugar baked in shell-like molds

madère, sauce au sauce made with Madeira wine

madrilène clear chicken soup with tomato; served chilled (becomes jellied)

maison a term applied only to recipes that are exclusive to the restaurant's owner or chef but usually used more loosely to mean in the style of the restaurant

marchands de vin, sauce brown sauce of butter and red wine

maître d'hotel headwaiter

médaillon meat cut into a round or oval shape

menthe mint

meunière method of preparing fish; the fish is first seasoned, floured, and sautéed in butter, then served with lemon juice, parsley, and melted butter

mornay white sauce with cheese added

moules mussels

mousse a light, airy dish made with cream and eggs; may be of fish, chicken, fruits, or chocolate or other dessert flavor; served hot or cold

moutarde mustard

nature plain; without trim; in its natural state

niçoise, à la a dish cooked in the style of Nice, often prepared with tomatoes, zucchini, garlic, potatoes, green beans, black olives, garlic, capers, and anchovies

nouilles noodles

oeuf egg

oeufs à la Russe hard-boiled eggs with a mayonnaise sauce of chives, onion, and a dash of tabasco or tomato flavoring

oeufs bénédictine in most American restaurants this refers to an egg and ham on an English muffin with hollandaise sauce and possibly a slice of truffle

oignon onion

omelette omelet; an egg dish

omelette aux fines herbes omelet made with parsley, tarragon, and chives or another combination of herbs

pain bread

palourdes clams

papillote, en steamed, enclosed in a sheet of parchment or foil

parfait an iced dessert

pâté any dish of ground meat or fish baked in a mold that has been lined with strips of fat

pâté maison a pâté unique to a particular restaurant

pâtisseries pastries

pêche peach

pêches Melba peaches that have been steeped in vanilla-flavored syrup, served over vanilla ice cream topped with raspberry purée

petit-beurre butter cookie

petite marmite clear soup made with meat, poultry, marrow bones, stock pot vegetables, and cabbage; usually served with toast and sprinkled with grated cheese

petit pain roll

pilaf rice sautéed in oil and cooked with a variety of seasonings

poisson fish

poivre pepper

pomme apple

porc pork

potage soup, usually with cream base

pot-au-feu French version of the boiled beef dinner

pots de crème au chocolat rich chocolate dessert

poulet chicken

poulet à la Marengo a method of cooking chicken by browning it in oil, adding wine, and serving it with a garnish of fried eggs, mushrooms, and crawfish

poulet chasseur chicken prepared with sautéed mushrooms, shallots, and white wine and tomatoes

poulet rôti à l'estragon roast chicken with tarragon

printanière, à la garnished with a variety of spring vegetables

prix-fixe at a set price

profiterole eclair-like pastry; may be filled with ice cream, any purée, or a custard, jam, or other sweet filling; usually served with chocolate or other sweet sauce

provençale, à la cooked in the style of Provence, usually with tomatoes, garlic, olives, and eggplant

purée food that has been mashed or put through a sieve or processed in a blender

quenelles dish made with ground fish or meat blended with cream

quiche Lorraine a tart made with eggs, cream, cheese, and bacon

ragoût a dish made from meat, poultry, or

fish that has been cut up and browned; may or may not include vegetables

ratatouille a mixture of eggplant, zucchini, squash, onions, tomatoes, and peppers; may be served hot or cold

ravigote a white sauce, hot or cold, highly seasoned with thyme and coarsely ground black pepper

reine de saba cake of chocolate, rum, and almonds

ris de veau veal sweetbreads

riz rice

Robert sauce of onion, white wine, and mustard; served with grilled pork dishes

rognons kidneys

saucisson large sausage; sliced for serving

saumon salmon

sec dry

sel salt

sorbet sherbet; made from fruit or liqueurs

soufflé dish made with puréed ingredients, thickened with egg yolks and beaten egg whites; may be made with vegetables, fish, meat, fruit, nuts, or liqueurs; served as an appetizer, a main dish, or a dessert

spécialité de la maison specialty of a particular restaurant

steak au poivre steak made with crushed peppercorns

steak tartare uncooked ground meat seasoned with salt and pepper and served with a raw egg yolk on top and with capers, chopped onion, and parsley on the side

sucre sugar

suprêmes de volaille boneless chicken breasts

sur commande made to your special order

tarte pie

thé tea

tournedos small slice of beef, round and

thick, from the heart of the fillet of beef; sautéed or grilled

tranche slice

truffe truffle, a fungus that grows underground

truite trout

varié assorted

vichyssoise a cream soup of leeks, potatoes, and chicken broth; served cold

vin wine

vinaigrette sauce of oil, mustard, and vinegar, seasoned with salt and pepper and, at times, herbs

volaille fowl, poultry

Foreign Restaurant

SEE ALSO *Chinese Restaurant; Eating in Africa; Eating in China; Eating in Europe; Eating in India; Eating in Japan; Eating in the Mideast; Japanese Restaurant; Foreign Menu Terms.*

Most so-called foreign restaurants are fairly Westernized, so you are unlikely to encounter much that is strange.

If the menu is written in a foreign language, there is usually a translation on one side. If there is no translation, never feel shy about asking a waiter to help you out. (Keep in mind, though, that it helps to know basic restaurant French and Italian.)

With the exception of Oriental restaurants, where chopsticks may be used, the method of dining in all other foreign restaurants will be what you are used to. Even if some exotic custom prevails (you may be encouraged to sit on the floor in some Oriental restaurants or to eat with your right-hand fingers in some African and Mideastern restaurants), you can always decline to participate and dine the way you usually do. Even restaurateurs who try to keep the spirit of their native cuisine know that not everyone will participate to the same degree or with enthusiasm, and they usually have facilities for traditional Western dining.

If the cuisine features hot dishes, and your palate or special diet does not permit this, remember that you can usually ask the waiter if the chef will tone down the seasoning. Say you would like "mild" seasoning, and the chef will usually get the message. Sometimes the reverse is true; and an ethnic cuisine will have been toned down too much for your taste. When this happens, the chef will be delighted to have a order to serve a naturally hot dish "hot."

Finally, enjoy yourself when you dine out in a restaurant that specializes in ethnic cuisine. Be adventurous and try some new or interesting dish that you would not ordinarily order.

Foreign Travel

SEE ALSO *International Business Manners.*

Not always known as particularly good travelers, Americans today are not only welcome as tourists throughout the world, but also are traveling in ever greater numbers and with ever-greater ease.

A good traveler is one who is curious,

eager to learn about other cultures, and not imposing about his own. To be all these things means that before you go, you must learn as much as you can about another country by reading books, attending lectures and films, and even taking a language class. Fortunately, there is always much more to be learned once you get there, and here are some hints that will not only help you learn but also will make you a good traveler.

LANGUAGE. It is helpful to know the language but not necessary. In most countries (the French are the primary exception), people are flattered—and patient—if you make any attempt to learn their language, and the wise traveler goes armed with a few phrases. "Hello," "How are you," "Please," and "Thank you" in the native tongue will do a lot to smooth the way.

LOCAL CUSTOMS. Customs vary from country to country just as they do from region to region in the United States. A careful observer can usually pick up enough to get by. Do people pass each other on the left or the right? Are they extremely courteous or a little brusque? Must you close a menu in a restaurant before the waiter will come to take your order? These kinds of things are sometimes mentioned in travel guides, sometimes not. Noticing them on your own and following local custom will make you fit in much better than you might otherwise.

TIPPING. Tipping customs vary throughout the world. Before you leave, memorize the currency denominations of the country-(ies) you'll be visiting. Travel guides usually mention current tipping practices and recommended amounts. Do not attempt to translate every tip into American currency, but keep in mind that just as our small coins are used for tipping, so, too, are the small coins in any currency. A pocket calculator or currency converter is invaluable if you will have to do a lot of moneychanging while abroad.

PHOTOGRAPHY. Some people do not appreciate having their picture taken, especially by curious tourists who fail even to ask their permission. Some groups object to pictures on religious or superstitious grounds. If you do take someone's picture, do so discreetly, if possible, so they do not know it is being taken. If you cannot manage this, then ask permission. And do not be surprised—or stingy—if the person expects some small remuneration for the favor.

MANNERS. Americans have casual manners, and most Europeans and Latin Americans have slightly more formal manners, at least by our standards. They make introductions more formally; shake hands or bow more often; do not use first names as readily as we do. Men occasionally show real gallantry by kissing a woman's hand, and certainly on all occasions, men tend to display more formal manners toward women than are currently fashionable in the United States.

I think Americans abroad would do well to tailor their manners to fit in with those of their guest country. There are limits, of course, and affectations that should be avoided. I think, for example, that any American man would look and feel pretty silly kissing women's hands, but we can curb our natural spontaniety and instant intimacy.

In addition, do not ask personal questions of people you just meet. An Arab man, for example, will be offended if you ask about his wife or children. The French will argue politics with a stranger, but will be reluctant to discuss their family lives or other aspects of their personal lives with a stranger or acquaintance. In some countries, usually where there is political upheaval, politics are a taboo subject. Money is still taboo in many parts of the world as a topic of conversation. Do not ask how much things cost, regardless of how curious you are. In all these areas, Americans would do well to tailor their naturally outgoing instincts toward more discretion and formality in their manners.

In many parts of the world, you will not often be invited into someone's home. Should you be lucky enough to receive such an invitation, you should consider it an honor.

Arrive promptly when you are invited to someone's home for dinner. Dress up a little as a compliment to the hostess.

Always take a present when you go to someone's home. In Western Europe, flowers are a welcome gift. Each country has various superstitions and taboos about flowers, but you can usually play it safe by buying a multicolored bouquet. Buy an even dozen or more than a dozen, but avoid the number thirteen. Red flowers, especially red roses, are sent only by lovers in some countries, and white flowers are sometimes a sign of mourning. Remove the wrapping paper before giving the flowers as a gift (unlike here, where the wrapping paper may be left on). The gift, whether it is flowers or something else, should be presented before dinner rather than afterward to avoid the impression of having waited to see how pleasant the evening was.

In Western Europe, presents to wives and children are a way to win your host's favor, but never give a woman an intimate gift of clothing or jewelry. Perfume is also considered very personal by Europeans. In an Arab country, where one does not even mention the host's wife, one certainly does not take her a present without causing an embarrassing and possibly hostile incident.

If you will be entertained very much in any country, it is a smart idea to check with their embassy before you leave to learn more about the etiquette of visiting someone's home, gift giving, and present wrapping. You may learn something that will help you avoid a minor gaffe.

All too often, we think we can bluff our way through the kinds of situations that occur when one travels in a strange country with little knowledge of the customs, and, admittedly, good instincts do go a long way. But more often than not, we have not won the bluff. Our hosts are just too polite and tactful to let us know we have given offense—or worse, made a buffoon of ourselves. Since Americans are traveling more and becoming more sophisticated at it, I think it behooves us to fit it in as much as we possibly can and to be as sophisticated travelers as we can be. A wise traveler gives into the greater formality and even enjoys it. He polishes up his or her best manners and does everything possible to avoid causing offense when traveling abroad.

Finally, if you know that you will be spending much time with hosts in the country you are visiting, consider taking some small typically American gifts to give them. The entry on "International Business Manners" lists some of the kinds of things you might give.

Forgetting Names

SEE *Introduction; Names.*

Fork

SEE ALSO *Flatware; Place Setting; Table Manners.*

Up to six forks could conceivably be encountered during the course of an elegant, formal dinner *(see Figure 26)*. Fortunately, on an average night, you are unlikely to encounter more than two, and the vast majority of families make do with one main fork for everything.

Forks go to the left of the dinner plate, with the exception of the dessert fork, which may be placed above the dinner plate, and the oyster (or seafood) fork, which goes to the right of the spoon(s). Never are more than three forks used at one time in a place setting. If more than three forks are required for a meal, some of the forks—the dessert fork, for example—are brought in with individual courses *(see Figure 27)*.

Knowing which fork to use is relatively easy, provided the table has been set correctly. Use forks in order of their appearance, starting with the oyster fork, if one is present, and continuing with the outermost fork and working your way toward the plate. If you are not sure which fork to use, take a cue from the hostess and use whatever fork she uses.

When finished using a fork, place it on a plate so its handle does not rest on the table. If you can avoid doing so, never put used flatware on the table.

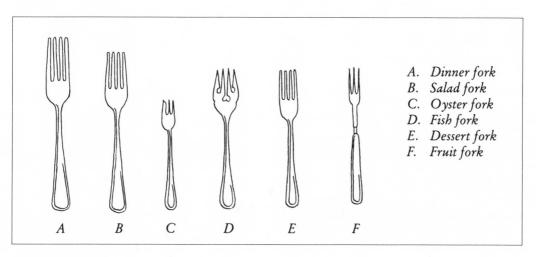

A. *Dinner fork*
B. *Salad fork*
C. *Oyster fork*
D. *Fish fork*
E. *Dessert fork*
F. *Fruit fork*

A   B   C   D   E   F

Figure 26. Forks

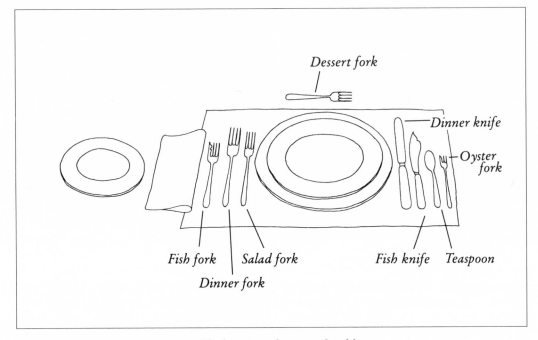

Figure 27. Correct arrangement of forks. Note that you should never use more than three forks (excluding oyster fork) at a place setting. This drawing shows placement only.

DINNER FORK. This fork, which is the largest in a place setting, goes next to the dinner plate.

The dinner fork is used for eating meat and vegetables. It is also used for eating salad, if there is no salad fork, and fish, if there is no fish fork. It is also used for transporting butter from the butter plate to vegetables or other foods on the dinner plate.

A dinner fork is held between the thumb and the first two fingers (see Figure 28). It should be held and used rather gingerly. You never want to look as if you are about to spear food with a fork.

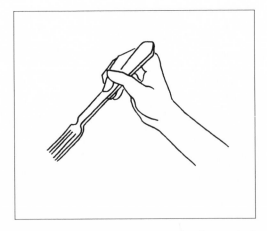

Figure 28. Correct way to hold a dinner fork

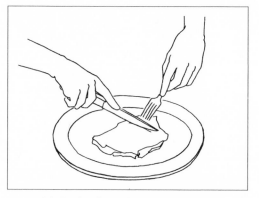

1. *Hold the knife and fork to cut meat.*

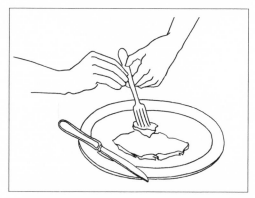

3. *Switch the fork from your left to your right hand.*

2. *Place the knife (blade toward the inside) on the plate after you have cut the food.*

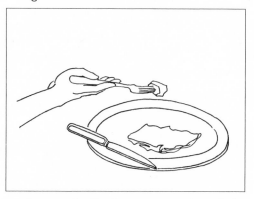

4. *Convey the food to your mouth with the fork tines up.*

Figure 29. American style of eating, for right-handed persons (left-handed persons reverse the process)

A fork may be used to eat American style *(see Figure 29)* or Continental style *(Figure 30)*. The American style of eating is most commonly used by Americans. *(See also Eating Styles.)*

When not using a dinner fork, rest it on the dinner plate, and leave it there when finished eating.

SALAD FORK. Smaller than a dinner fork, the salad fork may double as a fish, first-course, or luncheon fork. When buying place settings of flatware, these are the forks to stock up on, buying as many as two or even three per place setting if you can afford to do so. The salad fork is held the same as the dinner fork *(see Figure 28)*.

1. *After cutting the meat, continue to hold the knife and keep the fork in your left hand.*

2. *Take the food to your mouth in your left hand, with the fork tines down. You may keep the knife in your hand or return it to the plate until you are ready to use it again.*

3. *Your knife may be used to pile a small amount of food on the back of the fork's tines.*

Figure 30. Continental style of eating, for right-handed persons (left-handed persons reverse the process).

When finished eating, leave the salad fork on the salad plate.

The salad fork goes to the right of the dinner fork if the salad will follow the entree; it goes to the left if the salad will come first. If it is used for fish, as a first course, it goes to the left of the dinner fork. If it is used as a luncheon fork, it is the main fork in the place setting. If it is used as a dessert fork, it goes to the right of the dinner fork (and possibly salad fork) or above the plate.

FISH FORK. A true fish fork has broader tines than other forks, but many persons use a salad fork instead of a fish fork. The fish fork can be used, gently and with a light touch, to pick at a bite of fish to uncover bones.

Leave a fish fork on the plate when finished.

SEAFOOD FORK. This fork is used to eat oysters, clams, lobster in the shell, crab in the shell, mussels, and seafood cocktails. It is held the same way as a dinner fork. The seafood fork may be placed either to the far right or the far left in a place setting, depending on personal perference.

When finished, rest the fork on the service plate or the plate on which the seafood was served.

DESSERT FORK. A fork is used for any dessert that is not eaten with a spoon. In antique flatware, the fork has a distinctive look: It is larger than a teaspoon and slightly smaller than a dinner fork. In contemporary flatware, it is often identical to the salad fork.

The dessert fork goes nearest the plate or it may go above the dinner plate, with its handle facing to the right. Alternately, it may be brought in with the dessert plate. Then it rests across the top of the plate.

When finished, put the dessert fork on the dessert plate.

Formal Food Service.

SEE *Dinner Party.*

Formal Wedding Invitations.

SEE ALSO *Informal Wedding Invitations; Titles.*

The best and most accurate way to describe the current state of formal wedding invitations is to divide them into two categories: traditional and nontraditional. Nontraditional invitations are not to be confused with informal ones *(see separate listing).* Nontraditional invitations are variations on formal ones that have gained some acceptance and are fairly widely used today.

TRADITIONAL. These invitations, engraved, thermographed, or printed in black ink on white or ivory, paneled or non-paneled stock, are also formally worded in the third person. The invitations are printed on quality paper stock in one of two sizes. The first size, about 5½ by 7½ inches, is folded over once before insertion into an envelope. The other, smaller size, about 4½ by 5½, is not folded. Traditional, formal wedding invitations should be printed in either script or one of the block-style wedding faces such as Tiffany. A good engraver or printer can show you acceptable type samples.

If guests are being invited to the church ceremony alone, the invitation should read:

> Mr. and Mrs. William Smith
> request the honor of your presence
> at the marriage of their daughter
> Maria Elena
> to
> Mr. John Q. Smythe
> Saturday, the sixth of October,
> at four o'clock
> Church of St. John
> Bloomingdale, Indiana

Those who are invited to the reception also receive a small card, which reads:

> Reception
> immediately following the ceremony
> Bloomingdale Hills Country Club
> R.s.v.p.

If the wedding is held in the morning and the reception is several hours later, this reception card would be necessary.

The more frequently used invitation is the one that invites all guests to the ceremony and the reception:

Mr. and Mrs. William O'Reilly
request the honour of your presence
at the marriage of their daughter
Nora Jeanne
to
Mr. Michael Riley
Saturday, the fourth of June,
at ten o'clock
Church of St. Mary's
and afterward
at the Westbank Country Club
Westbank, Illinois

VARIATIONS TO FORMALLY WORDED INVITATIONS. If the wedding is held in a house of worship, the words "the honour of your presence" are used. If the wedding is held at home (see also Informal Wedding Invitations) or anywhere other than a house of worship, the wording may be changed to "the pleasure of your company."

You can use either the French abbreviation "R.S.V.P.," Répondez s'il vous plait (which translates literally as "Respond if you please") or the equally acceptable American "Please respond."

The year (spelled out) may be added to an invitation or not, as you choose.

Except for titles before names, a wedding invitation should contain no abbreviations. Note that the hour is spelled out and "o'clock" is used. "A.M." and "P.M." are not used because it is presumed that a "ten o'clock" wedding means ten A.M. since weddings do not normally begin at ten P.M., and that "eight o'clock" refers to an evening wedding.

If the bride's parents are divorced, the invitations can be issued in both their names, if they agree to do so, or they can be issued by the parent who is hosting the wedding. If the parents issue the invitations together, their names appear on separate lines regardless of whether or not either one has remarried:

Mrs. Walsh Riley
and
Mr. John Riley

Note that the use of "Mrs. Walsh Riley" is a combination of the mother's maiden name and her married name and signifies that she is divorced. If she were remarried, she would use her married name, and if she were widowed, she would use "Mrs. John Riley."

These designations apply only to the most traditional wedding invitations. On nontraditional wedding invitations, these days a mother may have chosen to retain her maiden name, may not wish to use the designation for a divorced woman, or may even have adopted some other name entirely—any of which are acceptable.

If the wedding is being hosted by someone other than the bride's parents, their names and their relationship to her (if there is a blood relationship) are given. If there is no relationship, they simply use their names. In the rare instance, for example, where the parents of the groom might be giving the wedding, the invitations would read:

> Mr. and Mrs. William Smith
> request the pleasure of your company
> at the marriage of
> Linda Sue Jones
> to
> Mr. Randolph Smith
> etc.

If the bride and groom are giving their own wedding, they may issue the invitations in their names. If they live together but wish to be discreet about it, and also because the envelope is tiny, they might include only the bride's name and address on the response card envelope.

> Marian Fox
> and
> William Harlan
> request the honour of your presence
> Saturday, the sixth of October,
> Nineteen hundred and eighty-eight
> at ten o'clock
> St. Sebastian's Church
> Layton, Louisiana

NONTRADITIONAL INVITATIONS. These are invitations to a "formal" wedding that are worded more casually than traditional ones, printed on pastel stock, or in a colored ink. They may even include a poem or saying. Unlike many etiquette experts, I don't oppose these informal invitations and even think that some of them are quite

lovely and warm. There is a point of overkill, though, when sentimentality and just plain bad taste take over. After describing two examples, I leave it to each reader individually to ponder this point and draw his or her own personal limits.

One lovely invitation I received looked and was traditional except for its wording. It read:

> Please share with us our joy
> and celebrate the marriage of our daughter
> Joan Elise Rankin
> to
> Randolph Jackson Borger
> Saturday, the fifteenth of June,
> at twelve thirty
> St. Stephen in the Fields
> Please respond   Jean and Harry Rankin
> 12 Tiverton Lane
> Forest Hills, Michigan

The second invitation featured a picture of the bridal couple's clasped hands, showing off her engagement ring. Under the photo was a sentimental poem by a bad poet. The ink was a bright pink; the paper, a pale pink.

Another nontraditional trend in wedding invitations, one that I do applaud, is the trend toward including the names of both sets of parents on the invitations. Before issuing invitations with both sets of parents' names on them, the mother of the bride or the bride should check with the groom's mother and father to see if this is acceptable to them. If they happen to be staunch traditionalists, or do not wish to convey the impression that they are paying for part of the wedding when they are not, then they may prefer that the invitations not be issued jointly. There is no obligation on either side to include both.

Having their names on the invitations does not obligate the groom's parents to pay for anything extra, nor need they assume any additional hosting responsibilities beyond what they would normally do.

Finally, I do not mean to imply by my comparison that nontraditional invitations are unacceptable, merely that they must be chosen with taste and skill.

THE ENVELOPE. In perhaps no other social correspondence does an envelope and its accoutrements carry so much weight as in the case of the wedding invitation envelope, or rather, the *two* envelopes. Wedding invitations have traditionally been inserted into two envelopes, but this custom is, fortunately, since trees are in scarce supply, on the wane. There is no reason to use two envelopes, and anyone who is ecologically oriented can comfortably limit himself or herself to one without committing any breach of manners.

Also on the road to extinction is the tissue that was traditionally used to cover engraved ink and thus prevent it from smearing. Today's engraving and printing techniques have improved to the point where the tissue is no longer a necessity, and since it, too, is made from trees, omitting it also falls in the realm of a good ecological deed.

If you do use two envelopes, the procedure for inserting the invitations is as follows: On the outer envelope, write the complete address of the guest. No abbreviations should be used, and the names of every person who is invited should be included. For example, if a couple's children are included in the invitation, their names should be listed on separate lines. Conversely, if their names are not on the invitation, the receiver should assume that children are not invited. Children over the age of eighteen should receive a separate invitation. If there are too many children to list separately, it is acceptable to write "Mr. and Mrs. John Smythe and Family."

On the inside envelope, write, again without using abbreviations, the names of those invited. An alternate method when inviting children is to address the outer envelope to the couple and then to list the children separately on the inside envelope.

Invitations are inserted fold first or, lacking a fold, with the printing toward the flap. A nonfolded invitation is inserted with the printing up.

The second envelope is inserted with its flap toward the outer envelope's flap *(see Figure 31)*.

Wedding invitations are always sealed and mailed first class.

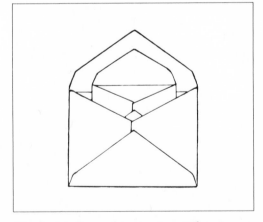

Figure 31. Formal invitation. When inserting the second envelope, both flaps should be at the top.

ENCLOSURES. Several possible enclosures may be required with a wedding invitation. With one exception *(see Canceled Wedding)* nothing should ever be written on the invitation itself, as it is a memento, but you may enclose response cards, pew cards, at-home cards, and maps and other directions to the wedding and/or reception. With the exception of maps and directions, which may be photocopied or instant-printed, enclosures should match the invitation.

RESPONSE CARDS. These used to be considered an insult, since a well-mannered guest always responded to a formal invitation. Experience has shown that even the best-bred guest does not always respond these days, and since weddings are expensive, it has become acceptable and sometimes even imperative to prod one's guests a little.

Not surprisingly, an etiquette has sprung up around response cards. To be polite, a response card must come with its own envelope, which should be printed on the front with a return address. It should be stamped. To preserve your guest list, I suggest using the following wording:

> _____accepts
> _____regrets
> May 6, 1987

The date listed should be the date of your wedding, not a deadline by which guests must respond. To issue a deadline *is* to insult your guests and should be used only in extraordinary circumstances, when, for example, the caterer has set an unusually early deadline for ordering the food.

If you use the alternate method and print "Number of guests," people will assume you are including the entire family. The above format makes it clearer that only those listed on the invitation are invited.

PEW CARDS. These are issued to close family members and friends to ensure that they are seated "within the ribbons" or in a front pew for the ceremony. Several pews are marked off with ribbons, thus reserving them for those with pew cards. A pew card can read "Pew number _____" (you fill in the number), or "Within the ribbons," the latter being an old-fashioned but lovely way of printing a pew card.

AT-HOME CARDS. These enclosures announce the address of your new home and when you will be at home to guests. They are not used by couples who have been living together before the wedding. An at-home card should read:

> Mr. and Mrs. John Jacobs
> will be at home
> after the sixteenth of July
> 20 Roundtree Lane
> Seattle, Washington 98100

Forms of Address—Spoken

FAMILY. *Aunts and Uncles.* In most families aunts and uncles, especially if they are a generation older than their nieces and nephews, are called "aunt" and "uncle," and these titles are usually combined with their fore-names, for example, "Aunt Susie," "Uncle Bill." If the two generations are close in age, as happens in some families, the titles are often dropped.

When aunts and uncles are introduced by their nieces and nephews, the relationship is mentioned and their surnames are used. If they are introduced to someone much younger, it is proper to say, "Aunt Lila, I'd like you to meet my friend Jane. Jane, this is my aunt, Mrs. Williams." If the two being introduced are close in age, it would be more appropriate to say, "Jane, I'd like you to meet my aunt, Lila Williams." (And of course, because of the similarity in ages, the introductions could be reversed: "Lila, this is Jane. Jane, my Aunt Lila.") You need not go into any detail about familial relationships other than to identify them briefly when making an introduction, but a good reason to mention them is that they provide immediate small talk.

Cousins. Except among old people and in certain parts of the country where the custom prevails, cousins are no longer addressed as Cousin Mary or Cousin Jack, but are simply called by their forenames.

When introducing a cousin, the same rules apply as for other introductions. If the cousin is much older than the other person, then people are presented to him or her. There is no particular reason to mention a cousin relationship, although you may, of course, if you choose to do so.

Grandparents. Every family has its own customs about what to call grandparents, and these are usually passed down from generation to generation. In one family I know, where the paternal grandparents immigrated from Germany, and the other set are American-born, the paternal grandparents are called *Oma* and *Opa,* the German equivalents of "Grandmother" and "Grandfather," and the others are called the familiar American "Grandma" and "Grandpa." In some families the titles are used with surnames, for example, Grandma Smith or Grandpa Jones, and in other families forenames are used, as in Grandma Sara. Many families use names of ethnic origin or family nicknames. Whatever the grandparents and parents work out is fine. Actually, to be completely realistic about this, it is not always the parents and grandparents who work this out, as many grandparents have been dubbed whatever their small grandchildren are able to pronounce.

Grandparents are always introduced using their surnames, and invariably people are presented to them as a sign of respect: "Grandmother, I'd like you to meet Jennifer. Jennifer, this is my grandmother, Mrs. Anderson." *In-Laws.* What to call in-laws is a somewhat touchy situation in some families, and far too many people fail to confront the subject and end up calling their in-laws nothing, which is only slightly better than "Hey, you."

The best time to work out what each will call the other's parents is shortly after marriage. Since the parents are older and perhaps more experienced in these matters, it is really up to them to take the initiative in discussing this, but it really does not matter who initiates the conversation as long as the matter gets settled.

Some adults feel awkward calling their spouse's parents "Mother" or "Father," having long since reserved those names for their own parents. Although "Mother-in-law" and "Father-in-law" were used until about the turn of the century, they sound stilted today and have taken on a pejorative tone as well. The style today seems to be to call parents-in-law by their forenames, especially if they are young.

All relatives other than parents-in-law are called whatever the spouse calls them, unless the person requests something else. One very tactful grandmother-in-law, who knew that her new granddaughter-in-law had been very close with her now-deceased grandmother, recognized that it might be awkward for this young woman to call her "Grandma." Many of her nieces and nephews called her "Mrs. M.," so she suggested to the new granddaughter-in-law that she, too, might feel comfortable with this nickname. The granddaughter-in-law was delighted.

When introducing in-laws, mention of the relationship is usually made: "Mother, I'd like you to meet Sandy. Sandy, this is Mrs. Johnson, my mother-in-law."

Technically speaking, your sister or brother's spouse is related to you only and is not an in-law to your spouse, but out of courtesy, this fine line is rarely drawn. You may introduce your sister-in-law's husband (or your brother-in-law's wife) by saying either, "I'd like to meet Eleanor, my sister-in-law," or "I'd like you to meet my brother's wife, Eleanor."

When you are divorced or widowed, your in-laws become your ex-in-laws, although it is a matter of judgment whether you announce this fact when you introduce them. If you are making a quick introduction, it is usually not necessary to say anything. If it becomes necessary to say something, keep it as simple as possible: "Mary, I'd like you to meet Diane. Diane was married to my son." There is no need to mention divorce if that is the reason you are ex-in-laws, and if death is the reason, simply say, "Diane is my son's widow. She is now married to John Summers."

Nieces and Nephews. Nieces and nephews are invariably called by their forenames and are introduced based on their age and status. The relationship is usually mentioned when the introductions are made.

Parents. When children are very young, parents are called by familiar names: "Mommy," "Mama," "Daddy," "Papa," etc. As children grow older, they naturally switch from these familiar titles to something more adult: "Mother," "Father," "Mom," "Dad." I find it something akin to talking baby talk to hear adult children routinely refer to their parents as "Mommy" and "Daddy."

As a sign of respect, a child always introduces others to his parents. The exception to this is when the person being introduced has some special status or authority, such as a mayor, a judge, or a clergyperson.

Parents always used to be introduced by their surnames ("Mother, may I introduce Judith, Judith, this is my mother, Mrs. Riley"), but in today's more casual world, they are sometimes introduced by both their names ("Mother, this is Judith. Judith, I'd like you to meet my mother, Elizabeth Riley"). Do whatever flatters your parent.

Siblings. Sisters and brothers call each other by their forenames, and it would be silly not to mention the relationship when making introductions. The same general rules for making any introductions apply to siblings, that is, if a sibling is much older than you, as a sign of respect, introduce others to him or her.

Spouses. Long gone are the days when a woman referred to her husband as "Mr. Jones." Spouses, of course, always call each other by their first names, and the only problems that arise are what spouses call each other in the presence of others.

One newly married friend of mine complained that he was using "we" too much. While he loved being married, he said, he hated to think he was giving up the "me" in himself. He wanted to use both, and asked me how most people worked this out. Once I started thinking about it, I realized that these days it varies with the generation. People who married in the Forties and Fifties and before do tend to think of themselves almost exclusively as "we." The "younger" generation, exposed to the self-realization movement of the Sixties, is more eager to hang on to "I" and "me" even in marriage. This should only give one pause when the intention is to somehow exclude one's spouse rather than promoting one's own sense of identity.

One thing I do know: It is always polite to identify your spouse by saying "my husband" or "my wife." This is a courtesy not only to your mate but also to others who will want to know who your mate is. And it is never polite to refer to your partner in such condescending themes as "the better half" or "the little woman." Even terms that are well-intended but diminutive are unacceptable.

In introducing a spouse, when a married couple has the same last name, most people say, "This is Georgia, my wife," or "Have you met Alec, my husband?" When a husband and wife have different surnames, they must be mentioned when making any introductions: "This is Georgia Jackson, my wife," or "Have you met Alec Rivers, my husband?"

Stepparent. Only a generation or so ago, a stepparent was someone who married one's parent after another parent had died. Today, because of divorce and remarriage,

"stepparent" has come to be used to describe any person to whom one's biological parent is married. Children even refer to the children of the "stepparent" as their stepbrothers and sisters. Since these new relationships exist with much greater frequency then they did a few decades ago, I approve of the changing use of the words, "stepparent" or "step-sibling" to encompass new family members.

Apart from describing the relationships, in practice, stepparents are almost invariably called by their forenames, unless the children have grown up in their home, had little contact with their biological parents, and think of the stepparent as the "real" parent.

While it may seem of little consequence to work out what a stepparent will be called when a child is suffering the loss of a real parent or going through a divorce, establishing titles and deciding what to call someone is part of the healing and acceptance process, and it is important to the continuity of family life. The issue of names can remain on hold for a short time, while children heal, but eventually, in an effort to complete the healing process, I think it is necessary to deal with names and who is called what in a reconstituted family.

Stepparents should be introduced in the same manner that parents are, that is, people should be presented to them as a sign of respect. It is a matter of your personal judgment whether you choose to mention the step-relationship. If a woman has acted as your mother for many years, and you feel comfortable doing so, simply say, "Mother, I'd like you to meet Sally." If it is obvious that this is not your biological mother, you might choose to clarify matters by saying, "Mother, this is Sally. Sally, this is my stepmother, Mrs. Riley." No one should ever feel uncomfortable mentioning the relationship, nor should anyone feel uncomfortable not mentioning it. Such things remain essentially personal.

NONFAMILIAL. *Distinguished Persons.* You will on occasion find yourself in the company of someone who fits into this category by virtue of being your town's mayor, a judge, or some other dignitary. If you are both adults, do not call this person "sir" or "ma'am" unless he or she is very elderly. Unless you are a good friend and/or relations are very casual in your community, you are expected to call him by his official title rather than his name alone: "Mayor Smith," "Judge Manor." And even if you are good friends, as a courtesy, in the presence of others and certainly when making introductions, use the person's official title and surname.

Beyond these obvious titles of respect, it is considered polite to refer to anyone whose job gives him a title by his title and his surname. A policeman or woman is thus "Officer Smith" or "Sergeant Smith."
Family Friends. Family friends used to be bequeathed with the honorary titles of "Aunt" and "Uncle." The use of these titles has diminished, however, and today most children call close family friends by their first names or by some special nickname the friend has suggested.
Live-In Lovers. Far too much has been made over what to call a live-in lover. As an etiquette expert, I could sit down and think of a title and then dictate it to my readers, but I am well aware that such attempts to railroad etiquette invariably fail. People who cannot stand the use of "Ms." for "Miss" and "Mrs." will never use it, for

example, and people who prefer it will use it regardless of what etiquette experts say. As of this writing, no acceptable terms for live-in partners have been devised. "Lover," as in "I would like you to meet my lover," has gained a foothold, particularly among gays, but I think it is too intimate and revealing to become a permanent fixture in our society.

In fact, I am not sure why we need a title for live-in lovers and I tend to favor discretion in these matters, not because I disapprove, but just because I think there isn't enough discretion in the world. The simplest solution, then, at least to my way of thinking, is to introduce a live-in mate by saying, "Mary, I'd like you to meet John."

If you and Mary are good enough friends, you will probably feel comfortable at some point disclosing to her that you and John are more than platonic friends, that you do, in fact, live with each other.

If you and Mary are not good enough friends, or there is some reason you are not particularly interested in her knowing about your living arrangements, then simply say, "John and I go together." Romantic relationships, like marriage relationships, should be clarified because it is more comfortable for everyone involved to know who belongs together, but announcing your relationship never means you have to describe all the details of it.

Forms of Address—Written

You may have occasion to write to persons of official importance, and there is an etiquette to using their titles both in writing and in speaking. The list that follows shows how to address dignitaries when writing to them and when meeting them.

THE PRESIDENT

Address: The President
The White House
Washington, D.C. 20500

Letter opening Dear Mr. President:
or Mr. President:

Closing: Respectfully,

Speak of him as: the President

Call him: Mr. President
or Sir

Introduce people to him as: "Mr. President, may I present . . ."

Say: "How do you do, Mr. President."

FORMER PRESIDENT A former president of the United States is addressed as "Mr. President" for the rest of his life. See suggestions under "The President."

THE PRESIDENT'S WIFE

Address: Mrs. John Adams
The White House
Washington, D.C. 20500

Letter opening: Dear Mrs. Adams:

Closing: Sincerely,

Speak of her as: Mrs. Adams

Call her: Mrs. Adams

Introduce people to her as: "Mrs. Adams, may I present . . ."
Say: "How do you do, Mrs. Adams."

To address them both The President and Mrs. Adams

UNITED STATES AND STATE SENATORS

Address: The Honorable James A. Michaels
United States Senate
Washington, D.C. 20510
or The Honorable John J. Carlson
State Capitol
Springfield, IL 31610

Letter opening: Dear Senator Michaels:

Closing: Respectfully,

Speak of him as: the Senator
or Senator Michaels

Call him: Senator Michaels

Introduce people to him as: "Senator Michaels, may I present . . ."

Say: "How do you do, Senator Michaels,"
or "How do you do, Senator."

*To address
Senator
Michaels
and his wife:* The Honorable James A.
Michaels and Mrs.
Michaels

MEMBERS OF CONGRESS
OR
STATE LEGISLATURE

Address: The Honorable
Elizabeth A. Scott
House of Representatives
Washington, D.C. 20515
or The Honorable
John A. O'Reilly
State Capitol
Des Moines, IA 50300

*Letter
opening:* Ms. Scott:

Closing: Respectfully,

*Speak of
her as:* Ms. Scott

Call her: Ms. Scott

*Introduce
people to
her as:* "Ms. Scott, may I
present . . ."

Say: "How do you do, Ms.
Scott."

*To address
Ms. Scott
and her
husband:* The Honorable Elizabeth
A. Scott and Mr. Scott

THE CHIEF JUSTICE OF THE
SUPREME COURT AND
ASSOCIATE JUSTICES

Address: The Chief Justice
The Supreme Court
Washington, D.C. 20543
or Associate Justice, Henry
Blackmun

*Letter
opening:* Dear Chief Justice:
Dear Mr. Justice (for
associates):

Closing: Sincerely yours,

*Speak of
him as:* Mr. Chief Justice *or*
Mr. Justice
or Mr. Warren

Call him: Mr. Warren
or Mr. Chief Justice *or*
Mr. Justice

*Introduce
people to
him as:* "Mr. Chief Justice (or
Mr. Justice)
may I present . . ."
or "Mr. Warren, may
I present . . ."

Say: "How do you do, Sir,"
or "How do you do, Mr.
Chief Justice."

*To address
the Chief
Justice
and his wife:* Chief Justice and
Mrs. Warren
or Mr. Justice Harry
Blackmun and Mrs.
Blackmun

HEAD OF STATE AND OTHER HIGH DIGNATARIES.

Follow the format for the President of the United States, only use the correct title, e.g., Prime Minister

AMBASSADOR

Address: Mr. Ambassador
or Mr. Lee Wong
Chinese Embassy
street address
city, state, zip

Letter opening: Dear Mr. (or Miss, Ms., Mrs.) Ambassador
or Mr. (or Miss, Ms., Mrs.) Ambassador

Closing: Respectfully,

Speak of him or her as: Mr. Ambassador

Call him: Mr. Ambassador

Introduce people to him as: Ambassador Wong

Say: "How do you do, Mr. Ambassador."

GOVERNORS

Address: The Honorable Carol E. Neely
Governor of California
The Governor's Mansion
Sacramento, CA 95800

Letter opening: Dear Governor Neely:

Closing: Respectfully,

Speak of her as: the Governor

Call her: Governor Neely
or Madam (Sir)

Introduce people to her as: "Governor Neely, may I present . . ."

Say: "How do you do, Governor Neely."

To address the Governor and her husband: The Honorable Carol E. Neely and Mr. Neely

THE MAYOR

Address: The Honorable David Lindbeck
Mayor of Kewanee
City Hall
Kewanee, IL 61443

Letter opening: Dear Mayor Lindbeck:

Closing: Respectfully,

Speak of him as: the Mayor or Mayor Lindbeck

Call him: Mayor Lindbeck
or Sir (Madam)

Introduce people to him as: "Mayor Lindbeck, may I present . . ."

Say: "How do you do, Mr. Mayor," *or* "How do you do, Mayor Lindbeck."

To address the Mayor and his wife: The Honorable David Lindbeck and Mrs. Lindbeck

MINISTER

Address: The Reverend Susan George

or The Reverend Dr. Susan George

Letter opening: Dear Miss (Ms. or Mrs.) George:

or Dear Dr. George:

Closing: Sincerely,

Speak of her as: Miss (Ms. or Mrs.) (*or* Dr.) George

Call her: Miss (Ms. or Mrs.) (*or* Dr.) George

Introduce people to her as: "Dr. George, may I present . . ."

To address a clergyperson and spouse: The Reverend Susan George and Mr. George

or The Right Reverend Susan George and Mr. George

PRIEST

Address: The Reverend Daniel W. Williams (*or* other initials indicating his order, if he belongs to one) Pastor, St. Peter's Church Chicago, IL 60657

Letter opening: Dear Father Williams:

Closing: Sincerely,

Speak of him as: Father Williams

Call him: Father Williams

Introduce people to him as: "Father Williams, may I present . . ."

Say: "How do you do, Father Williams," *or* "How do you do, Father."

RABBI

Address: Rabbi David (*or* Judith) Rosenberg

Letter opening: Dear Rabbi Rosenberg:

Closing: Sincerely,

Speak of him or her as: Rabbi Rosenberg

Call him or her: Rabbi Rosenberg

Introduce people to him or her as: "Rabbi Rosenberg, may I present . . ."

Say: "How do you do,
   Rabbi Rosenberg," *or*
   "How do you do,
   Rabbi."

French Fries

French fries are finger food only under casual circumstances. Most of the time, use a fork to cut each fry into bite-sized pieces, and eat it with the fork. It catsup is used, put it on the side of the plate; never pour it directly over the fries. Pour out only a little catsup, and replenish your supply as necessary.

French Restaurants

SEE *Eating in Europe; Foreign Restaurant*

Fruit

Fruit is the ultimate finger food, at least in the United States. Europeans cut up their fruit and sometimes even eat it with a fork. At most, you are liable to encounter a fruit knife in the United States. If you do, use it to cut a piece of fruit into halves or quarters, remove the core, pit, or seeds, and then eat it, using your fingers.

APPLES. Quarter with a knife, cut out the core, and eat with your fingers.

AVOCADO. If half an avocado is served filled with dressing, use a spoon to scoop out the fruit. If served with other fillings, use a fork, usually a salad fork.

BANANA. At formal dinners, peel completely, put on plate, and cut in bite-sized pieces with fork. Informally, you may peel halfway and eat; then peel remaining half and eat.

BLUEBERRIES. Since they have no seeds, simply eat them with a spoon or your fingers, the latter being the more casual method.

CHERRIES. If not served in syrup, pick them up with your fingers and pop in mouth. Remove the pit discreetly by dropping it into your slightly closed fist and replacing it on your service plate. If cherries are served with a syrup, eat them with a dessert spoon and remove the pit to the spoon and then to the service plate.

FIGS AND DATES. See Peaches.

FRUIT AND CHEESE PLATE. Pieces of hard cheese may be picked up and eaten with your fingers, as may be pieces of fruit that are too small to be cut gracefully with a fork. You also may cut all the fruit and cheese into bite-sized pieces and eat it with a fork. If bread or crackers are served, the cheese may be spread on it. At a casual dinner, you may spread cheese on pieces of fruit.

FRUIT COMPOTE/STEWED FRUIT. Use a dessert spoon. Neither eat nor drink the liquid that remains in the bottom of the dish. Drop the pits on spoon and place them on service plate.

GRAPEFRUIT. This is eaten with a spoon. The seeds may be returned to the spoon and placed on a service plate.

GRAPES. Put the whole grape in your mouth. Remove the seeds by making a small fist at your mouth into which you drop the seeds. Put seeds on a service plate. If you do not want to eat the skin, you may press the stem end against your teeth, and gently suck the pulp into your mouth. Put the skin on the service plate or to the side of the dinner or dessert plate. Grapes that are part of a salad are eaten with a fork, and the seeds are removed as just described.

MANGO. There are two ways to eat a mango. You may cut it in half and eat it out of the skin with a spoon, or you may quarter it lengthwise, lay it out flat in sections (flesh side down), and pull away the skins with your fingers. Cut the fruit into pieces and eat with a fork.

MELON. Use a spoon to eat a melon wedge. For melon balls or cut-up pieces, use a fork. Use a fork to pick seeds out of watermelon—as much as possible—before you eat it.

ORANGE. Peel it with sharp knife and eat in sections. Use a fork or your fingers.

PAPAYA. Usually served halved. Scoop out flesh with spoon.

PEACHES. Cut it in half, remove the stone, and use your fingers to eat it.

PEARS. See Peaches.

PERSIMMON. Place it upright, stem down, and cut it into quarters. Then eat it in small bites. Or cut it in half horizontally and scoop out with a fork.

PINEAPPLE. Eat with fork and knife. It may be resting on the skin, but it should have been cut away from it in the kitchen. If this has not been done, ask your waiter to do it for you.

PLUMS. See Peaches.

POMEGRANATE. Cut it in half, hold it in your hand, and pick out the seeds with spoon. Put them on the service plate. The seeds are edible, so you can eat some of them if you choose. Eat with spoon in small bites.

TANGERINE. Use your fingers to peel it. Break it into sections and eat one section at a time with your fingers.

Fruit and Cheese

SEE *Fruit: Fruit and Cheese Plate.*

Fruit Compote/Stewed Fruit

SEE *Fruit: Fruit Compote/Stewed Fruit.*

Funeral

SEE *Christian Mourning Customs; Condolences; Death; Gravestone; Jewish Mourning Customs; Memorial Service.*

Most people in our society have some kind of funeral or memorial service these days. Such services are a comfort for the living, as well as providing them with a sense of finality that enables them to go on with their own lives. Persons without deep religious feeling often dislike the religious aspect of funerals, and, of course, the desires of the deceased must be taken into account, but some kind of service can be planned that will respect the wishes of the deceased and provide comfort to the living as well.

DRESS. Black is the traditional color of mourning; white may be worn in the summertime and in the tropics. Today, black is not required at a funeral, either by family members or friends who attend, although many people will wear it. A mourner may quite correctly choose to wear an outfit that was favored by the departed, provided of course that it is not so bright a color as to appear gay. These days, even if a widow shows up at her husband's funeral in a red dress, it is safer to assume that it was his favorite and not that she is showing any disrespect.

Friends and family members other than the chief mourners may wear any clothes that would be appropriate for a religious service. Even if the funeral is not held in a church or synagogue, hats may be worn by women at Roman Catholic services and Orthodox and some Conservative Jewish services, and yarmulkes will be worn by men at most Jewish services.

WHO ATTENDS. Anyone—friend or acquaintance or merely interested party—may attend a funeral provided it is public. When a funeral notice or obituary notes that a private service is being planned, the funeral is not open to the public, and only those who have been specifically invited may attend. Funerals of celebrities are usually private, but a memorial service that is open to anyone who chooses to attend is sometimes held at a later date.

NEWSPAPER NOTICES OF DEATH. Many people will learn of the death via the notices that appear in local newspapers. Notices should be placed in all local papers where friends and family of the departed live. For example, a person who lived in New York for the last ten years of his life, but had formerly lived in New Orleans, should have death notices in both cities' newspapers.

The notice gives the date and time of the funeral, indicates whether it is private or public, and usually specifies whether flowers or donations are preferred. It also lists the survivors.

Garnish

The best garnishes are made of edible materials. In fact, garnishes that are not edible are a little tacky, to say nothing of disappointing. Garnishes may always be eaten.

Gays

Gays have become much more open than ever before about announcing their sexual preferences, which is a boon for the unsuspecting host or hostess. When entertaining a gay friend, treat him or her like any other friend, which means inviting him to bring his partner or another date on all social occasions. Wedding and other similar invitations may be sent jointly or individually to a couple who live together. If one invitation is sent, write the names on two separate lines.

Gay couples should be treated just like any other couples.

Note, too, that "gay" has become the acceptable term to describe homosexuals (of either sex), by their own choice. To persist in using older, however nondiscriminatory, terms is to risk giving offense.

However open we have become about matters of sex, it is still impolite to ask questions or exhibit any curiosity about a friend or acquaintance's sexual behavior.

Gift

SEE ALSO *Anniversary Party; Baby; Business Gift; Debutante Ball; Farewell Party; Graduation; Host/Hostess Gift; Housewarming; Money Gift; Teacher; Visits (Sick Friend).*

A gift is a wonderful way to express affection for a friend, and I urge you to give them not only on special occasions but also on nonoccasions—simply to show love and affection, to let someone know how much he or she is appreciated. I hope that husbands and wives continue to give each other romantic presents, and that good friends of the same sex show their appreciation of one another with the occasional present.

CHOOSING. Never give a gift you do not like yourself, but always try to fit the gift to the recipient's personality rather than your own. And never, ever give someone a gift because you think it is what they should like rather than what you feel they will actually like. Do not try to upgrade a friend's taste, in other words. The gesture is never without an element of insult, and it often leaves a friend wondering why you would give her something that is so unlike her.

Gifts must also be chosen with great tact. If someone shows little interest in cooking but you think he should learn this skill, a cookbook is not an appropriate present. If a man pays little attention to his appearance, he probably would not especially appreciate a gift of clothing.

WRAPPING. Presents should be wrapped and should have a card attached. Any color paper and ribbons are acceptable in America, but not in other countries *(see Business Gifts)*. Americans also typically send pre-printed cards, but these are less acceptable in Japan, China, and Western Europe. In place of a card, it is acceptable and even preferable on certain occasions (when you cannot find the right card) to enclose a note on your informal stationery.

OPENING. Americans usually open gifts when they are presented with them *(see Business Gifts)*. The exception is a wedding, where gifts are never opened during the reception, but are opened and acknowledged at a later time.

HINTS. Friends often ask for hints about what to get as a present. Since you may not know the friend's price range, the most tactful answer is a general one. Instead of saying, "I'd love a cappuccino maker," say, "We are great coffee drinkers, and love anything having to do with coffee." The exception to this is your mother, who, when she asks you what you wants expects a direct and specific answer, and who, furthermore, will probably get you exactly what you ask for.

CEREMONIAL GIFTS. Certain kinds of occasions—graduations, weddings, ordinations, baptisms, circumcisions—call for what I like to call ceremonial gifts, something of lasting value that truly serves as a memento of the occasion. Something in sterling silver, if you can afford it, is always an excellent ceremonial gift. A new baby might be given a rattle, a spoon, or a cup. An appropriate adult ceremonial gift would be a mug, letter opener, pen, key chain, or a piece of jewelry.

PRESIDENTIAL GIFTS. Every year the President of the United States is sent thousands of presents. He never sees most of them and is not permitted to keep most of them, either.

Almost as often, he presents ceremonial gifts to persons of special merit or achievement. Such a present need not be reciprocated, nor need a thank-you note be sent.

RECIPROCATING. Around holiday time, it is easy to suffer the minor embarrassment of being given a gift for which one has planned no reciprocation. The only solution I know for this awkward situation is to keep a supply of small presents on hand to give people who show up with an unexpected present for you. Candy and other food gifts are excellent for this.

UNWANTED GIFTS. Occasionally, someone will give you a gift that is for any one of a number of reasons unwanted. It may be too expensive, too tactless, too tacky, just too utterly wrong for you. In another not-too-rare situation, a friendship has dwindled to nothing, and you would feel more comfortable stopping the gift exchange altogether. Can you do anything about these awkward situations? Sometimes.

Expensive gifts from friends are embarrassing but there is little you can do about them. One only hopes the friend can afford the present. One need never reciprocate in kind, but should always buy what can be afforded. There is one time when an expensive gift can, and should be, refused, and that is when a man gives an expensive gift to a woman, unless the man is her fiancé or husband. A woman may also refuse a gift she finds too intimate.

Tactless gifts fall into the same category as expensive gifts, but most of the time one must grit one's teeth and accept them.

As for those friends who continue gift exchanges long after the friendship has dwindled to nothing, something can be done, if you are willing to take the initiative. Say, "Molly, we put in a new kitchen last year, and I know you spent a lot on the summer house, so why don't we skip the gifts this year. I'd love a long letter from you telling me all about the family and everything that is going on in your life. That will be present enough for me." If the friend lives in the same community, it is easier to taper off the gift giving. Begin by saying, "We've both got so many expenses this time of year, I know. Why don't we just treat ourselves to a nice lunch instead of exchanging Christmas gifts?"

RETURNING/EXCHANGING. An unsuitable gift may be exchanged or returned, provided you do not always exchange or return the gifts of any one person. That is *not* tactful.

If you have returned or exchanged a gift, it is better to admit it than to pretend you still have it when you do not. Most givers are more than happy to have someone exchange a gift for exactly what they want.

Wedding gifts may always be exchanged or returned, and, in fact, should be bought with the expectation that this may be necessary. (The risk of duplicates is high.) A wedding gift should be purchased at a store that accepts returns, and the store should enclose a receipt without a price that can be used for this purpose. Only a rare couple do not receive some duplicates, and keeping them would be highly impractical.

Gift Certificate

Although it is always more flattering to give someone something that has been chosen especially for him or her, gift certificates are acceptable presents in certain circumstances. An avid reader may appreciate the pleasure of choosing a book for herself. Someone who is hard to fit in clothing may be impossible to buy clothes for. And a couple who are marrying may appreciate a gift certificate if you do not know their needs or taste. But gift certificates are not acceptable as presents for family members year after year. To rely on gift certificates in this way betrays a lack of affection toward the gift recipients. The exception, of course, is the gift giver who is too elderly or housebound to do any shopping; for persons like this, the use of gift certificate is always acceptable.

Glasses

SEE ALSO *Glassware.*

At dinner, the possible glasses at a place setting include a water goblet and one or more wineglasses, maybe a champagne and/ or a sherry glass. They are placed to the right of the place setting above the knives and spoons.

When several glasses are encountered, it is easy to know which one to use, since the host or hostess will pour either water, red wine, or white wine into the appropriate glass. At the beginning of a meal, a table should be set with the water and wineglasses that will be used.

Stemmed glasses should be held by the thumb and a couple of fingers near the base of the bowl *(see Figure 32).* The only time this might be not advised is when a very good cold wine is being served and fingers on the bowl of the glass would warm the wine. A cognac glass is cupped in one's hands, which are used to warm the liquor *(see Figure 33).*

Glassware

Glass, which has been around for 3,600 years, is the most breakable of all tableware and is also the tableware that is touched most often. Most people buy sturdier, less expensive glassware for everyday use and

Figure 32. Hold a stemmed glass by the thumb and one or two fingers near the base of the bowl.

Figure 33. Hold a cognac glass or brandy snifter in your cupped hand to warm the liqueur.

save their crystal glassware for more formal entertaining.

CRYSTAL. All crystal is glass, but not all glass is crystal. The best crystal is clearer, brighter, more sparkling than other glassware. Crystal is stronger than ordinary glass, but it is also often thinner, and because of its design it is also more susceptible to breakage. The most expensive crystal is handblown and has a high lead content.

DESIGNS ON GLASS. Glass is adaptable to a wide range of designs. The most popular are:

Cut Glass. The most formal glassware, fine cut crystal is stunning looking. It is best—and most expensive—when hand cut. Cut-glass styles range from a simple band around the top of the glass to an overall cut pattern. If you cannot afford a quality cut-glass crystal, then plain crystal is to be preferred to cheap cut glass.

Engraved/Etched. Engraved or etched glass is out of favor now. It was popular when people liked to have their family crests etched on their formal glassware. Engraved glass is, for the most part, formal, and it sometimes looks quaint to our eyes today. Some lovely etched Victorian glasses—especially liqueur glasses—can still be found in antique shops. A glass that has too much etching or engraving on it looks frosted and cheap.

Molded/Pressed. Except for some antique glass dishes, which collectors favor, molded or pressed glass is, and always was, cheap glass, and you would do better to buy cut glass if the look appeals to you.

Painted. Painted glass must be selected very carefully, or it too looks cheap. It has been unfashionable for a few decades, but it is now making a comeback, and some designers are doing some witty things with this kind of glass.

CHOOSING A PATTERN. Glassware is available in a variety of styles, designs, and prices. It is usually chosen last, after china and flatware have been selected, and care should be taken to select a pattern that complements the other tableware. If the china is trimmed with metal, for example, the glasses, if metal-rimmed, should match the china. Thick, cut-glass crystal goes well with heavy silver and china, and delicate china and silver require delicate, less decorated glassware.

Plain glassware is very much in style right now, mostly because it is so versatile. A plain crystal wineglass goes with a traditional, formal china as well as a more casual, modern pottery dish. Colored glass in wineglasses is properly used only on Rhine wineglasses, which have a pale green bowl.

Glassware is not sold in place settings. Expensive glassware is purchased by the glass, and less expensive glass is sometimes sold in sets.

A table may be set with matched and unmatched glasses, although all the glasses for one use should be identical. Most women choose identical water goblets and basic wineglasses and branch out from there.

NEEDS. It is far more difficult to predict a family's needs in glassware than in flatware and dishes. As a general rule, you need more than you think you need rather than less. To get started in crystal, most couples buy the same number of wine and water goblets as they do place settings of china. If red and white wine are frequently served at the same dinner, double the number of wineglasses is needed.

For everyday, most households of four need a minimum of eight juice glasses, eight large tumblers (for water and soft drinks), and eight highball glasses for mixed drinks. More specialized glasses—Rhine wineglasses, sherry glasses, liqueur glasses, martini glasses, champagne glasses—are most useful in a minimum number of eight *(see Figure 34)*.

CARE. Everyday glasses are dishwasher safe; crystal glasses are not because crystal is so fragile and should be washed in warm water. Ideally, good crystal glasses should be stored upright (the rims are especially fragile) so they are not touching one another and only one layer deep, that is, so it is unnecessary to reach over one glass to get to another. Breakage can also be reduced by turning every other glass upside down.

Gloves

SEE ALSO *Men's Formal Wear; Women's Formal Wear.*

Gloves, once a necessary accessory for both men and women, are now worn regularly

Figure 34. Glasses, from left to right: juice glass; large tumbler; highball or old-fashioned glass; all-purpose wineglass.

by neither. Only a few occasions remain where women are considered improperly dressed if they are not wearing gloves.

BRIDAL PARTIES. Until very recently brides and bridesmaids were not considered properly dressed unless they were wearing gloves. These are no longer required, but, depending upon the style of the dresses, many brides still opt to beglove their wedding party. If gloves will complete the outfit, they are worn. If they are not needed to complete the outfit, they are not worn. When a bride wears a long-sleeved dress, she often chooses not to wear gloves.

PRIVATE PAPAL AUDIENCE. Women are expected to wear gloves to a private papal audience.

WOMEN AT RELIGIOUS SERVICES. Gloves never were required in the sense that hats were, but the time was when no well-dressed woman set foot inside a church without wearing gloves. Many women today still choose to wear gloves to religious services.

WHITE HOUSE. At formal White House dinners, women wear long (above the elbow) gloves.

Godparent

SEE ALSO *Gift: Ceremonial.*

A godparent is an honorary position during a baptism in which one agrees to sponsor or oversee the spiritual education of a child. In practice, godparents frequently form a special relationship with the child that has little to do with actual religious practice. A godparent, contrary to what many suppose, has no legal obligation to rear the child should he lose his parents; that is the responsibility of the legal guardian.

Roman Catholics are required to have godparents, and Roman Catholics may not be godparents to children of other faiths. Male Jewish children are sometimes given godparents at the time of their bris (circumcision), although the position is honorary.

Godparents hold the infant or stand close by during the cermony. They are usually among the parents' closest friends, and they are usually, but not always, of the same or a similar faith.

Godparents should present their godchild with a special gift, often of silver or silverplate, on the occasion of his or her baptism or his bris. A typical present might be a silver mug, spoon, or bowl, and occasionally savings bonds or money are given.

If the godparents live at some distance, proxies may stand in for them at the ceremony.

Golf

Individual clubs have rules regarding the use of a golf course, but there are also some basic rules of courtesy that are observed on any course.

Men often tee off first, since their tee is further back. If men's and women's tees are the same, it does not matter who starts first. After the first hole, the person with the lowest score on the previous hole tees off first.

When someone is teeing off or making another shot, absolute silence is a must (as is absolute stillness), and other players should stand back far enough so as not to distract the player.

On the green, the person whose ball is farthest from the cup putts first. Ask if that person wants you to mark your ball if it in any way impedes completion of his or her putt. Also ask if that person would like you to tend the pin. Always avoid stepping anywhere in the line between another player's ball and the cup, and, when waiting for another person to putt, stand so that your shadow does not fall across the line of putt or across the cup.

On the fairway, the person whose ball is farthest from the hole shoots first. Always watch where your ball goes and where other players' balls go, and volunteer to help look when a ball is lost.

Slow players should let faster players play through, and all players should take care not to hold up the game. Only a few minutes should be taken to look for a lost ball, players should not take an unduly long time to make a shot, and players should leave the green as soon as they have finished the hole.

Gossip

SEE ALSO *Office Gossip.*

I cannot deny that a juicy tidbit or two is not highly enjoyable fare on occasion, but gossip also does a great deal of damage to people's lives. While I have never been of the school that considered it a major sin, I do think it is to be avoided. If at all possi-

ble, keep gossip to a minimum, and never, ever, pass on gossip that you know will be harmful to someone.

Rumors about the state of a friend or acquaintance's marriage, finances, or career are especially damaging and should be avoided at all costs.

Grace

Pay attention at the start of the meal for the moment of silence that indicates that a family says a blessing over food. Grace may be said standing or sitting. If you are seated, do not touch your napkin or any food until after grace.

Custom varies within families but grace may be said by either parent, and it is nice to let children say it, too. If a clergyperson is present, he or she has the honor of saying grace.

Graduation

SEE ALSO *Gift: Ceremonial.*

High-school and college graduations are the ones that are celebrated with the most vigor, but in some communities there is a trend toward celebrating graduations from the lower grades, too. While children should certainly be rewarded for their academic achievements, I have often felt that overplaying the minor graduations somehow diminishes the importance of the major ones. Obviously, if your child's school is planning something, your child should participate, but when the celebration is up to the parents, I suggest that the major events be high-school and college graduation.

INVITATIONS. Invitations to the graduation ceremony are usually rationed by the school, which means that only the immediate families attend. Parents then typically plan a party after the graduation for the entire family and friends. It can be as elaborate or as simple as the family's means and taste dictate. An afternoon reception is acceptable, as is a more elaborate sit-down dinner with live music and dancing afterward.

Invitations can be printed, handwritten notes, or telephoned. Some parents choose to have one party for family and adult friends and another party for the new graduate and his friends.

ANNOUNCEMENTS. Printed announcements are frequently sent for high-school and college graduations. While anyone who receives one and is fond of the new graduate should send a present, this is not obligatory. A note of congratulations should be sent, though, whenever an announcement is received.

GIFTS. Those who are invited to a graduation party and/or honored to be included as a guest at the ceremony itself are obligated to bring a present to the new graduate. Close friends and relatives who do not attend will still want to send gifts. Gifts are usually something of lasting value—stocks, bonds, or money in some families, silver or jewelry, a dictionary or some other reference book, a rare book, a case of good wine (if the recipient is old enough to drink and appreciate it), a typewriter.

Grapes

SEE *Fruit.*

Grapefruit

SEE *Fruit.*

Graveside Service

Most religions have some kind of graveside service. The clergyperson who conducts the service will advise the family regarding what is usually done.

The most elaborate graveside services are those of military personnel buried with full honors. The chaplain who helps the family plan the funeral will explain the service.

Other than that, family members usually gather at the grave for a few prayers. They may or may not stay until the body is lowered into the grave, depending upon their own preferences and their religion's practice. In some Protestant and Catholic families, often only the immediate family goes to the cemetery. At most Jewish funerals, the custom is for everyone to go, and those who go form a line that the mourners walk through as they leave the cemetery.

Catholics and Protestants often return to the gravesite in the days and weeks that follow. Jews usually do not return for one year, at which time they have an unveiling ceremony as the gravestone is erected.

In addition to religious customs, each family has its own customs about visiting the graves of the departed. Some go only on traditional holidays such as Memorial Day, Veteran's Day, Mother's Day, or Father's Day. Others go whenever they feel the need to do so.

In any event, a person who is recently bereaved should not be dissuaded from visiting the cemetery if that will give comfort.

Gravestone

The type of gravestone erected over a loved one's grave depends upon one's personal taste and, these days, the dictates of the cemetery. Gone are the days when elaborate, highly individual, carved stones—monuments to art as much as to the departed—could be erected to immortalize one's family. Most cemeteries now strive for a kind of bland uniformity, and many even go so far as to limit the kind of plants and flowers surrounding a gravestone. Some ban flowers entirely! Gone, too, unfortunately, are the colorful and sardonic epitaphs that one sometimes comes across in old cemeteries. This is history's loss as well as our own.

In most cases, the gravestone that you erect will be the only memorial to your loved one, so it should be in keeping with his or her personal desires. If the departed expressed an interest in having a military title or some other honor mentioned, this request should be honored, if possible. Familial relationships are usually described. Most often, a marriage partner is mentioned, but children may also be referred to

on the memorial stone. Some examples are as follows:

1910–1988
John Mackey
Beloved husband of
Elaine Jones Mackey

or:

1910–1988
Eleanor Washington
Beloved mother of three
Adored wife of
Herbert Washington

Although one rarely thinks clearly in times of overwhelming grief, if possible, a gravestone should not carry a sentimental message expressing undying love—such an epitaph may prove embarrassing at a later time.

Christians erect a gravestone within a few weeks. Jews erect a gravestone or marker a year after the departed's death, at a ceremony called an unveiling. Usually, family members attend, prayers are said, and wine and some light food (cookies or crackers) are served at the cemetery or at home.

Gravy

When a ladle is passed with the gravy, use it; otherwise, the gravy may be poured directly from the bowl over the food. Gravy, which is a type of sauce, should not be used indiscriminately. It is primarily intended for meat, and a little may be dribbled over potatoes, if they are not highly seasoned or already sauced.

Greek Restaurant

SEE *Eating in Europe; Foreign Restaurant.*

Greeting Cards

SEE ALSO *Business Condolence Note; Christmas Cards; Condolence Note.*

ACCEPTABILITY. While there are times when a handwritten note is more gracious, the only time that a printed gretting card is not acceptable is when offering condolences. When offering your sympathy at the death of a loved one, the message must always be personally written.

APPROPRIATENESS. Greeting cards convey a wide range of messages, ranging from the cynical and sarcastic to the cloying and sentimental. People unfortunately tend to choose a card that matches their own personality, when they should actually choose one to match the sensibilities of the recipient. A sarcastic card that doubles you over in the store could seem hurtful and even mean to the person who receives it in the mail a few days later.

Grocery Store

Polite behavior in a grocery store consists entirely of common sense, and is best ex-plained with a short list of do's and don't's:

Do let people with only one item go ahead of you at the checkout whenever possible. Do pack your own groceries if there's no one else to do it. Do be polite to the people who work there. Do pick up any items you may have dropped or knocked over and do tell the manager or a stockperson if there's been a serious or messy spill.

Don't get in an express line with more items than you are permitted. Don't bump people's unattended carts out of your way, but rather, move them aside quietly. Don't put your cart in line and then go off to finish your shopping.

Groom

SEE *Bridegroom.*

Guest

A guest in someone's home occupies a special position of honor but also must take pains to fit in with the routine of family life. For example, as a guest you will most likely be given first shot at the shared bathroom in the morning, but you might do better to turn it down if your host or hostess needs to get an early start. You may be told to help yourself to snack food, but this is hardly carte blanche to eat anything and everything in sight.

On arrival, ask about the household routine—when meals are served, for example, or when bedtime is normally—and do everything possible to fit in. You may follow your own routine to some extent, but it should not inconvenience others.

As a guest you are responsible for keeping your room tidy, especially if there is no household help. (If there is household help, you need only pick up your personal belongings.) On the day of your departure, ask your hostess if you can strip the bed. Sometimes I do not even ask, but simply remove the sheets, fold them loosely, and leave them on the bed. Similarly, you should ask what you can do with the bathroom towels you have used.

If you are a long-term guest, there are small ways that you can help out. Offer to do simple household tasks. Offer to cook dinner, which means you should shop and pay for the food yourself. Bring home flowers, wine, cheese, or other small gifts.

If you do these things and anything else that seems appropriate, your welcome will wear out far less quickly than if you do not find some ways to make yourself useful.

Guest List

Putting together a guest list is truly an art. It is obviously more of an art to select the guests for an intimate setting than for a large party, but in either case some planning and thought should go into the guest list. Consider who will get along with whom, which new acquaintances would most enjoy meeting old friends and vice versa, what special friend or friends you might want to honor. Above all, think about how the people will mesh. Every hostess hopes for scintillating conversation at her dinner table or party, but no one wants painful conflict or deep dissension. And certainly no one wants so little chemistry among her guests that they start stifling yawns soon after they arrive. The solution is a well-thought-out guest list.

Never be afraid to be a little experimental with a guest list. One made up of the same old crowd soon loses its luster. Include some new faces among the familiar ones; have a dinner for an old friend who is in town for a few days; invite a couple of fairly well-behaved people with opposing political views. Barracudas with strongly opposing views can turn a party into World War III, but intelligent people who happen to be on opposing sides can make for some fascinating conversation.

Guest Room

A guest room is a luxury these days, but if you are able to devote a room exclusively to guests, it should be equipped for their comfort. Guest-room basics include a comfortable bed, made up with attractive linens; one or more good pillows (opt for synthetic if you can only buy one, since so many people suffer from allergies); a good reading light; a night table; a radio or television; a clock; and, if possible, a comfortable chair, small sofa, or chaise longue. The room should be inviting and comfortable. A plate of bedtime snack food is an especially nice touch; fruit or chocolates go over well. Stock the bathroom with extra toothbrushes, toothpaste, soap, body lotion, shaving lotion, and other items people frequently forget when they travel.

If, like most people, guests in your home

are more likely to take over the foldout bed in the den or a child's bedroom, you can still make them feel special with a "guest basket." I fill an attractive wicker basket with some of the aforementioned amenities and necessities and leave it beside the guest's bed. All my guests seem to love it.

What you need not feel obligated to do is give a guest the master bedroom. It is acceptable that the master bedroom stay with the master and mistress, even in a small house.

Hairdresser

Hairdressers are tipped except when they are shopowners. A hairdresser who has become a friend may appreciate a gift more than a tip. Something extra is usually given for the holidays. Tip the shampoo person fifty cents to a dollar, and the hairdresser 10 percent of services rendered.

Half Brother, Half Sister

A half sibling is one who shares only one biological parent with another sibling. If you have the same father, but different mothers, you are a half sister or half brother to someone.

Hand Towels

Hand towels are small towels that are used by guests to dry their hands. Hot, damp towels are also occasionally passed to diners in restaurants, and far less often, in homes. (The damp hand towel has gone the way of the finger bowl; neither are seen much these days except in Japanese restaurants.)

When entertaining, hand towels—one per guest and some spares—should be put out for the company. I think the nicest hand towels are terrycloth, but for a very large party, where a host or hostess obviously does not have enough towels to supply one to everyone, a very good grade of paper hand towels may be used.

I have noticed a tendency on the part of my guests to ignore the guest towels and use my face towel instead. While this may seem like a way to save me a little work (laundering the towels, I suppose), towels

223

are actually quite personal, and I think a truly good guest would do better to use the towels that are put out exclusively for his or her use.

A guest towel should be used by only one person. The person who uses it should leave it unfolded so its use is clear to everyone, and a host should check the bathrooms from time to time while entertaining to put out more towels and dispose of those that have been used.

AT MEALS. Hot hand towels are presented to guests in some Japanese restaurants and in some seafood restaurants, where they are passed after eating a messy food such as lobster.

Their use, particularly in a Japanese restaurant, where they are called *oshibori*, should not be declined. After using them, return them unfolded to the tray.

Handicapped Person

Handicapped people like to be treated, as much as is possible, like everyone else. For example, if a deaf person is attending a dance, he or she can probably hear or feel the beat of the music and would enjoy being asked to dance. Handicapped persons also do not like to have their handicap ignored totally, especially if this provokes great stress in those around them. No one knows better than a person in a wheelchair that he is in a wheelchair, and for you to ignore the fact while nonverbally expressing your total awareness of it is awkward for all involved. Only rarely are handi-

capped people totally adverse to discussing or having reference made to their handicap. It is rude, however, to stare at anyone, including someone who is handicapped.

Although many handicapped people are quite self-sufficient and need little assistance, when someone obviously needs help, it should be given. A blind person waiting at a busy intersection, for example, could use some assistance crossing the street, and whoever is beside him should offer.

Be as tactful as possible when offering assistance. If you are helping someone cross a street, let him take your arm and walk across the street with you rather than your grabbing his arm and guiding him across the street.

Finally, unless mental retardation is someone's handicap, his intelligence and feelings should be assumed to be unimpaired. Blind people, deaf people, spastics, paraplegics—all are just as intelligent and feeling as anyone else.

Handshake

SEE ALSO *Kissing; Street Manners.*

A handshake is an ancient, congenial greeting among strangers and friends alike.

AMERICANS VS. EUROPEANS. Americans shake hands less than Europeans do. The French, for example, always greet friends, even those whom they see regularly, with a handshake and frequently shake hands again when they depart. Americans tend to shake hands with friends whom they see infrequently, and are less likely to shake hands with close friends whom they see regularly.

CHILDREN. Children as young as four or five can be taught to shake hands gracefully; this is a charming gesture in a child, and they seem to enjoy it, too.

HOW TO. Unless you are infirm or otherwise incapacitated, always stand to shake hands. Remove the glove of your right hand if wearing one. Look the person in the eye, smile, and extend your right arm. Even left-handed persons shake hands with their right hands. Your handshake should be firm. No one likes to shake hands with a limp rag, nor should your grip be bone-crushing or overlong. Lean slightly toward the other person from the waist when shaking hands. The bow may be more defined when you are introduced to someone who is very elderly or a person with a great deal of authority, such as a head of state or a high-ranking clergyman.

MEN AND WOMEN. Men probably still shake hands more frequently than women do, but this custom is changing rapidly. In addition, a man used to have to wait for a women to extend her hand to him, but today, men generally assume a woman will want to shake hands with them and don't hesitate to initiate the gesture. This is particularly the case among young people. It is an insult for a woman—or anyone else—to ignore an extended hand.

Occasionally a man will offer a limp or fingertip-only handshake to a woman (and then there are those people who just do not seem to be able to manage a very enthusiastic handshake under any circumstances). I think a good solution for these situations is to slip your hand firmly into the other person's and give them a proper handshake. Maybe if they get enough of these, they will get the picture.

DECLINING TO SHAKE HANDS. There are times when a handshake is inappropriate. A handicapped person may offer the other hand or decline to shake hands. If the reason that one cannot shake hands is obvious, no explanation need be given. If it is not so obvious, an explanation may, but need not, be offered, unless of course the other person extends a hand and would feel hurt if something was not said. Arthritis, for example, can make shaking hands too painful to undertake. Simply say, "I'm sorry I can't shake hands; I've got a touch of arthritis."

Other times to beg off shaking hands are in very cold weather, when you have a cold or some other illness, or when your hands are dirty.

Hat

SEE ALSO *Religious Services: Dress.*

For a long time, a lady never appeared at certain social functions without a hat, and hats were required for attendance at some religious services. A well-dressed gentlemen also owned several hats. Nowadays, hats are *de rigueur* almost nowhere.

More and more men keep their hats on when greeting friends, and even in elevators. Women, of course, have always kept on their hats and should continue to do so with one exception: A woman should be prepared to remove a large hat at the theater or any public performance since it may block the view of those sitting directly behind her.

Heirloom

The precious belongings that have been handed down in a family do not, in a sense, belong entirely to the user; they belong, in a larger sense, to the family.

If you have been bequeathed heirlooms as a result of your marriage, make every attempt to be sure those items stay in your spouse's family when you die. If you have children, they should go to them. If you do not, your will should stipulate that your spouse's heirlooms be returned to his family.

Persons who have many heirlooms to dispose of do everyone a favor by having a carefully drawn up will that indicates the dispensation of their belongings. It is, I believe, the ultimate discourtesy to die intestate, thereby setting up your relatives to bicker over your belongings.

Hiring

SEE ALSO *Firing.*

Once a firm offer has been made and accepted, everyone stops negotiating and begins laying the groundwork for what all concerned hope will be a pleasant relationship. When you have made a firm offer, and

that offer has been accepted, an exchange of pleasantries should follow. Either of you may initiate it. The boss should tell the prospective employee how happy the company is to have him or her join them, how delighted they are with his qualifications, and what high hopes they have for his or her future with the company. The new employee, in turn, should remark on how delighted he is to join the team.

On the managerial and executive levels, the boss often arranges a small congratulatory lunch the day the job offer is accepted or on the new employee's first day or even before he comes to work, if this can be arranged. Especially congenial and helpful is to ask along some of the new employee's colleagues so they can begin to get acquainted. This is, of course, an expense-account lunch, and the prospective employee should neither expect nor offer to pay for the meal. If the boss and the colleagues do happen to divide the tab, the new employee should offer to pay for his share, but should also expect that this offer will be rejected and should accept the "gift" luncheon graciously.

WHEN THE DECISION IS NOT TO HIRE. If you decide that a certain interviewee is not what you are seeking after all, you owe it to the person to tell him or her yourself. Techniques such as suddenly becoming unavailable or leaving the talks dangling indefinitely or saying that your company won't be hiring right now after all, when you know you intend to hire someone else, are cowardly and rude.

Telephone the person or invite him or her to your office to say that you have decided not to offer the job. Avoid going into details that might hurt the person's ego unnecessarily, but give as honest an answer as you can. Instead of saying, "I don't think your personality will work in our company," you might say, "I feel that you might find yourself in conflict with the person for whom you would have to work. You are very different persons, with different management techniques, and would clash sooner or later. Your management techniques are excellent, but I would rather see you put them to work somewhere where they will be truly appreciated. Because of this, I have decided not to offer you this position. I hope you will understand."

If the person is obviously under- or overqualified, this is one of the easiest things of all to explain and hurts no one's feelings.

Hispanic

Persons of Latin American extraction today often refer to themselves as "Hispanic," although in some parts of the country the preferred term is "Latin" or "Latino." Considerate friends will use the term indicated as preferred.

Home

SEE ALSO *Household.*

A home is not a house. A house is the basic structure in which a home is created, but a home is a state of mind. The hospitable home is organized in a way that is comfortable and considerate for both family members and guests.

Consideration means many things, some of which are so little that they are noticed only in their absence. Outside, it is a house that is easily identifiable, with a well-lit entryway, steps that are secure, a welcome mat on which to wipe one's feet. Inside, consideration consists of carpets that one does not trip over, chairs that are not wobbly, tables that comfortably fit whatever number is seated at them (the exception is large holiday meals, when one somehow fits in as many as one must). Comfort is enough large, fluffy towels, hard beds, soft bed linens, good pillows, a temperature that is neither too hot nor too cold, with no draughts.

Not surprisingly, the decor of a house has much to do with how pleasant a home it is. The best homes are lovely visually but never overdecorated. Sometimes they are beautiful, witty, or amusing. Furniture may be shabby of slightly worn, but it must never be dirty.

Your home decor must also suit your personality. The "lived-in" look that so many people joke about is fine if that is what suits your family. It is more important, if you are the casual type, not to have a home so formal that you cannot relax in it, nor, for that matter, should you feel compelled to have an utterly casual home if you really prefer a little formality.

This only becomes a problem when a decorator is brought in to decorate a house. Then, the people living there must take care to communicate their likes and dislikes, their tastes and preferences, so that the home that emerges is the owners' and not the decorator's. One should never be in awe of one's possessions, but should enjoy them and live comfortably among them.

Home Wedding

Some of the loveliest weddings are small, quiet ones held at home or in a garden. If the bride's parents have a home or garden that can accommodate such a wedding, this would obviously be the first choice. If an aunt or grandmother has a home that is better equipped to handle a wedding or has a particularly lovely garden, the wedding could be held there. The fact that a wedding is held in a home other than that of the parents of bride does not change their role as hostess and host.

A home wedding, particularly one that will be held in a garden, should be scheduled for daylight hours. One does not schedule a raindate for an outdoor wedding, but instead moves the wedding indoors when the weather does not cooperate. Therefore, when considering a setting for a home wedding, this possible event must be taken into account.

Most home weddings are simple affairs, deceptively simple, in fact. Many a bride and her mother, justifiably concerned about keeping down costs, have overestimated the share of work that they can—or realistically should—take on in terms of organizing the home wedding. Although there are usually few enough guests so the food can be prepared by the bride's mother or the bride, weddings have a way of becoming more hectic than anyone ever thinks they will be, and the bride and her mother should seriously consider hiring a caterer rather than preparing the food themselves.

The logistics of the home or garden wedding must be worked out so that the ceremony can be held in one place and the food and beverages served in another. A lovely spot in a garden is the obvious backdrop for a home wedding, but an indoor setting can also be created with flowers or potted plants and a curtain or drape of some kind. The guests usually stand during a home ceremony, but chairs should be provided for elderly guests who may need them.

GUEST LIST. Unless the house is very large, the guest list at a home wedding is necessarily limited to immediate family and a few close friends. People are invited informally, either by telephone, handwritten note, telegram, or day letter, if there is time.

DRESS. The bride can wear a traditional wedding dress and veil if the wedding is formal, or she can wear street clothes if the wedding is informal. Even though women do not normally wear hats in their own homes, the bride may wear a hat and/or veil for her wedding. Her mother does not wear a hat. Nor do the bride and her mother wear gloves.

Guests wear clothes that would be suitable for any religious service.

FLOWERS. The loveliest flowers at a home wedding are those that look natural. Fill large and small vases with flowers that look as if they have just been picked from someone's garden, and no one could ask for a prettier display.

FOOD AND BEVERAGES. Food at a home wedding is usually served buffet style, but some houses are large enough to accommodate a sit-down breakfast or luncheon.

Keep in mind that the intimacy of a home is part of the charm of a home wedding, and nothing should be done to detract from that, either in the food served or the manner in which it is served.

MUSIC. If there is room to have musicians, a single musician or as many as a quartet are lovely. (If the wedding is outside or the house is large enough, an entire band could be hired if desired.) An excellent alternative for any small wedding is taped music.

Homosexual

SEE *Gays.*

Honeymoon

SEE *Wedding Trip.*

Hors D'Oeuvres

SEE *Appetizer.*

Host/Hostess

SEE ALSO *Business Entertaining; Single Entertaining.*

A host and/or hostess have certain responsibilities toward their guests, the most important of which is to ensure that their guests enjoy themselves while accepting their hospitality. More specific responsibilities vary depending upon the type of entertainment, but in general a host and hostess should make sure that every guest is introduced to others, settled in comfortably after arrival, and given food when it is served.

The best host/hostess is one who is relaxed and self-confident and—most important—able to enjoy his or her guests. A shortcoming of too many hosts/hostesses is to spend every minute providing food and services to his or her guests and never to sit down and enjoy their company.

Host/Hostess Gift

SEE ALSO *Business Gift; Gift.*

A small present should be taken to the host or hostess when you are invited for a meal. The usual gifts are a bottle of wine, flowers, candy, or some small memento.

It is not acceptable to bring dessert or any other food that the hostess might feel put upon to serve at the party, since she will already have carefully planned her menu for this occasion. The same is true for wine. While it is an excellent gift, never expect that the wine you bring will necessarily be served the night you bring it because the wine will already have been selected for the evening.

Flowers may be brought wrapped in paper when they are presented to the hostess or host. (In some European countries, it is rude to give flowers wrapped in paper, and certain kinds and colors of flowers are taboo. *See Business Gifts.*)

When selecting flowers as a gift (or for yourself, for that matter) buy as nice a bouquet as you can afford. I try to avoid the scraggly half-dozen flowers that sidewalk stands and grocery stores sometimes sell in favor of something nicer—a robust bouquet of daisies, three or four tulips or freesia—but not necessarily more expensive. Always be sure the flowers are long-stemmed; short-stemmed flowers do not last very long, and are likely to be old when you buy them.

Candy is a good hostess gift, but some tact must be exercised when giving it. It is not, for example, the most welcome of gifts when someone is dieting or diabetic.

Other gifts are also appropriate. For years, I gave my hosts an especially wonderful cheese grater I had discovered because I know that most cooks appreciate a serious cooking utensil. Small food gifts are also welcome—an unusual vinegar or a mustard in a decorative pot.

Americans usually give their host his present as they arrive. A hostess gift need not be wrapped, but I like to keep decorative bags on hand to present wine and other small gifts in. No card is included since the gift is presented in person.

HOTEL. See also Motel; Tipping Chart; Conventions. Hotels provide a greater range of services and are more centralized than are motels. For example, clothes can be cleaned and pressed, flowers and catered meals can be ordered, a physician is on call, morning newspapers are provided. If fact, in a great hotel there is no limit to the services available to guests. A hotel has a lobby where you may greet and sometimes even briefly entertain guests, several restaurants, and, depending on whether it is also a resort, facilities for sports and other activities.

CHECKING IN. When you arrive at a hotel, the first step is to check in and sign the register. The management at the majority of hotels these days have become sophisticated enough not to care who is signing the register and what their marital status is, so as a matter of safety and for emergencies, simply sign your own name regardless of whether or not you are married to the person you are sharing a room with. After checking in, a bellhop will be called to carry your luggage and escort you to your room. He opens the room and helps you become familiar with it. He should be tipped one to two dollars per bag at this time.

CHECKING OUT. When it is time to check out of a hotel, call the front desk and ask for a bellhop if you need someone to carry your luggage. Otherwise, you may carry your luggage to the front desk yourself. At the front desk, your bill will be presented to you. You will be expected to pay with a credit card, cash, or traveler's checks. A good policy is to check the hotel's requirements in advance of your visit. Personal checks are not usually accepted unless you are known to the management.

DRESS. Standards of dress in a hotel vary depending upon whether it is an urban or a resort hotel. In an urban setting, you can usually wear casual or business dress, although a jacket and tie may be required for men in the formal dining room. At a resort hotel, evening dress may be required or expected during dinner; sports clothes are acceptable during the daytime.

EUROPEAN. European hotels function along the same lines as American, although they provide a couple of extra amenities. Most European hotels, for example, have a concierge, who provides a range of services from booking tours to obtaining tickets for performances to accepting packages to just about anything that you need done. The concierge's services are usually listed separately on your hotel bill, or his bill may be presented separately. He or she need not be tipped, although an occasional gratuity will have its benefits. Concierges are beginning to show up in better American hotels.

Many European hotels do not have baths in the rooms. When you want to use the bath, you call the housekeeper or maid, and she will draw a bath for you or show you where to go. Tip the equivalent of a dollar in local currency for this service each time you receive it.

You will often return after dinner to find your bed neatly turned down and your nightclothes laid out. In some hotels, if you leave your shoes outside the room, they will be shined overnight. Tip the staff for these services when you leave or more often if you stay a long time.

TIPPING. Tip the bellhop when he delivers you to your room and about $1 per average-sized bag on departure, if you use his services. Tip extra for extra services. Waiters providing room service should receive a tip of 15 percent of the bill on top of whatever charge has been added for room service. The doorman does not receive a tip unless he provides a service for you. Either tip 50 cents each time he gets a cab or helps you with packages or luggage or tip him $2 to $3 per week if you are staying longer. Tip the room maid $1 to $2 per day for a short visit, $6 to $8 a week for longer stays. You can leave this in the room on a desk or bureau in an envelope marked "Room maid." Attach a brief note of thanks, if possible. The tip can also be left with the desk clerk, who, by the way, receives no tip unless he or she has provided some special, out-of-the ordinary service. Those who provide other services for which you would normally tip should receive the regular amounts. If you would not normally tip for a service—dry cleaning or flowers, for example—you need not tip in a hotel.

House Party

SEE ALSO *Guest; Guest List.*

Any time that guests come to stay for longer than overnight, the rules of guesting and hosting change a little.

When guests arrive, they should be shown to their rooms (or niches) and left alone for a few minutes to clean up, unpack, rest, whatever suits them.

Guests should be sensitive to when they have taken over someone else's room and should try to accommodate this person during the times when he or she may need the use of the room for a short while, for example, in the early morning and at bedtime.

Newly arrived guests should be told something about the family's daily routine (when meals are served, the normal hour for bedtime, for example) and whether any festivities have been planned. A guest in someone's home for longer than overnight should take extra pains to disrupt the family routine as little as possible.

In planning activities for guests who will be staying longer than overnight, keep in mind that it is impossible and extremely wearing to plan for every minute. Even guests are entitled to a few moments of quiet relaxation, an hour or so to read, during the course of the day.

For longer visits, the host and hostess also need not consider themselves on call every minute. They may retire to a quiet corner to read or to their room for a nap, and they should not be disturbed by their guests during such moments.

Another difference in the visit of a short-term and a long-term guest is the way food is offered. A house-party guest should be given run of the kitchen, or, if that is not possible, food should be offered at times other than meals. Providing a bowl of fruit or a dish of candy, as well as making afternoon tea or coffee, are excellent ways to ensure that a guest who may not feel free to grab something whenever he is hungry at least has a snack in between meals.

A hostess need not appear at breakfast when she has a houseful of guests, but may provide food for them or give them free reign to serve themselves in the kitchen.

The host and hostess should provide transportation for their guests, if needed.

In a household with no extra help, a guest should help out as much as possible, even over the host's or hostess's protests. On the morning of departure, the guest should strip the bed and ask if he could put clean linen on.

When staying only one night with friends, a warm thank-you note is all that is required; longer stays call for a thank-you note and a gift. Wine, a special food, a book, a record, tickets to a theatrical or sporting event are all excellent thank-you presents. The gift can be sent after the visit or brought along and given to the hostess upon arrival or departure. If a guest has displaced a child, a nice touch is to give the child a small present of appreciation, too.

Household

SEE ALSO *Bath Linens; Bed Linens; Dishware; Flatware; Glassware; Home; Kitchen; Kitchen Linens.*

A household consists of all the possessions that are needed to run a home efficiently and graciously. A home can be run efficiently with one basic set of dishes, with enough place settings to serve all the family members. It can be run graciously, and will be equipped to serve guests, if there are some extra place settings of the dishes, and, even better, if there is an extra set of dishes, perhaps good china or a set of pottery.

Years ago, households were more lavishly although not necessarily better equipped than they are today. A woman was likely to own several sets of china, and a very complete set of sterling silverware—twelve or more place settings. She replaced china and sterling by ordering plates or teaspoons or whatever was needed by the dozens. Today such items are ordered by the place setting, and most women consider their sets complete with eight, although some are lucky enough to own twelve place settings. Since few women have domestic help these days, eight is about as many people as they can comfortably serve at a dinner party. Stainless steel has replaced sterling flatware for everyday and casual entertaining.

Although the needs of any one household are highly individual and also dependent upon a couple's taste, household needs can be divided into several basic categories, all of which are described in detail in separate listings elsewhere in this book.

Bath linens
Bed linens
Dishware
Flatware
Glassware
Kitchen linens

Household Help—Full-Time

SEE ALSO *Companion; Household Help—Part-Time; Nurse.*

Few people are fortunate enough to have a fully staffed house, but as more women enter the workplace, more families once again are employing some workers in their homes. The usual full-time, live-in household positions are those of housekeeper and child caretaker.

HIRING. Always check references when hiring someone, but never hire someone with good references whom you do not like personally. This person either will be living in your home or spending many hours a day there, and you will want someone with whom you are compatible. Personality counts more than you can imagine, sometimes even more than a person's ability to do the job. aprat from that, a household employee must be honest and competent.

Outline the employee's duties when you hire him or her. Never play down what you will expect. If you have a child who is a handful, say so. If you expect child care to come first and household work second, make that clear. If you must come home to a clean house and child every night, say so.

Once you have hired someone, do not add to his or her chores without discussing it first and renegotiating his pay. The terms of the job that you discussed when you hired someone are the terms you should stick to. It is one of the best ways I know to hang on to household help.

Even though this person will live in, keep in mind that you have not hired a 24-hour employee. Today many household workers expect to work 9 to 5, or 9 to 6, although in households where both parents work and there are small children, this may not be possible. At any rate, a household employee should have enough free time to eat and sleep, in addition to time for recreation. Most employees want two days off a week, although these need not be consecutive.

When you are hiring someone, state the pay, be sure you are both in agreement about it, and also in agreement about when the person will be paid. Sometimes the method of payment—check or cash—is also part of the agreement.

UNIFORMS. If you want your household staff in uniforms, it is your responsibility to provide them and maintain them. If you do not require uniforms, observe how the person is dressed when you interview him or her, and discuss any basic requirements you have regarding dress.

LIVING QUARTERS A live-in employee must be provided with a clean, well-appointed room. It should have a bed and comfortable chair, adequate lighting, and a place to hang clothing. A television is a necessity.

ENTERTAINING. Employees should be permitted to entertain guests in their quarters, in some other private part of your house that is suitable for this, or, if there is no other place, in your living room when you are gone. If the employee uses your living room, den, or library, he should leave it in spotless condition.

NAMES. Most employees feel more comfortable being called by their first names. Employees usually call their employers "Mrs. Jones" or "Mr. Jones." Children are called by their first names. Even if an employee calls you by your first name, sign notes to him or her "Sally Jones."

If you really are more comfortable being called by your first name, even by your employees, then you may do so, but being overly friendly with employees does neither of you a favor. It cannot erase the fact this person works for you and must answer to you. Consider whether you will not both be more comfortable if a proper and polite distance is maintained.

FIRING. Any employee should be fired on the spot for certain serious offenses: robbery and other forms of dishonesty, rudeness, and being unkind or cruel to your children. As for minor offenses, it is often better to work with an employee to train him or her than to terminate employment.

When you must fire an employee, always give a good, concrete reason. If there is no major, serious offense, if he or she simply does not fit in with your family, then try, if possible, to give the employee some notice so he or she can find another position. Also, if possible, write a flattering letter of reference.

Household Help—Part-Time

SEE ALSO *Companion; Household Help—Full-Time; Nurse.*

At best, most of us consider ourselves lucky to have even part-time, live-out help these days. The part-time employees that most of us must know how to cope with are the babysitter, a cleaning person, mother's helpers, and caterers or others associated with preparing and serving food.

BABYSITTER. A babysitter is often the son or daughter of a family friend, and should be treated accordingly. Introduce him or her as you would any young friend and offer the same freedom of your home that you would offer to any other friend's child.

Explain what is expected from someone who babysits for you. Tell him or her what food may or may not be eaten, what the rules are for your children, how you feel about entertaining guests when you are out.

Never ask a babysitter to take responsibility for your's and someone else's children without first asking if he or she is willing to do so, and certainly not without offering extra pay.

MOTHER'S HELPERS. Mother's helpers are teen babysitters who sign on for a longer term of duty than one night. They may work regularly two or three afternoons a week, or, as is most common, may join your family for a summer. Their primary responsibility is to care for the children, although light housework is also sometimes part of the job.

Mother's helpers are treated as part of the family. They eat with the family and are invited on some family outings. The employer may even act as a parent in absentia to a mother's helper, enforcing a curfew or otherwise paying attention to the teen's social life. These matters are usually discussed with the teen's parents when the teen is hired as a mother's helper.

The duties of a mother's helper should be outlined carefully during the job interview. They typically involve daytime responsibility for the children, and may also include some nighttime babysitting as well.

Like other employees, mother's helpers are entitled to enough time off to eat, play, and socialize a moderate amount. When more is asked, they should be paid overtime or her fees should be renegotiated.

A mother's helper may share a room with the children or have his or her own room. Since the teen joins in family activities, this person need not have his or her own television or radio.

CLEANING PERSON. A cleaning person's work should be carefully outlined when he or she is hired, and specific assignments are then also made on a week-to-week basis. Most cleaning people are paid weekly, some in cash, and are also given transportation money and lunch. At the time you hire the cleaning person, ask what he or she wants for lunch and then what she needs to make it. Make it clear whether or not he or she may eat other food in your refrigerator.

The first few times someone works for you, it will be helpful if you are present to show the person around and to show how you want things done. It is your obligation as employer to provide cleaning supplies and a uniform if you want your cleaning person to wear one.

CATERER. Caterers, part-time cooks, bartenders, and waiters and waitresses are sometimes used on a freelance basis at parties and formal dinners. Always check references before hiring someone to work for you in this capacity. If the people you hire are incompetent, the entire event will be a failure.

Discuss the terms of employment when you hire someone—such things as what they will be paid, how they will be paid, what they must do specifically, and what you expect of them generally. Most professional caterers will not need much guidance from you, but if you want something done a certain way, then discuss this with him or her.

Caterers either provide uniforms for their staff or advise them to dress similarly, usually in black pants and skirts and white tops. You may want to discuss this in advance.

Caterers and their staff are tipped 10 to 15 percent of the fee for service.

Housewarming

SEE ALSO *Buffet Dinner; Cocktail Party.*

A housewarming may be given any time after a new home is presentable enough to receive guests. There is no real need to wait until the house is fully decorated, or even until you are fully settled, before planning a housewarming party. I once attended a charming housewarming party where the guests sat on packing boxes and the food was served from the kitchen counters. The spontaneity of the host and hostess in wanting to show off their new home to their friends before it was entirely in order was positively infectious, and a wonderful time was had by all.

A buffet dinner or appetizers are the usual food at a housewarming. Punch or mixed alcoholic and soft drinks should be served early on, and coffee and tea provided later, usually with dessert.

A housewarming may be held at night or during the afternoon. Invitations may be mailed or telephoned.

Guests who attend a housewarming need not bring a gift, but many will want to do so. Presents for housewarming gifts can be as simple as salt, a loaf of bread, and a bottle of wine, old traditional gifts to warm a new home, or something more elaborate that is needed by the host and hostess in their new home. A housewarming gift should be something that will be used in the home.

Humor

SEE ALSO *Public Appearance.*

Humor is ultimately personal. To a large extent one's sense of humor depends upon one's values and the way one looks at the world, yet a great deal of humor is also common to a culture. In most cultures, for example, certain things are found to be universally funny. The most obvious example is that a person slipping on a banana peel is considered funny in some cultures and not in others. If your humorous comments continually appear to go over the heads of others, you may simply have to accept the fact that you may not be a very funny person. The values you inject into your humor may, for example, not be the values your friends share. People often make the mistake of assuming that friends share their prejudices and that they can feel free to tell jokes expressing those prejudices. When you realize your comments are offensive to another person, and you value the friendship, you should refrain from making such comments.

ETHNIC. This type of humor, designed solely to denigrate various cultural, racial, and ethnic groups, has no place among kind people. Should someone insist on telling a joke of this type in your presence, you need not respond and can even express your dislike for this brand of humor.

PRACTICAL JOKES. Most practical jokes are carried out at someone else's expense. Before you prepare a practical joke, therefore, stop to consider how you would respond were the same gag pulled on you. If it still seems amusing, go ahead; if not, think about amusing yourself in some other manner.

Husband

SEE *Family Finances; Forms of Address—Spoken; Marriage.*

Informal

SEE ALSO *Business Card; Visiting Cards*.

The smallest writing paper, which is about 4 by 3 inches, is called an informal. Informals are always ordered and used with matching envelopes. An informal is never given out the way business or social visiting cards are. It is, in fact, not to be confused with a visiting card. An informal is larger than a visiting card and is folded in half in the center. It is blank on the inside, where you write, and may be printed with your name or monogram on the outside top.

An informal is used to write brief notes of thanks or congratulations. They are also enclosed with gifts instead of using a pre-printed card. Informals are also used for invitations, acceptances, and regrets.

All messages are written inside the card, usually on the bottom half, although if the message will be long, you may begin on the top half of the card. As a friendly gesture, you may cross out your name on the card; although this is not often done these days. It is a nice touch, though, and I like it.

When an invitation is written on an informal, it may read as shown in Figure 35.

Buffet dinner
Sunday, August 20 at 8 P.M.

Regrets only

Figure 35. An invitation handwritten inside an informal card

Regrets may be written on your informals or telephoned.

A conservative informal has panels, is printed in black on white stock, and may contain either your name or monogram.

A less conservative informal may be printed in a color on pastel stock, and may dispense your title and simply contain your name, Susie Gladson, for example, rather than Mrs. William Gladson or Miss Susie Gladson.

241

Informal Food Service

SEE *Barbecue; Clambake; Kaffeeklatsch; Tailgate Party.*

Informal Wedding Invitations

SEE ALSO *Formal Wedding Invitation.*

When a wedding is informal or is held on short notice, handwritten invitations may be issued, or people may be invited by telegram (or day letter, which is less expensive) or by telephone.

If handwritten invitations are sent, they are usually written in paragraph style, although they may also be written to resemble more formal invitations. One might read:

> Dear Aunt Marie,
>
> Michael and I are going to be married quietly in the Presbyterian Church in Kingston on Wednesday, August twentieth. We do so hope you will be able to join us for the wedding and breakfast afterward at mother's.
>
> Love,
> Suzanne

Intermarriage

Couples of all races and religions are intermarrying at higher rates than almost any other time in American history. The only other time when intermarriage rates between Jews and Christians were as high as they are today was during the colonial era.

Each couple must, of course, find their own way in what is essentially their own private cultural experiment, but I can make a few suggestions that I think will help.

Begin by acknowledging each other's differences and showing curiosity about them. While it may be rude to discuss someone's religion or race when you are not married to him or her, it is rude *not* to show curiosity when you are. Ask about customs and traditions. Read about them. Share what you learn with your spouse so he or she is aware of your interest.

Figure out ways that the two of you can merge traditions or celebrate a healthy balance for each of you. A Swedish woman I know who married an American black arranged for their newborn daughter to be baptized in her religion and in a traditional African ceremony. Her husband's family had been Americans for six generations, and he was at first skeptical, but he soon came to appreciate his wife's gesture. Each of you can attend the other's religious services and find countless ways to share your customs with one another.

Do not criticize the new customs and celebrations you see, even if your family does them in what you perceive to be a better way. This is a good rule for any marriage, but it is especially important in a mixed marriage.

Finally, relax and do not worry about any social blunders you might be making. You are entering a world that is different to one degree or another, and no one expects you to know everything. You will do some things right and some things wrong; you will learn about some customs and adopt them, and you will learn about other customs and discard them because they do not work for you personally. For example, one young woman I know, a Christian, was mildly chagrined after attending two Jewish funerals with her new husband to discover that one does not ask the chief mourners how they are. That was *all* she had asked them. After reading the Jewish tradition of leaving mourners alone (somewhat), she decided she felt more comfortable expressing her concern and that she would do nothing different the next time.

Each of you individually and as a couple must find your own way. To do this takes time, patience, love, and respect.

International Business Manners

SEE ALSO *Eating in Africa; Eating in China; Eating in Europe; Eating in India; Eating in Japan; Eating in the Mideast; Travel—Asia; Travel—Europe; Travel—Latin America.*

Americans are conducting far more business abroad than ever before, and although we are a naturally hospitable people, we do not necessarily conduct business gracefully—at least, not in the eyes of the rest of the world.

We seem to be culture-bound—bound, that is, entirely too much to our own culture. This is hardly surprising since we are a giant among countries geographically and further do not have the benefits of being bordered by many other nations the way most European and Asian nations are. Most Americans have had little exposure to people speaking other languages and little inclination as a result to learn the finer points of etiquette in other lands.

That same American get-up-and-go that has made us famous does not serve us well in the older cultures of Europe and the Orient. We do not have the patience for ritual and ceremony that is often so important in older cultures, even in the conduct of business affairs. Even our natural gregariousness can work against us. People in the rest of the world are slower to become friends and are sometimes put off by our casual manners and familiarity even with acquaintances. Almost without exception, the rest of the world cultivates one another a bit more than most Americans are willing to—or even know how to. The Chinese, for example, like to sip a little tea before they begin to talk shop. The French are eager to discuss politics and life for hours (as a way of getting acquainted) before they settle down to anything as serious as business. Latin Americans may invite you home to meet the family first, and the Japanese are likely to insist on an evening of elaborate entertainment (men only!). In most other countries—surprisingly even in Communist countries—much importance is placed on protocol and ceremony.

Americans who want to be successful in

other countries need to learn as much as they can about the other culture and adjust to its way as much as possible. We often think because we are so large and a world leader that others can adjust to our ways, but the rest of the world harbors some resentment toward our size and success. They want us to cater to them a little bit. This is not to say that our competitors have not studied our culture and determined the best way to do business with us. The Japanese and the French and even the Soviets have studied our culture and learned how to sell things to us, but if we want to sell things to them, we must learn the ways of their worlds.

We need not necessarily learn their languages (although this is not a bad start) but we must learn the etiquette of using their languages. The French, for example, do not have much patience with people who do not speak their language, but Spanish speakers are delighted when a foreigner tries out their native tongue.

Even more is involved in conducting business with those in other cultures. Once you know what country you will be doing business with, check with their embassy. One of the major reasons for the existence of embassies is to promote trade between their country and others, so the embassy staff will be happy to provide you with information on such things as entertaining, exchanging gifts, greetings, visiting, and what things are socially taboo. It is especially important to learn the few things in every culture that are insulting or simply taboo. Hand gestures are not international, for example, and in some countries it is an insult to raise the palm of your hand to someone—the way Americans wave would give offense. In Arab countries, crossing

your legs and showing the sole of your foot is considered an insult. In parts of Eastern Europe, it is discourteous to rest your hand in your lap while eating; both hands should remain on the table. In France, it is considered rude to converse with someone with your hands in your pockets. These are the kinds of small details an embassy can provide. In addition, they can supply information on how to conduct business and how to entertain for business.

Another excellent source of information is a business librarian, who will direct you toward books and articles on how to conduct business in a particular country.

Although every country has its own finer points of etiquette, some general rules can be followed that will ease relations between the American businessperson and his or her foreign counterparts.

Here are a few suggestions that will help you get by almost anywhere in the world.

- Be slow to use first names. Everyone else sticks with surnames longer than Americans do.
- Be prepared to shake hands (or bow, in the Orient) a lot. Americans generally shake hands when meeting strangers; the rest of the world that shakes hands uses the gesture as a general greeting.
- Watch your hand and body gestures. Some gestures are insulting, and the best way to avoid insulting someone unintentionally is to keep your hands quiet. For that matter, keep your feet quiet, too. Do not wave (that gesture really varies from country to country); do not make an okay sign by forming a circle with your thumb and forefinger, do not give the

thumbs-up sign. Keep hand gestures to a minimum.

- When you are invited to someone's home, take a gift. I'll suggest some gift possibilities later and discuss this in more detail.
- Treat women more formally than you treat American women. Almost anywhere else in the world you will encounter fewer women in positions of power than in the United States. Unlike American women in business, who have opted for more equal treatment, European women in business (there are few Oriental women in business at this time) prefer to be treated more like ladies than equals. Standing up to greet them, waiting for the woman to extend her hand, holding doors, helping with coats, all are signs of courtesy that European businesswomen consider basic good manners, as do the wives of businessmen. Most of the women you come into contact with in Europe will be in the latter category.

And although women want the preferential treatment, European women are less tolerant of intimacy than are American women. Do not ask personal questions, do not use first names, and do not give presents that are in any way considered personal. Perfume, for example, is considered too personal a gift, unless a woman has specifically requested that you bring some American perfume. Any kind of wearing apparel or jewelry will be considered too intimate. If you give flowers to a woman, a mixed bouquet is best. Red roses are for lovers, white is the color

of mourning in some countries, as are chrysanthemums, so play it safe with mixed flowers.

Do not be quick to compliment a woman; your words may be mistaken for an overture. Do not make overtures, for that matter. In many countries casual sex is unacceptable, and mixing business and sex is taboo.

In many parts of the world, women are more sheltered than the United States. In some countries, they are virtually considered property, belonging, of course, to the men to whom they are married. In an Arab country, never ask a man about his wife and children, even if you are a guest in his home. You probably won't even see them, and on the very rare occasion that your wife is invited to join you in dining in an Arab home, she will probably be shipped off to another part of the house to eat with the women and children. Japanese businessmen rarely include their wives in any business entertaining, and most business entertaining is done outside the home. (The Japanese have generous expense accounts, and do entertain publicly a lot, even before they have conducted any business with you.) These are extremes, but since many people in other countries tend to separate business and pleasure, they do not welcome inquiries about their personal life.

- To be on the safe side, let the other person take the lead in discussing business. The British, for example, do not like to discuss business at night, so while they may invite you out to dinner or out for an evening of entertaining, they will not be up to talk about the deal you are working on. The Chinese and the Arabs will want to sip a little tea with you before embarking on any kind of business discussion.

LANGUAGE. If you cannot speak a language fluently, it is a problem not only socially but also in terms of how accurately you are able to conduct business. In business dealings, it makes good sense to use a translator. Using a translator also lets you avoid giving inadvertent offense or looking like a fool for misusing a word. As a tourist, this would not necessarily be a serious matter, but as a businessperson, it can seriously affect your image. Americans are often willing to mock themselves. Saving face, however, is much more important in other parts of the world, and you should be equally concerned with this when conducting business.

GIFTS. When Americans give one another business gifts, they are as likely as not advertisements of one sort or another (logo-bearing at the minimum) or business-oriented gifts. In the world of international business, gift giving is a cultural exchange, and gifts take on much greater meaning.

A gift need not be expensive (around $25 is the average price), but it should be thoughtful.

The gift should be personally selected for the recipient. Often, it is related to something you have discussed—a product the customer admires, something that is typically American, something American that is highly valued in another country. Great care must be taken in selecting the gift. Too expensive a gift may prove embarrassing, as may too inexpensive a gift. A gift should never be so large or important that it seems to be incurring an obligation on the part of the recipient. It is true that gift giving "sweetens" the relationship, but the person who feels that he has been bought off may not be inclined to buy from you. Logos are not acceptable in most international business gift exchanges unless they are small advertising items.

The perfect gift, of course, which will satisfy all the requirements, is something that is uniquely American. I suggest, depending upon your client and your expense account, the following:

U.S. stamps
Maple syrup
Virginia hams (if the recipient eats pork)
Pennsylvania Dutch foods
American caviar, truffles, pâté de fois gras, nuts, or some of the other new, unique food products
Stetson hat
Indian jewelry or weaving
Eskimo carving
Scrimshaw
American antiques
Books, pens, or other desk accessories
Cigarettes
American-made sports equipment
Steuben glass
American candy
Photograph books about the U.S., a particular state, or region of the country
T-shirts
California wines

Regional art
American-made tools
Records and compact discs
Videotapes of American movies

Many experienced businesspeople say they never give a gift without making some advance announcement of it. ("I heard how much you enjoyed your last visit to Chicago, and I'm bringing you a small memento of our city.") A surprise gift may cause the recipient to lose face and thus would defeat the purpose of the gift entirely.

Also tricky is the timing of the gift. In some countries, it is not wise to initiate the exchange. Sometimes it is important to give a gift only if you have first been given one, which means you should travel armed with presents but not give them unless you receive a present first. Sometimes a gift may not appropriately be given until after business has been conducted. And sometimes gifts must be presented when you are alone with a client; at other times that would seem like a bribe and the gift must be presented in the presence of others. In the People's Republic of China, you do not present gifts in the presence of others, whereas in Arab countries, a gift must be presented in front of others if it is not to look like a bribe. In Western Europe a gift brought to someone's home should be given upon arrival, never after dinner, so the gift does not look like payment for the meal. In the People's Republic of China, a gift should never be given before the end of negotiations.

Wrapping is another tricky area. In Japan, where reside those masters of packaging, it can assume enormous proportions, and the wrong wrapping can be read as an insult. Gift wrapping is such an intricate art in Japan that all gifts should be wrapped by Japanese who are expert in these matters. To be on the safe side, gifts given in Western Europe should be plainly wrapped in white or pastel colors. Flowers, when given or brought to someone's home, should not be wrapped.

Always enclose a card with a gift, preferably your printed informal or plain informal stationery with a personal message written on it. Preprinted greeting cards are not as acceptable in other countries as they are here.

Here are some hints on gift giving in major regions of the world where Americans conduct business.

Western Europe. The French are slow to develop personal relationships, and gifts should not be given until one has developed. Then the gift should be something personal—a book, record, some business accessory. Do not give perfume or wine to the French unless it has been requested because those are their areas of specialization.

Unlike many other European businesswomen, French women in business do expect to be treated as equals with their colleagues, and business gifts presented to them should be the same or similar to gifts given to French businessmen.

The same general rules apply to gifts given to Germans, exept that gifts should never be wrapped in white, brown, or black. The Germans, less chauvinistic than the French, appreciate good American wine and other American products. The gift should always look as if it has been selected personally for the recipient.

The Germans appreciate an evening of entertainment that has been carefully planned with their interests in mind—an opera, a concert, for example.

The British do not give business gifts very often, perhaps because they prefer to keep business and pleasure strictly separate. They do enjoy a carefully planned evening of entertainment, although they prefer not to discuss business at night. Small gifts may be given, and this is one country where you can gain favor by giving a gift to a man's wife or children.

Japan. The giving of gifts is far too high an art to be gone into thoroughly here, but suffice it to say that gift giving is very much a part of Japanese business culture.

January 1 and mid-June are traditional gift-giving holidays, similar to Christmas, and you cannot go wrong presenting a Japanese businessperson with a present at these times of the year—provided you find the right gift.

A Japanese businessperson may present you with a gift on your first meeting. You need not, but you may of course reciprocate. Let him initiate the gift giving unless you are reciprocating from an earlier gift he gave you.

The Japanese do not open gifts in front of the giver. Do not expect a Japanese businessperson to open your gift, and do not open yours in front of him. Along the same line, do not give a Japanese businessperson a gift in the presence of others. Doing any of these things might force him to act as if he liked a gift he does not care for, and this would be very trying for him.

Do not surprise a Japanese with a gift; let him know in advance that you are bringing him something.

The Japanese are impressed with quality. If you buy an appliance or gadget, make sure it is a good brand name. The Japanese do not appreciate joke gifts (joke gifts are generally too risky in any culture), but they do appreciate small gadgets and electronic toys. They appreciate American liquor, candy, and food products. They favor scotch and do not particularly like bourbon, as a rule.

Always have Japanese gifts nicely wrapped by someone who understands the etiquette of Japanese gift wrapping. Bows are considered unattractive, and ribbons, depending upon their color, carry messages.

Presents of red are meaningful to Japanese; they signify good health. Do not give gifts with animal symbols on them; they, too, have symbolic meaning and may be misunderstood.

People's Republic of China. Gifts should be tokens; lavish gifts are frowned upon. The Chinese especially appreciate a small, personal memento.

Gifts should be given only for a good reason, at the completion of negotiations, for example. Always present gifts privately. Gifts that are uniquely American are appreciated, as are kitchen gadgets, a bottle of liquor, pens, and other inexpensive presents.

Latin America. Give a gift only after a personal relationship has been developed. An inexpensive personal gift is always preferred over something more lavish. Never give a knife or a handkerchief to a Latin American. The knife suggests the cutting of a relationship, and the handkerchief is associated with sadness and tears.

A gift should always be taken if you are

invited to a Latin American home. It is appropriate to take presents to the woman of the house and the children.

Do not give a gift during a business encounter. Since Latin Americans do not discuss business over lunch, this is often a good time to give a present. If possible, give a gift only after negotiations have been concluded; otherwise, it may be misinterpreted.

Logo gifts are not much favored, but a gift with a subtle logo or one that has something to do with the kind of business (a small model tractor for a tractor manufacturer, for example) are fine.

Latin Americans love giving and receiving gifts, and a well-selected gift can often pave the way for further relations. If a secretary or assistant has been particularly helpful, a gift will help ensure that you receive the same kind of help on your next visit.

Introduction

SEE ALSO *Business Introduction; Forms of Address—Spoken; Names; Receiving Line; References.*

Introductions enable two persons who do not know each other to make the acquaintance of one another. Beyond that, an introduction is the first impression you make on someone, so it is important that every person knows how to handle introductions graciously. Introductions used to be quite informal and full of ritual. Today, much of the formality is gone, although a few rules persist. These rules cause many people to panic at the mere thought of them, yet when you know the very simple guidelines for introducing one person to another, introductions are easily accomplished. These rules should become second nature to you, so you can concentrate on the people involved rather than the rules.

BASIC GUIDELINES OF INTRODUCTIONS. When introducing two persons to one another, keep in mind that one person nearly always takes precedence over another. For example:

1. Women always take precedence over men, which means that men are always introduced to women: "Ellen, I'd like you to meet Wilbur Agee. Wilbur, this is Mrs. Simon."
2. Elderly people take precedence over younger people, which means that younger people are always introduced to older people: "Grandmother, may I present Bill Jones, a school friend of mine, Bill, this is my grandmother, Mrs. Harrington."
3. Dignitaries always take precedence over nondignitaries: "Your Eminence, may I present my wife, Clara Smith. Clara, this is His Eminence, Cecil Cardinal Riley." Before you protest that America is not a class-oriented society, let me explain that dignitaries, at least for purposes of introductions are, for the most part, high-ranking elected or religious officials—a governor, a mayor, a judge, a clergyperson. These persons are accorded this respect because we respect the offices they hold, not because they as

individuals are better than others.

And there are two less-often-used rules to keep in mind when making introductions:

4. Guests, unless they are dignitaries or elderly, are always presented to a hostess or host.
5. Everyone is introduced to a guest of honor, with the exceptions noted above.

WHEN TO INTRODUCE. At social gatherings, you may always introduce yourself to any other invited guest. If the hostess or host invited you both, you have, in effect, been given what might be called a *de facto* preliminary introduction.

On all other occasions, make individual judgments about whether or not to introduce yourself or your companion. If you bump into a friend on the street when you are walking with another friend, there may be no need for introductions if the greetings will be short or the two persons have no reason to know each other. If the two friends would enjoy each other, by all means introduce them to one another.

Your partner (your spouse or otherwise) should almost always be introduced whenever you greet someone. The exception is the awkward moment when you cannot remember the name of someone whom you rarely see.

Children. Your children should be introduced to all business and social friends when you meet them. Until your daughter is eighteen, she is presented to others. After age eighteen, she should be accorded the status of an adult woman, and men are presented to her.

Relatives. See Forms of Address—Spoken.

Servants. As a rule, servants need not be introduced to guests in your home. The exceptions are nurses, companions, and others of professional status, who are usually introduced. In these days when your child's caretaker may well be a young woman with a master's degree who is in your employ until she finds something more suitable to her education, you may feel more comfortable introducing an employee to a guest. There is no reason not to introduce employees if you feel comfortable doing so.

WORDING OF INTRODUCTIONS. The most formal introductions are made with the phrase "May I present . . . ?" Less formal is to say, "Mary, I would like you to meet Jack Evans. Jack, this is my sister, Mary Hamilton." If you do panic and momentarily forget the precedence of introductions, you can always introduce in the least formal manner, using just names: "Mary, Jack Evans. Jack, my sister, Mary Hamilton." Introductions like this are so quick that no one really pays much attention to who met whom.

Always use full names when introducing persons. No one—not even children and teens—should use only first names. Never say, "Mary, this is John. John, Mary." There is a tendency for people to introduce themselves this way today. I can only say that if you do not trust the person whom you are either meeting or introducing enough to disclose complete names, you should not be making the introduction at all.

Except when introducing contemporaries, and young ones at that, always err on the side of conservatism, and use titles and surnames. For example: "Mother, I'd like you to meet Anita Epcot. Anita, this is my mother, Mrs. Lee." "Anita, I'd like you to meet Mr. Lee. Steven, this is Ms. Epcot."

What you call a person is somewhat irrelevant when making an introduction. If you call someone by his first name, use it in the introduction when you speak directly to the person even though you introduce him or her by title and surname. For example, you would say in introducing your friend Mary: "Mary, this is Anita Epcot." To Anita, whom you are introducing and who is much younger than Mary, you would say: "Anita, this is Mrs. Hamilton."

RESPONSES. The proper response upon meeting someone for the first time is to say, "How do you do" or "I am pleased to meet you." Never say "I am pleased to make your acquaintance," "I'm glad to know you" (you do not know this yet), "Charmed," "Pleased," or "Pleased to know you."

It is nice but not necessary to repeat the person's name, but do not respond with, "Ms. Epcot?" Far better to say, "How do you do, Ms. Epcot?" Repeating the name helps you to remember it.

And last but hardly least, it is always friendly to smile when meeting someone.

SHAKING HANDS. Most people shake hands upon meeting. A man used to have to wait for a woman to extend her hand, but this is no longer the case. Hostesses and hosts should shake hands with anyone who is presented to them. It is polite to wait for an elderly person or a dignitary to extend his or her hand first. If you see that someone is handicapped and cannot shake hands, do not offer your hand immediately but still be prepared to shake hands. Sometimes a handicapped person who cannot use his right hand will offer his left instead.

RISING. In these days of more egalitarian manners, I like to see everyone except the elderly and infirm rise for an introduction. I think it looks sloppy to remain seated when meeting another person, or for that matter when greeting another person. Unless elderly or infirm, a host and/or hostess always stands to greet their friends.

INTRODUCING ONESELF. When introducing yourself, always use your first and last name, but never your title. For example, never say, "Hello, I am Mrs. Smyth," but rather, "Hello, I am Amanda Smyth."

GROUP INTRODUCTIONS. When introducing one person to a group, there is no need to go around the group and mention every name, since the person being introduced will not be likely to remember them anyway. If the group is small enough, under five or six, you may mention every name. If it is much larger, introduce the person to a few people who are standing nearby. Or if one person is being introduced to a group of eight or ten, you can usually introduce the first few people, and let the rest take over and introduce themselves.

INTRODUCTIONS TO THE PRESIDENT OF THE UNITED STATES. Generally, an aide stands nearby and introduces persons to the President. If you handle the introduction yourself, the correct form is "Mr. President, I have the honor to present Mrs. Eleanor Sabot." Nothing further is said, for it is presumed that Mrs. Sabot is well aware of whom she is meeting.

The President is always the one to extend his hand in greeting regardless of whether he is meeting a man or a woman.

The correct response to meeting the President of the United States is to bow slightly and shake hands.

Invitation

SEE ALSO *Formal Wedding Invitation; Informal Wedding Invitation.*

Depending upon its degree of formality and the time involved, an invitation may be issued by mail, in person, or over the telephone.

FORMAL. Formal invitations are engraved or printed in black ink on white or off-white paper with a matching envelope. The paper may be paneled or plain. A second envelope and tissue are not required but are sometimes used, especially for wedding invitations, primarily because it is the custom to include them. The tissue dates back to the days when engraving was a messier task than it is now and the tissue was necessary to prevent the type from smearing. The second envelope is even older in origin and dates back to the days when mail was delivered by messengers. New methods of engraving have eliminated the need for the tissue, and messengers no longer deliver mail by hand, so both the tissue and the second envelope are no longer necessary, although, as noted, many people continue to use them. Usually sent for weddings,

anniversary parties, dances, balls, and other similar, major events, they are worded as follows:

Mr. and Mrs. William Garrity
request the pleasure of your company
on Saturday, the fourth of July,
at nine o'clock
347 Old Mill Drive
Washington, D.C.
R.s.v.p.   Black tie

Note that if the party were held in a club or some other public place and the replies were to be sent to the host and hostess, the R.S.V.P. would also include the address to which replies were to be sent.

Dress is included only when it is very formal—white or black tie.

The invitation may also state the reason for the party, for example:

in honor of my granddaughter
Eleanor Louise
or
in honor of our son's graduation

A couple giving a party for themselves, in honor of their own anniversary, for example, would not state a reason for the party, and the invitation would read as in the above example.

Formal invitations should be mailed at least three weeks before the event is scheduled to take place.

INFORMAL. Preprinted invitations may be used for less formal occasions and casual parties. These can be purchased in any stationery store. They come in a large assortment, in varying degrees of formality, and for various occasions. Some of the most useful are fairly plain white cards, often bordered in a color, with blanks to be filled in with the address, time, and so on. You may also use your own informal stationery to write out invitations. You may, for example, use a fairly formal format:

> Open House
> John and Nancy Neff
> New Year's Day
> 2 to 8 P.M.

Or you may write a short note:

> Dear Sally,
>
> John and I are planning our annual New Year's Day open house on Sunday, January 1, from 2 until 8 P.M. We do hope you and your family will be able to join us. No need to call unless you can't come. If we don't hear from you, we'll look forward to seeing you soon.
>
> Love,
> Nancy

Informal invitations also may be issued orally, either in person or by telephone. The host or hostess simply says, "John and I would like to have you come to dinner on Friday, August twenty-first, around 8 o'clock. We're cooking out, so dress casually."

An invitation should be accepted or declined as soon as possible after it is received.

If a reply card is enclosed with a formal invitation, that can be used to accept or a handwritten note, written in the formal third person on formal white stationery, can be sent.

A formal acceptance would read as follows:

> Mr. John Smith
> accepts with pleasure
> your kind invitation
> for Saturday, the twentieth of June

A formal regret should read:

> Miss Jeanette Jones
> regrets that she is unable to accept
> your very kind invitation
> or
> the kind invitation of
> Mr. and Mrs. Mark Hitchcock
> for Saturday, the fifth of June

Since a formal reply does not include an explanation, if the invitation has come from a close friend, you may also want to telephone and explain briefly why you must miss the event.

If an invitation is issued in person, and you cannot accept right away, simple say so, but then get back to the person who invited you as soon as possible with your response. A host or hostess is within his or her rights in asking you to reply by a certain date so someone else can be invited if you must decline.

When a written invitation includes a phone number, that is the proper way to respond, although a note may be sent if there is enough time.

Regardless of whether you accept or decline an invitation, always do so graciously. Do not simply say, "Okay, I can come," or anything to that effect. Far more gracious is to say, "A dinner party! What a splendid idea! I'd love to come." If you must decline, sound genuinely sorry: "I'm so sorry I'll have to miss your dinner on the eighth. John and I were just saying the other night how long it's been since we've seen you. Unfortunately, we're going out of town that weekend, so we won't be able to come." You need not supply detailed reasons for why you cannot attend, but it is polite to give some brief explanation when declining an invitation.

Italian Restaurant

SEE *Eating in Europe; Foreign Restaurant.*

Japanese Restaurant

SEE ALSO *Eating in Japan.*

Many Japanese restaurants in large cities invite diners to sit cross-legged on the floor *(tatami)* during the meal. If this is not your idea of a way to dine, you should ask for a regular table when you make a reservation or request one upon arrival. Only a rare Japanese restaurant does not have both kinds of seating.

Japanese restaurants are not set up to serve food communally as Chinese restaurants are, and individual dinners are usually ordered. These frequently include soup, a main dish, dessert, and tea.

If chopsticks are provided, feel free to request a fork if you want one.

A small, hot hand towel *(oshibori)* may be presented to diners before the meal begins. It is rude not to accept it, even if you have just washed your hands and applied hand lotion. After using the towel to wipe your hands, return it unfolded to the tray on which it was presented.

Jewelry

SEE ALSO *Class Ring; Club Jewelry; Ear Piercing.*

ON WOMEN. A woman's taste in jewelry is highly personal and idiosyncratic. Some women are known for their beautiful jewelry, while others wear little or no jewelry. How and when a woman wore jewelry not too long ago was considered a reflection of her breeding, which is to say that too many diamonds or brightly colored stones were considered garish and diamonds were definitely not daytime jewelry.

Jewelers have gotten smart, though, and have persuaded women that diamonds are daytime stones, and that not only brightly colored real stones but also brightly colored costume stones are appropriate anywhere a woman wants to wear them.

I confess that I still attempt to follow a couple of rules my mother set down regarding the wearing of jewelry. The first is to wear no more than three pieces at any one time, and the second is to put on the jewelry for the day and then remove one piece. There are few limits, of course, when it comes to a fancy ball—one can almost never wear too much glitter on such an occasion.

Whether or not you decide to follow such quaint rules is entirely up to you. I believe that each woman should evaluate and cater to her own personal jewelry style. If large, brightly colored stones are in style but you have always worn a simple gold chain and pearl earrings, you need not adopt a style that doesn't suit you. A woman can also maintain her own personal sense of style and still follow fashion. When big earrings are in, buy slightly larger ones, but not the largest, most outlandish ones you can find if that is not you. When jewelry is pared down, pare down, too, but again, do not pare down entirely if this look just isn't you. There is something wrong about a woman wearing jewelry because it is fashionable when it does not suit her personality.

Then, too, I think a woman should wear the best jewelry she can afford. Better to wear a simple 14-karat gold chain than a thick gold-plated one. If you cannot afford much jewelry, buy the best quality you can and make do with fewer pieces. You can always fill in with good costume jewelry once you own a few good pieces.

HEIRLOOM. Finally, I would like to discuss the custom of wearing family engagement and wedding rings other than your own—mother's or grandmother's, for example. These are often worn clumped together on the right or left hand. When rings are worn for the sake of sentiment, I can hardly object, but I do think that these often unaesthetic clusters of unmatched rings might be shown off to greater advantage reset into other pieces of jewelry or even into one ring.

ON MEN. I think the less a man wears, the better he looks. Gold chains, bracelets, and pinky rings are all in bad taste.

A man's basic jewelry should consist of a watch and his wedding ring. Other rings are appropriate as long as they are kept simple. The most classic is a signet ring.

Only a few years ago, one mark of a gentleman was that he wore a very simple, plain gold or leather-banded watch. Today, however, watch design has progressed so far (both in digital and traditional styles) that I think there is a great deal of leeway in the kind of watch a person wears. A man whose hobby is diving may take great pleasure in wearing a diver's watch all the time, and why shouldn't he? A man who loves technology may choose one of the interesting new digital watches.

For dress occasions, however, the best watch is still a plain gold or a very classic leather-banded one.

ON CHILDREN. SEE ALSO EAR PIERCING. Popular taste in terms of what is acceptable jewelry for children has changed, too. Children did not used to wear much jewelry, only very simple gold or silver pieces. Today, however, preteen and even younger girls wear some very sophisticated jewelry.

Apart from pierced ears in those groups where they are the custom, I still do not like to see much jewelry on a baby or a little girl. A delicately wrought gold or silver necklace or bracelet is a nice touch, however. By the time a girl has reached the age of ten or eleven, she usually has developed her own taste in jewelry, and probably should be permitted to exercise it. Or, to be more accurate, the girl's parents likely will not be able to stop her from exercising her taste and may as well spare everyone the arguments by acquiescing. A young girl can be encouraged to appreciate fine jewelry, though, often by being given some nice pieces that are appropriate for a person her age.

Jewish Birth Ceremonies

BRIS. A *bris,* or *brith milah,* as it is called in Hebrew, is the circumcision ceremony performed on the eighth day after the birth of a son. Only the health of the baby prevents its being held then. A *bris* can be held in a hospital, synagogue, or, as is most often the case, the home.

A *moyel,* the man who performs the circumcision, will tell the parents what he needs for the ceremony. A table should be covered with a cloth, and in many families the cloth that covers the table and or the baby's cover have been handed down for several generations.

Since a *bris* is usually performed in the morning, the reception that follows is a brunch or luncheon. As a rule, only close family and friends are invited. Invitations are issued by phone. Guests bring presents to the baby—whatever they usually give a newborn. Godparents usually give the baby something lasting, which usually means a gift of sterling, but any of the things that new babies need will be a welcome gift, and stocks and bonds as well as contributions to a trust fund are also acceptable presents.

PIDYON HABEN. A son's arrival may also be celebrated by Orthodox and some Conservative Jews at a *pidyon haben,* which occurs thirty-one days after his birth. The son is dedicated to the service of God and then redeemed by his parents. The ceremony is held in a synagogue and a reception is held later in the synagogue or the parents' home.

NAMING CEREMONY. The naming ceremony for a girl, held anywhere from the first Sabbath after her birth until several weeks afterward, is usually a simple ceremony held in the synagogue and followed by a reception in the synagogue or at home. As is the case for a boy, appropriate gifts may be brought to the reception. If a gift has already been given, another one is not necessary.

Jewish Mourning Customs

SEE ALSO *Christian Mourning Customs.*

In the Jewish religion, the formal, public period of mourning is observed after the funeral. Jews are buried as soon as possible after their death, often on the next day. An announcement of funeral plans is made in the local newspaper(s). Flowers are not sent to a Jewish funeral as a rule, but contributions to charity are often appreciated. Check the newspaper announcement for the family's preference.

Often everyone present at the funeral attends the graveside service, at which several prayers will be said. At the end of the graveside service, all attendees except the chief mourners form two lines that the family members walk through while a funeral prayer is said.

After the funeral, the family often retires to one relative's home for several days (seven for most Conservative and Orthodox Jews, three for Reform Jews) of public mourning, during which time friends call. Friends who attended the funeral often stop by the home after the graveside service. At the cemetery or, more often, at home, a pitcher of water is provided so that guests may rinse their hands before entering the house.

This period of mourning is referred to as "sitting shivah." Food, typically consisting of coffee and a sweet table, is provided for people who pay a shivah call during the week, but as the mourners do no work when they sit shivah, guests are expected to help themselves.

Whereas Christians often show great concern for the well-being of the chief mourners, asking them repeatedly how they are doing, the Jewish tradition is to grant the mourners their privacy. Usual greetings, such as "How are you?" and shaking hands, are traditionally dispensed with during a shivah call.

Job Interview

Entire books have been written about job interviews (see Marian Faux: *The Executive Interview*. New York, St. Martin's Press, 1985), and a great deal goes into a successful job interview, one that culminates in a job. Here we shall deal only with the behavior that will help you to get the job or at the least will not cause you to be rejected. To appear well mannered in a job interview, you must do the following:

1. Arrive on time.
2. Be appropriately dressed. You must also be immaculately dressed: with clean, manicured hands; shoes properly heeled and polished; clothes spotless and in good repair.
3. When the interviewer greets you, either in the reception area or in his or her office, stand up and extend your hand in greeting.
4. Do not sit until you are invited to do so, and then sit where you are asked to sit.
5. Do not place anything on the interviewer's desk. Obviously if you are showing samples, you may put them on the desk, but, in effect, when you were invited to show your work, you were invited to use the desk. Even so, say, "May I?" before you intrude on someone's turf.
6. Ignore all interruptions. If the interviewer takes a call or talks with someone who comes into the office, act as if you have heard nothing. If the interviewer talks as if you were listening,

say, "Oh, I wasn't really paying that much attention."

7. Take your cues from the interviewer. He will usually shape the interview. If he does not, then you may ask him questions about the job and the company. In fact, at some point during the interview, it is appropriate for you to ask questions to find out any details you want to know.

8. Realize that a little bragging, or what may seem like bragging to you, is acceptable. If you want to get the job you will have to present your credentials as well as the reasons why you should be hired. You need not brag excessively, but should not be shy about discussing what you have done and can do.

9. Let the interviewer end the interview. He will signal that it is over by summarizing what you have discussed, talking about the next step, or simply by standing up and concluding it.

10. Be polite to everyone you meet. The receptionist may be as responsive to you as a light fixture, but she may be a spy for the interviewer. She can report back that you were (a) extremely congenial or (b) rather snobbish, brash, or whatever else and this might cost you the job. Remember that about 90 percent of getting through an initial job interview is how you present yourself.

Kaffeeklatsch

As the term suggests, this is a morning gathering over coffee and coffeecake. The participants are usually a group of neighborhood women. I've often wondered whether the early women's consciousness-raising groups were not the direct descendants of kaffeeklatsching.

Kaffeeklatsching is usually done somewhere around 10 or 11 A.M., and it is often a group effort. One women offers her home and usually provides the coffee and tea, and one or more women bring the sweets.

A kaffeeklatsch can be as informal as you like, with the table set with mugs and paper napkins, or it can be a little more elegant, with china cups and saucers and cloth napkins.

Kissing

Apart from the handshake, kissing is probably the next most popular form of greeting, although it is not without its disadvantages, namely it is an excellent way of spreading germs and thereby prolonging the usual bouts of winter colds and flus. If you are in fact ailing, it is undoubtedly more courteous not to kiss than to kiss. And even when you are in a state of perfect health, it is probably healthier to kiss someone's cheeks than to kiss on the mouth.

REGIONAL VARIATIONS. Kissing customs vary from family to family, region to region around the country, and even from country to country. Some families are real kissers, and kiss each other hello and goodbye when only a few days have elapsed since their last visit. Other families are more formal and kiss one another only after a long absence (and I suppose some sad families are so formal that they do not kiss at all). New Yorkers and Californians are famous for greeting their most casual acquaintances with kisses; Southerners, too, enjoy kissing. Midwesterners and Westerners are too reserved to indulge in much kissing, certainly not with virtual strangers. In Western Europe and some Eastern European countries, a greeting kiss is actually two kisses: one on each cheek. In Arab culture, as in some others, men greet each other by kissing on each cheek.

Kitchen

The kitchen is often the hub of the home, and most cooks like their kitchen to be a warm, friendly place. In some parts of the country, much is made of the eat-in kitchen, that is, a kitchen large enough so the family can take meals in it.

Formal dining, however, does not take place in the kitchen, nor need informal dining, for that matter. The housekeeper who refuses to use her dining room for any but formal occasions misses the joy of providing a lovely setting for the people she most loves—her family. I fully understand the efficacy of eating breakfast or a quick lunch in a kitchen or a breakfast room, but I think that family dinners, even the most casual ones, should take place in the dining room.

Kitchen Linens

SEE *Table and Kitchen Linens.*

Knife

SEE ALSO *Table Manners.*

At a formal dinner or in a restaurant specializing in steak or seafood, you may encounter a variety of knives *(see Figure 36).* For casual dining, a dinner knife is the only knife in the place setting. With the excep-

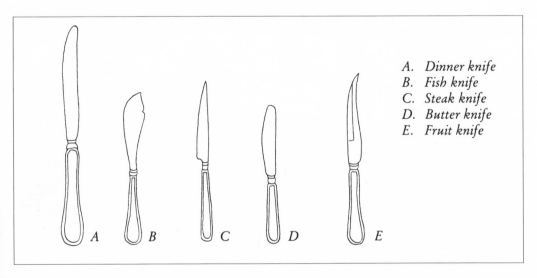

A. Dinner knife
B. Fish knife
C. Steak knife
D. Butter knife
E. Fruit knife

Figure 36. Knives

tion of the butter knife, knives go directly to the right of the plate in a place setting. The sharp edge of the blade should be turned in, facing the plate.

DINNER KNIFE. This is the biggest knife in the place setting, and it goes right next to the plate *(see Figure 37)*. The dinner knife is used for cutting meat, vegetables—any food on the dinner plate, actually—and it also may be used, if necessary, to cut salad greens. Use of the dinner knife and fork is shown in Figure 38.

FISH KNIFE. The fish knife, which is specially shaped to make cutting around fish bones easy, goes next to the dinner knife in a place setting. This knife is held slightly differently from the dinner knife *(see Figure 39)*.

STEAK KNIFE. This knife has a sharp, serrated edge that is used to cut beef, especially steaks. Many flatware knives are sharp enough to handle most cuts of meat, and the steak knife is not used very often these days. It occupies the same position as the fish knife in a place setting.

BUTTER KNIFE. After the dinner knife, this is the most frequently used knife. Rarely used for informal family dining, it is a staple in many restaurants and at formal dinners. The butter knife rests across the butter plate, which is to the left above the dinner plate. Its blade should face in, and the handle end points toward the knives—in a way that makes it easy for a right-handed diner to pick up the knife. When a butter knife is passed with the butter, it is considered a serving utensil and should

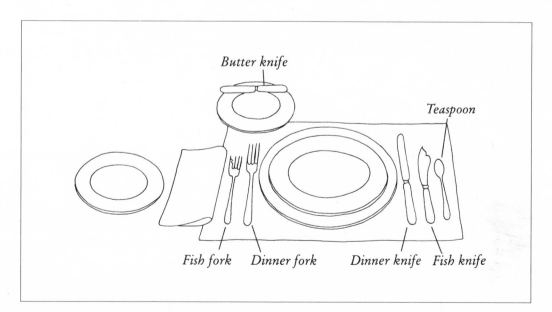

Figure 37. Correct arrangements of knives at a table setting

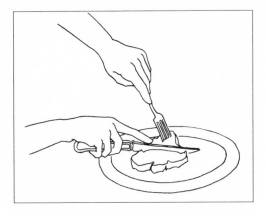

Figure 38. Correct way to use a dinner knife

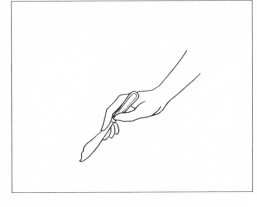

Figure 39. Correct way to use a fish knife

only be used to remove butter from the serving dish to the butter or dinner plate. The place-setting butter knife is then used to butter the bread or roll.

Once you have used any knife, always rest it on a plate. Never, if you can avoid doing so, place a utensil that has been used on a tablecloth. The butter knife rests on the butter plate and all other knives on the larger plates in the center of the place setting.

Kosher

SEE *Eating Habits of Guests.*

Late Arrivals

Late arrivals are rude arrivals. Not only that, but at some public performances, late arrivals may find themselves unadmitted arrivals. Those who arrive late at a live performance may not be seated until an appropriate break in the action. Unfortunately, at $40-plus theater tickets, management has gotten far too lax about admitting latecomers. They may think they can't keep people who spend that much money standing in the lobby very long, but it would be more sensitive to feel that they could not interrupt the far greater numbers of persons who are seated and already engrossed in the show.

In some denominations and religions, religious services are also another inappropriate occasion to arrive late. Late arrivals at Protestant religious services can expect to be seated during an appropriate break in the service. Anyone who enters a house of worship and finds the congregation praying or in a special contemplative moment should refrain from taking a seat until a break in the service.

There is even one occasion when arriving late can cause you to miss the whole event, and that is a wedding. Most wedding services are only about twenty minutes long, and the bride and groom are expected to be the center of attention throughout the service. Late arrivals may find themselves watching the entire service from the back of the sanctuary.

Latino

SEE *Hispanic.*

Lemon

Woe to the unknowing person who squeezes a lemon with abandon and ends up squirting his dinner partner. To avoid this admittedly minor disaster, shelter the lemon in one hand while squeezing it with the other *(see Figure 40).*

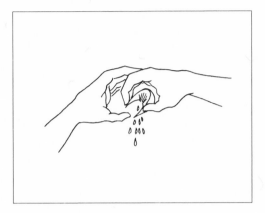

Figure 40. Correct (and safest) way to squeeze a lemon

Lesbian

SEE *Gays.*

Letter of Introduction

SEE *References.*

Linen Monogram

Monogramming has become expensive, and is considered something of a luxury these days. Monogrammed linens are a lovely present for a couple who are setting up housekeeping because it may be the only time they indulge in this small luxury. Tastes in monograms vary greatly, though, so it is always a good idea to check with the couple before giving them a monogrammed

Figure 41. Monogram styles for linens

gift to see whether they like monograms and what kind they prefer. Monograms vary in style from the elaborately scripted to a modern block printing *(see Figure 41)*. One initial or three may be used; two is usually considered a bit awkward in terms of design.

Another very good reason to check with the couple first is that they may not use the same surname, and this can pose problems in working out a monogram. Years ago the bed, bath, and table linens in a woman's trousseau were monogrammed—always with *her* initials. Even after a woman was married, her maiden-name initial adorned their household items. The woman's name alone is not usually used today. Instead a combined monogram of his and her first initials with their surname initial is preferred. If they use different surnames, a good idea is to use both surnames with a dot or other mark separating them. Seemingly "cute" monograms, like "His" and "Hers," are in poor taste.

Liquor

SEE ALSO *After-Dinner Drinks; Brandy; Champagne; Cocktail Party; Dinner Party; Wine.*

Whether or not to serve liquor is a personal decision; however, it is served with great frequency these days in homes and restaurants.

Alcoholic beverages have a way of being (or not being) trendy. From the 1920s through the early 1960s, cocktails were all the rage, and a sophisticated host was the one who could make the driest martini. In the 1960s, drinking tastes began to change. Health-conscious souls opted for white-wine spritzers, and vermouth on the rocks became popular. An entire generation of youngsters grew up without ever having tasted a martini. The trend away from hard liquor accelerated in the 1980s, and many hostesses and hosts today, particularly young ones, feel comfortable with a bar that consists entirely of red and white wine, soda water, soda (for the teetotalers), and a couple of vermouths and apéritif wines. A more complete bar would, of course, also contain scotch, whiskey, gin, and vodka, along with several after-dinner liqueurs.

SERVING MINORS. No hostess/host should take it upon herself or himself to serve a minor alcoholic beverages. It is against the law, and furthermore the minor's parents are the ones who should decide when and under what circumstances their child should be served liquor.

TEETOTALERS. Teetotalers and drinkers should strike a bargain: Those who prefer for one reason or another to abstain will spare everyone a sermon about their abstinence, and the gracious host/hostess will quietly offer a soft drink as a substitute to those who wish to abstain. Many people abstain these days for reasons that have little or nothing to do with disapproving of alcoholic beverages. Pregnant women should not drink, reformed alcoholics should not, nor should persons taking certain medications. In fact, enough people are abstaining so that a home bar should always be well stocked with soft drinks.

HOST'S/HOSTESS'S RESPONSIBILITY. In the past few years, many states have launched rigorous campaigns to educate people about the dangers of drinking and driving. The burden of blame has also shifted from the already drunken driver, who can rarely be stopped, to the person who served the drinks. As a host, you should be aware of when a guest has had too much to drink to drive. Tact should at first be used to dissuade the drinker from driving his or her own car. Arrange a ride and insist that the inebriated guest accept it; offer to drive the car around yourself the next day; call a taxi and put your guest in it. If all else fails, take the car keys away from a person who is in no condition to drive.

Living Alone

SEE ALSO *Singles' Entertaining; Singles' Friendship; Singles' Intimate Relations.*

Only in the past two decades have single women and men moved out from under their parents' roofs to establish households on their own. Many of those persons live with roommates, but a growing percentage of young adults over the past ten years have established their own households. If you decide to go this route, then by all means do so with a flourish. Set up a real, fully stocked household, one in which you can entertain your friends and thoroughly enjoy your moments of solitude. *(For more information on setting up your own household, see entries on Bath Linens; Bed Linens; Dishware; Flatware; Glassware; Home; Household; Kitchen; Kitchen Linens.)*

HOUSEWARMING/HOUSEHOLD SHOWERS. When you move into a new home, you should feel free to have a housewarming party just as a married couple might. A household shower, which has become a fad in some parts of the country, is another matter. Friends should not be permitted to hold a shower per se, but several friends could join together to buy a housewarming present for a friend.

PARENTS AND SINGLE HOUSEHOLDS. Some parents have difficulty understanding that their single children have their own households, and, by association, their own lives. A child's moving out inevitably redefines the parent-child relationship, just as a child's going off to school also changes the relationship by bringing in a new degree of independence. Each parent and child must work this out on an individual basis, but this is also one of those times when manners, being nothing more than rules for getting alone with one another, can offer some assistance.

Parents should respect their children's right to run their own households. The child is responsible for himself or herself now, and has a right to (1) choose his own brand names when grocery shopping; (2) eat frozen food—and no vegetables—for weeks on end; (3) live with as much mess as he can tolerate; and (4) wear reruns if the laundry does not get done on time. However offensive or disgusting these facts may be to a parent, they must be tolerated by the parent. In fact, the wise parent will wear blinders and an invisible gag when it comes to matters like this. This should be done not only out of respect for one's child but in order to preserve one's sanity.

Also important is for a parent to respect the child's privacy. Parents had a right to enforce house rules when a child lived at home, but they lost this right when their child established his or her own household. Respecting a child's privacy boils down to restraining oneself from prying phone calls at odd hours and unannounced visits.

CHILDREN AND PARENTS AND SINGLE HOUSEHOLDS. Children who establish their own households can also do several things to make their relationship go more smoothly with their parents. Begin by offering them some reassurance. Parents are often concerned about a child's physical safety, and you will do better to emphasize the safety of your new neighborhood than to tell horror stories about the latest mugging or street incident. Tell them you see a police car on your block about ten times a day and have just been befriended by the local beat cop. Try to reassure them on a more mundane level, too, by describing the great butcher you just found right around the corner or the drugstore that will deliver at all hours of the day and night.

Another way to assert your independence and at the same time reassure your parents of your abilities to take care of yourself is to invite them for dinner just as you would any other friends. Let them see that you know how to plan and organize and clean and cook for company.

Living Together

SEE *Cohabitation.*

Lobster in Shell

You won't encounter this at a formal dinner, but if you have any palate at all, you will arrange to encounter it somewhere. It's messy, and you are expected to use your hands. Eating lobster is probably the only time an adult can be seen wearing a bib; if the restaurant supplies one, do yourself and your dry-cleaning bill a favor and use it. See Figure 42 for the five steps to indulging in this gustatory delight.

1. Twist off the claws. Crack each with a nutcracker. Use pick or oyster fork to remove and eat the meat.
2. Break tail (culred-up end) off body. If tail is split, use fork to get at meat. If not split, break back flaps with your hands and push in with fork.
3. Twist off legs. Suck meat out gently.
4. Use fork to get small, accessible pieces of meat in body.
5. Use fork to eat tomalley (green matter) and roe (coral).

Lodging and Out-of-Town Guests

Persons who travel to attend a wedding, graduation, or other gala event should not expect their host and hostess to put them up either in their home or to pay for a hotel. The thoughtful host and hostess will check out several hotels and motels and make

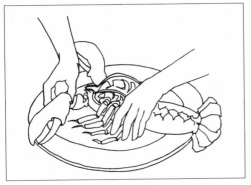

1. *Twist off the claws. Crack each with a nutcracker. Use a pick or an oyster fork to remove and eat the meat.*

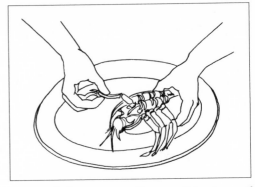

4. *Use fork to get small, accessible pieces of meat in body.*

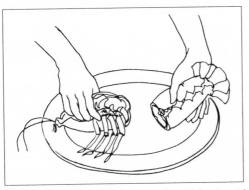

2. *Break tail (curled-up end) off body. If tail is split, use fork to get at meat. If not split, break back flaps with your hands and push in with fork.*

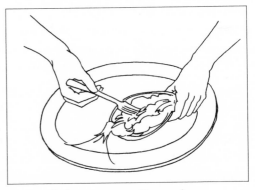

5. *Use fork to eat tomalley and roe.*

3. *Twist off legs. Suck meat out quietly.*

Figure 42. Correct way to eat a lobster

suggestions to their guests, even book rooms for them, but they should not feel obligated to pay for their out-of-town guests' lodging, nor should their guests expect them to do so.

Luggage

AIRPLANE. Skycaps are usually available at curbside to take the luggage of arriving passengers. Their services may be declined. If used, the tip should be a minimum of $1 per bag, more for large luggage.

BUS. A porter may be available in large bus stations to carry travelers' luggage to the gate. Tip bus porters 50¢ to $1 per bag and as much as $2 to $3 for handling a large trunk.

SHIP. Luggage is checked by a porter at the pier. Tell him which pieces should go into stowage and which ones should be delivered to the room. When sharing a cabin, it is considerate to bring as little luggage as possible to the room.

Tip the porter no less than $2 total and at least $1 per regular-sized bag. For trunks, tip $3 to $5.

TRAIN. Train porters greet passengers as they arrive and accompany them to the train platform. They store large bags at the end of the sleeping car and put a small bag or overnight case in the roomette. Basic prices for train porters are sometimes posted, but a small tip should be added to that. Between a listed price and tip, the porter should receive a minimum of $1 per a bag, more for a large bag or trunk.

ON FOREIGN TRANSPORTATION. Porters are not so readily available in other parts of the world, and you should always travel with the expectation that you will carry your own luggage. They should be tipped, in local currency, an amount equivalent to what American porters receive.

Lunch

SEE ALSO *Business Lunch; Wedding Reception.*

Ladies used to lunch; these days they are more likely to brown-bag it at their desks or grab a salad after a workout at the health club. Regardless of workstyle or lifestyle, we should all still make time in our social calendars for the occasional lunch. Not breakfast, not brunch, but an old-fashioned lunch.

MENU. Lunch is rarely formal, which is not to say that one could not get out the best china and set the prettiest possible table. Lunch food is usually lighter than that served at dinner, but it is appropriate to serve an entree and side dishes, usually salad and/or a vegetable, and a dessert. Some typical "lunch" dishes are quiche, omelettes, chicken breast in a light sauce, a lightly seasoned curry, anything served in a light pastry shell.

One way to keep lunch fairly light is to reduce the number of courses that are served. The most popular first course is a light broth or cream soup, followed by an entree. Dessert is often omitted in these diet-conscious days, or it may consist of fruit and cheese.

Alcoholic beverages may be served, or they may just as easily be omitted. Typical luncheon drinks, however, are Bloody Marys, screwdrivers, and mimosas, although anything may be properly served except for heavy cognacs and similar liqueurs, which are reserved for more formal evening meals. A good, light wine is an excellent choice at lunch.

INVITATIONS. Luncheon invitations may be extended in person, over the phone, or in writing. A lunch can be large, as when an entire group or organization holds a luncheon meeting, or it can be as delightfully intimate as two or three or four friends sitting down together to catch up on one another's lives over the course of a leisurely afternoon.

When asking someone to lunch, specify the time. Lunch is served between 12 noon and 2 or 2:30 P.M. Earlier than that and it is breakfast or brunch (although in some communities, the hours for lunch and brunch are the same); later, and it is tea.

Lunch Counters

Tips used not to be required at a lunch counter. This custom never made sense since lunch-counter waitresses and waiters work just as hard as those who wait on tables. Therefore it is only polite to show appreciation by tipping 10 to 15 percent of a lunch-counter bill.

Lying

Socially, lies are sometimes regrettably necessary. Each of us must decide for himself or herself how much is acceptable and under what circumstances.

White lies, as small social lies are dubbed, are told to spare the feelings of another. You have told a white lie when a friend asks you how you like her new—and as far as you can tell, perfectly unattractive—dress, and you respond by telling her that she looks great in it. A more honest white lie is to tell her that the color or fit or style is flattering without commenting on the dress overall. At the other end of the scale is the plain and often painful truth: "I think that dress looks awful on you. Is it too late to take it back and get something else?" The value of such honesty should be weighed on two levels: the degree to which it will hurt a friend and one's conscious, and possibly even subconscious, motives in exhibiting honesty that will surely hurt another person.

Ma'am

SEE ALSO *Women's Social Titles.*

"Ma'am," a shortened form of "Madam," is still used by children in certain parts of the country, mostly in the South, as a title of respect to their elders. A girl who has been taught to use this should be told that she may stop using it about the time she is 18 or 19, lest she begin to give offense. These days, it is mostly reserved for elderly women, and is not a welcome title for a woman in her forties or fifties.

"Ma'am" is also used in addressing royalty. By contrast, the First Lady would never be addressed as "Ma'am," except, again, by very small children.

Maid/Matron of Honor

SEE ALSO *Wedding Attendants.*

The bride usually asks the sister closest to her in age or the sister to whom she is closest personally to be her maid or matron of honor. The term "maid of honor" is reserved for an unmarried woman, while "matron of honor" is used for a married woman.

A bride also may ask a good friend to be her honor attendant. Usually a bride has only one honor attendant, but there is no reason the duties could not be shared if the bride so desires.

The maid or matron of honor assists the bride during the wedding ceremony. She takes her bouquet at the appropriate moment, lifts her veil, and holds the groom's ring until it is needed.

The maid or matron of honor usually is distinguished in some way in her dress. She may wear a dress of slightly different style from the bridesmaids; more often she wears the same dress in a different shade or color. She also may carry a slightly different bouquet. Or there may be no distinctions in her dress, according to the bride's preference.

Maiden Name

SEE ALSO *Names; Women's Social Titles.*

A "maiden name" is a woman's surname before she marries. Today, women have several options with regard to the use of their maiden names. Women use their maiden names until they marry, at which time the majority take their husband's surnames. A growing number of women today are electing to keep their maiden names after they marry, and even more working women resolve the problem by using their maiden names professionally while adopting their husband's name socially.

A few women combine their maiden name with their husband's surname to create a hyphenated name. For example, Mary Jones weds John Smith, and she becomes Mary Jones-Smith. He may or may not become John Jones-Smith. In some Latin cultures, families use both surnames in a similar manner, but this has not yet taken hold in the United States, and this solution probably creates more social problems than it resolves.

There is also a growing trend for a young woman who is divorced to resume using her maiden name.

Mango

SEE *Fruit.*

Marine Corps

Commissioned officers and warrant officers of the Marine Corps are called by their titles, which are parallel to those in the army. Their insignia is the same. Warrant officers' bands are scarlet enamel. Noncommissioned officers and other enlisted men wear sleeve badges of scarlet on a forest green background.

The ranks are as follows:

1. Sergeant Major—3 chevrons above 4 arcs, star in center
   and
   Master Gunnery Sergeant—3 chevrons above 4 arcs, exploding bomb
2. First Sergeant—3 chevrons above 3 arcs, diamond
   and
3. Master Sergeant—3 chevrons above 3 arcs, crossed rifles
4. Gunnery Sergeant—3 chevrons above 2 arcs, crossed rifles
5. Staff Sergeant—3 chevrons above 1 arc, crossed rifles

6. Sergeant—3 arcs, crossed rifles
7. Corporal—2 chevrons, crossed rifles
8. Lance Corporal—1 chevron, crossed rifles
9. Private First Class—1 chevron
10. Private—no insignia

Marriage

Marriage is the relationship with the greatest intimacy, and also the relationship that provides the greatest opportunity for abuse of intimacy. A smart couple realizes these pitfalls of intimacy and strives to preserve the more civilized side of their relationship.

It may seem oddly formal to think about being "polite" to one's spouse, who is, after all, the person around whom you are supposed to be able to be totally yourself, but treating a spouse with courtesy does a lot to keep a marriage lively. Even maintaining some small and rather formal courtesies—saying "Good morning," "Good night," "Please," and "Thank you"—is helpful.

One way to show love for one another is to make a concerted effort to maintain the manners that you used during courtship. I am convinced that we never quite let down our hair around someone until we are married to him or her, and then we too often do it to the detriment of the marriage. Everyone fears being taken for granted, but despite this, we begin to take our partner for granted almost immediately after we marry him or her. Manners can help us avoid this.

If a couple makes a concerted effort to maintain all the little courtesies they showed to each other before they got married—holding doors, exchanging small presents, carrying each other's packages, yielding to the other's taste for a certain kind of food or a desire to see a certain movie, consulting with each other before making plans—they will have gone a long way toward not taking each other for granted.

Courtesy also helps to keep the lines of communication open. Partners should try to make time in each day to sit down and talk with each other. A tendency exists once one is married to settle in and assume that one's spouse will always be the same, that nothing will change. But humans are not necessarily made this way, and the loving couple should never take each other for granted to this degree. Neither partner should assume, for example, that the other partner is satisfied with his or her career, or for that matter, with any other element of his life, but should occasionally make the time to sit down and talk about life goals, desires, wants, and needs, new interests and waning interests.

Courtesy can also be used to ensure that each partner gets some privacy. There is a period in every relationship when the intimacy is so intense that neither partner can imagine that the other one would want even a few minutes alone. Marriages fare better in the long run, though, if each partner feels free to take whatever solitude he or she needs. Some people need an hour or more a day; others need only a few minutes. Regardless of the amount of time that is needed, each spouse should learn to read the other's signals that he or she needs some time alone. A closed door, for example, should always be a sign that some privacy is desired. A spouse should knock on the bedroom door when it is closed, just as he or she should knock before entering a bathroom his spouse is using. A partner's need for privacy or solitude should never be cause for resentment on the part of the other spouse.

A spouse should also never snoop in his partner's life. Some couple's read each other's mail; others find this annoying. These things should be discussed, and each partner must abide by the other's wishes. A spouse should never assume that he has a right to read his partner's personal mail. Similarly, if one person has a special drawner, corner, or room in a house, the other one should respect it as his partner's turf. Obviously a wife can go to her husband'd desk to borrow a pencil when she needs one (and vice versa), but she should not feel free to snoop through the drawers of his desk or anywhere else among his personal belongings.

HOUSEHOLD WORK SHARED. Particularly when both partners work, a division of labor often exists at home, too. Some couples divide the labor formally, only after much discussion and rearrangement of their lives, and others just seem to fall naturally into a pattern of sharing work. Either way, once the household work has been divided, each partner should do his share without complaining or subversively undermining his responsibilities.

Marriage Vows Reaffirmed

On an important anniversary, a couple may decide to reaffirm their marriage vows.

There is a ceremony in most Western religions for doing this.

The ceremony itself is simple, with the wording of the reaffirmation vows being quite similar to the marriage vows.

Often a celebration is planned for afterward, although usually a couple only celebrates the reaffirmation of their vows with a big party once or on very large anniversaries, such as the twenty-fifth and the fiftieth (see also Anniversary Party).

Married Couples' Social Lives

In the eyes of the world, a man and a woman are never again regarded quite so separately as they are before marriage. Even a couple who live together are not viewed in the same light nor treated in the same way socially as a married couple.

Each marriage is highly individual, and what is expected of a married couple varies from generation to generation. Even a generation ago, a married woman was rarely seen lunching, much less dining, alone in public with a man who was not her husband. Today, when so many married women have careers, no one would ever think that a woman's marriage was on the skids simply because she was seen in the company of another man. The more likely conclusion would be that she was working!

Your marrieds today also tend to lead more independent social lives than their parents did. They often maintain separate friendships with persons of both sexes.

Their friends and families must always

invite them out as a couple, however, and it is up to the couple themselves to establish the extent to which they wish to pursue separate social lives. If you want to maintain a separate friendship with an old chum, your friend cannot suggest to you that the two of you have dinner without your spouse. To be polite, he or she must always extend the invitation to both of you. It is up to you, as the married person, to say, "Oh, we haven't seen each other alone for ages. Let's just have dinner alone tonight."

Most couples have decided on the extent to which they will lead separate social lives, but a polite partner still goes out of his or her way not to exclude his spouse. When Jack wants to have dinner alone with his old college roommate, he will still call his wife and say, "Dear, Bill is in town tonight, and he and I thought we would have dinner at the club. I haven't really sat down to talk with him for months, and I'm looking forward to catching up on his life. Do you want to join us, or would it be too boring for you?" Jack's wife will get the picture, and unless she has a special reason for wanting to join Jack and Bill, she can bow out.

Sometimes a partner will take the lead in bowing out. Jack's wife might say, "Oh, you men are awful to be with when you're reminiscing. Why don't just the two of you go to dinner and spare me?"

Another major change in married couples' social lives revolves around who handles the social calendar. All social invitations, until the past few years, were handled by the wife. If an employer wanted to invite a man who worked for him to dinner, his wife called his employee's wife and extended the invitation. A man who received an invitation at work or anywhere

else invariably said he had to check with his "social secretary" before responding.

Couples today, however, are much more likely to share this responsibility. Most couples do like to check with each other to make sure their calendars are clear, but invitations are now extended to either spouse, and either spouse may decline or accept.

As you can see, there is great flexibility in the way that a couple decides to handle their social life. It is up to each couple to set its own rules and draw its own boundaries.

Mass Cards

Roman Catholics often arrange for a mass to be said in memory of someone who has died recently. A card giving the date and time of the mass is sent to the family, who need not attend. A handwritten thank-you note should be sent to anyone who arranges a mass for a family member.

Meal Tray

Providing a meal tray (see Figure 43) to a family member who is ill or who would simply enjoy the luxury of breakfast in bed is a special, loving task. A meal tray can also make a lovely present for a family member, giving him or her a chance to luxuriate in bed a little longer than usual.

If the meal is a present, by all means use

Figure 43. Suggested arrangement of a meal tray

your prettiest linens or something bright and cheerful. If it is going to a sickbed, bright, cheerful colors will be appreciated. At any rate, the tray should be covered with a place mat, then set with a single place setting, including a napkin. It may be helpful to tuck in some extra napkins as they may be needed. A pretty flower in a bud vase is a nice touch, too.

Since balancing a tray in bed is not the easiest thing in the world, the food served should be simple. Broths and soups can be served in mugs to make them easier to handle.

The main course is brought in first on the tray, and if dessert is served, it and coffee or tea are brought in later.

Meetings

REFRESHMENTS. Refreshments are often served at meetings of social or charitable organizations. If a meeting is small and is held in someone's home, the host often assumes responsibility, including the cost, for serving a light snack. If a large group is meeting, either in someone's home or outside, the organization or group provides the refreshments, although the physical responsibility for getting them may fall on the shoulders of the person in whose home the meeting is held. Alternately, a refreshment committee may take charge.

ROBERT'S RULES OF ORDER. A meeting usually works best if it has some structure. The best and most widely used guide to conducting meetings is a book entitled *Robert's Rules of Order*. Based on parliamentary law and procedures, it is used by social and charitable clubs, as well as businesses, to conduct meetings. It can be borrowed from any library or purchased in any bookstore.

Melon

SEE *Fruit*.

Memorial Service

A memorial service may be held in addition to a funeral or in place of one. The body of the deceased is not present, the setting is some place other than a funeral home, and the regular funeral service is not used. The service may or may not be religious, usually depending upon the departed's and/or the family's preferences. Instead of the regular funeral service or eulogy, friends and relatives often give personal tributes to or share their memories about the departed.

A memorial service may be public or private. In some cities, a public memorial service is held some days or weeks after the death or a well-known person, particularly if the funeral has been private. Usually, the public is invited to attend these memorial services.

It is the Quaker practice to hold memorial services rather than funerals.

Men's Formal Wear

SEE ALSO *Wedding Attendants; Women's Formal Wear.*

The two kinds of men's formal wear are "black tie," also called "dinner jacket" (and less correctly called a "tuxedo"), and "white tie," sometimes casually referred to as "tails."

An invitation may or may not specify the kind of formal dress that is required. In general, when an invitation is formal or specifically states formal dress, black tie is worn. Only when an invitation specifically says "white tie" is white tie worn.

Most formal occasions call for black tie; only rarely is white tie the order of the night. Most men who buy their evening clothes (as opposed to renting them) invest in a dinner jacket. I always advise choosing a classic, traditional line that will not look dated as fashions change. Black, of course, is the preferred color for both black and white tie.

Black-tie evening wear consists of the following:

- A black jacket, in lightweight wool, double- or single-breasted, depending upon what flatters you. The collar may be plain with peaked labels or shawl. the lapel may be trimmed in satin or grosgrain faille.
- Matching pants, without cuffs, with a stripe of satin or grosgrain faille down the outside leg seam.
- A vest or cummerbund (never both), in wool to match the jacket. A belt is not worn.

- A white, front-pleated shirt with a classic fold collar or a white (but not button-down) dress shirt.
- A bowtie made of dressy fabric, usually satin or silk. The tie is traditionally black, but some men opt for a colored—often red—tie and cummerbund.
- Plain black oxfords or evening pumps with grosgrain bows.
- Thin (but not overly sheer) black socks, usually silk or nylon.
- Optional items include a black Homberg, gray suede gloves, a white silk scarf.

In warm weather, a white lightweight wool (or some blend) is substituted for the black jacket, but all other clothes remain the same. A cummerbund is always worn in place of a vest.

White tie consists of the following:

- A tailcoat with satin lapels. Properly fitted, the tails reach to just behind your knee.
- Matching pants, without cuffs, with a stripe of satin or grosgrain faille down the outside leg seam. (Note that the same pants that work for black tie can be used for white tie.)
- A white waistcoat. The traditional fabric is piqué, but cotton and even satin blends are sometimes seen.
- A white shirt with a wing collar. Studs are used in place of buttons. Very plain gold cufflinks are worn if the shirt has French cuffs, as most do.
- A white bowtie.
- Plain black oxfords or evening pumps with grosgrain bows.
- Thin (but not overly sheer) black socks, usually silk or nylon.

- Optional items include a silk top hat, a white scarf, and white gloves.

White tie is not properly worn before 6 P.M. Black tie is basically evening dress, too, but it is sometimes worn for a late afternoon wedding. Daytime formal wear is rarely worn today, except at weddings and occasionally when an ambassador presents his credentials. *(For daytime formal wear, see entry on Wedding Attendants).*

Men's Social Titles

SEE ALSO *Esquire; Names; Physician; Signature; Sir.*

The only social title that is widely used for men is "Mr." A boy under the age of twelve is addressed in correspondence as "Master." After the age of twelve, he is addressed as "Mister," which is, without exception, abbreviated (Mr.).

Menu Planning

There are, of course, all those things your mother taught you about meals: They should be nutritionally balanced; always include a green vegetable and a starch, and so on. Beyond that, there is a great deal more that should be taken into account when planning a meal, especially a company meal. It is perhaps easiest to think of a meal in courses, even if that is not necessarily the way you will serve it.

FIRST COURSE. Tried and true appetizer first courses are quiche, pâté, and cold fish or shellfish. Less traditional but popular today are such items as vegetables in vinaigrette or some other sauce or a small portion of pasta with sauce. While we all got pretty tired of fruit as a first course (there were all those ubiquitous grapefruit halves, either served plain or stuffed with crabmeat), there are some fresh, enticing fruit combinations (and sometimes fruit and vegetable combinations) that take advantage of the new array of fruits that are available practically year round these days, and many creative cooks have begun to serve fruit as a first course again. With the exception of a few, obviously unsuitable dishes such as stews and curries and the like, many entrees can be pared down and served as appetizers. The trick is to serve smaller portions. Most entree pastas work equally well as appetizers, provided the rest of the meal is not overpoweringly heavy.

The first course should be balanced against the rest of the meal to come. If a heavy entree is planned, for example, it should be light—or even omitted. If fruit is served for dessert, a first course of fruit would be overkill.

SOUP. Although considered a first course, soup deserves discussion on its own merits. Soups are an excellent way to start a meal, and some kind of soup is suitable before almost any entree.

Soup are heavy or light. Heavy ones are often made with a base of puréed vegetables and cream; light ones with a clear broth base. When a heavy soup is served, many cooks prefer to omit a starchy food with the entree. A cream of cauliflower soup, for example, would go quite well with roast beef and lightly sautéed vegetables, but it would be too much if potatoes or rice were also served. A light, broth-based soup would be excellent with a pasta dish, though.

Soups also may be served either hot or cold. Some soups only work when hot, and some only work when cold, and there are others such as potato-and-leek soup, that are delicious either way. I personally tend to serve hot soups during cold weather and cold soups during hot weather.

ENTREE. The entree is usually the first course chosen when planning a menu. All the other courses should be planned to complement it. To use a rather extreme example, if you are serving a curry that has a chicken-broth base and is of Indian origin, the menu would not be enhanced by hot-and-sour soup. You need not serve mulligatawny (the classic Indian soup) either, but should choose something that does not fight with the curry—a cream soup made with a green vegetable and cream base would be an excellent choice. The curry probably does not contain many, if any, green vegetables, nor does it contain cream.

Conversely, if you served a curry with a cream base, you would not then serve a cream-based soup. Watercress soup might work well.

SALAD. As I have said before, I like the salad to follow the entree (see also Dinner: Menu). I also favor a fairly simple green salad.

DESSERT. Dessert, too, should be keyed to the rest of the menu. If the meal has been heavy, the dessert should be light—cheese and fruit perhaps. If the meal has been fairly light, a rich, succulent dessert—chocolate mousse—is the perfect end.

More and more health-conscious cooks are abandoning dessert entirely, serving nothing or serving only fruit and perhaps cheese. This is fine at a casual dinner or if everyone knows this is what you do, but at a formal dinner your guests will usually expect dessert of some kind. One alternative is to offer dessert to those who want it, along with fruit for those who do not indulge in sweets.

Mexican Restaurant

SEE *Foreign Restaurant.*

Military

SEE *Air Force; Army; Marines; Military Title; Military Wedding; Navy and Coast Guard.*

Military Title

SEE ALSO *Air Force; Army; Marines; Navy and Coast Guard.*

The top positions in the armed forces—Joint Chief of Staff, Chief of Staff of the Army, Chief of Staff of the Navy—are filled by Presidential appointment. These appointments are made from among top-ranking officers, who continue to be called by their titles: General in the Army, Air Force, and Marine Corps, and Admiral in the Navy.

Women are addressed in the same manner as their male counterparts in the services.

Students at the military academies are addressed socially as "Mr." or "Miss," "Ms.," or "Mrs."

Military physicians and dentists are addressed by their official rank, although they may use "Dr." socially if they are junior officers. Naval physicians below the rank of Commander are addressed as "Mr.," as are all Coast Guard doctors.

Military chaplains are called "Chaplain" or by their military title, whichever is most flattering. In the Navy, "Chaplain" is the only correct title for a clergyperson below the rank of Commander.

Reserve officers, if inactive, do not use their titles socially. A high-ranking reserve officer who served for a long time is the exception; he is addressed as "General Franklin."

All retired officers in the Army, Air Force, and Marine Corps may continue to use their titles socially if they choose to do so. Only retired Naval officers above the rank of Commander may use their titles.

An officer's rank can be identified by his insignia, which are worn on all but formal mess uniforms *(see individual service listings).*

Military Wedding

When the United States is at war, military men must be married in uniform. During peacetime, being married in a uniform is an option that many professional military men like to exercise. Now that women have begun to make the military their career, it remains to be seen how many dual-uniform weddings or weddings with the bride in uniform we shall have. Formal dress uniform is appropriate at any kind of wedding.

The only time a problem arises with a professional serviceman who wishes to be married in uniform is when some of his wedding attendants are in the service and some are not. Either all the ushers must be in military dress uniform or none must be. The groom can, however, wear his uniform when his ushers wear traditional wedding dress or dark suits.

The bride and/or groom also may wish to use his or her title on the wedding invitation. If the groom's rank is Lieutenant Commander or above in the Navy or Coast Guard and Major or above in the other armed forces, it precedes his name on the invitation:

> Lieutenant Commander James
> Martin
> United States Navy

Noncommissioned service personnel may use their titles or not as they prefer, but they are identified this way:

> James Martin
> Corporal, United States Army

> *or*

> James Martin
> United States Army

> *or*

the marriage of their daughter
Alexandra Jane
Ensign, United States Navy

One other custom distinguishes a military wedding from others, and that is the arch that the military officers form with their swords. It is occasionally formed at the altar, in which case the bride and groom walk under it and the ushers then break ranks and escort the bridesmaids down the aisle after the couple, but it is more often formed outside on the church or synagogue steps. When it is formed here, the ushers escort the bridesmaids in the recessional and then escort the other guests outside. The ushers then go outside, form the arch with their swords, and the wedding couple walks through it. Only the bride and groom pass under the arch.

Miscarriage, Abortion, and Stillbirth

The woman who has a miscarriage or an abortion need not offer any explanations to anyone, unless she wants to, except possibly close family and friends who knew she was pregnant and will be concerned about her.

No one should be anything but sympathetic to a woman who has miscarried, or who, as a result of amniocentesis or for any other reason, has had to make the painful decision to have an abortion.

If the woman wants to talk about it, she should be given a sympathetic ear; if she does not want to talk, she should be left alone. Above all, she should be permitted to mourn in her own way. Never suggest to a woman who has miscarried or had an abortion or a stillbirth that this is a minor loss or that she needs only to get pregnant again right away in order to feel better. Comments like this, which have traditionally been used to console women in these situations, really show great insensitivity.

Monument

SEE *Gravestone*.

Motels

CHECKING IN. To check in, drive to the main office and sign in. You may be required to use a credit card as identification and proof of ability to pay. You will be given a room key, and you then return to your car and drive it directly to your door. When signing the register, sign the names of all persons who will be staying in the room. This is a safety precaution.

CHECKING OUT. Checkout procedures are equally simple. Pack your luggage into your car, and drive around to the main desk to check out.

TIPPING. While there are no porters to tip, you should leave something for the motel maids. A tip of one to two dollars a night is adequate. Room-service waiters should be tipped 15 to 20 percent of the bill.

Mourning

SEE ALSO *Christian Mourning Customs; Funeral; Gravestone; Graveside Service; Jewish Mourning Customs.*

Formal mourning customs, which have largely fallen by the wayside in the past few decades, make the decision of how to mourn the loss of a loved one entirely personal. Black is no longer socially required of the immediate family, either at the funeral or in the months following it; black armbands are virtually never worn except possibly on the day of the funeral. Nor need someone restrict his or her social activities after the loss of a loved one. One may, but society will not disapprove if one does not. Since mourning is an internal process, each person must find his or her own way of dealing with death. If you do not feel like going out socially for a few weeks after the death of a loved one, and few persons do, feel free to reject the well-intended invitations of friends. If you do not feel like wearing brightly colored clothes, then do not wear them. On the other hand, if your late husband loved you in a bright red dress, and you feel close to him wearing it, by all means, wear it. Wear it even to the funeral it if will help.

The immediate family does usually wear black or dark-colored clothing to the funeral of a loved one. Jewelry should be conservative; traditionally only a watch and wedding rings are worn.

Jews do not wear unrelieved black to funerals, as a rule.

Anyone attending a funeral should behave in a dignified and somber manner. Boisterousness, laughter, and other displays of gaiety are inappropriate. Certainly, if you are a chief mourner, you will not feel joyful, and if you are a friend or acquaintance, your behavior should be appropriately subdued out of respect for the family and other mourners.

In the weeks after the funeral, friends should respect the wishes of mourners regarding their need to mourn, and should offer only appropriate forms of consolation, taking their cue from the bereaved person. A widow may be offended by the suggestion that she attend a party within weeks of her husband's death, but she may be deeply appreciative of the friend who asks to come by and merely spend some time with her or the friend who calls to ask if she would like to take a drive or go for a walk.

As noted earlier, a mourner should be permitted to avoid social commitments until he or she is ready to resume them. The only exception is a wedding. Except for the death of a parent, a wedding need not be cancelled. Even when someone in the immediate family has died, a wedding may still take place. A person in mourning may always attend a wedding, perhaps bowing out of the reception festivities.

Christmas cards may be sent to persons in mourning, but they should be specially selected so they are not frivolous.

tially public entertainment, and because of this, all movie patrons have an obligation to be considerate of others.

If possible, arrive before the movie begins so you don't have to crawl over people who are trying to settle into the mood of the movie.

The most offensive behavior these days at movies comes from people who talk right through the show. A little quiet conversation is fine before the film starts; a few soft whispers are even acceptable as the credits roll ("Oh, I saw that actress take a bath in *The Big Dive*."), but no—repeat *no*—conversation is acceptable once the film has begun. Even if you don't want to concentrate on the opening credits and hear the introductory music, others do.

If you must leave during a movie, do so quietly. Good reasons to leave during a movie include the following: (1) This isn't your cup of tea and you don't intend to watch it; (2) you have a cold and a coughing fit comes on you (you may return as soon as the coughing is under control; (3) ditto, a sneezing fit; (4) you took a chance and brought your two-year-old who promised to be quiet and is now keeping up a steady patter. A bad reason to leave during a movie is that you suddenly decided ten minutes into the film that you must have popcorn. Be polite and get it before the movie starts. And if you do eat in a movie, do so as quietly as possible.

Movies

However much a movie may resemble watching television, it remains an essen-

Ms.

SEE *Women's Social Titles.*

Museum

Museums and art galleries are places for quiet enjoyment, but because they are public places, cooperation among visitors is necessary. Always talk in a quiet voice. Few things are more obnoxious than someone lecturing a friend and anyone else within hearing distance about a piece of art or some other museum display.

Children should be kept under control at all times. They should not be allowed to roam around by themselves, run through the rooms, or talk in loud voices.

Unless you simply cannot avoid it, never pass in front of someone who is looking at a display. If you must pass in front of someone, excuse yourself.

Never monopolize a particular display. Take the time you need to look at it, but move on so others can enjoy it, too.

If someone is looking at a display, treat him with the same courtesy you would like to receive if you were looking at something. Do not crowd in, make comments, or otherwise act impatient.

Musicians

SEE *Anniversary Party; Ball; Dance; Wedding.*

Mussel

Eat steamed mussels the same way as you would steamed clams. Eat mussels in the shell the same way as clams on the half shell.

Names

SEE ALSO *Baby; Men's Social Titles; Women's Social Titles.*

FIRST NAMES. Americans are quick to use first names. They often begin using them as soon as they are introduced to someone. Among peers, this seems to be acceptable practice, and there are occasions when the use of surnames is offensive, but I think those quick to use first names often run a risk of giving offense when they do so with older persons. Then I always recommend staying with a title and surname (Mrs. Evans, Mr. Benson) until the older person asks you to use his or her first name. Employees below a certain rank in many offices are still expected to use titles and surnames, even though in many offices employees are on a first-name basis with their employers from the first day of employment.

Of course, one need not go along with the excessive intimacy that prevails these days. Parents may wish to teach their children to call adult friends "Mrs. Jones" and "Mr. Smith," although I must warn you that you will be swimming against the current. I still feel it is a genteel sign of respect for children to call adults "Mr. So-and-So" and "Mrs. So-and-So" until they are invited by the adults to do otherwise.

Unfortunately, the fad for familiarity has extended throughout our society, and I find that all manner of people who serve me these days, from the doorman at my daughter's apartment building to the grocery delivery boy seem to think it acceptable to call me by my first name. Of course, in better stores and restaurants, no well-trained salesperson would dream of addressing a customer by his or her first name. If you wish, you can resist the first-name syndrome by sticking with your title and surname when announcing yourself or introducing yourself to someone who will work for you or be selling you something. Simply say "I am Miss Moss" or "Please tell Mrs. Jones that Mr. Addington is here to see her" when you are asked your name.

FORGETTING. It is always awkward to encounter a casual acquaintance or even a friend and be unable to recall his or her name. If you are unaccompanied when this happens, your momentary block may go unnoticed.

If you are with someone who must be introduced, it is difficult to bluff. Besides I don't believe in bluffing in such situations; I think misdemeanors only escalate into major crimes when they are not dealt with immediately. It is acceptable, however, to stall for a few minutes in hopes that the conversation will provide you with enough clues to deduce the person's identity or that your brain cells will somehow miraculously reorganize themselves and save you, but after anything more than a few minutes, the problem threatens to escalate and you run the risk of giving more offense by not making the introduction.

There are times when an introduction can be avoided entirely, such as when you are with a casual acquaintance and bump into another casual acquaintance. You simply say hello to the second casual acquaintance, exchange a few pleasantries, and go on about your business. If you are with your mate or your child, it is almost impossible to avoid an introduction.

When the moment comes that you simply must introduce someone to another person whose name escapes you, just confess the problem. Apologize and say, "I am so sorry, but your name has slipped my mind."

Sometimes the problem is reversed. If you bump into someone and sense that he or she does not remember your name, it is kind to help out by saying, "I don't know whether you remember me or not. I'm Joshua Wright and I worked with you on the Red Cross fundraiser last year."

Spouses and other good friends can often sense when their partner or friend is at a loss for a name. When this happens, and you sense the other person foundering, you can gracefully save the situation by introducing yourself. If you say "I'm Joshua Wright," the other person invaribly responds with, "I'm Sally Jones." and the introductions are accomplished, at no loss of face to anyone.

NICKNAMES. Some people enjoy nicknames, and other people have a serious aversion to them. Before you take it upon yourself, therefore, to dub someone with a nickname, check with the person. Better yet, don't take it upon yourself to dub someone with a nickname. Call each person by the name that he chooses to use. If someone introduces himself as "Michael," for example, do not decide to call him "Mike" or "Mikey" and if someone introduces himself as "Mike," it is not up to you to call him "Michael." Even when other people call someone by a nickname, do not assume that you know the person well enough to use it, too.

Children and teens especially love creating and using nicknames with one another; this is part of their peer development. Eventually there comes a time, though, to stop using these childish names. Your friend, whom you fondly remember from grade school days as "Rat," and who has now become a Wall Street corporate lawyer, may never say it, but will undoubtedly gnash his teeth every time you bump into him and insist on addressing him as "Rat." Ditto the childhood custom of addressing peers by their surnames. Once we all become adults, the only genteel thing to do is call each other by our forenames. Do not wait for someone to tell you to stop using a childish nickname; just do it.

PARENTS' AND CHILDREN'S NAMES. SEE ALSO SINGLE PARENT. In these days of reconstituted families, it is not unusual for parents and children to have different names. An unmarried woman (divorced or never married) with a child may not want to use the child's father's name, but the child may use that name. The child also may use the mother's name. Regardless of the reason, the child has a different name from at least one of the parents, and this is too often a source of curiosity to others. No explanation about a difference in name need be given to anyone except close friends, and if the two names are different, only a brief explanation is required: "I use my name, and he uses his father's name."

MARRIED WOMAN. Most women base their decisions about whether or not to change their names on their and their partner's personal feelings, their careers, and their social standing. By the latter, I mean that if all the women in your social circle are know as "Mrs. John Doe," you may be fighting a losing battle to insist on retaining your maiden name socially. I am not saying that you should not do it, merely that you will encounter resistance if you do.

Whatever name you choose to use when you marry, it is necessary these days to announce it, not in print but casually to friends, acquaintances, and business colleagues. Simply say, "By the way, I've decided to keep my name instead of using John's." Especially tactful if your husband or fiancé is present is to include him in the announcement: "John and I have decided that I will use his name socially and keep my maiden name professionally." As a matter of courtesy and because he may have feelings about it, and most certainly will want to be part your decision, you should discuss the name you plan to use after you are married with your fiancé.

DIVORCEÉ. SEE ALSO FORMS OF ADDRESS—SPOKEN; DIVORCE. A divorced woman may take back her maiden name or continue to use her ex-husband's name. If she goes back to her maiden name, she is Mary Jones, having been born with the surname Jones. If she uses her ex-husband's name, she is Mary Jones Smith or Mary Smith. In any case, she no longer uses Mrs. John Smith.

WIDOW. A widow who continues to use her husband's name is known as Mrs. John Jones. She may also choose to be known as Mrs. Mary Jones or simply Mary Jones. Few widowed women have any desire to resume use of their maiden names, but there is no reason a woman could not if she chose to do so.

Napkin

I still favor cloth napkins, but I sympathize with the homemaker who uses paper napkins for family dining. Except for very large groups, I think cloth napkins also provide a nich touch when entertaining. If I can persuade you to use cloth napkins *en famille*, I suggest also buying napkin rings so family members can reuse napkins for several meals. That way, each family member can put the napkin back in the napkin ring at the end of each meal. One-time guests will obviously be given a clean napkin, but guests who stay longer than one meal may be assigned a napkin ring.

If the family uses cloth napkins, they should be changed as soon as they show signs of wear, within three days for some families and as long as a week for others. The napkins should match or at least complement each other. If a guest comes, new napkins should be put out for everyone if necessary for them to match. Unmatched napkins may be used when large groups are entertained, although they should all be color-coordinated.

PLACEMENT. At a formal dinner, napkins should be placed in the middle of the place setting, on the service plate. If the first course is on the table when the dinner guests sit down, the napkin should be placed beside the forks.

At less formal dinners, a creative hostess may find many different places for napkins. They may be tucked into a water or wine glass or go anywhere else in the place setting.

USING A NAPKIN. As soon as you are seated, put your napkin in your lap. If grace is said, do not put your napkin in your lap until after the prayer.

A small napkin should be opened, and a large napkin may be opened only partially. Napkins always go in the lap. With the exception of paper bibs supplied by lobster restaurants and those under the age of two, a napkin should never be used as a bib.

A napkin should be used to blot one's mouth gently to remove any crumbs or food particles before taking a drink. Note that the proper action is blotting. A napkin should not be used to wipe the mouth. It should go without saying (but does not in these days of abundant paper napkins) that a napkin should *never, under any circumstances* be used as a substitute handkerchief. I can think of few things more inconsiderate to one's hostess or a waitress or waiter than to have to clear away a napkin that has doubled as a handkerchief.

Lipstick presents its own problem when cloth napkins are used. If paper napkins are used, there is no need for worry, but cloth napkins may be stained by lipstick. On the other hand, a woman who wears lipstick has every right to wear it to lunch or dinner. I suggest that a woman blot her lipstick carefully before coming to the table, and that she take great care to dab very lightly at her mouth when wearing lipstick.

When you are finished with a napkin, refold it loosely and place it on either side of the plate. It should not be meticulously refolded.

National Anthem

When the national anthem of the United States, "The Star-Spangled Banner," is sung or played, all present are expected to stand quietly at attention or sing along. When another nation's national anthem is sung, and you are a guest in the country, it is polite to stand quietly at attention. You may sing along if you know the words. Members of the armed services stand at formal attention.

Navy and Coast Guard

The ranks are the same in both branches, except the Navy has the title of Fleet Admiral and the Coast Guard does not. Navy personnel wear rank pins similar to those worn by the Army, but the enameled bands are navy blue. Commissioned officers also wear stripes, anchors, stars, and corps insignia embroidered on their uniforms.

In the Coast Guard a shield is used in place of the star. The ranks are as follows:

Commissioned Officers

1. Fleet Admiral (Navy only)—1 broad stripe, 4 full stripes; 5 gold stars
2. Admiral—1 broad stripe, 3 full stripes; 4 gold stars
3. Vice Admiral—1 broad stripe, 2 full stripes; 3 gold stars
4. Rear Admiral—1 broad stripe, 1 full stripe; 3 gold stars
5. Commodore (wartime rank only)—1 broad stripe; 1 gold star
6. Captain—4 full stripes
7. Commander—3 full stripes
8. Lieutenant Commander—2 full stripes, 1 half-stripe
9. Lieutenant—2 full stripes
10. Lieutenant (jg)—1 full stripe and 1 half-stripe
11. Ensign—1 full stripe

Warrant Officers

12. Chief Warrant Officer (W-4)—1 full stripe, broken by 1 blue interval
13. Chief Warrant Officer (W-3)—1 full stripe, 2 blue intervals
14. Chief Warrant Officer (W-2)—1 full stripe, 3 blue intervals
15. Warrant Officer (W-1)—1 half-stripe, 3 blue intervals

Noncommissioned Officers and Other Enlisted Men:

Sleeve insignia of petty officers are blue with red stripes and white emblems; seamen wear white stripes on a blue background.

16. Master Chief Petty Officer—2 stars (or shields), eagle, 1 arc above 3 chevrons
17. Senior Chief Petty Officer—1 star (or shield), eagle, 1 arc above 3 chevrons
18. Chief Petty Officer—eagle, 1 arc above 3 chevrons
19. Petty Officer 1st Class—eagle, 3 chevrons
20. Petty Officer 2nd Class—eagle, 2 chevrons
21. Petty Officer 3rd Class—eagle, 1 chevron
22. Seaman (and other titles such as Airman, Fireman, Stewardsman)—3 stripes
23. Seaman Apprentice (or Airman Apprentice, etc.)—2 stripes
24. Seaman Recruit (or Fireman Recruit, etc.)—1 stripe

New Job

The first days on a new job can be trying indeed. If the office is friendly, your head will spin with trying to keep straight so many new, smiling faces. And then there are those offices that simply do not take note of someone new. They leave you wondering if you showed up at the wrong address by mistake. If you know how to handle yourself, you will make the first days on a new job fairly easy to handle regardless of how they are treating you.

DRESS. Plan to wear something fairly conservative your first few days on the job, until you can survey what others wear and see what goes and what does not. Also keep in mind that employees with tenure can get away with more than new employees. Everyone is watching a new employee, and you are expected to pay your dues.

INTRODUCTIONS. Introductions will be your main activity as a new employee the first few days on the job. Don't worry if you forget a few faces. They will begin to sort themselves out. Do whatever you can, though, to help this process along. This is one situation where you can say, "I'm so sorry I've forgotten your name, but I've met so many people the last few days."

MAKING FRIENDS. Every office has someone who tries to move in a little too quickly and befriend the new person. This helpful soul may turn out to be a true friend and a valued colleague, or he may turn out to be the office troublemaker. As a result you are better off holding back a little, at least until you have sorted everyone out somewhat, during your first few days on a new job.

By all means, accept luncheon invitations because that is how you get to know people, but be a little slow to settle down to regular lunching with one clique. Respond with friendliness to all these helpful and not-so-helpful overtures, but do not fall in with the first person or group to befriend you. Doing so may hurt your chances with other groups and with your career. Do not let the office gossip corner you and fill you in on everyone; wait and learn these things for yourself.

Newspaper Announcement

There used to be a saying that a well-bred woman had her name in the paper only three times: when she was born, when she was married, and when she died. Even though we now live in an age of celebrity when more publicity is often welcomed, and sometimes solicited, these remain the three occasions in most people's lives when formal announcements are made to the press.

BIRTH ANNOUNCEMENTS. It is still a popular practice in most communities to announce local births. Usually, the parents need do nothing (although in some large city dailies, they are paid announcements), and reporters will report recent births from the hospital records.

DEATH ANNOUNCEMENTS. SEE ALSO DEATH; FUNERAL; OBITUARY. Death announcements, not the same as obituaries, are paid announcements. Death announcements are placed by the funeral director, based on information he has collected from the family.

ENGAGEMENT. SEE ALSO ENGAGEMENT. Engagement announcements are submitted to local newspapers, who may publish them if they choose to do so. In some communities, almost any announcement that is submitted is published; in large city dailies, such as *The New York Times*, only a select number of a engagements are announced in the editorial pages of the paper.

Call the newspaper to which you want to submit the announcement and ask them to mail you the submission forms. If they do not have any prepared forms, discuss the required format for an announcement.

Engagement announcements usually describe the bride's and groom's education, their current employment, their parent's social position and current employment, and may even describe several generations in the family lineage.

If you prepare the announcement, try to duplicate the format of the announcements the newspaper usually publishes. The announcement should be neatly typed, double-spaced, on 8½-by-11-inch white paper. Type your name, address, and a telephone number where you can be reached during the day at the top of each page. Include an identification line at the top of each page: McCloud engagement, for example.

PERSONALS. SEE SINGLE LIFE.

SOCIAL ACTIVITIES. Leading an active social life can land you either in the social columns (desirable in many people's eyes) or the gossip columns (not so desirable in many people's eyes, unless you are a celebrity personality and need publicity as a boost to your career).

To get this kind of attention, you probably must know or be known to the colum-nist or writer who covers the society beat in your local newspaper. If that is the case, you can also to some extent manipulate the kind of publicity you receive, for example, by inviting a reporter in to cover a large dinner but declining to have a small, intimate dinner covered. In general, if you play fair with the writers who cover society and help them write some of their stories, they will leave you alone when you wish to be left alone, provided, of course, that you are not a celebrity for whose activities the public has a voracious appetite.

Finally, keep in mind that no publicity is sometimes its own form of publicity—and is often far more tantalizing than too much publicity.

Nurse

A nurse employed in one's home is a professional. The relationship is that of employer-employee and not one of servant-employee.

If a nurse lives in, she should be given her own room, and her hours should be set by mutual agreement. Her work assignment will be limited to caring for the person she is hired to care for, and she should not be asked to perform household tasks. She may take her meals with the family or by herself, whichever she prefers.

TIPPING. Since a nurse is a paid professional, she or he will not expect tips. If someone has worked for a family for a long time, however, affections develop, and most employers find they want to give some kind of gift on occasion.

Obituary

SEE ALSO *Newspaper Announcement.*

An obituary is not the same as a newspaper notice of death. Obituaries are newspaper reports on the death of a famous (or infamous) person. The family cannot request or buy them. If someone in your family is prominent enough to warrant an obituary, you may want to gather the information (including his or her résumé) shortly after death so it can be correctly given to the reporter who calls. This is not a particularly good time to rely on memory.

Obscenities

SEE ALSO *Humor; Profanity and Vulgar Language.*

Foul language, which has become all too common and even chic these days, is none-theless not to be admired or respected. Many of us use it for years, beginning early in adolescence and it is only when we have children of our own that we begin to realize that we do not want our children to pick it up. Pick it up they will. The only question is whether they will learn it from their peers or hear it at home. Parents have about ten years to influence their child's development before peer pressure begins to play a competing role, and I advise them to teach their children to express their thoughts and emotions clearly without benefit of obscene language.

Office Assistant

Somewhere in rank between a secretary and a peer colleague is the assistant. In some offices, an assistant is merely a glorified word for secretary, but in others, an assistant is far more than that and merits a different kind of treatment. The assistant who deserves more professional behavior from you is the one who truly assists you—who provides you with assistance you need to do your job properly and even takes over some of your work.

GENERAL RELATIONSHIP. As is the case with anyone who works for you, you will be better off maintaining a certain professional distance. The temptation to make an assistant—particularly a good one—a sort of personal extension of you is always there, but it is not a good step for either of you.

An assistant may well be privy to some of your personal secrets—a promotion you are after, even the fact that you are looking for another job, or a special assignment you will both work on. In fact, it is a good idea to make an assistant feel that the two of you are a team. You will be repaid with hours of work and loyalty, and both are exactly what you want from a good assistant.

There are, however, limits to the loyalty you can expect—and should cultivate—in an assistant. No one should expect an assistant to take on his likes and dislikes, move to another department with him (unless the move is also a clear promotion for the assistant, too) or in any way alienate an assistant so that he will feel he has to leave the company when his boss does. And to the extent that no one should do this to an assistant, the savvy boss has to know how to maintain a certain amount of warm and friendly yet distinctly professional distance in the relationship. The assistant will not know to do this; it is up to the higher-ranking person.

It is also important to keep in mind that, however close you are or however much you see an assistant as your protegé, you are still the boss. If you are unnecessarily friendly with an assistant, upper management may observe that you are more comfortable in the ranks of lower and middle management and may cease thinking of you as upwardly mobile. Even if they do not do this, they may question your management skills if you are seen as unusually soft on the people who work for you.

As a general rule of thumb, you should be friendlier to an assistant than to most other people in the office, in a sort of parental way, but you should not make him or her your best friend.

It is important to recognize the degree of control you have over an assistant, as well as the extent to which you do not control him or her, so that you can work together compatibly. Assistants have some independence in many offices, and they may even report to your boss rather than to you. His or her job responsibilities may have been clearly defined by your boss or you and your boss working together.

Regardless of whom the assistant reports to, though, you are probably responsible to some degree for his or her work habits—whether he arrives on time, whether he dresses appropriately for the office, whether he handles his work well. If an assistant repeatedly arrives late, for example, you would only be doing him a favor to point this out and tactfully request that he get to work on time.

What is inappropriate behavior on your part and will most likely cause offense is to ask an assistant to do things that are outside his defined areas of responsibility. Just as secretaries will willingly type and file but won't willingly get the boss coffee and run personal errands, an assistant will not like being asked to do filing and typing that is quite properly secretarial work. It is bad form even to ask. If an emergency arises and you must ask an assistant to do work that is beneath him or her, make sure the request is accompanied with an explanation and an apology. Another way to enlist an assistant's assistance is tactfully to suggest that he or she help you solve a problem. For example, you might say: "We are desperate to get this report typed since it is due tomorrow morning, but John has already left for the night. Do you know anyone around here who might handle it?" That leaves the assistant with two options: finding a willing pair of hands to type the report or offering to type it himself. It also leaves him or her feeling that he or she is part of a team that has a problem to solve, rather than feeling that he or she is the hired hand who is ordered to do something.

If you have no choice but to order an assistant to do something he or she will consider a menial task, try to recognize these feelings when you make the assignment: "Sally, I hate to ask you to do this, but this report is due tomorrow. Could you do us both a big favor and lend a hand by typing it tonight?" Any smart assistant knows that this politely couched request is actually an order.

Courtesy and tact are called for in other areas of the relationship. In some offices, everyone is on call around the clock, and your assistant cannot turn you down and expect to keep his job for very long, but a well-mannered boss also recognizes that his employees have a life outside work and plans in advance, when possible, for overtime.

If you must ask someone to work late, and cannot give advance notice, couching your last-minute request as if it were a favor will go a long way toward soothing hostile feelings.

Also helpful is occasionally to offer a polite bribe to an assistant who takes on last-minute or excessive amounts of overtime. This greasing-of-the-wheels keeps everyone happier in the long run. For example, if you must ask your assistant to work overtime, and you know he has theater tickets or tickets to some special sporting event, offer to pay for the tickets or gift him with tickets to something else as a way of compensating for his loss. You need not do this every time overtime is required, but doing it once in a while buys you a lot of goodwill. Note that it may be company policy to pay for things like this on occasion, or it may have to come out of your own pocket, but either way, it is worth it.

INTRODUCTIONS. Think of introductions as a kind of small perk. When a VIP visits you in your office, particularly someone who will be of interest to your assistant, introduce them to each other. Not only should you introduce them, but take advantage of the opportunity to show off and compliment your assistant. This is the time to say: "I'd like you to meet John Riley, Mr. Chairman of the Board. He is the person who put together that report on new products that you liked so much." A fair and even generous ackowledgment of others' contributions makes you look good.

Always introduce a lower-ranking person to a higher-ranking person. Nowhere is this clearer than in an office, where hierarchies are carefully set forth. An assistant and other staff members are presented to all VIPs. ("Mrs. President of the Company, I don't think you've met Joe Helpful, who is my assistant. Joe is working on the ABC acquisition with me. In fact, he's really been burning the midnight oil putting together a report on the annual profits in the X sector." "Mr. Big Client, I'd like you to meet Sally Efficient, my assistant. Sally has been gathering some very interesting information on the XYZ Project.")

Joe or Sally should stand for the introduction. The lower-ranking person usually waits for Mr. or Ms. Big Shot to extend his hand. As he shakes hands with the VIP, he should say something congenial such as, "I'm delighted to meet you. Yes, that project has been keeping us busy." Note the use of "us" rather than "I." This is definitely a time to act like a team player.

LUNCHING WITH AN ASSISTANT. Whether the company pays or it comes out of your own pocket, treating an assistant to an occasional lunch pays big dividends. And, yes, the boss always pays. Lunches are very useful for getting to know employees better and building personal ties.

It is a good idea to organize lunches along hierarchical lines. For example, there will be times when you will lunch with your staff, i.e., your secretary and any assistants. But there should also be times when you lunch individually with assistants; a one-on-one lunch with the boss is a valued perk. These lunches also afford an opportunity to get a progress report in a fairly informal, relaxed setting. A savvy boss will plan both individual and group lunches on a regular basis.

Office Decor

Just as all companies have dress codes, many of them unwritten, so, too, do all offices have decorating codes. In some ways, then, the company with the rigid decorating hierarchy is the easiest to fathom. At least you know what is expected of you. In corporations like this, office decor is tightly controlled, and you must petition the Great Corporate Decorator in the Sky if you wish to add so much as an ashtray. You almost certainly will not be permitted to hang that watercolor of a sailboat that you acquired at last summer's street fair, and you may even have to choose your wall decorations from among a selection of prints that are available to those on your level of employment. (Corporate art in and of itself has become Big Business, and with rank comes privilege, like the privilege of hanging an oil painting rather than a drawing or watercolor.)

As for office furniture, this, too, may be strictly regulated by rank. Rank A gets you a small sofa, Rank C, two rather uncomfortable chairs for guests placed in front of your desk. In almost all companies, in fact, employees are not free to choose their own office furniture. Even if the exact pieces of furniture are not regulated by rank, you must still choose furniture that conforms to the overall look of the office.

If you are permitted free reign in decorating your office, keep a few things in mind, the first and most important of which is that this is your office. It is not your den or study. Keep knickknacks and mementos of personal activity to a minimum. The man who is an avid tennis player and who chooses to display photos of himself playing tennis and other tennis mementos should also realize that he may be sending a direct message to his boss. The message, unfortunately for him, is this: I'd rather be playing tennis. Such messages have been known to adversely affect one's climb up the corporate ladder.

Among the other no-nos' in office decor, apart from those that announce your strong interests outside work, are very domestic decorating accessories (anything needlepoint or embroidered, especially anything with a motto or cute or funny saying on it), small games and other executive toys, any kind of toys (unless you happen to manufacture them)—in short, anything that is too cute. Women especially should take care to avoid domestic touches in their offices.

A trickier problem is whether to display photos of your family. Many young working mothers have told me how much they enjoy having photos of their children on their desks, yet I think this smacks of announcing your outside interests too much. The boss may wonder how dedicated you are to work if you spend much of your time gazing at a photo of your child. Unfortunately, it is women who are most suspect for having photos of their children on their desks.

With men, family photos often work the other way around, that is, they serve to remind the employer of what a steady, stable fellow he has in this man. Particularly today, when a high value is placed on family life (not so in the Fifties, when the ultimate corporate man tended to put his family after his career), a man can use photos to send his employer a very positive message.

Too many photos for anyone are overkill, however. Before placing photos in an obvious place on your desk, consider your situation (did you have to convince your boss that children would not interfere with your job?), and what other people seem to

be doing. If yours is a friendly, family-oriented office, and everyone has a picture or two of his family on display, then by all means, join the crowd. If photos are not displayed, take a hint. This company is too tough for that sentimental stuff.

Office Gossip

SEE ALSO *Business Friendship; Gossip.*

All offices have a grapevine, and unfortunately about 90 percent of all rumors have some basis in fact. Despite that, these rumors can do a lot of damage and hurt a lot of feelings before they come to fruition as fact. People have learned from the grapevine that they were being passed over for promotions, or, worse, fired. Companies have lost out on bids and projects and have otherwise been damaged by office gossip.

The best strategy, both in terms of being a kind person and in terms of looking out for your own career, is to avoid spreading gossip. Listen to it, if you must, but let it stop with you.

Office Guest

RECEIVING GUESTS. You may either greet guests personally, by walking out to the reception area to greet them, or you may ask an assistant or secretary to greet them and bring them back to your office.

When a guest arrives in your office, stand to greet him or her. Walking out from behind your desk is a particularly gracious gesture. Bosses and other high-ranking employees deserve guest status, but they are also more likely to be in and out of your office many times during the course of a day. If this is the case, you need not stand to greet them every time you see them, and they, of course, are free to sit without a specific invitation from you.

Shake hands and offer the guest a seat. Beverages are often offered to office guests. This is one time when it is appropriate to ask a secretary or assistant to serve coffee or tea. That way, you do not lose valuable time conducting business.

In the course of conducting business in their offices, some people like to come out from behind their desks and sit on the same level with their guests; others like to maintain the power position at their desks. This is a matter of personal style.

WHEN YOU ARE THE GUEST. As a guest in someone's office, you should stand until you are invited to sit down. Never sit until you are invited to do so, particularly if you are on a job interview or in a superior's office. When you do sit down, place your briefcase and/or purse in an unobtrusive spot near you. Never put anything on the desk. In fact, always consider the desk the other person's space. Even when you are making a presentation, wait until the other person suggests that you use his desk.

If you are ushered into an office, and its occupant is not there, never sit at the desk and never snoop, not even to examine bookshelves. Many people have jobs of which all or part are confidential, and any nosing around could easily be misread as snooping,

so do not feel free to look around when you arrive in an office.

When the "host" takes a phone call or has a conversation in your presence with someone who comes into the office, act as if you heard nothing and resume your conversation where you were when you were interrupted.

You may feel free to accept a beverage if it is offered to you, but do not ask for one. It is fine, under most circumstances, to ask where the restrooms are. The best time to do this is when you are leaving.

Be quick to take a cue from the person whose office it is when it is time for you to leave. When he or she stands up or makes some concluding or summarizing statements, the meeting is coming to an end. Gather up your things, say a speedy goodbye, and leave. Never prolong goodbyes in an office environment. It is simply not businesslike.

Office Life

SEE ALSO *Business Friendship; Client Relations; Office Gossip; Office Love Affair; Office Politics.*

The grind of day-to-day office life requires the same empathy and tact that is required to live year in and year out with one's family. In fact, in many instances you will find yourself spending more time with your colleagues than with your family. The same good manners that carry you through the vagaries of domestic life will serve you well in the office.

GREETINGS. In most offices people exchange greetings the first time they see each other every day, and they say goodnight to their colleagues when they leave for the day.

Beyond that, each office has its own mode of relating. In some offices, everyone is chatty throughout the day; in others, everyone works fairly quietly throughout the day, and people may only nod when they pass each other in the hall or meet at the water fountain.

CONVERSATION DURING THE DAY. The atmosphere varies from office to office, but since you are there to work, most people indulge in less rather than more chitchat during the day. While you want to remain friendly, you do not want to fritter away your valuable work time or have your boss think you are doing that. Occasionally someone will become a bit of a pest and you will have to handle this tactfully.

If you are the boss, you can be fairly direct about telling this person to talk less and work more. If you are a colleague, a more tactful approach is called for. Try not responding, or responding with only the barest nod. If that does not do the trick, say, "I'd love to talk, but I'm really too busy to right now" or "I can't chat now because I have to get this done right away."

ANNOYANCES. Worse than the excessive talker is the co-worker with an annoying habit, such as chewing gum noisily, cracking his or her knuckles, or smoking excessively. Rather than suffer in silence and always being a little cold to the offender, try having a frank discussion about what it is that bothers you. The gum chewer and knuckle cracker probably have no idea how

their habits annoys others, and once you point it out they may make an effort to stop.

The smoker and nonsmoker may have more to work out since there is so much animosity between the two groups. Lucky you if yours is one of those offices that has smoking restricted to certain areas only. If this is not the case, you will have to take matters into your own hands. Begin by explaining that the smoke annoys you, say you are sympathetic to his or her desire to smoke (even if you are not), and ask the person if the two of you can work out a compromise, that is, if the person can smoke somewhere else or smoke fewer cigarettes a day. Let the offender make a few suggestions first, if he or she is willing to work with you on this, and then add your suggestions. Since you have to co-exist, it is in your both best interests to compromise, and most co-workers find a way to live together peacefully.

Another person who rouses everyone's ire is the newspaper borrower. Frankly, I would prefer to lend a newspaper to an out-and-out freeloader, when it is convenient to do so, rather than to waste my time and energy stewing about it, but if you cannot accept this situation so placidly, then you probably should say something such as, "Sure you can borrow it, but how about chipping in to buy a daily paper since we both enjoy it so much?"

There are other bad habits that drive co-workers up the wall, and in every situation some kind of compromise can be reached. Remember your co-workers are, in a sense, your family. Certainly, you are expecting to have a lengthy relationship with them and will want to keep that relationship on as friendly a level as you can. Tact, friendliness, and everyday good manners can go a long way toward achieving this goal.

Office Love Affair

Office love affairs, once strictly taboo, have become acceptable in recent years. In fact, a recent survey shows that relationships among co-workers last longer than relationships started under more casual circumstances, most notably, health clubs and singles bars—and that more than half of all women have been involved with a co-worker. Despite this good news, those who indulge must do so with care. And by office affair, I am speaking of a liaison between two unmarried persons. Goings-on between a couple where one or both are married are dangerous under any circumstances, but particularly so in an office, where careers often come tumbling down over such infidelities.

Some persons choose to keep an office affair so quiet that no one knows what is going on. Others are unable to do so, for any number of reasons. Discretion, however, is the key to any office affair.

Any boss will quite correctly draw the line when the affair starts to interfere with business. So keep in mind that *any* displays of affection at work—furtive loving looks as well as lover's spats—are unwise.

The exact amount of discretion that is called for varies from office to office. In some offices, the couple who are involved tell no one, plan dates in out-of-the-way places where they are not likely to encounter anyone from work, and always make sure to come to work separately, even though they have spent the night together.

In other offices, everyone would consider this a lot of unnecessary subterfuge. Couples who are known as couples and who may even possibly live together come to work together. With any office affair, you gauge the tolerance for such activity in your particular office to know how to conduct the affair.

BETWEEN SPOUSES. Many professional couples these days find they can sell themselves as a team and both work for the same company. Not surprisingly the same rules of discretion apply to them. Obviously they may walk in together in the morning and leave together at night, but the married couple who work together must take care to keep their domestic life and their love life out of the office. As would be the case with any other couple, they must avoid lover's looks, rendezvous, and quarrels during office hours. They must also avoid much discussion of their domestic arrangements or too much time spent on the phone with each other. Neither of their bosses will be happy to have a conference interrupted with a call from one spouse asking the other spouse if he can stop by the grocery store on the way home or pick up little Johnny at day care. The married couple who works together, like the unmarried couple who plays together, must realize that their every action will be subject to special scrutiny.

Office Politics

SEE ALSO *Office Life.*

My advice about office politics is to rise above them. They are like bits of dirt on a piece of lettuce in a salad that you are served in someone's home. If at all possible, pretend they are not there.

Of course, not everyone is in a position to ignore office politics. If you must play, try to do so honestly and fairly, all of which will get you a reputation as a very well-mannered person.

Of those who do play office politics, most are ambitious. And while there is nothing wrong with being ambitious, you will get along better if you temper your ambition with courtesy. It is important that other people like you for you to get ahead, and being courteous is one of the best ways to make others like you.

Old-Boy Ties

Old-boy ties are those with someone who has attended your college or belonged to the same clubs as you. The ties are most strongly associated with Ivy League schools. These bonds are often counted on in business, when, for example, it is acceptable to call someone whom you do not know personally but who attended your alma mater to request some information. Old-boy ties are particularly useful in building a client list and checking out prospective employees and employers.

Open Fly

An open fly is always embarrassing, but provided you know the person well enough to say something, the kindest action is to let the person know about it rather than ignoring it. The moment of embarrassment when someone learns that his fly is open is far smaller than the embarrassment suffered when returning home hours later and discovering it. A woman who does not feel comfortable telling a man she knows only slightly might enlist the aid of another man whom she does know.

Open House

An open house is a form of entertainment in which one's home is opened with great hospitality during a set number of hours. Most open houses last three to six hours. During that time guests come and go as they please, feeling no obligation to arrive at a scheduled time or stay for the duration of the party. A good guest, however, does not arrive right on the dot of the scheduled time, nor does he stay until the very end, unless he is a good friend of the family or close relative and can offer assistance serving food and cleaning up.

While being a guest at an open house is easy, a considerable amount of effort is required of the host and hostess. Each guest, regardless of the time of arrival, must be greeted, supplied with a drink, introduced to others, and eventually fed something, usually a buffet lunch or dinner. Ten guests may arrive at the same time or two guests may arrive over the course of an hour; all must be welcomed, settled in, and served food and drink. If the guest list is very large, staggering the time on the invitations will help somewhat.

Guests may be invited in person, but written invitations are often sent. Those invited to an open house need not respond unless a response has been requested on the invitation.

An invitation to an open house should specify the time of the party, including a time when it ends. For example, the invitation should read "two to seven P.M." or "seven to eleven P.M."

An open house is an excellent way to entertain for a housewarming, a party for out-of-town guests after a wedding, and around the holidays. Christmas Day or New Year's Day open houses are traditional in some families and communities.

Opera

Opera is the showiest of the performing arts, so it is only fitting that the audiences wear more plummage than at other kinds of performances. Years ago, the custom was always to dress for opera; today, black tie and evening dresses are seen mostly at opening nights and gala performances.

For opera, you must be in our seat for the curtain or you may not be permitted to go there until an appropriate break in the action, which could be well into the first act.

The players are rewarded with applause at the end of each act and for a more extended period of time at the end of the performance. Particularly lovely or strenuous arias are also applauded, and the singers may take bows for them. Cries of "brava" (for a female singer) and "bravo" (for a male singer) will be heard for particularly splendid performances.

FLOWERS. Opera lovers are known to dote on their favorite performers, and flowers may be thrown on the stage or bouquets delivered to favored prima donnas as they take their final bows for the evening. A florist will also deliver a bouquet backstage. It should be addressed to "Miss Prima Donna, Backstage, The Metropolitan Opera House." Enclose a note or an informal, but be forewarned that such cards are often lost in the happy confusion that prevails after an exciting performance. Alternately, a bouquet can be delivered in person, provided the prima donna is receiving visitors after the performance.

Orange

SEE *Fruit*.

Outdoor Entertaining

SEE ALSO *Barbecue; Picnic; Tailgate Party*.

Lucky you if you have a setting in which to entertain outdoors. By all means make the most of it, whether you have a picnic, a barbecue, a beach party, or an elegant dinner party that just happens to be served outdoors.

Outdoor entertaining as a rule can be far more casual than other kinds of entertaining. Paper plates and napkins are definitely acceptable, as are plastic glasses. Plastic utensils may be used, but I find them too flimsy and suggest instead that you invest in an inexpensive set of flatware for outdoor entertaining. Note, too, that there is nothing wrong with entertaining elegantly outdoors—using real dishes, glasses, and flatware—but merely that something less is quite permissible.

Outdoor entertaining is usually scheduled during daylight hours, but if you have the facilities to entertain after dark, there is no reason not to. When planning to entertain outdoors, you must have either a rain date in mind or alternate plans to move the party indoors should the weather be bad.

Out-of-Town Date

SEE *Teen Dance*.

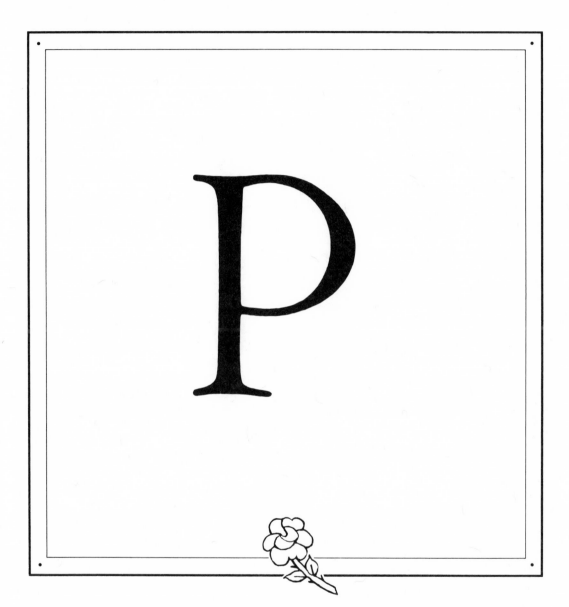

Pallbearer

SEE *Funeral.*

Papal Audience

Anyone who wants to can arrange to be invited to a group papal audience. Hundreds appear at these audiences.

Arrangements should be made well in advance of a trip to Rome. The person who wants the audience must ask a priest or a well-known layperson to submit a letter of application to the North American College, the proper authority. When the audience is granted, a letter is mailed to the person who requested it. Upon arriving in Rome, you must obtain directions for submitting your letter of acceptance at the Vatican. After this, a day and hour for the audience are assigned, and an invitation is sent to you. The concierge in your hotel will be able to advise you in greater detail on these procedures.

General audiences take place in the morning on Wednesdays at St. Peter's. If you have not been assigned a reserved seat, arrive early so you can stake out a good viewing position.

Dress conservatively even if you are one of hundreds. Women wear dark-colored dresses, with unrevealing necklines and long sleeves, and cover their heads. Men wear conservative business suits; in the reserved section, some men will wear formal morning dress, and most women will be in black with gloves and mantillas.

Some people—those who can do so—prefer to arrange for a private audience. These are granted to prominent persons of all religious persuasions. This still does not necessarily mean that you will meet the Pope alone, but you will not be among the throngs for the Wednesday-morning audiences at St. Peter's.

When the Pope approaches a visitor at a private audience, the visitor is expected to kneel and kiss his ring. If you have some religious objection to doing this, other arrangements may be made if you speak to the monsigneur in charge when you arrive.

Dress is very conservative at a private audience. Some men will be wearing formal morning dress, but most will be in dark blue, black, or gray suits. Women wear black dresses, gloves, and mantillas. Jewelry is considered inappropriate; men and women wear only wedding rings and watches.

Papaya

SEE *Fruit.*

Party

SEE *Anniversary Party; Bachelor Dinner; Ball; Business Entertaining; Business Entertaining at Home; Caterer; Card Party; Children's Party; Clambake; Cocktail Buffet; Cocktail Party; Dance; Debutante Ball; Dessert and Coffee; Dinner Party; Entertaining Style; Farewell Party; House Party; Housewarming; Invitation; Kaffeeklatsch; Outdoor Entertainment; Open House; Reception; Supper; Sweet Sixteen Party; Teen Dance; Teen Party; Wedding Reception.*

Pasta

There are those who claim that "real" Italians eat pasta by holding a fork against a soup spoon and wrapping the pasta around a fork, while others maintain the spoon is never used and the fork should be placed against the plate while the pasta is wrapped. The truth is that pasta is eaten in different ways in different parts of Italy. Proponents of both schools miss the point, however, which is to eat pasta without making a fool of oneself by letting it hang from the mouth and/or slurping it. One thing is known: Pasta is most manageable when wrapped around a fork, and it matters not how this is accomplished.

Passing Food

When food is served family style, it is passed around among the diners so that each person may help himself. Food is supposed to be passed counterclockwise, but far more important than this fine point of etiquette is that all the food be passed in the same direction simply because this makes good logistical sense.

If something is within easy reach, and you do not have to stretch your arm in front of someone else to get it, you may simply reach for any dish that you wish. If something is not within easy reach, simply ask, "Would you please pass the spinach, Jackie?" When Jackie passes the spinach, thank her.

Care should be taken to pass a serving dish in a way that is convenient for the person who will serve himself or herself from it. For example, one person might balance a very hot or heavy dish while the person to the left takes food from it.

Some people are superstitious about the passing the salt and pepper shakers; they do not want to accept them directly but prefer that they be placed on the table. And, yes, the two should always be passed together even though only one is requested.

The correct way to pass a cream pitcher or any small pitcher or dish with handles is to pick it up by the handle with one hand, grasp it with the other hand on the side opposite the handle, and turn it so the handle is presented to the person who requested it *(see Figure 44)*.

Pay Calls

Whenever you make a long-distance or a toll call from someone's personal telephone, offer to pay the charges. Certainly for long-distance phone calls, do not take no for an answer, and, if need be, leave the money where it will be found with a short note explaining what it is for.

When using a coinless phone in someone's business, offer to pay for the call. Usually your offer will not be accepted, especially if you are a customer, but it is presumptuous not to offer.

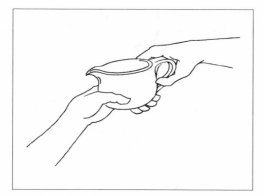

Figure 44. Correct way to pass a small pitcher or a dish with handles

When using a pay phone in a public place, try to be courteous to others. Use the telephone only for brief calls; lengthy personal calls should be made on your own phone in the privacy of your own home. People who conduct business in public pay-phone booths are especially annoying. Shorten a conversation when someone is listening. If you finish one call and must make another, either offer to let someone waiting squeeze in his or her call or tell the person you will be only another minute.

If you find yourself waiting to use a pay phone, do so patiently. Do not tap your feet, sigh, or otherwise harass the person who is talking.

Peach

SEE *Fruit*.

Pear

SEE *Fruit*.

Persimmon

SEE *Fruit*.

Personal-Ad Date

The "personals," long considered a déclassé way for two people to meet each other, have now become acceptable and as hot as singles bars were in the 1970s. Not surprisingly, an "etiquette" for using the personals has also emerged.

When making a date with someone whom you found through a classified ad, you need not obligate yourself to more than a quick get-acquainted meeting. A drink or cup of coffee should be enough to see whether you want to pursue this further. Certainly, as a matter of safety, that first meeting should be in a public place. After the ritual cup of coffee, a decision must be made about whether or not to go on to dinner together. If the two of you are getting along well enough, there is no reason not to. If you want to leave dinner optional when you make the date, that is fine, but do not say you have plans and then let them magically vanish when you make an on-the-spot decision to have dinner. Far better to be honest when making plans and say, "Why don't we just have coffee and see how that goes." If you do not feel comfortable going to dinner, then it is acceptable to say that you have dinner plans or something else you must do that evening.

Many people who respond to personals use the telephone for their introductory date. If you do this, you should do yourself and the other person a favor by being completely honest, in as tactful a way as possible. If you sense that this is not someone you want to get to know better, say so gently. For example, you might say, " I'm so glad we've had this time to talk, but I don't think it would make much sense for us to get together. We don't seem to have much in common, although I can tell you're a very nice person." And do not let yourself be talked into a meeting that you

can tell won't be very pleasant or fruitful in terms of generating a new friendship.

Personal Correspondence

I find it a sorry situation that so many of us have arranged our lives so as to almost never have to write a letter or note of any kind to a fellow human being. This is a most uncivilizing custom, and I wish I could convince you all of the warmth of personal written communication with friends and family. It is, of course, quite acceptable these days to telephone congratulations, news, and thanks, but the telephone never, to my way of thinking, is as gracious as the written word.

OBLIGATORY VS. GRACIOUS LETTERS. There are a few occasions when not writing a letter is rude. A letter or note is always expected under the following circumstances.

1. Thank you for wedding present
2. Thank you for spending night or longer in someone's home
3. Thank you for presents not opened in the presence of the giver
4. Letter of acceptance or regret to all formal invitations
5. Letter of condolence to any friend who has lost a member of his immediate family

A written letter or note is especially gracious under the following circumstances:

1. Note of congratulations in response to any important event, honor, or award, or other accomplishment in a friend's life
2. Thank-you note to anyone who has done a favor for you
3. Thank-you note to hostess after a party or dinner

APPEARANCE OF PERSONAL LETTER.

Personal letters, like business letters, have a definite format. If there is a letterhead, the date goes under it. If there is no letterhead, write the date in the center of the page or in the upper right-hand corner.

A personal letter begins "Dear Jack" or "My dear Jack," followed by a comma. Closings for personal letters are highly variable and depend upon your relationship with the person. "Love" works for family, lovers, and close friends. "Fondly" and "Yours" (or "Yours always") are always appropriate for letters to acquaintances with whom you aren't especially intimate but toward whom you feel warmly.

"Sincerely" is used most often to close personal business letters.

Here is a typical personal letter:

June 6, 198—

Dear Chauncey,

Thought the enclosed clipping might be of some interest to you.

We were both delighted to see you the other night, and we think these reunions are much too far apart.

Hoping to see you soon.

All best,
Joan

APPEARANCE OF A PERSONAL BUSINESS LETTER.

Business letters are used to order services and goods, to complain, to return unsatisfactory merchandise, and to make recommendations.

The format for a personal business letter is slightly different from strictly personal correspondence. The heading must include not only a date but also an address. Of course, if there is a letterhead, you need only type or write in the date. Here is a typical format for a personal business letter:

April 22, 198—
123 W. 98th Street
New York, N.Y. 10025

Dear Mr. Holmes:

Enclosed is the invoice for last month's meat. I am sorry about the mixup. Now that you know our new address, I assume there will be no problem with next month's bill.

Sincerely,
Mrs. Donald Foxx

You will occasionally use your personal business stationery to write a letter of recommendation. They are usually written for someone who will be joining a club or group that you belong to. Here is a typical one:

(letterhead)
February 2, 198—

Dear Mrs. Nelson,

I am delighted to recommend Natalie Windell for membership in the Tuesday Club. I've known Natalie for years. She has been a close personal friend and I've always known her to be kind and supportive.

In addition, Natalie and I have worked together in the League of Women Voters. Natalie, you may remember, organized and introduced the political debates last year. If you saw them, I am sure you will agree with me that Natalie will make an excellent addition to our club.

If I can answer any other questions, please feel free to call me.

All best,

All personal correspondence may be either typed or handwritten with two exceptions: thank-you notes for wedding presents and condolence notes should always be handwritten.

If you do write your personal correspondence by hand, your handwriting should be legible.

You should also take some pride in the look of your personal correspondence. The writing in handwritten letters should be legible. Make sure the writing goes in a straight line and does not roam uphill or downhill. Always choose the best paper you can afford for your stationery.

ADDRESSING ENVELOPES. A formal response—and these are always handwritten—is addressed as follows:

> Mr. James Hill
> 38 Oak Lane
> Indianapolis, Indiana 46234

An alternate method of addressing is this:

> Mr. James Hill
> 38 Oak Lane
> Indianapolis, Indiana 46234

On formal correspondence, everything is spelled out, with the exception of Dr., Mr., Mrs., Ms., Jr., and Sr.

If your return address is not printed on the back of the envelope, write it in, centering it on the back of the flap:

> 261 Elm Street
> Columbus, Indiana 37645

On other less formal correspondence, abbreviations may be used for streets and states.

People ahould always be addressed with the names they use, that is, a married couple who use two different names should be addressed that way:

> Mr. William Gross
> Ms. Janet O'Connor

No personal message is acceptable on the outside of an envelope, but some other messages are:

Personal. This is correctly used only when you send mail to someone's business address. Then "personal" informs the office staff that the letter is to be delivered un-opened to the person to whom it is ad-dressed. Never write "personal" on an en-velope sent to someone's home; it implies that family members cannot be trusted not to open one another's mail.

Please Forward. When someone has moved and you know only the old address, you can request that the letter be forwarded to the new address.

Please Hold. This is written on mail sent to a hotel or address at which the recipient has not yet arrived. The message asks that the letter be held for the person's arrival.

Courtesy of is written on a letter or pack-age that is delivered in person. It serves to introduce the messenger to the recipient of the letter or package. (Of course, if you have hired a messenger, there is no need to make this introduction as this is purely a business transaction.)

FOLDING THE LETTER AND STUFFING THE ENVELOPE. Small stationery may be

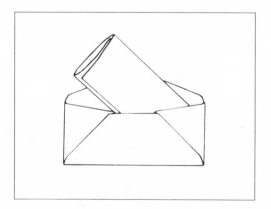

Figure 45. Stationery that is folded in thirds is inserted into an envelope so that the wrong side of the top sheet faces toward you.

folded in half horizontally, and larger sta-tionery is folded in thirds.

It should be put in the envelope so the note or letter will fall open ready to read *(see Figure 45).*

Pest in Food

A pest in your food is annoying, and how it is dealt with depends upon whether one is in a restaurant or someone's home.

In someone's home, some discretion is called for. One option is to eat around the offender. Another is to quietly ask the host-ess for another serving. A savvy hostess will not ask why; she will simply comply. If circumstances don't permit you to do this, it may be necessary to eat around the of-fender.

At a restaurant, simply ask a waiter to bring a new plate of food, but do so quietly so other diners are not subjected to the same offense.

The same method may be used when one is confronted with a spotted glass or dirty piece of flatware. Very quietly ask the host-ess or waiter for a substitute.

When someone requests a new serving, polite companions do not inquire into the circumstances.

Pet

Pets can be taught manners the same as other living creatures, and if you want peo-ple to like your pet, you will teach it some basic rules of good behavior. For example, a dog should be trained not to jump on people or otherwise annoy them. In public, the animal should always be on a leash. And the dog owner should obey the law and clean up after their animal. Not to do so is to display the most basic contempt for one's neighbors and community.

Keep in mind also that some people simply do not love animals. When you sense that such a person is uncomfortable around your pet, the kind thing to do is to keep the animal away.

If possible, people who have allergies to animals should take an antihistamine before they visit a home with cats or dogs. The owner may be able to keep the pet(s) away, but since there is animal dander and hair around this may not solve the problem entirely and thus precautions are sometimes necessary.

Pew Card

SEE *Wedding Invitation.*

Phone Machine

SEE *Telephone Answering Machine.*

Photographs

SEE ALSO *Wedding Photography.*

Photographs make excellent presents under certain circumstances. Couples in love, for example, often exchange photographs of each other. A bride often gives her new husband a framed photograph of her wedding portrait. Parents and grandparents adore receiving and viewing pictures of their children and grandchildren.

Public figures, particularly politicians and actors, often distribute photographs of themselves to those who have done them favors. These photos are always signed, and are all the more valuable if they are signed with a distinctly personal message. Only public figures can get away with presenting a photograph as a gift and not also giving a frame. As a rule, when you give someone a photograph of yourself, particularly a portrait, it should be given in a frame. And that frame should be chosen to match the individual's taste and style of decor.

Of course if you have taken some candids of a friend's children or other family members, these need not be framed and you may give simply a set of prints. A lovely gift, though, is to present a matted frame with several candids.

GREETING-CARD PHOTOS. Families often enjoy having an annual portrait taken and then using this photo to create a Christmas card that is sent to all the friends and acquaintances of the family. I see no objection to this practice, and I enjoy receiving such cards, but I would caution that they are most appropriately sent to close friends only. It is not particularly appropriate to send such personal greetings to business associates and acquaintances.

Physician

SEE *Doctor; Military Title; Title.*

Picnic

SEE ALSO *Barbecue; Outdoor Entertaining.*

A picnic is an outdoor meal that usually consists of cold dishes or simple grilled foods. It can be eaten in the backyard or on some special outing to a beach or park.

When a picnic is eaten in a public place, care must be taken to leave the site as clean or cleaner than it was before the picnic. This helps to ensure that the next group has an enjoyable time.

Pineapple

SEE *Fruit.*

Pizza

Pizza, although primarily a finger food, may be eaten with a knife and fork. This pronouncement will undoubtedly be a relief to those who do not like orange-colored oil sliding down their forearms but who feel silly using utensils to eat what most of the world views as finger food.

Methods of eating pizza vary throughout the country, and there is no one "correct" way to eat it. New Yorkers generally fold their pizza slices lengthwise, while those in the rest of the country tend to hold the pizza slices flat while eating them. Whatever works for you is right.

Place Card

Place cards are used at any dinner where the host/hostess want or need to have a plan for seating their guests. Blank place cards can be purchased in most stationery stores. If the party is large, and last-minute cancellations can reasonably be expected, the wise hostess does not waste time filling out place cards very far in advance. This is one task that is best relegated to the last minute.

The names of the guests should be written in black or gaily colored ink; black is the correct color for a formal dinner. If there is likely to be any confusion over guests' names—two women are named Mary, for example—last names should be used. At a formal dinner, titles are often used: Mrs. William Smyth, Mr. Robert Johnson.

Placemat

Placemats come in a variety of shapes and materials, and each hostess must choose ones that suit her style of entertaining and personal tastes. Placemats, acceptable at a formal dinner, are proper at a formal lunch, where a damask tablecloth is considered too much.

Now that you know the rules, I propose doing what pleases your eye. At a formal lunch or dinner, white linen placemats can be lovely. On more casual occasions, a wide range of less formal woven cotton, hemp, and synthetic placemats are available. (For that matter, I see no reason not to set a luncheon table with a tablecloth—white damask or something else—if that suits you.)

To please the eye, the shape of placemats should accommodate your dishes and the size of your table. Placemats should never overlap, and ones that are designed to hang over the edge of the table are often awkward to use. A placemat may be round and so small that it holds only the plate, in which case the rest of the place setting goes directly on the table. Alternately, it may be oval or rectangular and accommodating enough to hold an entire place setting.

Except for family dining with very young children, I think plastic placemats are best avoided. Good synthetic fabric ones resist stains well enough to be practical for everyday; woven ones are also practical, as are inexpensive natural-fiber ones, and all these are far more pleasant to the senses than plastic.

Place Setting

SEE ALSO *Dishes; Fork; Knife; Napkin; Spoon.*

A place setting *(see Figures 46 and 47)* is the arrangement of individual dishes, glasses, and flatware for each diner. All tables are set alike, which means to accommodate right-handed people. The flatware is not reversed for someone left-handed or for any other reason.

All place settings should be equidistant from one another, and enough space should be allowed between them to make eating a comfortable experience. About 12 to 18 inches space is best, but this will vary, depending upon the size of the table, the number of diners, and the shape of the chairs.

Figure 46. Basic informal place setting

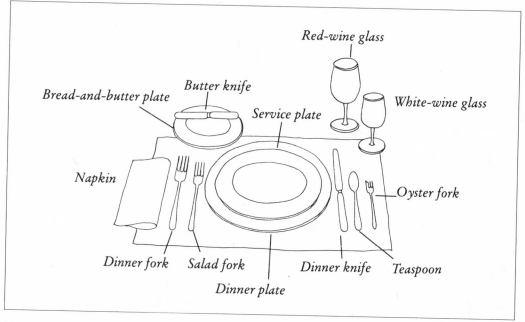

Figure 47. Basic formal place setting

If placemats are used, the place setting is centered on them, although they need not be large enough to accommodate everything in the place setting. Put the plates in the center, with any picture or design facing the diner. The flatware goes on either side. Forks are always placed on the left, and knives and spoons on the right. (There are some exceptions; see the listings under Fork; Knife; and Spoon.) The blades of the knives are always turned inward, facing the plate. The napkin goes on the plate or to the left of it (never under the fork except with paper napkins at a picnic, where the wind might blow them off the table). If a decorative fold is used, it may go anywhere that is attractive—in the wineglass, for example. Glasses go to the right above the knives. The bread plate goes on the left above the forks.

Line everything up about one inch from the edge of the table or placement. Figure 47 shows a formal place setting. For less formal settings, remove utensils and dishes as necessary to suit your dining style.

FORMAL VS. INFORMAL. SEE ALSO CENTERPIECE; DINNER PARTY. A formal table setting is usually (but not always) set with the best china, sterling, and crystal glasses. An informal place setting makes use of pottery dishes, stainless flatware, tumblers instead of water goblets, and so on. The choices are entirely up to the individual host or hostess. To my mind, the only thing that is inexcusable is to set an unattractive table. Casual need never mean unattractive, nor need formal ever mean stuffy.

In planning how to set a table, keep in mind balance, convenience, and attractiveness. Do not be afraid to use color or unusual objects to create the table decor. I've seen several collectors draw on their collections to create unusual and stunning centerpieces. The only limit is your imagination.

Plastic

I admit to a prejudice against most plastic when used in home decor. I dislike plastic flowers certainly, and also most plastic dishes, glassware, and table linens. I like the beauty of real (and, sometimes, fabric) flowers and the feel and touch of real dishes and glassware, to say nothing of table linens. I say this with full awareness that some excellent household designs have been done in plastic.

Increasingly I acknowledge that there is a time and place for some plastic—at a picnic or when dining with small children, to name just two occasions—but I still believe that good taste dictates that plastic items not be used to any great extent and certainly not when entertaining.

Plate

SEE *Dishes; Dishware.*

Play Date

Children as young as three or four who live in cities and cannot easily go outside to play with their friends frequently arrange "play dates" so they can visit with them. The children often ask each other, at school or over the telephone, but only with their parents' permission, and it is usually the mothers who make the final arrangements.

Arranging play dates is a gracious way to teach your child about reciprocation, and it also ensures that your child has a social circle of friends and acquaintances. The play date itself gives children an opportunity to learn group social skills, and thus I encourage parents to make these social arrangements.

Playground Behavior

SEE ALSO *Pointing; Staring.*

I am convinced that playgrounds are a great civilizing force. It is in them that children begin to acquire the skills they need to get along with their fellow humans. Children must, of course, be guided by adults, so it is necessary that parents teach their children to share toys as well as the public equipment. Children should be expected to leave playgrounds as clean, or cleaner, than they found them.

Finally, because most playgrounds are in public parks, children are liable to encounter people from many different walks of life. Through this experience they can begin to understand that they must treat all people with respect. More specifically, they can begin to learn that they must not stare, point at, or otherwise comment on other persons in their presence.

Plum

SEE *Fruit*.

Pointing

In our culture, pointing a finger at another person is considered an offensive gesture. As soon as they are old enough to understand, children (who are particularly prone to such activities as pointing and asking in a loud voice, "Mommy, why is that woman walking funny?") should be taught that it is rude to point a finger at (and ask such questions about) a fellow human being.

Pomegranate

SEE *Fruit*.

Postponed Wedding

SEE *Canceled Wedding*.

Pregnancy

ANNOUNCING. People used to delay announcing pregnancy until a woman began to show, but many couples now leap to make the happy announcement as soon as they know, which these days, thanks to home-testing kits, is about two weeks after conception. When to announce a pregnancy is a personal decision, but I think a couple should, for their own sakes, take their circumstances into account when deciding when to tell people. If the woman has had several miscarriages or is older—when there is a possibility that the pregnancy might not proceed well, in other words—a couple might feel more comfortable delaying their announcement at least a few weeks and perhaps a couple of months.

Although the woman's husband is usually counting the days with her, if the pregnancy is a surprise, she must, of course, share the joyous news with him first. The next person to be told are the grandparents-to-be. If they are taken into the couple's confidence early on, they may be asked to keep the news quiet for a while. They must respect the couple's wishes in this matter.

MATERNITY CLOTHES. Maternity clothes, which used to be decidedly unattractive, are now quite the opposite. Most pregnant women need maternity clothes sometime during their fourth or fifth month. A woman no longer need change her style of dressing to accommodate pregnancy. If she is the sweater and pants type, she can usually find chic sweaters and pants to wear during her pregnancy. If she is a professional who must wear tailored suits to work, she can find these, too.

Pregnant women are advised to choose clothes that draw attention to their faces rather than their burgeoning waistlines, but I think this is silly advice. It is rather difficult to deemphasize a pregnancy when one's belly precedes one everywhere, and most pregnant women are proud of their expanding waistlines, anyway. In addition, some pregnant women experience a bloating around the face that is not particularly flattering, and they may want to play that down. I think a pregnant woman should wear whatever is comfortable and makes her feel attractive.

The days when a pregnant woman did not dare to show her face (or body, actually) at the beach are long gone. A variety of well-designed and flattering bathing suits make pregnant women look attractive at the beach.

WORK. The days when women quit their jobs early during a pregnancy are long gone, too, and many women work right up until they deliver.

A woman who plans to work throughout her pregnancy should plan her wardrobe accordingly, that is, buy the pregnant woman's equivalent of whatever she would normally wear to work. Since maternity clothes are expensive and are worn for only a short time, most women buy fewer outfits than they would normally own. A smart idea is to buy separates that mix well with one another and to create as many outfits as possible from them.

A woman who is planning to resign or take a pregnancy leave should discuss her plans with her employer as soon as possible so alternate plans can be made for her absence.

QUESTIONS AND COMMENTS. People seem to think pregnant women belong to the community, and this is a time in a woman's life when she often has to fend off more than the usual number of nosy questions ("Did you and your husband plan this baby?" "Are you married?" "Did you have a miscar-

riage?"). When the questions are painful and no one's business, a woman need not answer them. In these situations, I suggest the Ann Landers Counterquestion: "Why do you want to know that?" It usually puts nosy souls at an appropriate distance.

As for the butcher, the mailman, and the counterman in your local deli, all of whom want to tell you what to eat, not to drink coffee, and what they think the baby's sex is, they are best fended off with a little good humor since they mean well.

Prejudice

SEE ALSO *Profanity and Vulgar Language.*

Prejudice unfortunately reflects the ignorance of the speakers. Also unfortunate is the fact that tact often does not work well around prejudiced persons, who seem to assume that the entire world shares their views. This is, therefore, one of those rare occasions when a cold shoulder is the best—and sometimes the only possible—treatment. If the person does not sense your discomfort in discussing such subjects, you may say, "I disagree with what you're saying, and this is not a subject I am willing to pursue."

Preparatory School

SEE *College and Dormitory Life.*

Private Club

SEE ALSO *Professional Membership.*

GUEST. When you are a guest at someone's club, there are only a few things to keep in mind. If you arrive first, you will usually be greeted by a doorman or someone whose job is to screen nonmembers. If you identify yourself and say that you are a guest, you will usually be directed to a waiting room. Do not roam around on your own in a private club; this could lead to some embarrassment. And although it will probably not be offered, do not order food or beverages until your host or hostess arrives.

After you have eaten, and when the bill arrives, do not offer to pay. Many private clubs do not accept cash, and only members may sign the checks. You are always a guest when someone invites you to lunch or dine at a private club—or for that matter to use any of its facilities. The one exception might be if you have a standing athletic game played at someone's club; you might, after a few times as guest, suggest that you pay your own way. More desirable would be for you to return the invitation at your own club. Or you could also repay your friend in some other way.

Don't let yourself be put off if the club is very fancy or exclusive. Always act perfectly at ease, as if your name has been omitted from the membership list due to some kind of minor typographical error.

Suggestions to sponsor someone at a private club always come from the member, never from the hopeful prospective member. Do not drop hints about joining, and do not ask about fees or expenses connected with the club membership.

HOST. Since you are more clearly the host at a private club than in a public restaurant, it is tactful to arrive a few minutes early so you are there to greet your guest.

You may offer to show a guest around, particularly if the club is well known and has some historical associations, but take care to avoid any appearance of bragging about the club or any sense of superiority regarding your membership.

The host at a private club picks up the tab. If you have a regular athletic game with someone, and your club has the better facilities, you both may decide to play at your club, but it is snobbish (and no truly well-mannered person wants to give the impression of being snobbish) to insist on eating or playing at your club to the exclusion of another's club if your reason for doing so is that your club has more status. That is as rude as insisting that someone always come to your house rather than your going to his because your house is the nicer of the two. Be sure your motives are above suspicion.

If you think that someone is eligible and would like to join a club you belong to, discuss it with him or her and offer to submit his name to the membership committee. That might be the appropriate point to discuss dues.

Prix Fixe

SEE ALSO *Table d'Hôte.*

A prix-fixe menu is one in which the price is preset, or fixed, for the meal that is served. The meal is usually served in several courses, and substitutions are not allowed, although one may skip a course. Sometimes a restaurant will offer several different levels of prix-fixe menus, that is, one for $15.95, another for $25.95, and still another for $35.95.

Profanity and Vulgar Language

SEE ALSO *Obscenities.*

I am well aware that standards of using language have changed considerably over the past few years, and that words that would never have been acceptable in polite conversation are now broadcast into our homes via television. I fully understand peer-group pressure and profanity, namely, that it is difficult to resist peer-group pressure when the only thing you have to do to belong is use vulgar or profane language. Having said all this I would still like to repeat what my father taught me about vulgar language because I think it applies as much today as it did several decades ago.

If you rely on profanity or vulgar language, you are cheating yourself of the opportunity to develop your vocabulary, that is, to find other words that are more descriptive or expressive.

If you start to use vulgar language, you will find it difficult to break the habit, whereas if you never develop the habit, you will not need to break it.

Even if you have the foulest mouth imaginable, when you become a parent, you will probably want to shield your chil-

dren from vulgar language at least during their early years. This will be very difficult to do if you yourself use vulgar language routinely.

Finally I would like to add something I do not think my father thought of, but which I have discovered to be true: If you only rarely resort to profanity or vulgar language, then on the occasions when you do use it, it will carry more force. My children rarely heard me swear, but when they did, they knew that *Mother meant business.*

Professional Membership

SEE ALSO *Private Club.*

A professional membership is much like any other membership except that you must keep in mind that you are always representing your company when you participate in any professional organization's activities. You should always seek to put your company in as good a light as possible. Your choice of activities, and even your degree of participation, may be guided in part by your company's interest in the organization. If your boss headed up the major fundraising effort last year and brought you into the organization, he may at some point want you to volunteer to head up the same project, particularly if doing so is good public relations for the firm.

And before you decide to tackle any major projects that will be very time consuming, you should, as a matter of courtesy and to be sure that you will have the cooperation you need, check with your boss to see if there are any objections to the amount of time that will be required. Most employers do not raise any objections to employees doing any form of public service that puts the company in a good light, but they like to be kept informed about these activities.

Professor

SEE ALSO *Teacher.*

"Professor" is a title usually reserved for someone who has received a doctorate. At some schools, it is used more loosely to address any instructor. You may simply follow the custom on whatever school you are attending or visiting, keeping in mind that no one is ever insulted to be addressed as "Professor."

Prom

SEE *Teen Dance.*

Public Appearance

During the course of daily life, many of us have occasion to make a public appearance of some sort, either as a speaker, on radio or on television. Those who regularly make public appearances may want to use the services of a consultant who can advise them on their appearance and help them improve their performance. Numerous self-help books also offer advice for public speakers. One excellent book is *How to Write and Give a Speech* by Joan Detz (St. Martin's Press, New York: 1984).

SPEECHES. Few persons are natural extemporaneous speakers, and it is generally a kindness to an audience to prepare for any speech longer than two or three minutes. The speech should be centered around the audience's interests and not the speaker's. With a live audience, eye contact is especially important. If you are too shy to look directly at members of the audience, scan their faces rapidly every so often. If you want the sympathy and attention of an audience, dress in a way that appeals, interests, or at minimum does not alienate them.

RADIO AND TELEVISION. Both these mediums run on carefully calculated timetables, so you must arrive on time, which means at least ten minutes before a radio show and fifteen to thirty minutes before a television show. Dress is irrelevant on a radio show, and on a television show, it is important to wear something that photographs well. White and other bright colors can be too glaring. Pastels, if they are not so pale that they look washed out, work best.

Public Displays of Affection

SEE ALSO *Farewells.*

These always have been and probably always will be in poor taste, never more so than today when couples have complete freedom to seek out privacy. Hand holding, which used to be taboo, has now become acceptable, with some limits. A couple can feel comfortable holding hands or walking arm in arm when strolling down a street or even in a movie theater. They should not feel comfortable—or at least should feel highly unsophisticated—holding hands during a concert, a live theater performance, or a ballet—in other words, during any performance when courtesy demands that their full attention be given to the players.

Anything beyond hand holding or walking arm in arm is in poor taste—without exception.

Public Grooming

Combing hair in public and other kinds of grooming are tacky behavior, especially when it is done around food. It is always a good idea to excuse yourself and retire to the nearest restroom for personal grooming tasks.

Public Parks

Behavior in a public park requires only that people respect their neighbors and the environment. Respecting the neighbors means keeping noise to a minimum, keeping children in tow, keeping pets under control, and, in general, not treading on others' turf. Respect for the land means leaving it in as clean, or cleaner, condition that it was.

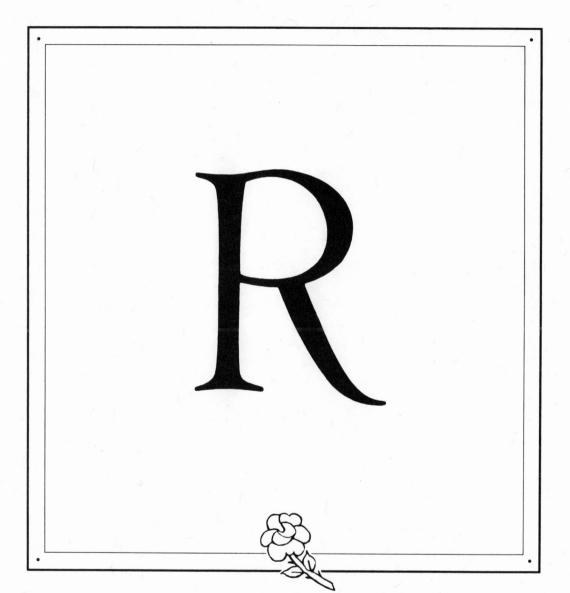

Racquetball

SEE *Racquet Sports*.

Racquet Sports

Individual clubs have rules regarding the sports that are played there, but some basic rules of courtesy are observed anywhere:

- Wear appropriate clothing. In general this means white, although many clubs have relaxed this rule.
- If you are evenly matched with your opponent, you may play as hard as you like. If you are not evenly matched, it is rude to slam balls or otherwise take advantage of the other player's lack of skill.
- If you are not sure whether your opponent is ready for your serve, find out by asking, "Ready?"

- Whichever player is closest to the line calls balls "in" or "out." If there is some question about a play that earned you a point, offer to play it over.
- Your court is your territory when you are playing on it. No one can enter it without your permission, nor should you enter a court on which others are playing. If their ball comes into your court, it is a courtesy to return it, but you need not interrupt your game to do so.

Ramekin or Individual Casserole

In restaurants and sometimes in private homes, food is served in a ramekin or an individual casserole *(see Figure 48)*. It may be eaten in the serving dish or lifted onto a plate. If the casserole is accompanied with a

Figure 48. Ramekin resting on service plate with serving spoon at side

large spoon, that is a sign that the food is meant to be transferred out of the ramekin and onto another plate. Most often these days, except in fine restaurants, the serving spoon is missing, and the food is meant to be eaten right out of the individual casserole. Should you be served a casserole without a spoon that you wish to transfer to a plate, simply ask the waiter for a serving spoon. Transfer the food in two or three servings to your plate. Rest the serving spoon in the casserole.

Reaching at Table

SEE *Passing Food.*

Reception

SEE ALSO *Wedding Reception.*

Receptions these days are a favored form of entertainment only among government officials, most notably diplomats. They are held at the White House right down through local levels of government and at embassies. A reception is usually held in honor of someone or something. Of course, private citizens and organizations also have receptions, but they are more likely to be called cocktail parties or simply parties.

Invitations are usually printed and sent out well in advance, although responses are rarely required. There is no obligation to arrive on time for a reception; you may attend anytime during the hours you were invited, and you may stay forty-five minutes or several hours without giving offense. Dress is usually business clothes—suits for the men and suits or dresses for the women, unless something even more formal is requested.

Drinks will be served, and they may or may not be accompanied by food. Usually some kind of cocktail food is served.

Because a reception is in honor of someone or something, there may be a receiving line. If so, all guests must go through it.

Recruitment Services

Your behavior is especially important when you are working with an executive recruitment service, or a headhunter, as executive recruiters are called.

An executive headhunter (and headhunters, by definition, deal with executives) will be interested in how you present yourself socially. At the upper levels of management, being presentable is almost as important as having the right experience and professional skills. Companies also want team players, and since the headhunter will be vouching for you in every area, he will want to be sure that your social skills are polished. So if you find yourself being wined and dined by a headhunter, or, more likely, wined and lunched, it may not be so much because he is trying to woo you as it is because he is checking to see if you know how to use a fish fork and make small talk.

The best thing you can do is to watch your manners. Whatever you do, do not stiffen up (the best manners are always relaxed manners), but do not fool yourself into thinking that this is a carefree occasion. Sit up straight and keep your elbows off the table! Go prepared with some conversational topics to show that you are capable of carrying on an intelligent conversation about more than just "the job." Do not try to impress, but do not be afraid to show that you are an impressive candidate.

Rectory Wedding

A wedding in the rectory, or clergyperson's study, is the religious equivalent to a civil ceremony. A couple may choose a rectory wedding because they want an intimate, private ceremony or because they cannot, for one reason or another (usually because one of them has been married before or because of religious differences), be married in a church or synagogue. Either way, the rectory wedding is small and informal, with only immediate families and possibly a few close friends present.

The bride wears street clothes rather than a wedding dress, although she may wear a fairly simple white bridal gown, preferably street length. She may wear a hat, if she chooses to, and when she does wear a hat, it often has a small veil. The groom wears a suit, usually of dark gray or navy, a white or pastel-color shirt, and a tie. Guests wear the same kinds of clothes they would wear to any religious service.

Little pomp is attached to a rectory wedding. There is, for example, no recessional or processional. The couple's family and friends all gather at the appointed time.

Two friends may serve as witnesses, or the couple's parents, siblings, or children may stand up with them. The number who may be invited is limited by the size of the room. After the wedding, everyone usually goes to lunch or breakfast together. Rectory weddings are held during the regular working hours of the clergyperson. They are often scheduled in the late morning, so that a brunch or lunch may be served afterward.

The bride's parents may give the wedding celebration, or, since many rectory weddings involve second marriages or couples who cohabit, the couple themselves may give the wedding breakfast or lunch.

Reference

SEE ALSO *Business Reference.*

CASUAL. When a friend is moving or traveling to a new city, he or she may appreciate introductions to people who live there. The most—the only—considerate way to make this kind of introduction is to call your friend yourself to pave the way for the person whom you are introducing. Your call is the seal of approval, and it obligates your friend to see the new acquaintance at least once socially.

Everyone is put in an awkward situation when someone gives one friend a name and tells him to get in touch on his own with another friend. I always think calling someone cold is the most difficult introduction for those who must take advantage of it, and that the least the introducer can do is telephone or write a note in advance alerting the person to be expecting the call from a virtual stranger.

If you must call someone cold, so to speak, to introduce yourself, try to call at a convenient time and get to the point as quickly as possible. Say something like this: "You don't know me, but I am a good friend of Sally Shreve. She suggested that I call you. My name is Becky Jackson, and I recently moved here." The person to whom you introduce yourself should take it from there, and will usually make plans to get together with you at least once.

When someone has moved to a new community and been introduced to a friend of a friend in this manner, the friendship is often transitional, that is, the friend of the friend stays in touch long enough to help the new friend become settled in the community. Depending upon how much they have in common, they may or may not pursue the friendship much beyond this point. Neither party need feel embarrassed about letting the relationship die a natural death.

FORMAL. Formal, written personal references are used more rarely these days than in the past, when a person traveling abroad was quite likely to carry with him several letters of introduction. Today, when a friend is moving or traveling to a strange city and you wish to introduce him to another mutual friend, it is much easier to pick up the telephone or write a short note than to write a formal letter of introduction.

When a formal letter of reference is used today, it fulfills the same purpose, to introduce one person to another. Your two friends meet in person, with you, the person supplying the reference, introducing them in writing. A letter of reference carries with it your seal of approval of this person; it is intended to open social doors.

A formal letter of reference should be written or typed on your social stationery (your business stationery if this is a business introduction). It may be short and should be reassuring:

Dear George,

This letter is to introduce John Maccoby. John and I met several years ago when we both worked at Standard, and we've been good friends ever since. I can vouch for the fact that John is an amusing dinner companion, and I hope you will take him under your wing while he visits your city. I promise you won't regret it.

I hope all is well with your family. Lydia sends her love.

All best,
Jack

Put the letter in an unsealed envelope, and on it, write out the name of the person to whom it is to be given. Once the letter of introduction has been given to the person who needs it, he or she delivers it in person, after having called for an appointment, or may mail or messenger it to the addressee. If the later method is used, a short note should be included, saying:

Dear Mrs. Pryce:

Mary Ames gave me this letter of introduction to you. I am staying at the Fillmore, and will be here through Saturday. I am looking forward to meeting you.

Sincerely,
John Maccoby

No one should request a letter of introduction. It must be offered. And such offers should take into account whether the recipient of the letter of reference will find its bearer compatible and pleasant company.

Regrets Only

SEE ALSO *Invitation.*

When "regrets only" is written on an invitation, it means you need reply only if you cannot accept the invitation. If you do not reply, the assumption will be made that you have accepted the invitation. "Regrets only" is mostly used for large parties, such as cocktail parties, barbecues, and buffet dinners, where an accurate head count of the guests is not necessary.

It is rude to ignore a "regrets only" invitation, that is, to not answer and not attend. Even if you find you cannot attend a party at the last moment, the kind thing is to call the host or hostess to let her know.

Religious Services

SEE ALSO *Baptism; Chapel Wedding; Christian Birth Ceremonies; First Communion; Funeral; Jewish Birth Ceremonies; Rectory Wedding; Sanctuary Wedding.*

Religions have different rules about behavior and dress during their services, and while the rules have generally become more lax in the past ten years, because of immigration, there are now more religions being practiced in America than ever before. The best way to know what will be expected of you in a house of worship is to ask. Find out about any dress restrictions or customs and how the service will go.

DRESS. Although I see women wearing pants suits to religious services, I adhere to a more conservative and, I feel, respectful stance. I think women should wear dresses, however casual, when attending a religious service. If you are traveling and visiting a church, then pants are acceptable, and should you get caught up in a service during your visit, then whatever you are wearing would also undoubtedly be acceptable under the circumstances. A man or boy attending a religious service should wear a jacket or at least a shirt and tie.

Hats are no longer required in Roman Catholic churches, but the well-equipped traveler always carries a head scarf for those times when a woman's head must be covered. In an Orthodox synagogue, the women wear hats or other head coverings. In religions that require head coverings for men, such as the Jewish faith, skullcaps, called yarmulkes, are usually provided in the sanctuary. In general, you should try to comply with any dress code or custom as a sign of respect.

BEHAVIOR. You may participate in as little or as much of a religious service as you feel comfortable with. Join in the singing of hymns and the responsive readings if you feel like doing so. But you need never feel obliged to recite a creed of beliefs or do anything else that makes you uncomfortable. If your religious practice is not to kneel and you are in a church where kneeling is part of the service, you may remain seated. It is considered polite to stand when the congregation stands. In many churches, you may not take communion if you are not a member of the congregation.

Apart from the general guidelines, each congregation seems to have its own unwritten rules regarding behavior during the service. In some congregations, for example, people do not chat informally before or during the service; in other congregations, people greet their friends as they enter the sanctuary. As a guest, you should take the lead from those around you.

OFFERING. If possible, make a contribution, however small, when the offering is made. The money is put to good use, often without discrimination, to feed and clothe the poor.

COMMUNION. While some Protestant sects invite anyone worshipping with them to share in communion, other sects, particularly Roman Catholic, wish to give communion only to their own communicants. And while some Protestant sects encourage anyone worshipping with them to join in communion, they don't encourage their congregants to take communion with any other sect. Jews, Buddhists, and those of other non-Christian faiths obviously are not interested in taking communion under any circumstances. To be safe, therefore, take communion only during your own religious services. You will offend neither your conscience nor your (or anyone else's) clergyperson.

Relish

SEE *Condiment.*

Remarriage of Divorced Persons

SEE ALSO *Chapel Wedding; Civil Wedding; Home Wedding; Informal Wedding Invitations; Rectory Wedding; Second Wedding.*

Not so infrequently as one might imagine, divorced persons remarry their original spouses. When a wonderful reunion like this occurs, a celebration certainly is in order.

A party or even a small reception may be held, but it should not imitate the traditional formal wedding reception, mostly because friends and relatives are not expected to give gifts again. The relatives and friends who want to give the loving couple a present may do so, but are under absolutely no obligation to do so. The couple pays for their own party or small reception.

The bride should avoid wearing a dress or outfit that makes her appear even remotely like a first-time bride, although she may carry flowers or wear a corsage. She is not given away a second time. She is not even escorted by her father, and, in fact, there is usually no processional or recessional. Instead the couple often walk together down the aisle, or else they come out of a side room off the sanctuary with the clergyperson and walk to the altar. Remarriages are often held in the clergyperson's study if a religious ceremony is desired, or in a judge's chambers if the ceremony is civil. Only immediate families and close friends attend, as a rule. Children may always be present at the remarriage of their parents, as it is a particularly joyous occasion for them, too.

Guests wear what they would wear to any religious service.

Basically, all the same guidelines that apply to a second wedding apply to the remarriage of divorced persons.

Reservation

SEE ALSO *Business Lunch.*

Reservations are most often required at restaurants, but they also may be required at some performances and other activities. Once made, they should be honored. The practice of making reservations in four or five restaurants and choosing one at the last minute or letting your guests choose the one they prefer quite justifiably angers restaurateurs—so much so that many restaurants in large cities now require their patrons to reconfirm on the day of the reservation.

Resignation

A resignation, whether from a job, a club, or an organization, should always be handled as graciously as possible. Often this means delivering the resignation in person, even though a written letter may follow as a formality.

Always resign, if possible, to the appropriate person. At a job, this is your immediate boss; in an organization or club, it is the president or chairperson of the membership committee. It is a serious breach of etiquette, particularly at work, to let your boss hear about your plans to leave from other people. Always formally resign before making any kind of announcement to anyone.

To resign in a huff or a fit of anger from anything is to burn a bridge behind oneself. Even if you are angry or hurt, it is far better to say tactful things when you resign. You may, of course, give your real reason for resigning if it is politic to do so, but also try to say something good about the job or club at the same time. And sometimes it is best to bury the real reason for your resignation and tell a white lie instead.

When resigning from a club or organization, make sure that your affairs are in order and that all bills are paid.

Response Card

SEE *Formal Wedding Invitations.*

Restaurant Meal

SEE *À la Carte; After-Dinner Drinks; Belching; Business Lunch; Children's Table Manners; Coffee;*

RESTAURANT MEAL (con'd)

Condiments; Doggy Bag; Eggcup; Elbows; Food Courses; Food Stuck in Teeth; Fork; Knife; Liquor; Napkin; Passing Food; Place Setting; Plates; Prix Fixe; Ramekin or Individual Casserole; Salt and Pepper; Smoking at Table; Soup; Spoon; Table d'Hôte; Tea; Toothpick; Waiter/Waitress; Wine.

A restaurant meal should be no different from any other meal in terms of the manners that one uses, but in truth the manners that are permissible when a family dines together at home may have to be polished a bit in public, even in the most casual restaurant. Restaurants offer varying levels of quality, with the food and service often, but not always, matching one another. Manners, unlike the food and service, should not come in varying levels of quality. Diners should be courteous in their eating habits and their treatment of those who wait on them regardless of whether they are eating in a four-star restaurant or the corner coffeeshop.

With some variations, the routine of eating in a restaurant is much the same in all restaurants.

ARRIVING. New arrivals at a restaurant are usually greeted by a host, more often called a *maître d'hôtel* (*maître d'*, for short), or a hostess, who is responsible for seating diners. Coffeeshops and other inexpensive, casual restaurants often dispense with headwaiters, and customers are free to seat themselves at any available table. If you are unsure about the seating policy in a restaurant, ask the cashier or a waiter whether you may seat yourself.

In expensive restaurants, the *maître d'hôtel's* responsibility toward the diners does not end with meeting them. He may take the order; he will supervise the service, often preparing a dish at the table himself; and he should return to the table at some point during the meal to inquire discreetly whether everything is going well.

Some people like to tip the headwaiter in advance, feeling that this will ensure better service than they might otherwise obtain, but this is not necessarily so. A good *maître d'* will not want to be seen taking bribes and may not be in a position to seat you ahead of other diners or give you the best table in the house, the primary service that people seem to want when the tip comes before the meal. If you do want to tip the headwaiter first, do so discreetly for your own sake. As a rule, $5 to $10, depending upon the community and the fanciness of the restaurant, will suffice.

ORDERING FOOD. Once you are seated, someone, a waiter or the *maître d'hôtel,* will bring menus, which you can then study preparatory to ordering your meal. It is correct to ask the waiter about any foods you are unfamiliar with; you may also ask how certain foods are prepared.

If the menu is in courses *(table d'hôte,* in other words), you will have to decide what courses you want to eat. If you are paying for your own meal, this is no problem, and you may order whatever you like, but when you are someone's guest, it is polite to confine your meal to two courses, an entree and dessert and coffee. Since many entrees come with vegetables, you might want to inquire about this before ordering anything more than an entree and dessert in any event. If the host or hostess encourages you to have more ("The appetizers look delicious. I'm going to try one. Why don't you?"), then you may order more if you choose to do so.

In many restaurants, particularly in some foreign countries, the waiter will not come to take the orders until the menus have been closed; this is a sign of courtesy to the diners, who are left alone to make their selections.

More often, it is now the practice for the waiter or waitress to show up at the table and do a little song-and-dance while explaining the specialties of the day. Anytime a waiter approaches with a large smile, and says, "Hi, I'm Jeremy," you are probably in trouble. There is no way to turn off these overeager food promoters entirely, but failing to respond does help somewhat. Be warned, though: This new breed of waiter thinks he is adorable, and will not only attempt to provide your preprandial entertainment but also will nudge his way into your evening in other ways. He will return at utterly inappropriate moments (when you and your friend have agreed that the romance is definitely O-V-E-R or when you and your friends are in the middle of heated debate as to just what comprises a good mortgage deal) to cheerily inquire whether you like the overpriced, overcooked, and undersized entree he has convinced you to order. As for taking your order, the waiter may be asked politely to return in a few minutes if you have not yet decided.

Of course, in a great restaurant, which by definition provides you with both excellent food and excellent service, the service will be so subtle and flawless that you will barely notice it. The waiter will magically appear at a lull in your conversation to take your order. He will not introduce himself, nor will he attempt to become your friend. He will describe dishes in detail only when you ask him to do so, making recommendations only when asked, removing all dishes as soon as you have finished the food on them, and most important, anticipating your every need, sometimes even before you yourself know what it is that you want. He will never condescend; he will not correct your French (or if he does, it will be done with great tact).

As a rule, the waiter will establish the way in which he would like to take the orders. If there is a large group, he may even dispense with taking the women's orders first and simply progress around the table. Most formally, the women's orders are taken before the men's.

When a man and woman are dining together, and she is his guest, the most old-fashioned way of ordering is for the woman to tell her host what she would like and for him to give the waiter both their orders. Often the woman does not speak to the waiter at all during the meal; her requests are conveyed through her host. But many women are not comfortable with this and prefer to give the waiter their own orders, which is fine. At a business lunch, the woman always gives her own order and speaks directly to the waiter, even if she is the guest. Of course, when two friends of either sex are eating together and are ordering the same thing, one person may order for both. It is fast and efficient to say, "We'll both have the salad niçoise." There is no obligation to do this, of course, but neither is there anything wrong with it.

When you order your food, the waiter will also take any special requests, such as how you would like something cooked, how spicy you would like a food to be, or whether you would like your salad served before or after the entree. Sometimes when one diner is eating light and has ordered only an appetizer, he or she must tell the waiter to bring it with the other person's entree so their meals will be timed to be eaten together. If a dish will be shared, let the waiter know this, too.

It is acceptable to ask a waiter to speed up or slow down the meal service. The best time to do this is when placing your order. ("Waiter, we have theater tickets. Can we get the grilled fish fairly quickly, or would you suggest we order something else?" or "Waitress, we're hoping for a leisurely dinner, so I think we'll sip our drinks awhile longer before we order.") One way to slow down the meal service is to delay ordering until you have sipped your predinner drinks first.

When several people are dining together, it makes sense to settle on the main course first, so you can discuss the kind of wine you would like with the meal.

ORDERING DRINKS. The waiter will offer to take drink orders at the same time he delivers the menus. It is appropriate to order drinks at this point if you want to. You may order something alcoholic or non-alcoholic, whatever your preference. You may also decline to order anything. Many people who know they will want wine with dinner prefer to wait; if you mention this to the waiter, he or she will send the wine steward to take your order. In some restaurants, the *maître d'hôtel* is also the wine steward.

Usually people dining in a restaurant, especially one where the food promises to be good, do not have more than one or two predinner drinks. It is rude to order several drinks when none of the other diners is doing so because this holds up everyone's meal.

The *sommelier,* or wine steward, will present you with the wine menu, make suggestions at your request, and serve the wine. The markup on wine in a restaurant ranges from 100 to 200 and sometimes is as high as 300 percent, so no one should be embarrassed to ask the wine steward to suggest something within a specific price range. And considering the markup, no *sommelier* should ever make a diner feel cheap for refusing to order a bottle of wine for sixty dollars that he could perfectly well buy in a wine store for twenty.

When dining with a small group, you may need to coordinate entrees so you can order a bottle of white or red wine. Remember, though, that wines are much more flexible than we tend to think. If everyone has ordered fish and is clearly headed toward a white wine, one diner can still order chicken or veal and drink white wine with it. When there are enough diners, both red and white can be ordered, and the problem is solved.

If you are someone's guest, it is courteous to let them suggest ordering wine, and they, of course, will do the actual ordering.

SERVICE. Unless the restaurant serves family-style, food will be brought in courses. You will be served food at your left, and empty dishes will be cleared from your right, unless it is inconvenient to do this, in which case it is acceptable to clear from the left, too. Occasionally a table is too crowded for a waiter to manage any kind of correct service, but he should still avoid reaching in front of diners to serve food.

If a food requires sauce, the waiter may serve it. You should signal him when you have had enough. Fresh-ground pepper may also be served in this way, and if you are not offered some, you may ask the waiter to bring the peppermill.

Unacceptable food, that is, food that is overcooked, undercooked, and the like, may always be sent back. Simply call over the waiter and explain the problem and what you want done. ("Waiter, this fish is a little undercooked for my taste. Would you have the chef grill it a little longer, please?")

As you finish each course, the waiter will remove it from your place setting. You can signal him that you have finished eating by placing your knife and fork parallel to one another on the right or left side of your plate. Crossing your knife and fork over one another indicates that you are merely resting and have not yet finished eating.

When you have finished, and the dishes have been cleared, the waiter will return with the menu so you may select dessert if you choose to do so. At that time you order (or decline) dessert; coffee and tea are also ordered. In these diet-conscious days, it is acceptable, even in a very good restaurant, to share a dessert. If the waiter does not bring them, ask for two forks and plate, divide the dessert in two, and place it on the plates. The waiter also may do this for you.

In restaurants, coffee and tea are sometimes served in individual pots. If the teabag is on the side of the service plate, put it in the teapot (not your cup) and let it brew until it is the strength you want.

Remove the teabag with your spoon, wrap the string around your spoon, if you wish, to drain off any excess tea, and place it on the service plate or the saucer. When the teabag is served at the side of your cup, the teabag goes directly into your cup and is treated the same way when it is removed.

Those who serve you should be treated with courtesy at all times. If you are in a club or a restaurant where you dine frequently, you will probably know the names of those who wait on you and should address them accordingly. If not, get the waiter's attention by calling out "Waiter" or "Waitress." A waitress may also be called by saying "Miss," but a waiter should never be called "Mr." or "Sir." Never attempt to get a waiter's attention by snapping your fingers, clapping your hands, banging a spoon on a glass, or whistling. When the waiter does arrive to take your order, do not become overly friendly and take up too much of his or her time. Ask whatever questions you may have and then place your order swiftly.

Ask for the service you need politely, saying "Please" when you place your request and "Thank you" when it is filled. Thank the waiter occasionally, not every time he does the slightest thing for you, but from time to time as he serves you.

Do not argue about house rules; the waiter does not make them. For example, if you want to substitute one food for another, and the waiter says this is not permitted, however silly this rule is, do not argue with him over it. If you want iced coffee, and the chef isn't serving it, do not take out your frustrations on the waiter. It is not his fault.

On the other hand, never let a waiter bully you. If the service is not good, let him know it, and do so in a way that lets him know you expect better service. If you request something and it is not done, ask the waiter a second time, this time in a firmer voice if need be.

When there is a serious problem, do complain, first—but politely and unobtrusively—to the waiter. If he cannot provide satisfaction, ask to speak to the *maître d'hôtel*, and if necessary, to the owner.

There is another type of complaint that I have more difficulty with, and that is the diner who launches into a full-scale attack on a restaurant when a waiter, *maître d'*, or owner stops by the table at the end of the meal to inquire how everything was. If something specific is wrong with a food at the time it is presented, and it can be corrected, then take steps to correct it so your meal will be more pleasant. If, though, you have found the entire meal to be below your standards, I think little can be accomplished, other than the expansion of your ego, by haranguing the waiter or anyone else about the sorry state of affairs. You are not going to return to this restaurant anyway, so why bother? If a restaurant that you patronize regularly drops in quality, that is another matter, and you might do the owner a service by speaking up—tactfully, of course.

ENDING THE MEAL. In a restaurant, as at home, many diners like to linger over coffee and dessert. In a quality restaurant, no objection will be raised to this, and reservations will have been carefully timed to allow diners to enjoy a leisurely meal.

In many other restaurants, though, diners are not encouraged to linger. You can buck them on this, or acquiesce and leave when they want you to. Signs that you are not to linger in a restaurant consist of everything from whisking away your dishes the second you have finished eating to presenting the check promptly and then standing by to collect the cash to the waiter or owner stopping by repeatedly after you have finished eating to ask whether everything is okay. I frankly think, if for no other reason than to save wear-and-tear on yourself, that you should eat quickly and leave in restaurants where this is what is expected of you (coffee shops, delis during their rush hours, pizza joints, and Chinese restaurants in New York City), and save the lingering meals for those restaurants where it is acceptable. I also think it is rude to prolong your meal unduly when a line of diners is waiting to eat. If you really want to linger over a meal, go to a restaurant where this is acceptable.

When you have finished, ask the waiter for a check if he has not brought it to you. It is always acceptable behavior to look over a bill carefully before paying it to make sure that it is correct. Do this at a romantic dinner, as well as at a business lunch. You will not be thought cheap; you will be thought careful. A few years ago, two women I know were dining in a posh and highly recommended restaurant in New York. When the check was presented, and one woman began to study it, the waiter hovered over her, asking if anything was wrong. When she pointed out a charge she did not understand, the waiter became defensive, accusing her of not liking him. My friend was not one to be easily bullied, however, and she asked to see the manager. The two of them determined that the waiter had indeed added a 15 percent surcharge to the meal, probably because he thought that two women dining alone would not tip him

sufficiently. I wish I could report that the two women declined to tip him at all, which was what he deserved, but graciously, they let the tip stand. At any rate, the moral remains the same: Always check the bill carefully before paying. If there is a problem, quietly call it to the waiter's or manager's attention.

The standard restaurant tip is 15 percent, 20 percent in an excellent restaurant, provided the service has been up to snuff. You may add the tip to a credit card receipt, and the staff will divide it among themselves. The general breakdown is 5 percent to the *maître d'hôtel*, and 15 percent to the waiters. The *sommelier* is tipped 15 percent of the wine order if he has personally helped you choose the wine. He will come over to the table when he sees you preparing to leave. The waiter's tip is left on the table, usually on the tray on which the bill is presented. You may tip the *maître d'hôtel* on the way out. In most restaurants, the 15 percent tip is left on the table. You should tip in a coffee shop, even if you eat at a counter.

If the service has been really poor, you may reduce your tip or tip nothing at all. This should be done in dire circumstances, though, and not routinely, and you should not reduce the waiter's tip for things over which he has no control. If you really dislike a restaurant, the ultimate way to express this is never to return.

If you are dining with several friends and wish to split the bill, a waiter will sometimes write separate checks, although this request is more thoughtfully made at the start of the meal when you place your order. Occasionally, a waiter will split a check between several credit cards, if asked to do so. The waiter will return with the credit card or your change. A good waiter never assumes that the change is his tip even if the amount is correct, but a diner may leave as soon as the waiter has taken the money if the change will be the tip.

Ring Bearer

SEE *Wedding Attendants.*

Roman Catholic

SEE *Christian Birth Ceremonies; First Communion; Naming Customs; Religious Services; Sanctuary Wedding.*

Roommates

SEE ALSO *College and University Life.*

SELECTING. A roommate may be selected from your pool of friends and acquaintances or from a less personal source, such as a roommate service. Obviously, compatibility will put the relationship on firmer ground, but many persons with different tastes and customs also find enough common ground to live together satisfactorily, so do not rule out living with a stranger or bare acquaintance. In fact, if you like your privacy and would prefer to be living alone,

finances permitting, a stranger or acquaintance may be preferable to a close friend as a roommate.

Whether you opt for friend or stranger, the roommate relationship should be viewed in part as a business relationship. You should take care not to be swayed by friendship when choosing a roommate. Make sure the person is able to carry the responsibilities of the household, because you will feel far more obligated to help out a friend than a stranger.

Whether the roommate is a friend or a stranger, certain areas of compatibility must exist for you to coexist amicably. For example, you should probably both be smokers or nonsmokers. You should both be either slobs or neatniks. Depending upon the size of the apartment, it may be necessary that you both love or hate television, and similar tastes in music also may be necessary, unless the rooms of your house or apartment are soundproof.

If you use a roommate service, be sure that it is a reputable one. The best way to be sure of this is to have recommendations from persons who have been successfully matched with roommates. When filling out an application, be as specific as possible about your taste in someone to share a home with. You can always make exceptions later when you meet someone whom you like.

You can also advertise on your own for a roommate in the classified ads. Remember that you will do your own prescreening if you take this route. It is a good idea to have a friend whose judgment you admire sit in on at least the final interviews to add another opinion to yours. Also, check references, especially financial ones, before signing on a stranger as a roommate.

GETTING ALONG. The roommate relationship is probably most akin to a sibling relationship. You need not—cannot—always be on your best behavior, but good manners go a long way toward smoothing over the minor skirmishes that arise when two people live together. Do not, for example, assume that you can blast the stereo without asking; do not take over possession of the television; do not spend hours in the bathroom without concern for the other person's schedule.

Sit down with any roommate, friend or stranger, and work out a relatively short list of rules and guidelines that cover the contingencies of your life together—entertaining, use of the bathroom, use of the kitchen, division of expenses, and responsibilities for maintenance.

RIGHTS. Whoever holds the lease on the apartment has the primary right to be there. Whoever holds the lease also has a greater right to establish rules and guidelines, such as use of the common space and division of the rent and utilities. If you will share the apartment equally, make sure both your names are on the lease.

MALE–FEMALE ROOMMATES. Occasionally, a man and woman will decide to room together on a purely platonic basis. This relationship should work the same way as any other roommate relationship, and the only major social problem that may arise is when either of you have dates. Dates may have a little difficulty at first imagining that this is indeed a platonic relationship, so it is smart to describe the nature of the relationship to a date before he or she meets your roommate. If you fail to do this, you may find you do not hear from someone in whom you are interested, simply because he or she has misread the roommate situation.

R.S.V.P.

SEE *Formal Wedding Invitation; Invitations; Regrets Only.*

Sailing, Yachting, Boating

A boat is its owner's domain. No one ever goes aboard without having been invited. Even when you have been invited for a sail, upon arriving at the dock, do not come aboard until specifically asked to do so. The captain (owner) is the first person to board and the last to leave a boat. Other than that, men may embark and disembark first to help women and children.

Appropriate clothing must be worn; this means, at minimum, rubber- or rope-soled shoes. (The exception is a large yacht, where one wears whatever one would wear to a resort or country club.) If the weather is ominous, wear your own foul-weather gear or inquire whether there is an extra outfit. Many boats do not carry enough for guests, though.

When the captain is busy, do not talk to him, and get out of the way when an operation is underway by him or other crew members. If you are asked to do something, do it quickly without asking questions.

Boat owners must, of necessity, be fastidious. Make sure you are, too, while aboard as a guest.

If the sail is a long one or you have been aboard several times take "the boat" a present. Liquor, special dishes, a small piece of equipment is always welcome.

As a matter of modesty, one always plays down the size of one's own boat. A boat is actually a small rowboat or dinghy, but most owners refer to their craft as boats, or if it is very large, as a cabin cruiser. A yacht is a large boat that is used for sailing or cruising, but one never properly refers to "my yacht," although others' boats may be referred to this way.

Salad Plate

SEE *Dishes.*

359

Salesperson

It is difficult to tell who is coming out ahead in the current and disgraceful battle of discourtesy between customers and salespersons. Salespeople claim that customers have reached new heights of arrogance and rudeness, and customers feel that service has reached new lows. The solution is for both sides to strive to behave graciously.

Salespeople may be there to serve the customer, but they do have feelings. Being a paying customer never exempts one from such minimal niceties as saying "please" and "thank you" and phrasing requests as questions whenever possible: "Would you please get me another size (color, style) of this garment?" As a rule, basic and minimal kind treatment has its own bonus, in that it is guaranteed to warm the heart of even the toughest salesperson and will, in turn, provide the kind of service we all deserve.

If, despite all your efforts, a clerk does not seem to understand that he is employed to serve others, little is accomplished by taking it out on him or her. Never, under any circumstances, permit yourself to get into a shouting match with a clerk. If there is a complaint, always ask, in your most civil voice, to speak to a manager.

There is more to the art of being a good customer. Don't interrupt a clerk who is obviously involved with another customer. After all, you will want the exclusive attention of the clerk when you are being helped, and it is only fair to let the clerk bestow it on others when it is their turn. Do not compare a store's service or stock unfavorably with that of another store. If something is against store policy, such as writing checks without identification, don't expect a clerk to rescind the rules just for you. Finally, when browsing, do not take up a clerk's time, and if you do intend to buy but will require time to make a decision, do not monopolize the clerk's attention while you decide.

Salt and Pepper

Salt and pepper are put on the table and need not be passed unless someone requests them. Fresh-ground pepper, much favored by many people, is often served in a restaurant by the waiter, who comes by with a peppermill and asks if you would like pepper. If you would, he will serve it until you motion for him to stop, usually by thanking him. In someone's home pepper may be offered in a peppermill, in which case you grind your own in the amount you desire, or it may be offered in a shaker, along with salt. At an informal dinner, one salt and pepper or one peppermill suffices; at a formal dinner, a small salt and pepper shaker is placed between every two diners. These are usually made of clear glass and silver.

There used to be a question of whether it was polite to season food before tasting it, implying that the cook did not know how to season food, or after tasting it, when it was clear that the cook had not seasoned it properly. Now that salt is in such disfavor, medically and nutritionally, many cooks quite deliberately cut down on salt or do not use it at all, a fact that should be shared with unsuspecting dinner guests, and diners can now comfortably salt and pepper food whenever they choose. Since these seasonings can always be added but can never be removed, I think a wise diner still tastes a food before reaching for the salt and pepper.

In addition to the peppermill, which is never put on the table during a formal dinner, old-fashioned salt containers and small spoons for serving salt are making a comeback. These are used for formal and casual dining, mostly in people's homes. Individual salts may be placed at each place setting, in which case you may use your finger to scoop up a pinch and sprinkle salt over your food. Alternately, one salt is shared by the table, and a small spoon is used to serve it.

Salt is always sprinkled over food, except for certain finger foods, such as carrots, radishes, and celery. With these foods, it is more appropriate to sprinkle a small amount of salt on a plate (your bread-and-butter plate or a dinner plate if there is no bread-and-butter plate) and dip the individual pieces into the salt just before each bite.

Sanctuary Wedding

SEE ALSO *Chapel Wedding; Rectory Wedding; Wedding Attendants; Wedding Flowers; Wedding Guests; Wedding Music; Wedding Photography.*

The most formal wedding ceremonies take place in the main sanctuary of a church or synagogue. Guests are seated in a prescribed way before the ceremony, and there is a processional and a recessional.

SETTING THE DATE AND TIME. The date and time of a wedding depend upon the religion. No religion encourages a wedding on its Sabbath, and in some religions, this is forbidden. Catholics and some Episcopalians sometimes do not marry during Lent, and Jews do not marry during Passover and at some other holidays, although practices vary with the individual clergypersons. Because the Sabbath falls between sundown on Friday and sundown on Saturday, Jews often marry on Saturday night or Sunday. Christian weddings typically take place on Saturday because their Sabbath is Sunday.

The time of day for a wedding has everything to do with fashion and little with religious practice. Large, formal weddings are held at night, especially in the South. In large, sophisticated cities, 4:30 P.M. is a fashionable hour to be married, and Catholics are often married in the morning, although this is no longer required. Often the time of a wedding is tied to the kind of reception that is desired. If a brunch or luncheon is planned, the wedding should take place at 11 A.M. or 12 noon. If a formal sit-down dinner is planned, the wedding will be held at 6 or even 7 or 8 P.M.

PLANNING WITH THE CLERGYPERSON. As soon as you know you want a sanctuary wedding, call the church or synagogue and schedule a meeting with the clergyperson who will marry you. Some religions have guidelines about dress for the bride (she must wear long sleeves, for example) or music (only sacred music is permitted). You will also probably discuss the wording of the ceremony, and this is when you should make any special requests you have (you want a favorite poem read or you would like a particular passage from the Bible or Torah). The clergyperson will also tell you whether the bride can dress at the church or must arrive ready for the ceremony.

You will also need one or more meetings with the church musician to plan the music for your ceremony.

ARRIVING AT THE SANCTUARY. Guests begin to arrive approximately thirty minutes before the ceremony. They are usually treated to a pre-ceremony concert of religious music.

Members of the wedding party should arrive an hour to thirty minutes before the service begins, especially if they are going to dress there. The bride and her attendants usually retire to a private room, and the groom and his attendants usually pace nervously in the vestibule. At some Jewish weddings, the bride receives guests in her room before the wedding.

If the bride has dressed at home, she may arrive just before the ceremony. By tradition, she drives to her wedding alone with her father, but there is no reason she could not be escorted by her mother, a brother, or anyone whom she chooses. It is not uncommon for a couple who live together to arrive together.

The parents of the bride and sometimes the groom have remained out of sight before the service, but there is a trend today— a very gracious one, I might add—for the parents (or the couple, if they are giving the wedding) to greet their guests outside the church as they arrive. I like this warm gesture. It is convivial, and that is what manners are really all about. Besides, wedding guests often include old family friends and relatives whom one does not see very often, so why not spend as much time with them as possible?

SEATING GUESTS. Ushers seat guests as they arrive. Members and guests of the bride's family are usually seated on the left side of the church, possibly because this makes it simpler for her father to retire to his pew after he has given her hand in marriage. Members and guests of the groom's family are seated on the right. This seating arrangement works well when the bride and groom are from the same community, and approximately equal numbers of their relatives can be counted on to show up. Today, when couples often live a great distance from their families, and their families may not travel in equal numbers to the wedding, the seating rules often are observed more in the breach, which is just fine.

If the guests will be unevenly divided between the two families or if the guests will primarily be friends of the couple, the ushers should be instructed to dispense with the traditional, and unnecessarily rigid, way of seating guests.

If the seating becomes unbalanced (there are far more people on the bride's side, for example, than on the groom's side), ushers can and should seat guests on either side. An usher might say to an arriving guest (provided he or she is not a member of the immediate family), "We're seating people where they can have the best view rather than on the left and right, and I can give you a much better seat on the right. Is that all right with you?" Or if the guest says, "I'm a friend of the bride, the usher can say, "Oh we're not worrying about that today. How about a good seat right here?"

Ushers offer their arms to the female guests and escort them down the aisle. If two women arrive together, he offers his arm to the more elderly of the two. If the two women are so close in age that one might be insulted, the usher should offer his arm to the woman closest to him. He may escort one woman down the aisle and return for the other one, or he may offer his arm to one woman and the rest of the party follows behind. An usher also should offer his arm to an elderly, frail man. The usher is also supposed to offer his arm to a married woman who arrives with her husband, but a more tactful and modern way to usher in a couple is to let them walk arm in arm behind him to their seats.

The ushers generally make polite conversation with the guests as they walk them down the aisle, and guests often talk quietly among themselves before the ceremony begins since many are friends and relatives who may not have seen each other since the last family celebration.

SEATING THE FAMILY. About ten minutes before the start of the ceremony, grandparents may be seated; they also may be seated when they arrive. Shortly after that, the parents of the groom are seated. And immediately before the ceremony is to begin, the mother of the bride is seated. If a close relative is an usher, he, of course, seats his mother and grandmother.

If a bride's or groom's parents are no longer living, other close relatives are designated to sit in the first pew in their place.

According to strictest wedding etiquette, no one else may be seated after the mother of the bride or the bride's closest relative has been ushered in. In reality, while no one should scurry in as the mother of the bride is walking down the aisle, late arrivals may be seated quietly and quickly at the back of the sanctuary provided the wedding party has not yet lined up for the processional, or, if they have, a side aisle may be used. Guests, take note: It is very rude to arrive late, as you may hold up the wedding or interrupt some part of the ceremony.

After the mother of the bride has been seated, an aisle carpet runner is laid if one is to be used.

PROCESSIONAL. If a sanctuary has a double aisle, one aisle is used for the processional and another for the recessional. In many services, the congregation stands throughout the processional.

When the processional is about to begin, the bride, her father (or the person who is to give her away), and her attendants gather at the back of the sanctuary. The processional music begins, and the clergyperson takes his or her place at the altar and is followed immediately by the groom and his best man, who have usually been waiting in a small side room off the sanctuary.

The ushers are the first to walk down the aisle (see Figure 49). Then come the bridesmaids. Ushers and bridesmaids may walk in twos if there are a lot of attendants; if there are only two or three bridesmaids and ushers, each walks alone. During the rehearsal, the attendants should have been paired off, usually according to height, for the recessional. The maid or matron of honor walks alone, followed by the flower girl or girls if there are any. The bride, on her father's arm, follows. In the rare instance where the

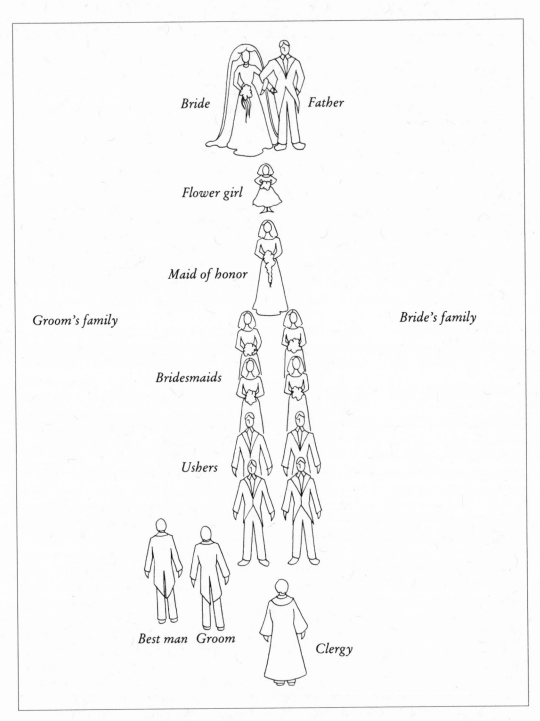

Figure 49. Processional for formal or semiformal wedding

bride has pages carrying her train, they, of course, follow her and her father down the aisle.

Note: In Orthodox, Conservative, and some Reform Jewish ceremonies, the bride and groom are escorted down the aisle by their parents, who then stand on either side of the chuppah during the ceremony *(see Figure 50).*

As they walk down the aisle, attendants should maintain a rather stately pace (although the hesitation step is rarely used these days) and should be about four paces apart. As a rule, no one has to remind the bride or her proud father to stand up straight.

The bridesmaids and ushers divide at the altar, half going to one side and half to the other. If there are steps on the altar, they may line up on the steps. During the rehearsal, the clergyperson will position everyone according to his or her preference and the guidelines of the religion.

THE CEREMONY. When the bride reaches the altar, she turns from her father (often after bestowing a parting kiss on his cheek) and takes the arm of her groom. They step forward to position themselves in front of the clergyperson. The maid of honor moves into position next to the bride and may even take her bouquet at this point or may wait to do this until the ring exchange begins.

The best man stands next to the groom so he can be ready to hand him the ring at the appropriate moment. If a ring bearer is part of the wedding party, the maid of honor and the best man carefully take the rings from him. (They should be firmly attached to a pillow, and a small child should not be permitted to handle them

because of the likely possibility that he will drop them.)

After delivering his daughter to the altar, the father of the bride does one of several things. He stands beside or slightly behind her until he gives her away, if this is to be part of the service, or he returns to the pew where his wife is seated because he will not give his daughter in marriage. If the ceremony is Jewish, the bride will not be given away, and both the father and the mother of the bride are likely to be at the altar, so they take their places behind the chuppah facing their child.

The clergyperson will signal the guests regarding when to sit, stand, and kneel during the ceremony. (Wedding guests who do not kneel in the practice of their faiths need not kneel at a wedding.)

At the end of the ceremony, the clergyperson will pronounce the couple husband and wife. The bride will take her bouquet back from the maid of honor, who will then lift her veil if it has covered her face, and if they have planned to kiss at the altar the bride and groom now do so.

If the couple have no attendants, as is often the case at a small, informal, or second wedding, each wears the other's ring until it is time to exchange them. A bride with no attendants may want to carry a small bouquet or wear a corsage because she will probably end up juggling it while she puts the ring on her groom's finger.

The bride wears her engagement ring, if she has one, on her left hand during the ceremony and replaces it outside the wedding ring after the ceremony.

THE RECESSIONAL. Immediately after the ceremony, the couple turn and move up the church aisle at the head of the reces-

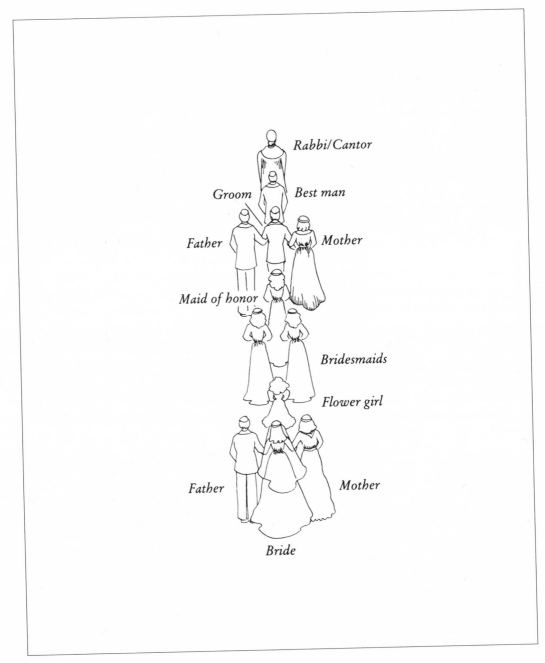

Figure 50. Processional for a Jewish wedding

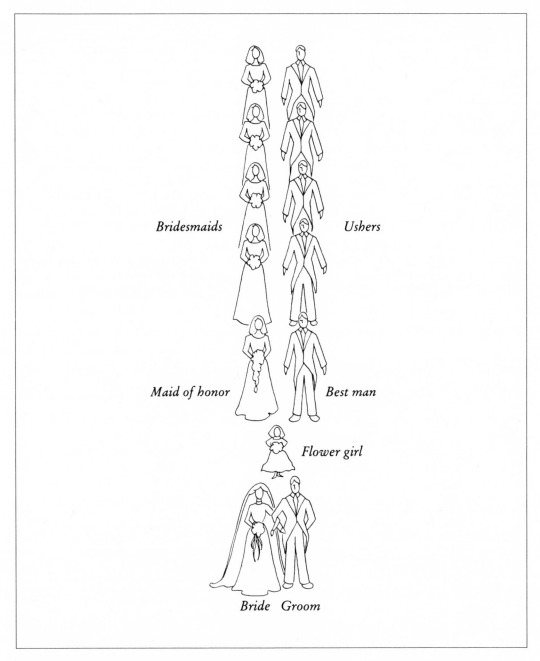

Bridesmaids

Ushers

Maid of honor

Best man

Flower girl

Bride   Groom

Figure 51. Recessional for formal or semiformal wedding

sional *(see Figure 51)*. They are followed by their attendants (children first, then the maid of honor and best man, then the others); bridesmaids pair off with ushers for the recessional.

The music is livelier, and everyone walks at a brisker pace.

The guests remain seated until the ushers return to release them row by row. If the receiving line is to be held at the back of the church, it forms to greet the guests as they leave the sanctuary. More often the wedding party returns to the church after the guests leave for wedding pictures on the altar and then departs immediately for the reception.

Sandwich

A sandwich composed of two pieces of bread can always be picked up in one's hands and eaten that way. A sandwich on one piece of bread, topped with the fillings, is called "open face" and is eaten with a fork and knife. A two-piece-of-bread sandwich that you convert to open face by removing the top piece of bread should also be eaten with a fork and knife.

Sauce

When sauce is passed, always use a spoon if one is passed with the sauce. Never pour a sauce unless there is no other way to serve it. Gravies and other so-called thin sauces go directly over the food for which they were intended. For example, hollandaise sauce should be put on vegetables, eggs,

and meats, not rice or potatoes. Gravy is intended for meat, and meat alone, but I sympathize with the urge to add a good gravy to rice or potatoes. It is acceptable to dribble just a little on the potatoes at an informal family dinner, but when eating out, the sauce should not go on anything but the food for which it is intended. Do not smother a food in sauce, either. The sauce is merely an accompaniment.

"Hard" sauces such as catsup, tartar sauce, jams and jellies, and many dessert sauces go at the side of the plate. Dip each bite of food into the sauce just before eating it. Sandwiches may be spread with the sauce before eating. You may spread the sauce on the entire sandwich if it is one piece. If it is cut into smaller pieces, or if you plan to cut it into smaller pieces, put sauce on only one piece at a time.

Seconds

Most hostesses offer seconds. If the hostess does not offer, and you see that there is enough food for seconds, you may simply say, "That was delicious. I believe I'll have another helping. Would you pass the spinach soufflé, please?"

Second Wedding

SEE ALSO *Remarriage of Divorced Persons; Wedding; Widow; Widower.*

With the divorce rate as high as it is, there are a lot of second weddings these days, and the rules and customs have accordingly undergone great relaxation as more and more people have worked out for themselves how they want to celebrate their second marriages rather than following what are actually some rather rigid etiquette rules.

Second marriages, in which either the bride or both partners had been married before, used to involve little or no fanfare: The marriage took place at city hall or at home, no reception was held, and the bride did not even consider wearing white. Fortunately, we now accept and celebrate second marriages as the joyous occasions they are.

Many couples opt to have a second wedding with all the trimmings either because they never had one the first time or they simply want it again, especially if the groom has never been married before. The criticism that has traditionally been rendered against a second big wedding is that guests who have already contributed to one household should not be asked to do so again. Yet most friends and relatives are delighted to see someone they love enter into a happy relationship—and they want to give a gift to celebrate. If, however, you suspect that your great Aunt Bessie will be much chagrined at the thought, or if she already gave you a silver service or some other especially generous gift at the time of your first wedding, then take her aside or drop her a note and let it be known that while you would dearly love to have her company at this wedding, you are still using the beautiful silver that she gave you, and you hope she will not feel obliged to give you a present again. She may do so despite your request, but she will also appreciate your graciousness and tact.

If you plan to go all out for your second wedding, then you may. That means the bride may wear a white wedding dress, complete with train and veil. The couple may have attendants, and there may be a processional and recessional. They may have a reception complete with all the trimmings and traditions that go with first wedding receptions. The bride may throw her bouquet, and the groom may toss his wife's garter.

If you do decide to have a more "traditional" second wedding, it will be much quieter than that just described. The bride may wear white or any other color that flatters her. Her dress may be made of a dressy fabric or long, but it will not be too bridish, or if it is bridish, it will be "second bridish." The brides' magazines have begun to accommodate the number of second weddings, and their pages show many dresses that are lovely and appropriate for a second wedding. The good news is that a bride can look sophisticated for this one! She usually wears a hat with a small, non-bridish veil. She may carry a bouquet or wear a corsage, whichever she prefers. The groom wears a dark suit. Attendants are usually limited to a best man and maid or matron of honor. The best man wears a dark suit and the maid of honor a pretty dress. Since there is only one attendant for the bride, there is usually no need to choose a bridesmaid dress; the bride usually tells her sister or friend to select something pretty to wear.

There is usually no recessional or processional at a quiet second wedding, but ushers may seat guests if a large number have been invited. The bride, in any event, is not given away a second time. At either a full-dress or a low-key second wedding, the bride may be escorted to the altar by her son, if he is old enough (thirteen minimum); her father; or another close male relative; or she may walk to the altar alone. If the couple are giving their own wedding, as is often the case with a second wedding, they may be mingling with their guests before the wedding, in which case they simply walk to the altar or over to the person performing the ceremony to begin.

For either kind of second wedding, the sanctuary may be decorated with flowers and the attendants may carry bouquets or wear flowers.

Usually the bride and groom stand alone after the wedding to receive their guests. After all, they are frequently older and may even have paid for the wedding themselves. The bride's parents are under no obligation to pay for a daughter's second wedding, however elaborate it is, although they may help out if they choose to do so.

The bride and groom may have a traditional wedding cake and share their first piece of cake and their first dance as husband and wife. The bride may throw her bouquet, and her guests may throw rice as she and her husband leave the reception to wish them fertility. If the bride and groom are the host and hostess of their own reception, as is often the case with second weddings, then they may not want to leave until their guests have departed. Alternately, they may ask a good friend to fill in for them and take their leave just as any other bride and groom do.

Secretary

A few years ago, office etiquette was far more formal. Even after working together for twenty years, a secretary and boss used "Mr.," "Miss," or "Mrs." and surnames with each other. Today, office life is far more informal—and harder to keep under control. First names are frequently used throughout a company—the only one who seems to be able to command the respect of "Mr.," "Ms.," or "Mrs." these days is the company president or chairperson of the board, and even he or she does not always manage to do so. Such informality is not a cause for complaint; after all, co-workers spend seven or more hours a day together year after year. In retrospect, it seems ridiculous that persons could be so closely associated with one another for so long and maintain so much formality.

A boss is the one to make the decision whether or not to call a secretary by his or her first name; just keep in mind that if you decide to do so, he or she may well respond by calling you by your first name.

Since you will see your secretary frequently throughout the day, there is no need to rise when he or she comes into the room. It is polite to gesture for a secretary to sit down whenever he or she has obviously come in to talk with you at any length, particularly if your working relationship is new and your secretary is not sure what to expect from you.

Bosses today do take their secretaries for lunch—and these are not necessarily working lunches. It is simply a gracious gesture to ask a secretary or assistant—or any other subordinate, for that matter—to be your guest at lunch on occasion. Birthdays and secretaries' appreciation days offer excellent opportunities to show your appreciation in this way.

When appropriate, introduce a secretary or assistant to visitors to the office. If you are in conference with a client, and your secretary brings you sandwiches or coffee, for example, it is only gracious to make introductions when you thank him or her.

A good rule of thumb when making the introduction is to use whatever form of the names you think the persons involved will use later. For example, if a very senior and older executive is in your office, it is only gracious to say: "Ms. Riley, I would like you to meet Mr. Baden, my secretary." If the person in your office is a peer and your office is informal about using first names, you could say: "Bob Jones, I'd like you to meet Sandra Wilson."

Take care not to monopolize a secretary's time. It is his or her right to have lunch with whomever he or she pleases, so while an occasional working lunch may be acceptable, asking for working lunches on a regular basis is rude. The same thing applies to asking a secretary to work overtime; it may occasionally be necessary, but to do so on a regular basis infringes on his or her privacy. If a great deal of overtime is expected, say, at particular times of the year, this is something you should discuss when you are describing the job to a potential employee.

Above all, show respect for the work a secretary or assistant does for you. Secretaries' work is important and in many ways eases your workload. Although secretaries today have become vocal about their demands, a good boss can do a lot to ease relationships by offering fair and gracious treatment before it is demanded.

Any number of important and not so important tasks belong to a secretary or assistant. He or she will handle your correspondence, book appointments, make travel plans, do filing and typing, and carry messages and memos to others; a bright secretary may correct your spelling or do some slight editing of an obviously ungrammatical sentence. He or she should not be expected to wait on you or perform personal services. Personal services include such chores as bringing coffee (unless the secretary is going to get some for himself or herself or you are in an important meeting with someone), balancing your checkbook, or lying about your whereabouts. Your secretary may, of course, answer your phone, and he or she may well protect you from unwanted callers by saying that you can't take a call or are in conference. Just do not ask him or her to tell obvious lies, particularly those that relate to your private life.

Separation

SEE ALSO *Divorce.*

It is always a sad occasion when a marriage does not work out, and most of us will work hard to save an ailing marriage. For some couples, a separation is necesary to sort out a few things. Many couples separate unofficially, on a trial basis, before making any decisions about what to do next. Usually the husband moves out, but either partner may. Sometimes the wife takes the children for an extended visit to her family.

No formal announcement is made of a separation, and many couples try to keep their separation as quiet as possible as long as they are still trying to patch things up. They may see each other or not, as they prefer. If there are children, whichever person has moved may come home to help with them or may take them out to visit for visits. Both parties continue to wear their wedding rings, and do not date other people if they are serious about saving the marriage.

The wife turns down all social invitations, although a couple may appear together at family dinners and other family functions. Obviously their families and a few close friends will need to be told about the separation. Anyone who knows the couple should take care not to show partiality at this stage, not to criticize either partner, and not to invite the separated couple to a party or dinner without first consulting with them. In other words, do not interfere.

If attempts at a reconciliation fail, a couple usually go ahead and get a divorce. If their religion does not permit divorce, but there is no possibility of reconciliation, they usually have their lawyers draw up a legal separation, which sets forth the terms of support and child custody and divides their property.

At this point, each begins living a separate life as if they were, in fact, divorced, and they usually inform friends and family of the permanent separation. No one need ever confide details of one's personal life to acquaintances or business associates.

Servant

SEE *Household Help— Full-Time; Household Help— Part-Time.*

Serving Food

SEE ALSO *Buffet Dinner; Cocktail Party; Dinner Party; Food Courses; Menu Planning.*

Food may be served in one of three ways: formally, family style, and buffet style. Serving in courses is the most formal manner of serving, and the most casual is family style.

FORMAL SERVICE. In formal service, food is brought around to individual diners on platters, and they help themselves. This is the least common form of service today, and is seen in fancy restaurants and at formal dinner parties, particularly in homes with servants.

FAMILY-STYLE SERVICE. In family-style service, food is put on the table in serving dishes, which are then passed counterclockwise around the table.

At a dinner party, one often sees a combination of formal and family style, that is, the host or hostess brings around the entree, and side dishes are served by passing.

BUFFET SERVICE. In buffet service, food is put on a serving table and diners help themselves. A buffet may be either seated or stand-up. The two terms are often confused, and with good reason. Although a seated buffet refers to one in which all guests are provided with seats at a table, and a stand-up buffet would seem to refer to a meal where all the guests stand up while they eat, this is not, strictly speaking, the case. At a sit-down buffet, guests take their food from a service table and go to another table to sit down and eat. Often eating utensils are already in place settings at the table or tables. The diners need not wait for the table to fill up, since everyone will move fairly slowly through the buffet line, but may begin eating right away or as soon as one or two other diners have joined the table. Any kind of food may be served at a sit-down buffet since everyone is seated.

Service at a stand-up buffet is the same as for a sit-down buffet. Diners go to a service table, where they receive food and also pick up eating utensils, which are usually wrapped in a napkin. Diners then eat standing up, or they may sit on chairs or at tray tables. A host need not provide enough chairs or tray tables to go around, though, and those should obviously be reserved for the elderly, a mother with a young child, or someone who is handicapped or will have some difficulty eating in a standing position. The menu should consist of food that can readily be eaten with a fork while standing—food that is already in bite-sized pieces, in other words.

Sex in the Office

SEE ALSO *Office Love Affair.*

For those of you who thought sex and the office were mutually exclusive, it may come as a shock to learn that a certain level of sexual vibration is present, on and off, sometimes more and sometimes less, in just about every office. These days, there is probably more rather than less sexual vibration as more women have assumed positions of responsibility in the workplace. Much of the time, the sexual overtones are no one's fault; they just occur whenever men and women are thrown together in intimate surroundings, and short of family life few surroundings are so intiamte as those of the office "family."

BANTER. Certain offices, or rather those who work in them, seem to invite sexual banter. If it is harmless, and if you feel comfortable participating, go ahead. Realize, though, that such innocent banter can easily escalate, so keep it on a light level. This kind of banter is no more serious than frivolous joking about any other subject.

One woman I know reports on a method of dealing with the banter that works especially well for her. When a colleague who obviously had a bit of a crush on her repeatedly and flirtatiously asked her out for an after-work drink, she responded by saying, "I've wanted you for a long time. Why don't you leave your wife and run away with me?" Her banter, outrageous as it was, also conveyed a serious message, which was that she was aware of his ulterior motive in inviting her. It also served to remind him that she knew, and he should remember, that he had a wife.

SAYING NO. Sometimes the banter turns into a more direct invitation that must be dealt with in a more direct fashion. Since the invitation usually (but not always these days) comes from a man, it must (usually) be dealt with by a woman.

In such situations, I think the direct response is the most effective and, in the long run, the kindest. And throwing in a little flattery helps. If you are dating someone, you can always say, "I really find you very attractive, but I'm involved with someone right now." If you are not dating someone, it may not be wise to claim you are since you will then have to keep up the pretense at work. Your colleague is also constantly around and capable of checking to see how your affair is going.

A better response if you are not involved with someone at the preesnt time and have no wish to see a colleague romantically is to say honestly (or if not honestly, then tactfully), "I find you very attractive, but I don't go out with people I work with." It is a little cliché to offer friendship when someone is lusting after you, but in many instances, a work colleague does become a good friend once he or she finds out there is no chance for anything else.

SEXUAL HARASSMENT. Occasionally someone encounters true sexual harassment. Before you cry "harassment," though, be very sure that you are indeed being harassed. Most office flirtations are *not* harassment. Harassment is when you are threatened with losing your job or status if you do not become sexually involved with the person.

If possible, try to handle the harassment yourself before going to the harasser's boss. Sometimes just the threat that you will go to his or your superiors to complain about his actions is enough to end the harassment.

If the situation becomes untenable, go to the person's boss and explain what has been going on. Do not threaten a lawsuit until you have exhausted every other avenue of action. Most complaints of sexual harassment are taken very seriously these days, but companies also like to resolve their internal problems without publicity. As a loyal employee you should give them an opportunity to do just that.

If the person harassing you is your boss or is the top person in the company, you will first have to deal with that person directly and firmly yourself. If this fails, unfortunately, no other option may be open to you than to resign from what promises to continue as an unpleasant situation. It is unfair that a woman employed in a small company with no one to shield her from the boss may have to resign her job, but there is no other solution that relieves the day-to-day pain.

Sexual Harassment

SEE *Sex in the Office.*

Shellfish

SEE *Clams; Lobster; Mussels; Oysters; Shrimp.*

Sherry

SEE ALSO *After-Dinner Drinks.*

Sherry, which may be either dry or sweet, is served with clear soups, as an apéritif, and as an after-dinner drink. Dry sherry is most appropriate before a meal and sweet sherry afterward. It may be served at room temperature in a V-shaped glass or over ice. Guests should be asked their preference.

When sherry is served with a soup, the glasses are removed with the soup dishes. Other wineglasses are left on the table throughout the meal.

Ship Travel

BON VOYAGE PARTY. Guests may arrive at your stateroom for a surprise or planned bon voyage party. They traditionally show up with champagne or wine and fruit or other edible delectables for you to enjoy en route. You can either entertain them in your stateroom, if it is large enough, or in one of the ship's dining rooms. Either way, call your steward or a headwaiter and let him know that you will need glasses and ice in your room or a table in the dining room.

CAPTAIN'S TABLE. It is an honor to be asked to dine at the captain's table, one that should not be refused without a good reason. Dining with the captain, who is always referred to as "Captain Jones," is similar to attending any other private dinner party. Arrive on time and don't start eating without him, if he is late, which captains often are. If he will be very late, he will probably send word that his guests should go ahead without him.

DRESS. Sports clothes, even bathing suits, are acceptable during the day on a cruise ship. Women generally change into a dress for dinner and men wear sports jackets and tie or open sports shirts. Take along casual clothes

and a pair of good walking shoes for the ports of call.

On a transatlantic luxury liner, people tend to dress in casual daytime clothes (pants or skirts for women and sports shirts for men), and do not wear sports clothes except when they are participating in a sport. Even if formal wear is not required for dinner, a dressy dress for women and suit or sports jacket and tie are for men are the appropriate choices. Passengers in first class dress for dinner every night except the first and last. Generally, this means black tie, but depending upon the liner, it may mean something less dressy.

RESERVATIONS FOR DECK CHAIR AND DINING ROOM. Both deck chairs and dining room tables should be reserved shortly after boarding. Sign up with the deck steward and the headwaiter. If you do not sign up early for a deck chair, you may not get one—or may get one in a poor location. If you do not sign up for a dining table, you will be assigned a table in the dining room.

SOCIALIZING. Shipboard friendships are like summer romances: You can be best pals for as long as it lasts, but there is no obligation to pursue the friendship once you have arrived at your destination unless you have enough mutual interests or acquaintances to form a lasting friendship.

Feel free to strike up a conversation with anyone you encounter; simply introduce yourself. If you do become friendly with people and want to dine with them, ask the headwaiter to arrange this. (Similarly if you are assigned to sit with obnoxious people at dinner, speak to the headwaiter about a reassignment, unless of course you're at the captain's table.)

If you wish to entertain guests, usually over cocktails, during the voyage, make the same kind of arrangements you made for the bon voyage party.

TIPPING. On a transoceanic voyage, plan to tip about 10 percent of the bill, 10 to 15 percent on a cruise ship. Tipping is traditionally done on Friday evening on a long voyage, before ports of call on shorter voyages. Approximate amounts may also help you plan tipping: $2 per day to the cabin steward or stewardess, $10 to the dining room steward, and $5 to the headwaiter. The deck steward receives somewhere between $4 and $12, depending upon his services. Tip him more if he has an assistant so he can split the tip. When a bath steward is used, he should be tipped $1. Bartenders and the wine steward should receive 15 percent of the bill, as they render services. These are the typical tips for first-class travel; passengers in other classes may reduce their tips proportionately. Staff who provide special services or run errands should receive a tip of no less than 50 cents to $1.

Shivah

SEE *Jewish Funeral Customs.*

Shower

A shower is a special kind of party that, as its name suggests, "showers" the honored guest with presents. The most popular showers are bridal and baby, but in some locales, a growing trend exists to shower single women starting their own households and grandmothers at the birth of their first grandchild. Although I do not really approve of "showers" for these events, I see no reason that three or four friends cannot go together on a housewarming gift and present it at a small gathering, if they choose, and a grandmother's close friends can similarly gift her with some presents for her grandchild, but such events should not assume the proportions of a full-blown shower.

BABY SHOWER. A baby shower should take place when an expectant mother is far enough along in her pregnancy that there is little chance of miscarriage and enough before her delivery date that there is equally little chance she will miss her own party because she is giving birth. In some parts of the country and among some ethnic groups, showers are not held until several weeks after the baby's birth.

As a rule, a shower is given only for a first child, and only close friends and relatives are invited, since those invited are expected to bring a baby gift. An exception can be made if a woman has moved to a new part of the country or has many new friends who want to "shower" her before the birth of her second or third child. The point is that the friends who gave presents at a shower for the birth of the first baby are not asked to give presents again. Obviously those who are close to the family will feel free to give a present to a second and third child, but they are doing so because they wish to and not because they have been asked to.

Many women who work are given a shower by their office friends and another one by their close friends outside work. If a friend overlaps in both areas, the expectant mother may invite the friend to both showers but suggest that she not bring a gift to both. (The thoughtful friend, not wanting to show up empty-handed, may feel more comfortable with some kind of compromise, such as bringing a big gift to one shower and a small one to another or a small gift to each shower. She may do whatever suits her pocketbook.)

A baby shower may be given by any close friend of the expectant mother but is usually not given by members of her immediate family such as her mother, sisters, sisters- or mother-in-law, or aunts. Family members should not solicit gifts for one another.

Baby showers are often women's social occasions, but there is no reason that a baby shower could not include the expectant father and the couple's friends, both male and female. A coed shower would be held during the evening (as opposed to afternoon for most all-female showers) and a buffet supper might be served.

Bridal showers are often surprise parties, but a hostess who is planning to surprise her guest of honor should do so as tactfully as possible. Many pregnant women do not feel their most attractive toward the end of their pregnancies, and to put a woman at further disadvantage by letting her show up for a shower in her grubbiest clothes is to risk having a dismayed guest of honor. It is far kinder to ask the guest of honor to come to lunch or some other social occasion so she will arrive looking her loveliest.

Guests invited to a baby shower are expected to bring a present. Alternately, sometimes all the guests chip in to buy one major present. If the shower is given before the baby is born, gifts should be of neutral color so that they are appropriate for either sex. If you are invited to a shower and cannot attend, you need not send a gift, but since only close friends are invited, most will want to do so anyway. The present may be left at the hostess's house a day or so before the shower or delivered in person or by mail to the expectant parents after the shower.

In the sad event that a woman loses a baby after she has been given a shower, she may return the presents. Should she find this task unbearably painful and instead put away the presents with hopes that she will have another baby soon, no kind person should fault her. If a woman has a baby who is severely ill and whose survival is in question, it is sometimes tactful not to give her a shower until the baby is out of danger.

If a woman has a physically or mentally impaired child whose life is not in any immediate danger, after she has been given a few weeks to learn to cope, a close friend should offer to give her a shower—and she should feel perfectly free to accept. If she seems reluctant, she might be offered some gentle persuasion to accept a party celebrating the birth of a child whom she has presumably come to love a great deal.

BRIDAL SHOWER. Showers to honor a woman who is getting married should be scheduled far enough in advance of the wedding so the bride is not harried with last-minute details and close enough to the date of the wedding so plans do not change. Several showers may be held, but the bride should attempt to keep the number to a minimum, and should permit only close friends to be invited. With the exception of her wedding attendants, no friend should be invited to more than one shower, and unless the wedding will be very small and intimate, all friends invited to showers should also be invited to the wedding and reception.

Bridal showers may be given by any close friend of the bride, but they should not be given by close relatives.

Bridal showers, which often are given for the happy couple rather than just the bride, are sometimes planned around a theme. A woman might be given a kitchen shower, a lingerie shower, a wine shower (particularly good if men are included), or a linen shower. There are any number of other possible themes for such showers. A surprise shower also may be given.

If an invitation is accepted, a friend is obligated to bring a gift to a shower. Even if a friend cannot accept, he or she may choose to send a gift anyway but is not obligated to do so since anyone invited to a shower will also probably be invited to the wedding and will also be obligated for a wedding gift.

PLANNING THE SHOWER. A shower can be held at any time of day that is convenient for those gathering. The food should be appropriate to the time of day. Decorations may be elaborate or simple. Flowers on the buffet table and tables where guests sit are always a lovely touch. Cake is the traditional dessert at any kind of shower.

THANK-YOUS. The guest of honor thanks her friends for their gifts as she opens them, and she also should send a handwritten thank-you note as soon as possible.

Shrimp

COCKTAIL. Eat the shrimp with an oyster fork. If the shrimp is too large to eat in one bite, then eat it in two or three bites from the fork. It is impossible to cut up shrimp in a cocktail dish. You may eat the celery; leave the lettuce alone, because it's too hard to get to and you don't want to look too hungry.

FRIED. Use a knife and fork for American-style fried shrimp. For Oriental-style split-tailed fried shrimp, pick them up with your fingers, or with your chopsticks if you prefer.

IN SHELL. Pick up with fingers and shell. Hold by tail and eat.

Shyness

Shyness causes a lot of discomfort, but fortunately you can learn to control it rather than letting it control you. I have one favorite technique for conquering shyness. Shy people often assume that they are the only ones who suffer from this problem. Yet if you look around, you will see someone else who is as shy as you, and sometimes even more in need of help. My solution to curing your shyness, then, is to take it upon yourself (because you know the anxiety of the situation) to walk over to someone else who is shy and try to put him or her at ease. The beauty of this small social assignment is that if you do your job well, you won't have time to think about how shy you are.

Another trick that is useful before going out with other people is to prepare a mental list of things to talk about. Newspapers and magazines and television news will provide lots of thought-provoking topics of conversation.

Signature

According to the *American Heritage Dictionary,* your signature is your name the way you write it; it is, furthermore, your distinctive mark. I would like to add that it should be legible. Not letter-perfect, but legible enough to serve as your identifying legal mark.

You must make some personal decisions regarding your signature. Do you want to use your full name, your forename and middle initial, your initials and surname? These are matters of personal preference, and you may do whatever you prefer.

Unlike men, who settle on a signature and need never change it, women have occasion to change their signatures. Many women who use their middle names until they marry then drop their middle names from their signatures and use their surnames: "Eleanor Mary Neely" becomes "Eleanor Neely Randolph." Alternately, she could become "Eleanor Mary Randolph."

SIGNATURE VS. TITLE. As a point of etiquette, many people think that signatures and titles are the same thing, but they are not. The interplay between titles and signatures does not assume any significance in personal correspondence, where you simply sign your name:

Love,
Sally
or
John

In both your professional business correspondence and your household and personal business correspondence, however, your name, and under certain circumstances your title, is typed beneath your signature, or in the case of medical and legal titles right next to your name. A man no longer types out "Mr." under his signature, but titles such as "Professor," "Esquire," "M.D.," and "D.D.S." are used in business correspondence. For example:

William Smith, M.D.

Note that while titles are used in the typed line, they are never properly part of your signature. Thus Dr. William Smith is always "William Smith" or even "Bill Smith" in his signature, never "William Smith, M.D.," at least not unless his last name is "M.D."! Similarly, lawyers (both male and female, according to current practice) sign their names only and then type in their titles:

Joy Moses, Esquire

When you sign your first name only or even a nickname in business correspondence, your full title is still typed beneath your name:

William Smith
Chief Executive Officer

WOMEN. The title vs. signature problem becomes more complicated for women, who have the option of using either "Mrs.," "Miss," or "Ms." in their typed signature—or none of the above! It is further complicated by the fact of women's changing roles and perceptions of themselves.

Married women always used to use "Mrs." in the typed line under their signatures, and any woman who did not use "Mrs." was assumed to be single, so single women never used "Miss." Today, one is safest making no assumptions regarding marital status from a woman's signature.

The simplest method is for women to adopt the practice of men, that is, to sign their letters and type in their names sans marital status underneath them:

Eleanor N. Randolph

For lack of any better terms to describe the situation, a married woman would conservatively sign her personal business correspondence:

Mrs. Stephen Randolph

Less conservatively, she might write:

Mrs. Eleanor Randolph

Choosing to completely downplay her marital status, a married woman might also sign and title herself:

Eleanor Neely Randolph

A single woman who wanted to identify herself as such might write:

Ms. Eleanor Neely
or
Miss Eleanor Neely

A divorced woman who wishes to use an ultraformal, conservative title designating her status would write:

Mrs. Neely Randolph

Few divorcées use this title, however, with the vast majority preferring to return to their maiden names or to use their surnames and married names, as in "Mrs. Mary Randolph."

DOUBLE SIGNATURES. A spouse never signs her or his partner's name to any correspondence. For example, when Eleanor Randolph writes a letter to her and her husband's good friends Stanley and Margery Wilmot, she may send her husband's best wishes along with any personal messages he wants delivered, and she may refer to "we," but she does not sign the letter "Eleanor and Stephen." Only if Stephen adds a few lines does he sign his name.

The only exception to this is greeting cards, where one spouse may sign both names or the entire family's names if there are children. It is still more gracious for each spouse to sign his and her name separately.

The same guidelines apply for cohabiting couples and for gay couples. The correspondence of cohabiting and gay couples is handled just as any married couple's is. Letters may be written on behalf of both partners ("John and I were delighted . . ."), but only the actual writer signs, and the writer signs only his or her name.

Single Parent

Ten or even five years ago, most "single" parents were unmarried women, and they were discriminated against socially. A woman often went to some lengths to disguise her real situation. Today, the stigma against having a child while unmarried has largely vanished, or at least it has in many circles. Since people tend to gravitate to those groups that are accepting of them, few single unwed mothers today encounter much social discrimination. Also, many men and women are single parents today as the result of divorce.

Most single parents today need feel few qualms about their social status. I say few qualms, because it is impossible, I feel, for a single parent, especially a woman, to experience no qualms. Awkward situations do arise, and they must be dealt with. Here then are some suggestions for handling some of those touchy moments.

ACKNOWLEDGMENT. People will express curiosity about your situation, and they will pry. Therefore, a savvy single parent has a few stock answers at the ready. You need not give more details about your life than you want to give, however, and rude questions can be dodged with or without tact.

The simplest explanation when asked about the whereabouts of your nonexistent spouse is to say noncommittally, "I'm a single parent." If more questions follow, Ann Landers has an excellent tactic for keeping unreasonably inquisitive questioners at bay, which is to say, "Whyever would you ask such a question?"

If you and your child have different surnames, you can respond to inquiries about that simply by saying: "He uses his father's name, and I use my name." If your names are the same, you can offer another equally simple, noninformative, and accurate explanation: "She uses my surname."

ADOPTIVE. SEE ALSO ADOPTION. More and more women and men these days

are opting to become single parents through adoption. The adoption of a child by a single person should be just as joyous an event as the adoption of a child by a couple. Send announcements; permit your friends to give you a shower; and enjoy all the privileges that would be conferred on you if you were a natural parent.

DIVORCED. Unfortunately a divorced single mother's status is often in some communities only slightly less a matter of curiosity than that of a single, never-married mother. After all, you probably won't continue to wear your wedding ring, and you may have retained or taken back your maiden name, so that you and your children have different surnames. When awkward questions arise, you can simply say, "I'm divorced," or you can respond with the less informative answers suggested for single parents.

SOCIAL LIFE. The social life of a single parent, whether divorced, widowed, or never married, is always viewed with some suspicion by the outside world in general and possibly by an ex-spouse who may want custody in particular. Because of this and to protect their children's feelings, single parents find they often must be more circumspect than other single people. They may have to avoid having a lover spend the night, or they may have to ask a lover to leave discreetly or at an early hour. This is a matter of manners only to the extent that a single parent may welcome some guidance in handling these awkward moments. The first thing to do is to stop thinking of them as awkward moments. You have every right to protect your reputation and your children's feelings. If you must make an "unusual" request of a lover, explain the situation and give reasons as much as possible. A considerate lover will tolerate any conditions that must be imposed and will even cooperate.

Singles

SEE *Cohabitation; Divorced Person; Roommate; Single Parent; Singles' Bar; Singles' Co-Host; Singles' Entertaining; Singles' Friendships; Singles' Intimate Relations; Widow; Widower.*

Singles' Bar

An institution that arose in the late 1960s, the first singles' bar was called Butch McGuire's and was located in that quintessential swinging singles' neighborhood, the Near North Side of Chicago. Singles' bars have proliferated since then, and have become less rather than more subtle in their intent.

Singles' bars for the most part are frequented by people (not necessarily singles) who are looking for a one-night liaison. Before going into one of these bars, you should understand that this is the ground rule. You can decline to play the game, but you should not be surprised that this is the game.

Apart from this, various singles' bars have different auras, and most are very cliquish. You will have to make a considera-ble investment of time and energy to become a regular.

Singles' Co-Host

Either a man or a woman who lives alone and is entertaining friends may ask a friend of the opposite sex to act as co-host, but it is also perfectly acceptable not to do so. In other words, a woman or man should feel perfectly comfortable being the sole host even when entertaining couples.

When someone does help out, he or she is often assigned certain tasks—to mix and serve drinks, for example, or start the grill.

Finally, keep in mind that the role of co-host is a rather honorary one. If you are having eight persons for drinks and would like to flatter your present heartthrob, by all means ask him or her to help you greet guests and serve drinks and hors d'oeuvres while you check on the food. But if you are having a cocktail party for twenty, then it's not fair to ask a friend to serve drinks. You need to hire a bartender.

Singles' Entertaining

A single person today incurs all the obligations that a married couple do with regard to entertaining friends. Gone, too, is the stigma attached to entertaining singles, and only a rare hostess pays much attention to the number of single persons she invites or to whether there will be an equal number of men and women. Men unfortunately may still be slightly more desirable as extras on a guest list, but an interesting single woman will find herself in great demand socially. The single who enjoys an active social life precisely because he is the "extra person" at a party no longer gets an entirely free ride; at some point, he or she is expected to reciprocate.

While you must reciprocate, you need not entertain people in the same manner in which they entertain you, but can adjust your plans to accommodate your lifestyle. A single may entertain in his or her own home, just as couples do, or if he or she has an apartment or home that is too small to accommodate many people may entertain in restaurants or other public places. One woman who lives in a studio apartment in a city rarely entertains there, but once a year she "borrows" a friend's large apartment and gives a wonderful party for everyone who has entertained her throughout the year. A single man who never really set up his apartment to handle guests entertains friends on his sailboat, and those who do not sail in restaurants. An enterprising young woman rents out a local art gallery every year and gives an elegant holiday party.

Singles' Friendship

There is really nothing to set apart a single person's friendships from those of married persons, although a few different problems come up. Some singles, for example, tend to make only casual plans, which they feel free to cancel if they decide to work late or if they decide to accept a date. For some reason, a date often takes precedence over dinner with a treasured friend, even though a friend is far more likely to be around after a lover has departed. A considerate single values plans with friends as highly as, and sometimes even more highly than, dates.

Then, too, everyone knows the single person who drops out when a new love affair begins and does not bother to see old friends until it ends. While all persons in a new love affair will, at least initially, spend a lot of time with their lover, it is never wise to drop old friends or permanently relegate them to second best. Each should have a special place. Enjoy the honeymoon period, but stay in touch with old friends and eventually introduce them to your lover so you can all merge into one social circle.

Singles' Intimate Relations

Whether and when one chooses to be intimate with another person is a highly personal decision about which I shall make no value judgment. My only concern is that the situation be handled with tact and consideration for both partners. Etiquette books often touch upon the need for consideration between marriage partners, but little is written about how a nonmarried but intimately involved couple can handle their relationship. Ultimately, of course, it is up to each couple to work out their own ground rules, particularly since they will presumably, at least initially, maintain some independence and separate residences. It is considerate and helpful for a couple to discuss their hopes and expectations at the outset of their relationship. Once intimate relations have begun, each should make an effort to treat the other according to the guidelines they have set up.

Singles' Living Arrangements

SEE *Cohabitation; Living Alone; Roommate.*

Sir

"Sir" is a term of respect for men. It is used to address the President of the United States, royalty, and elderly gentlemen. In the South, children are often taught to address their elders as "Sir" and "Ma'am," and I applaud this custom, although I suspect it is fading. An adult woman never properly addresses a man who is her peer as "Sir."

Sitting Shivah

SEE *Jewish Mourning Customs; Mourning.*

Skiing

Good manners on the slopes mostly consist of ensuring safety. A skier must ski in control at all times, and if he causes someone to fall, he must stop to make sure he is okay and to offer apologies. When skiing around someone, call out, "On your left" or "On your right" so the other skier is alerted.

When standing alone in the chairlift line, call out "Single" or tell the person monitoring the line that you are alone so that he can pair you off with another single skier.

Smoking

SEE ALSO *Job Interview; Office Life.*

Smoking has become a major social battlefield these days, with neither side willing to give an inch. A few guidelines will make life more comfortable all around for everyone.

AT TABLE. The touchiest scenes for smoking occur over meals in restaurants. Restaurants could help considerably by dividing their seating areas into smoking and nonsmoking, but few have been inclined to do this, so it is up to individuals to work out the rules of civil behavior.

The nonsmokers at one table do not want smoked food they did not order, and the smokers at the next table, who do not have their food yet, want a preprandial smoke. The solution? Smokers should be observant of when food arrives at the surrounding tables and should put out their cigarettes. If they do not extend this basic courtesy, nonsmokers should request this or at minimum that the cigarette smoke be directed elsewhere. I am not necessarily antismoker, please understand, but I do know that smoke and food do not mix.

When dining in someone's home, a smoker must ask permission to smoke at the table, and smokers be forewarned: These days the absence of an ashtray often means that smoking is frowned upon. If you do want to smoke during dinner, the only acceptable time is at the end of the meal.

EVERYBODY'S RIGHTS. Only a couple of years ago, relations were chummy enough so that nonsmokers could ask smokers to refrain in public places, and they did so graciously. Today, the situation has deteriorated to the point where requests are no longer received graciously, nor for that matter are they lightly made. The solution? As is often the case where civilized behavior is concerned, everyone should give a little. Nonsmokers should not ask someone to put out a cigarette purely on principle but because it is truly troublesome. Smokers should make sure their smoke does not blow in anyone's direction and might even ask if it bothers someone, especially when food is brought to the table. And everyone—smokers and nonsmokers alike—should ask in every restaurant if there are smoking and nonsmoking sections. The more often restaurateurs hear this request, the more likely they will be to arrange their restaurants to accommodate everyone.

DENYING PERMISSION. If you are the host or hostess and someone asks you if they may smoke, you may decline to let them do so. Certainly, whenever someone is present whose health would be affected, permission to smoke should be refused. An alternative can be offered when smoking is not permitted in a home. If a guest asks

your permission to smoke, and you cannot let him, simply say, "Oh, thanks for asking, but I would rather you didn't. Frank's asthma kicks up around smoke. If you like, you can step outside (on the back porch, or wherever) and have a cigarette."

Smörgåsbord

SEE ALSO *Cafeteria.*

This import from Sweden, which literally means "sandwich table," is used to describe a type of meal that may be served in one's home or in a restaurant. A smörgåsbord menu usually consists of sandwiches, salads, and food that is considered typically Swedish, such as Swedish meatballs and noodles.

In a restaurant, a smörgåsbord meal means that the service is similar to that of a cafeteria. Diners walk up to tables or counters laden with food, make selections, and carry their plates back to their tables. When a restaurant serves smörgåsbord-style, this usually means that diners may return for seconds if they like.

Snail

SEE *Escargot.*

Sneeze

Superstitiously speaking, a sneeze puts a healthy person as close to death as a healthy person is likely to get, and that is the reason for blessing the sneezer. That is why we say *Gesundheit*, which literally translates as "Good health" or "Bless you."

Sneezing is an excellent way to spread germs, so sneezers must exercise some basic consideration toward those around them. When you feel a sneeze coming on, reach for a tissue to cover your nose and mouth or cover them with your hand. Turn your head away from others, and excuse yourself after you sneeze. No further explanation is needed, but "Thank you" is the appropriate response to "Gesundheit" or "Bless you."

Snobbishness

SEE *Street Manners; Unintentional Snub.*

Soup

SEE ALSO *Consommé Cup; Crackers; Soup Plate.*

Soup is often served as a first course. If it is a clear broth it is served in a consommé cup; if it is a cream soup, it is served in a bowl or in a soup plate.

Soup is almost always eaten with a soup spoon, even though a consommé cup is designed so the diner can pick it up and drink the soup.

Move the spoon away from you as you fill it. Similarly, tip the bowl away from you so you do not spill any soup on yourself or the tablecloth. Soup should never be slurped. If a spoonful of soup is too hot, blow gently on it to cool it and then wait a minute or two for the rest of the soup to cool.

If crackers are served, they are meant to be eaten with the soup, not in it. Do not dip crackers into the soup, and do not crumble the crackers and put them in the soup. This is acceptable only with the under-two set and on days when you are suffering from the flu and lunching alone at home on chicken soup. Then the crackers broken into small pieces and dropped into the soup may be considered medicinal. In public, the exception is oyster crackers, which may be added a few at a time to chowder.

Occasionally, in an Oriental restaurant you will be served soup in a handleless cup with no spoon. Sip this soup as you would a cup of tea.

Soup Plate

SEE ALSO *Soup.*

Any soup other than a clear broth (and even some clear broths) is served from a soup plate, which is a wide, shallow bowl. A soup spoon is used to eat such soups.

Spoon

SEE ALSO *Fork; Knife; Place Setting; Table Manners.*

As is the case with other flatware, you should never encounter more than three spoons at any one time at a place setting.

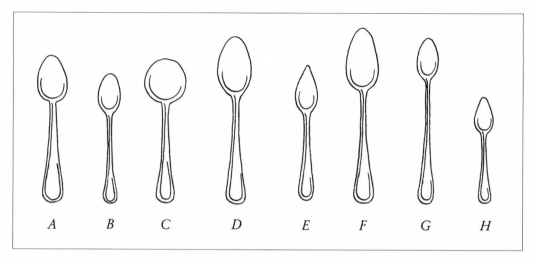

*Figure 52. Spoons A. Dinner spoon B. Teaspoon C. Consommé spoon D. Soup spoon
E. Grapefruit spoon F. Dessert spoon G. Iced-tea spoon H. Demitasse spoon*

The spoons that may be used to make up a place setting are the dinner or place spoon, the teaspoon, the soup spoon, the grapefruit spoon, the iced-tea spoon, and the demitasse spoon *(see Figure 52)*. Most place settings consist of the teaspoon alone. All spoons are held the same way *(see Figure 53)*.

Spoons go next to the knife on the right side of a place setting *(see Figure 54)*. When more than one spoon is used, they should be placed in order of use, that is, a teaspoon that will be used for coffee goes next to the knife and a soup spoon goes next to the teaspoon on the outside. A grapefruit spoon goes on the far right, while a spoon to be used for eating cereal goes between the grapefruit spoon and the knife because the grapefruit presumably would be eaten first.

DINNER SPOON. In most modern flat-ware, the teaspoon replaces the dinner spoon, but it is found in old sets of silver. The dinner spoon, which is larger than a teaspoon, is used to eat cereals, soups, and desserts. It goes to the right of the knife.

TEASPOON. When a dinner spoon is not used, the teaspoon is the third piece of flatware, along with the knife and fork, to

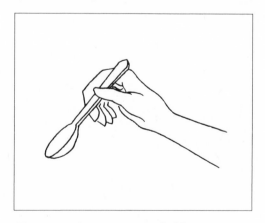

Figure 53. Correct way to hold a spoon

Figure 54. Correct arrangement of spoons at a table setting

make up a place setting. Even if the tea-spoon will not be used, it is put on the table to finish the place setting. The teaspoon often substitutes for a consommé spoon when soup is served in cups, and it is used for cereal, eggs in cups, and coffee and tea. The teaspoon goes to the right of the knife.

SOUP SPOON. Actually, there are two soup spoons: a large one that is used for thick soups served in bowls or soup plates, and another smaller spoon that is intended for use with consommés. When you are done with a soup, rest the large soup spoon in the bowl unless there is a service plate underneath. Do not leave it on your dinner or luncheon plate. Most consommé cups come with a service plate, and the spoon should be placed on that plate.

GRAPEFRUIT SPOON. This spoon has a sharp, slightly serrated top that facilitates the eating of grapefruit. A teaspoon is often used instead for eating fruit.

DESSERT SPOON. This is actually the dinner spoon that was described earlier. The dessert spoon either goes to the right of the plate, immediately next to the knife, or it may be placed above the plate. When placed alongside with a dessert fork at the top of the plate, the spoon goes on the top with its handle toward the right. The dessert spoon is also sometimes brought in with dessert.

ICED-TEA SPOON. This is a long, skinny spoon that is used for iced tea and also to eat sundaes and other desserts that are served in tall glasses. An iced-tea spoon is brought when iced tea or dessert is served.

DEMITASSE SPOON. This miniature spoon is used to stir espresso. A demitasse spoon is brought in with a demitasse cup and saucer. After use, it should always be placed on the small saucer under the cup.

Sports

SEE *listings of individual sports.*

Sportsmanship

The degree of sportsmanlike behavior that one displays, either as a spectator or as a player, is one real mark of a gracious, civilized person.

SPECTATOR BEHAVIOR. While spectators are certainly expected to display great enthusiasm toward their own team, they should never boo or in any way hassle or disparage the other side. Always remember that however glorious it feels to be on the winning team, in a rematch the outcome could change completely. That is why rematches are held and what makes sports so much fun.

If spectators know one another, as is often the case at local sporting events, the winners should offer polite consolation to the losers, commenting on how well they played.

PLAYERS. Any player is obliged to follow the rules of a game, but sportsmanship consists of an attitude that takes the rules one step further. It is an unwritten code of behavior that is tied to a person's character and sense of decency.

To the extent that it can be summarized, sportsmanlike behavior consists of giving an opponent the benefit of the doubt and extending every possible courtesy to him or her during the playing of the game. It might, for example, involve not calling a foul for a ball that was perhaps on the line, perhaps not. It involves being a gracious loser, and what is sometimes more difficult, a gracious winner. Sadly, sportsmanlike behavior among professionals in some sports has largely gotten lost in the undertow of fierce competition.

If you have won, always be gracious to the loser, assuring him or her that the game was played well. A gracious winner may even diminish his or her own victory by drawing attention to the role that luck played in his winning. For example, it would be polite to say, "Well, I really had luck on my side with those line shots" or something to this effect.

The loser, of course, must also be gracious in defeat. He should move quickly to shake the winner's hand, thus being the first to offer congratulations, and should compliment the winner on a game that was "well played." The loser would be ungracious to refer to the role that luck may have played in his loss.

Spouse

SEE *Family Finances; Forms of Address—Spoken; Marriage; Married Couples' Social Lives.*

Squash

SEE *Racquet Sports.*

Squid

If small and fried, pick them up and eat them with your fingers. If served in sauce, use a fork. On Italian menus, these will be called *Calamari, totani,* or *seppie.*

Staring

It is rude to stare at another person for any reason. Small children, of course, must be taught not to stare, and also not to make comments about others' appearances, but even adults need to remind themselvs on occasion that staring is rude and offensive behavior.

Stationery

SEE ALSO *Bread-and-Butter Note; Business Correspondence; Condolence Note; Informals; Personal Correspondence; Reference; Signature; Thank-You Note; Visiting Card.*

The well-dressed stationery wardrobe consists of formal writing paper, everyday writing paper for personal correspondence, and business writing paper. Men's and women's paper are usually different in size, design, and color.

FORMAL WRITING PAPER. This is used to respond to formal invitations, and it may be used to write condolence notes. Formal writing paper should be plain white or off-white, of the finest, heaviest paper stock you can afford.

If you do not receive many formal invitations, and would have little opportunity to use this paper, then there is no need to buy any. But if you can buy only one paper, and you do think you will be receiving formal invitations, this might be the one to invest in. It should not be monogrammed but may be engraved with your name and address. It also may be plain, with no printing. Formal writing paper is about 5 by 7½ inches and folds over once horizontally.

EVERYDAY WRITING PAPER. Everyday writing paper is used to write letters to friends, thank-you notes, letters of congratulation, and so on. A woman's everyday writing paper may be of a pastel shade or even one of the more vivid colors that are available. Everyday writing paper should be of the best quality you can afford, but it need not be as good as formal writing paper. It may be monogrammed or printed. Personal writing paper may be any size that appeals to you; it usually measures about 5 by 7½ inches.

If your everyday writing paper will also be used for condolence notes, it should be white, pale blue, or gray. You may also select a fairly conservative personal paper that can double as business writing paper.

Figure 55. Monogram styles for stationery

BUSINESS PAPER. You may also want a writing paper on which to conduct your personal and household business. This should have a businesslike appearance, that is, be white, gray, or beige, and fairly plain. Business paper is usually 8½ by 11 inches in size.

HIS, HERS, THEIRS, AND CHILDREN'S. Writing paper also varies depending upon whom is using it.

Women's paper, especially everyday stationery, is usually smaller than that of men, may be of pastel or bright color, and of a more frivolous design.

Men's paper is usually larger, at least 7 by 10 inches for everyday paper, and sometimes 8½ by 11 inches if the paper will double for personal business as well. It is white, gray, or beige.

Finding paper that a couple can share, especially if their names are different, is sometimes difficult. I suggest what used to be called house paper, that is, stationery that was used in a particular house by anyone—family and guests—who wanted to use it. This paper is at least 7 by 10 inches, and it is printed or engraved with the ad-dress alone. It may be printed with the street name, the street name and city, or, if this is a country house, with the name of the house rather than an address or in addition to the address. Personal names, however, are not engraved or printed on it. The paper is usually white, beige, or gray. I think this offers a practical solution to the couple who want some joint stationery but who do not share a joint surname.

Children's paper may be utterly frivolous, with funny drawings and lines—whatever pleases them. I think letting children choose their own paper, and letting that paper be as wild or colorful as they like, is an excellent way to interest children in letter-writing. A large sheet is probably better than a small one because it is easier for a child to handle.

MARKING STATIONERY. If you wish, you may print or engrave any of your writing papers. Engraving is far more expensive than printing, and good printing can look almost as fine as engraving. It is certainly acceptable today.

Women have a choice of using their monogram or their name and address, and men may have their name and address printed on their stationery. Men do not use monograms on stationery. If a monogram is used, no other printing is used with it, although the address may be printed on the envelope.

The printing either is centered at the top of the sheet of paper (be sure to order plain extra sheets) or it may go in the upper left-hand corner. Printed and engraved addresses usually go on the back flap of the envelope.

Monograms and printing come in a great variety of styles *(see Figure 55)* so you can easily choose one that suits your personality.

Stepbrother

SEE *Stepsister.*

Stepsister

If you are a sibling to someone by marriage, but have no biological relationship, you are a stepsister or stepbrother. When, due to death or divorce, parents marry someone who has children, the new marriage partner's children become your stepsiblings.

Stillbirth

SEE *Miscarriage, Abortion, and Stillbirth.*

Strawberry

SEE *Fruit.*

Street Manners

A century ago, an elaborate code of etiquette dictated people's behavior on the streets. A man did not greet a woman, for example, unless she acknowledged him first. Once greeted, a man was expected to remove his hat in the presence of the woman who greeted him (even if the temperature was minus 30 degrees), and he could be waylaid from his errands for as long as she chose to keep him in her presence. Fortunately, today, street behavior is more casual—and egalitarian.

Many older men still choose to follow the custom of removing their hats when talking with a woman, and they should be rewarded with a smile or some other small acknowledgment. But removing one's hat is no longer expected, and in very cold climates it can be deleterious to one's health.

A man may greet any woman to whom he has been properly introduced and strike up a conversation with her. He can also feel completely free to break off the conversation when it is convenient for him to do so.

A woman's street manners should parallel those of a man, that is, she may greet anyone whom she knows, and may feel free to initiate and end a conversation at her convenience. A woman is never obliged to respond to the comments or overtures of a stranger on the street.

On most public conveyances, special

seats are designated for the handicapped and the elderly. These should always be surrendered to those who need them, but beyond this it is only common courtesy to offer a seat to anyone who needs it. Men no longer automatically offer their seats to women, and there is no reason that a woman should not offer her seat to a man who may need it.

Some older men try to walk on the outside near the curb when they are walking with a woman, although I think they should give up this custom, which no longer serves any good purpose and simply is awkward for everyone. In the days before dry cleaning, men used to walk on the outside to protect women from the mud and water splashed by speeding carriages. We no longer have these vehicles to contend with, nor do we have to wash clothes by hand.

I admit I do not mind the protection of a man on those occasions when I am about to be accosted by something a little more crazed or dangerous than a carriage, as often occurs on the streets of our larger cities. Then I am appreciative of the man who steps around me to place himself between me and whatever obstacle has come our way. But the man who constantly trips over his own feet and mine, too, so that he can always be curbside is following some outdated notion of good manners.

Supper

A supper is sometimes served in place of a heavy dinner for a pre-theater or post-theater dinner party. Supper is also served at balls and dances, where the meal is presented around midnight. Supper is lighter than a formal dinner, often served buffet style, and, as noted, served very late at night on occasion.

MENU. Supper is often a buffet meal *(see Buffet Dinner)*. If it is a sit-down meal, omelettes and other brunch-type foods are suitable. Stuffed crêpes are excellent. Champagne is an excellent beverage to serve with supper, as are red and white wines. If the meal is served at the end of a big evening, wine may be a better choice than mixed drinks.

Surprise Party

SEE ALSO *Shower.*

A surprise party is most often given for a wedding or baby shower or a birthday, although there is no reason one could not be given for other events. Except for the element of surprise, nothing sets the rest of the party apart from other similar parties in honor of someone.

Invitations for a surprise party may be telephoned or mailed, but they must mention that the party is to be a surprise so the invited guests are cautioned not to ruin the surprise by mentioning the party to the guest of honor.

This is one party where the guests absolutely must arrive at the appointed hour so they are there to participate in the surprise when the guest of honor arrives. If you must go late to a surprise party, discuss this with the host, who will tell you when you may come without interfering with anything.

Persons planning a surprise party usually go through any number of machinations to arrange the surprise. The party may be held in the home of the guest of honor, in which case he or she is taken out for a while, to permit the guests to congregate, and then brought back to the assembled group of friends. An alternate method of surprise is to hold the party somewhere other than the guest of honor's home and lure him or her to that place at the appointed hour.

Swearing

SEE *Profanity*.

Sweet Sixteen Party

Turning sixteen is a *rite de pasage* in our society, one for which a teen, especially a girl, may enjoy a special birthday party. Although Sweet Sixteen parties are traditionally given for girls, there is no reason not to give one for a boy.

The best Sweet Sixteen parties have a note of elegance to them, but they should not be as sophisticated as an adult party. The party is, in a manner of speaking, an announcement that a child is approaching adulthood, not an announcement that he or she has reached it.

The teen should be consulted as to the kind of party he or she wants. Girls favor fancy parties—a slightly dressy dance, even a dinner dance, with real musicians, while boys often want a swimming or skiing party, something involving an activity.

Teens of both sexes also enjoy parties planned around activities.

It is fun to go all out on the decorations for this kind of party. A girl's Sweet Sixteen party is traditionally decorated in pink, and the decorations for a boy's party should be decidedly masculine.

The guest of honor should have a corsage (or nosegay) or a boutonnière if a dance is held.

Swimming

SEE *Swimming Pool*.

Swimming Pool

PRIVATE. Guests at a private or club swimming pool must follow any house rules, most of which are designed for safety. They provide their own bathing suits and any other equipment, and it's polite to bring a towel, although these are often provided at a friend's home.

PUBLIC. At a public pool, written rules are established for purposes of safety, and a few unwritten rules are followed out of consideration for others. Good unwritten rules to follow are:

1. Don't tread on others' space. If a towel reserves a chair or sunbathing space, don't remove it.
2. Be considerate about noise. Don't play a radio loudly in the presence of others.
3. Be aware that not everyone intends to get

near the water when swimming. Take care not to drip water on those who are sun-bathing. (Obviously, if people are sun-bathing at the edge of a swimming pool, it is their problem if they get wet.)

Synagogue

SEE *Religious Services.*

Table and Kitchen Linens

People entertain in such a wide range of styles that it is almost impossible to predict any one household's table linen needs. Table linens are available in a wide array of colors, textures, and styles.

Those who entertain formally will want white or pastel damask table linens, perhaps a mixture of cloths and placemats, and matching napkins.

Those who entertain casually, using pottery dishes and stainless steel, will want a more casual collection of table linens—brightly colored cloths and placemats in a variety of textures and materials. A stock of napkins that can be mixed and matched with various placemats and tablecloths works very well for informal dining. Even those who entertain casually may want one good white damask or lace tablecloth for special occasions.

Tablecloths come in standard sizes and fit the shape of the table. They are round, oval, square, or rectangular. A tablecloth should be approximately 10 inches longer than the table size all around. Thus, if you have a table that is 36 inches and round, you will buy 46-inch round tablecloths.

Napkins also come in sizes, but they are not standardized. Even though small napkins are favored for lunches, I think large napkins—what are called dinner napkins—always do the job better. The very best napkins are 24 by 24 inches square, if you can find them that large. There is a tendency to scale down the size of napkins these days. The large ones are luxurious and will cover any lap. Smaller napkins are perfectly adequate, of course. Very small napkins, about 4 by 4 inches or slightly larger, are used for serving drinks. Paper napkins may always be used.

Here are the basic table linen needs for a household of two to four that entertains fairly regularly:

- 1 white or pastel damask tablecloth or 1 lace tablecloth
- 8 to 12 matching napkins
  or
- 6 to 8 white damask placemats with matching napkins
- 2 sets (4, 6, 8 each) casual placemats
- 2 sets matching napkins
- 8 to 12 cocktail napkins

Kitchen linen needs are:

- 6 terrycloth dish towels
- 6 flat-weave dish towels (cotton, linen, synthetic)
- 4 dish cloths
- 2 to 4 potholders

The mixture of terrycloth and flat-weave dish towels is necessary because they have different uses. Terrycloth works well on pottery and pots and pans, while the flat-weave towels are good for glasses.

Tablecloth

SEE ALSO *Placemats; Table Linens.*

The most traditional tablecloth, always correct at a formal dinner, is white damask. The next most formal, a lace tablecloth, may be used alone or with a liner. Tablecloths come in a wonderful variety of colors, textures, and fabrics.

A tablecloth used for dining is different from one used for decorative purposes. When tablecloths are part of decoration, they may extend to the floor, whereas a dining tablecloth should extend only 12 to 18 inches over the edge of the table. Tableclothes come in standard sizes; measure your table, and add 20 inches to obtain the correct size.

If your table is a lovely wood, a pad may be needed for protection when a cloth tablecloth is used. If the table is not a standard size, the pad may have to be custommade. It is worth the investment to protect a fine wood table.

Never put a plastic liner on top of a tablecloth no matter how precious the material. To do so destroys the beauty of the table setting and detracts from lovely cloth itself.

Table d'Hôte

SEE ALSO *À la Carte; Prix Fixe.*

A table d'hôte menu is one in which a complete meal is offered for a set price. The meal may be several courses or one entree served with vegetables and a salad. When ordering table d'hôte, it is acceptable to skip a course if too much food is offered for your taste.

Table Manners

SEE *After-Dinner Drinks; Belching; Business Lunch; Children's Table Manners; Doggy Bag; Eggcup; Elbows; Food Courses; Food Stuck in Teeth; Fork; Knife; Passing Food; Plates; Ramekins and Individual Casseroles; Relishes; Restaurant Meal; Salt and Pepper; Smoking at Table; Soup; Spoon; Toothpick; Wine.*

I am of the minimalist school of table manners. Not that I do not like to see elegant manners at the table. I do, indeed. But I also like relaxed diners at my parties, and I despise stiffness in any area of etiquette.

After all, if manners really are nothing more than treating others kindly, which I firmly believe they are, then table manners should be kind both to those who must view them and those who must display them. Keeping this underlying premise in mind, what, then, is expected of the well-cultivated adult at table?

Many people, of course, will exhibit more casual manners when dining with their families than they do when they are guests at a dinner party. Dining alone or with your children is another matter entirely, and you may feel free to indulge in any kind of bad or so-so manners under these circumstances. Dining with your spouse falls somewhere in between, I suppose, but I firmly believe that a marriage always does better when some minimal standards are maintained; however, if you and your spouse agree to lower them on occasion at table, that is entirely between the two of you.

To paraphrase (badly, I admit) what young doctors are taught (First, do no harm), I would say this about your table manners: First, offend no one. Fortunately most of the rules about table manners that have endured through the decades are designed to accomplish this purpose. For example, the rigid rule that denied elbows access to the table has fallen into disuse largely because elbows casually resting on the table between courses do not cause any real offense. They are hardly an eyesore and do not interfere with anyone's eating. The taboo against talking with your mouth full of food, on the other hand, has persisted simply because it does offend and does interfere with the dining pleasure of others. Herewith, then, are a few basic rules of dining that should be followed at all times:

- Sit up straight (not rigidly, but avoid slouching).
- Keep your elbows off the table when eating (this is part of sitting up straight), although they may be rested on the table between courses or when you are not eating.
- Do not talk with your mouth full of food.
- Do not wave around a fork or any utensil with food on it.
- Once you have put food on a utensil, eat it. Do not hold it in midair while you talk . . . or listen.
- Cut food into small, bite-sized pieces, one piece at a time. No one over the age of two should cut all his food into small pieces beofre eating it.
- Eat slowly. Do not inhale food, but rather chew it.
- Chew it quietly. Do not slurp or make any other unattractive noises when eating.
- Reach for foods that are easily within your reach. Ask others to pass foods that are not near you.
- Always say "Please" and "Thank you" when foods are passed to you or when accepting or declining food.
- If you are eating in someone's home, remember that someone prepared the meal, and compliment the cook.
- If you must leave the table during the meal or before everyone else has finished, excuse yourself.

The following sections contain more specific information about table manners.

SERVING. When eating in a restaurant or dining in someone's home, the food will be served.

At casual dinners, food is often served family-style, which means that it comes to the table in communal bowls. Your obligation, along with that of other diners, is to pass the food to everyone. It is easier to pass food to the right because most people are right-handed, but food may be passed in either direction. All the food, however, should be passed in one direction to avoid confusion. Usually, the hostess says, "John, do you mind starting the broccoli?" but if she is too busy or does not notice, anyone may start passing dishes.

To be absolutely correct, no one should begin eating until all the food is served, and everyone should wait for the hostess or the host to take the first bite. For many years, the only exception to the hostess-first rule was when a large number of persons were at the table, for example, at a banquet or Thanksgiving dinner, and some people's food would get cold if they did not start eating it. Then people began eating as soon as they and others around them had been served. Anyone may start. Today, even at a small dinner party of eight to ten, the host or hostess may encourage those who have already been served to begin eating so their food does not get cold, and it is perfectly acceptable for guests to begin when so encouraged.

When more formal service is used, either the hostess or a servant will bring the food, which is on trays or in serving dishes, to each individual diner. The food will be brought to your left. Either the waiter will serve you or you must help yourself, using the utensils on the serving plate or tray. Your dishes will be cleared from your right, most of the time, so you should expect this.

If you know someone's servant, it is correct to say hello to him or her when he first serves you, and it is always kind to thank anyone who serves you, but you need not thank the server every single time he does something for you. An occasional "Thank you" will suffice, whether you are in someone's home or a restaurant, whether you know the server or not.

BREAD. When bread is served, take some and put it on your bread-and-butter plate, if there is one, or on your dinner plate. Americans, unlike the French, do not put their bread directly on the table, although when in France (or when dining informally *en famille*), you may feel free to follow the French custom. Where to put the bread is not an issue unless your dinner plate is laden with other food, and then tucking in that piece of bread does become a problem.

NAPKIN. Unless grace will be said, put your napkin in your lap as soon as you sit down. If grace will be offered, do not put the napkin in your lap until it has been said.

At a very fancy restaurant, the waiter may shake out your napkin and drape it across your lap for you, but there is no reason to wait for this infantilizing gesture if you do not want to.

Your napkin remains in your lap throughout the meal. You use it, as required, to gently pat your mouth, removing any crumbs that have lingered there. It is always advised that you dab gently at your mouth before taking a drink so as not to leave unsightly food on the glass.

Women who wear lipstick are often—and quite correctly—reluctant to use a cloth napkin since the lipstick will stain the napkin. I also think lipstick stains on glasses and utensils are ugly, too, but I can only offer two solutions, neither perfect. One is to blot your lipstick with a tissue before sitting down at the table, and the other is to pat your mouth very gingerly.

At the end of the meal, place your napkin to the right of your plate. It should not be neatly refolded, nor should it be crumpled mercilessly; a loose drape is what is called for.

UTENSILS. Forks, knives, and spoons are arranged in order of their use. Thus, you start with the outermost fork or spoon in a place setting, and work your way in, using one per course as a rule. Never should there be more than three of any one utensil at a place setting, if that helps. Usually, the utensil and the course will obviously correlate. For example, you will be served soup as a first course, and *voilà*, when you look down, the large spoon will be the first one. If an unusual food is served, and you are not sure how to eat it, you need suffer no loss of face. Since your hostess or host is supposed to take the first bite, simply wait until she or he does and watch to see which utensil is used and what the line of attack is.

Once you have used a utensil, it should never be put anywhere except on a plate. And it should not rest half on the plate and half off.

(I deplore the custom in so many restaurants of unceremoniously dumping the fork and knife they want you to "keep" on the tablecloth, but there is not much that can be done about it. It would be so much more gracious, I feel, to take the diner's used fork away and bring a clean one, or to have the table set with enough flatware in the first place.)

Your flatware can be used to signal a waiter (assuming he or she knows his trade) regarding whether you have finished eating or not. When you are merely resting between bites, place your knife and fork (tines down or up) across one another *(see Figure 56)*. When you are finished, place them parallel to one side or the other on your plate *(see Figure 57)*.

Figure 56. Rest position

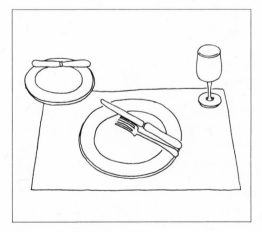

Figure 57. Finish position

SECONDS. You may feel free to ask for a second serving—it is always a compliment to the cook, after all. At a formal, multi-course dinner, though, you would do well to pace your eating so you can eat something of each course. It is not particularly polite to decline a course on the grounds that you have just stuffed yourself on an earlier one. The savvy diner knows that more is coming and tries not to get full too soon.

SHARING FOOD. It used to be considered rude to share food in public. Today, as Americans have become more involved in and appreciative of good food, it has become more accepted to share food.

If you want to share something—dessert being the most commonly shared course—ask the waiter to bring extra plates and utensils. You may then divide the food into smaller portions and give each person a plate. Only in the most casual restaurant should two or more people eat from the same dessert plate, and they should never share any other plate in this manner.

If one diner wants a bite of another diner's food, he or she should take it, after a small piece has been cut away, with his or her own utensil. No one should ever feel obliged to eat from another's fork or spoon. If the food is messy, the sample piece should be transferred to the sampler's plate before it is eaten rather than dripping food across the table as one tries to aim directly for the mouth.

No one should ever eat anyone else's food without a specific invitation. And no diner should ever feel obligated to offer food he has ordered to another diner.

Needless to say, if someone has a cold or any other communicable illness, he or she should beg off on sharing food or drinks.

Table Setting

SEE *Place Setting*.

Tailgate Picnic

A tailgate picnic, held on the tailgate of a station wagon, is a special kind of picnic that originated at football games, but they are now popular before any kind of sporting event, outdoor concerts, and the like.

The menu can consist of anything that works as picnic food. A tailgate party may be elegant—special food served on fine china and glassware—but most times is casual, as befits a picnic.

A tailgate picnic is held before the event. Trying to eat in a parking lot full of cars that are leaving is too hectic, to say nothing of being a somewhat unhealthy proposition. Those holding such a picnic should arrive an hour or more before the scheduled time to enjoy their party.

Tangerine

SEE *Fruit*.

Taxi Driver

Passengers are under no obligation to have any kind of conversation with a taxi driver, although the driver may not see it that way.

If you don't want to talk when the taxi driver does, simply nod curtly and say nothing to advance the conversation. Most cab drivers will take the hint. Be wary of starting a conversation with a cab driver because it is likely to last until you reach your destination.

As the passenger of a cab, you are entitled to choose the best route to your destination, to request that the cab driver not smoke (and he can make the same request of you), and to request that music be turned down if not off. Such requests should always be made politely, but no explanation is needed.

Tea

SEE ALSO *Coffee.*

The very best tea is brewed with fresh tea leaves and lots of hot water. Teabags are acceptable under less formal circumstances.

To properly brew tea, bring enough water to fill a teapot to a boil. Some purists insist that the teapot should be rinsed in hot water to prepare it for the boiling water. Fill a tea ball with fresh tea and put it in the pot, taking care to attach it to the outside so it can be easily removed. Let the tea brew for a period of three to five minutes, depending upon how strong you want it. Remove the tea ball. If you are serving tea to more than one person, you may find it helpful to brew it strong (the full five minutes), and then pour some boiling water into a small pitcher to be served with it. The water can be added to dilute the tea. Some people take milk (never cream) with their tea; most Americans take lemon. Those

who are offered milk are never offered lemon, and vice versa.

You may but need not offer a choice of teas if you are brewing. A Darjeeling or English or Irish breakfast is a good all-purpose tea. Some hostesses also keep herbal teas, in teabags, on hand for those guests who prefer a caffeine-free drink.

Hot tea is consumed in the same way as hot coffee, that is, it is served in cups and saucers. It may be served in mugs, but tea is never served in demitasse cups and saucers.

Iced tea is served in tall glasses. Because moisture accumulates on the glasses, a coaster may be necessary. Iced-tea spoons can be removed and placed on a plate (never on the table), or they can be held against the rim of the glass with your finger as you drink the tea.

Teacher

SEE ALSO *Professor.*

GREETING. Teachers are accorded an added degree of respect because of their academic status. Except in progressive schools, where the use of teachers' first names may be encouraged, children address their teachers as "Mr. Willke" or "Miss (Ms. or Mrs., based on the teacher's preference) Farley." Those with the doctorate degree are addressed as "Dr. Farley" or "Professor Farley." Although they do not use these titles socially, parents who are seeing their children's instructors in a professional capacity should address them the same way their children do unless asked to call them by their first names. Life having reached a very casual state, many parents do end up calling their children's instructors by their names and vice versa, but only after both parties have mutually agreed to do so. Of course, if you have a personal acquaintance with your child's instructor and have always called him or her by a first name, there is no need to change.

GIFTS. Especially at holiday time, children like to give gifts to their teachers. This is a charming gesture, and I would only encourage you to try to come up with something that reflects the teacher's personal interests, or, if you are unable to do that because you do not know the teacher well enough, to come up with something other than the traditional and utterly cliché gifts of perfume and after-shave lotion. Most teachers will be endlessly grateful for a record, a book, writing paper, even tickets to some special event, instead of yet another bottle of cheap cologne or a scarf or a tie.

ENTERTAINING. The custom of inviting teachers to dinner is a lovely one, and when your children show an interest in doing this it should be encouraged, provided it is the custom in your community or at this particular school. Send the child to school with a note from you extending the invitation.

Since teachers are usually invited to dinner during the week so as not to infringe on their weekend social life, which is theirs to keep strictly private, the dinner can be a "company" meal, if you choose, or a more simple family dinner. It will be nice for your child if you make the occasion somewhat festive. However delightful the evening is, be a little guarded about building a friendship. The teacher does have a social life of his or her own, and it will be severely hampered if he or she is expected to dine on any regular basis with the children in her class. As a result, each family usually invites a teacher to dine once each year.

Teenagers and Manners

SEE ALSO *Children and Manners; Teen Party; Teen Social Life.*

The teen years are often rebellious ones, when the good manners and graciousness that have been so carefully inculcated seem to vanish almost overnight, at least for periods of time. It is a time when the parent-child relationship is renegotiated, and parents have to give up some of the control they have maintained over their child for so many years.

At the same time that parents are learning to let go, they also have to realize that teens are not yet adults and that they do still need some supervision and discipline. It is important to set curfews, limit allowances, and expect a teen to perform certain chores around the house. The parent of a teen, while striving to let go, should always feel free to say no when something does not involve a child's best interests.

COURTESY TO YOUR CHILD. All the ground rules that apply to a small child also apply to a teen. Although most parents feel some sense of loss and may even be frightened by their teenage child's newfound independence, it must be respected. No parent has a right, for example, to read a teen's diary or otherwise snoop through his belongings. Unless a parent has a good reason to be in his child's room, the room should be as off limits to the parent as the parents' room is to the teenager.

A teenager is also old enough to spend some time without supervision and to make some of his own decisions about social plans. The world will not end if he misses a few family outings. While I do not recommend leaving groups of teens alone for a very long time, most teens are responsible enough to take care of themselves for periods of time when their parents go out.

One of the most important things a parent can do for his teen (and his own peace of mind) is to get to know his child's friends. You need not be omnipresent (teens do not need on-site chaperoning in most situations), but you can make the time to sit down occasionally and talk with your son's or daughter's friends. Remember, though, that it is rude to grill someone—especially a child—about his background. And if you decide that one of your teenager's friends is not your cup of tea, keep your feelings to yourself as much as possible. Certainly, do not let it affect how you treat the friend when he or she is a guest in your home at your teen's invitation. Be as hospitable as possible to the friend.

Teenage guests in your home will be more comfortable if you explain the house rules to them when they arrive. If a teenage guest does something wrong in your home, you may correct him or her. The best action is to correct the teen gently on the spot, and then keep it between the two of you. Do not mention the incident to your child if he or she was not around to observe it, and unless the situation is serious enough to warrant it, do not call the other child's parents. Staying accessible to your teen and his or her friends means they will be more likely to come to you when they need help.

A teen is also old enough to choose his or her own clothing. You may not like the selections, but give your child time; he or she will learn. And in the meantime, the teen is entitled to freedom of choice. It is important to teens to look like their peers, and peer taste is sometimes outlandish, but nonetheless it should be respected, or, at minimum, tolerated. Let your teen figure out for himself that a Mohawk haircut and dirty jeans are not acceptable everywhere, and he will discover this far more quickly than if you enforce many stringent rules about his dress. I am not saying that a parent should never suggest and occasionally put a foot down about how teens dress, when, for example, the style of dress will offend someone else, but in general the less fuss made about outlandishness the sooner it passes.

WITH COMPANY. The teenager should take on more responsibility than a small child when there is company. He or she is old enough to answer the door, introduce himself or herself, and entertain family guests for a short period of time. Parents should encourage their teenager to make at least a token appearance when they are entertaining because it gives the teen experience in dealing with adults.

Teens should be taught to stand when their elders enter a room the first time, to make introductions smoothly, and to perform basic small courtesies, such as serving tea, coffee, or a soft drink to a guest or offering a seat to someone older or infirm on public transportation.

WITH THEIR FRIENDS. Teens are old enough to entertain their own friends at home with little or no supervision. Some ground rules should be established first, though. These rules can only be based on each individual situation, but in general, you must decide whether your teen must seek your permission everytime he or she brings someone home or only when he or she is bringing someone for dinner or to spend the night. You might decide whether your teen may entertain members of the opposite sex in the bedroom. The answer is usually yes these days, especially if that is where the computer or electronic games are. You must also decide whether your teen is allowed to go to someone else's home when no parents are there to supervise.

When your teen does entertain, you would be wise to let him or her assume the extra responsibilities involved—changing the sheets on the guest bed, cleaning up after the midnight snacks, and so on. It saves you work, and it also teaches your teen something about entertaining guests.

When teens are having a party, by all means let them plan it themselves—and do most of the work.

WITH THE FAMILY. Because they are so self-involved, teens often go through an inconsiderate stage. You must decide how much you are willing to, or can, tolerate. Certainly, a teen who shares a bathroom with other family members needs to be considerate of the amount of time he or she spends in it. Ditto the telephone; a teen should realize that other family members may want to make or receive calls. Teens need to learn to clean up their messes throughout the house like every other fam-

ily member. They should understand that noise levels should be moderate.

At the same time, the family should be considerate of the teen's emerging needs, too. The phone cannot be tied up, but it is also unreasonable not to acknowledge that telephone life is important to teens. When a situation reaches an impasse, sit down with your teen, discuss the situation, and try to work out a compromise.

The bathroom is another battlefield when children become teens. If a child who has been neutral if not downright negative about personal grooming suddenly takes over the family bathroom and spends hours primping, you may not feel like discouraging it. Instead, talk to the teen about when it is okay to occupy the bathroom and when it is not.

Teen Dance

Big, formal teen dances and proms are back in style, and they are more lavish than ever.

People usually line up dates for these big nights three or four weeks in advance. Boys invite girls to their proms, and girls who want to do so may invite boys from other schools to their proms.

Girls can also occasionally invite boys from their own school to go to big dances with them, but the circumstances for doing so are tricky. And a girl should take the initiative only when she knows the boy likes her and would like to go with her and is too shy to ask her. Even then, it is best to let the boy think he did the inviting. A girl can bring up the dance in general terms, and if she sees that he is having trouble coming out with an invitation, she could suggest, "Why don't we go together?" I promise he will be relieved, and will probably swear he did the inviting anyway. Most of the time, though, girls should wait for boys from their own schools to invite them to school dances that are boy-ask-girl.

EXPENSES. Proms and big dances are not inexpensive. If they are formal, boys usually rent evening clothes, and girls often buy a new dress—and all the accessories that go with it. Tickets can be expensive, and then there is dinner beforehand, a snack afterward, flowers for the girl, and possibly the cost of transportation. In some communities, proms are all-night affairs, so there may be tickets to a post-prom bash to buy too.

When a boy and girl date regularly, they often share the expenses of these big events. Otherwise, I am afraid it is the boy who usually pays. When a girl invites a boy from out of town to her dance or prom, she buys the tickets and any clothes she may need, and he pays for everything else.

FLOWERS. SEE ALSO CORSAGES. For most big dances, boys give their dates flowers. Flowers can be delivered by the florist the afternoon of the dance, or the boy can bring them with him when he comes. If a girl wishes to do so, she may treat her date to a boutonnière.

OUT-OF-TOWN DATES. If you ask someone who lives in another community to be your date, he or she is expected to pay his own transportation costs and should even pay for a room, but if possible, find lodging for an out-of-town date so he or she is spared the expense. He or she can stay with your family or with another friend. If possible, when her date does not have a car, the girl arranges to double-date or borrow her family's car.

DRESS. SEE ALSO MEN'S EVENING DRESS. For formal dances and proms, boys usually wear black tie, and sometimes white tie. Girls wear evening dresses, often floor-length. They may or may not wear gloves, depending upon the style of their dresses. An evening dress calls for special accessories—an evening bag, glittery jewelry, a fancier-than-usual hairdo, glowing makeup.

BEHAVIOR. There is something very special about being all dressed up for a prom or formal dance. The mood is romantic, and you should enjoy every moment of it. One way to make the most of such a special night is to use your best party manners. Walk a little slower, stand a little taller, enjoy wearing your fine clothes. Let your date pay a little more attention than usual to you, and make sure you pay more attention to him, too. Whatever you do, don't let the mood of the evening get away from you. This is a big night in your life, and it should be treated as such.

Teen Party

Teen parties are among the simplest to plan and carry out. Written invitations may be sent, or your teenager may prefer to invite his or her guests in person or by telephone. Teens are old enough to issue their own invitations to parties, although no teen should plan a party without first consulting with his or her parents and obtaining their permission to entertain.

Dancing is the main activity at most teen parties. A dance floor can be provided, but unless you can afford the latest "in" rock band, there is no need to use anything but recorded music. It is helpful to make a prerecorded tape of favorite pieces of music, and since the guests will be teens, it should be their music regardless of how cacaphonous it sounds to adult ears.

MENU. Food may be simple, as long as there is a lot of it. It is far more important to have huge quantities than to have anything elaborate. Chips and dips are just fine most of the time. Pizza, cheese, and other appetizer foods are also fine. If a cookout or outdoor party is scheduled, hot dogs and hamburgers will always hit the spot.

Soft drinks are the favored beverage, but mineral water and fruit drinks should also be available. Alcohol should never be served to minors, and should be served with discretion and some degree of supervision to young people who are only recently old enough to drink. When some teen guests are old enough to drink and some are not, you may have a problem. If you do not want alcoholic beverages at your child's party—and I can imagine few parents who would want this responsibility—simply tell your teenager that a ground rule for having the party is that there will be no booze. Make it clear that this also means that no guests will be permitted to bring alcohol. Realistically speaking, this is hard to enforce, but you will have a better chance of controlling this aspect of the party if you are very clear with your teen about your expectations that there be no alcoholic beverages.

Unless you live on thirty isolated acres, the neighbors should be forewarned.

CHAPERONES. Adults should chaperone any teen party, although they need not stay in the same room, an arrangement that pleases everyone. The chaperones should make an appearance several times during the party and be available should trouble arise. The most common problems at teen parties are crashers and drinkers. Crashers can be included if they are not there to make trouble, but the adults should put in an appearance when they first arrive to make sure that they are welcome. A teenage drunk needs attention. He may feel ill and certainly should not, under any circumstances, be permitted to drive home.

The chaperones also may have to be the ones to end the party. When they sense deafness coming on, they can suggest that a slow song be played and the lights be turned up. (I am not suggesting that the lights will have been turned off, merely dimmed for atmosphere.) Removing the food and beverages is an excellent way to empty a room of teenagers.

Teen Social Life

SEE ALSO *Dating; Prom; Teen Party.*

As a teenager, your social life will become more like that of the grownups. You will begin to make plans by yourself with your friends, go out without your parents, and at some point in your teens, you will probably begin to date.

DATING. Keep in mind that, like so many other new things in life, there is no right time to start dating. It will happen when you are ready to handle it. Then, too, these days boys and girls seem to spend a lot of time going out in groups rather than pairing off in twos.

If you find yourself romantically interested in someone, the first thing you must do is let him or her know about it. Start by saying hello, and try to talk to the person. Do not worry about what you will say, just say something: "Hello. How are you today?" "Did you think the biology test was hard?" "Did you go to the game Saturday night?" Or better yet: "Are you going to the game this Saturday night?" Teasing, jabbing, and otherwise harassing someone is not the best way to let him or her know that you care.

Boys still do most of the asking for "official" dates, but a girl who is interested in a certain boy can ask him out, within limits. She can invite him to a party that a friend of hers is giving, or better yet, she can ask a friend to give the party and invite him so she can bump into him casually. A girl may comfortably ask a boy for a casual date, that is, a study date, or to get a soft drink or take a walk after school. Girls may invite boys from other schools to their regular school dances, and they may invite boys from any school to girl-ask-boy dances.

Whoever does the asking should have some activity in mind, but a couple usually plan a date together. A boy may ask a girl to go to a movie, but they should decide together what movie they would like to see. The boy may ask the girl to get a snack with him, but then they should discuss where they will go.

It is rude for a boy not to make every attempt to pick a girl up at home, particularly on their first date. It is even ruder to show up in front of the girl's house and honk the horn while waiting for her to come out. When picking up a girl, the boy should expect to meet her parents.

When you meet a girl's parents, you need not say much. Introduce yourself if she does not answer the door. Mention your plans to reassure them. If you know the girl has a curfew or her parents mention it to you, say, "That's no problem. We'll be home by then." Mostly a teen girl's parents want to know that their daughter is in good hands for the evening.

It is difficult for a boy to know how to behave around a girl on a date. Girls appreciate boys who have nice manners, but they do not like to be treated as if they are fragile. They like boys who hold doors for them and help them on and off with their coats. Except on very formal dates, most teen girls do not like waiting in a car for a date to come around and open the door for them. That, they say, makes them feel too helpless. And girls, in turn, should provide the same courtesies toward boys that they would toward any friend. If a boy is weighed down with books, then the girl should open the door for him. If a boy is having trouble getting out of his coat in a movie theater, then the girl should give him a hand. After all, this is really what manners are all about—helping each other when we need it.

Who pays on a date depends on several things, namely, who asked for the date, how much money each person has, and how long the couple have been dating. As a rule, whoever does the asking pays for the first date. If a girl asks a boy out for a casual date, and she does not have much money, he may offer to pay. A girl should not, however, offer to pay for dates simply because she may have more money than a boy. To help his budget, she may occasionally buy tickets to some event they both enjoy and treat him. When a couple date regularly, they often go dutch, which means each person pays his or her own way. When a girl dates a boy who will not let her go dutch, she should still treat every once in a while, and he should let her.

Many teens have curfews, a time when their parents expect them to be home. Their dates should respect this curfew, and make every effort to get them home on time.

GOING STEADY. Different generations call it different things, but teens have been pairing off in "steady" relationships for a long time. There is nothing wrong with going steady, and it does seem to suit some teens, but it is also limiting, and it is worth considering what you give up when you decide to tie yourself down in this way. Your teen years are a wonderful time to meet and get to know many different kinds of people. They are a time to date a variety of people, and a time to build solid friendships with peers and others. If you limit yourself to just one person, your social life with both boys and girls will be much more restricted than if you remain free to get to know lots of different people. You will have less time for platonic friendships and no experience dating lots of people. This may

not change your mind about going steady, and that is not my purpose anyway, but I hope it gives you some things to think about before you make the big decision to pair off on a regular basis with someone.

CHAPERONING YOURSELF. Except among some Hispanic groups, the days when girls were chaperoned every time they went out on a date are over. What this means, though, is that each teen is responsible for chaperoning himself or herself.

There will be times when you will be tempted to do something foolish or crazy, and some of those impulses are probably harmless. What you should not do are dangerous things, things that can injure your health, your grades, and, most important, your future. Since you alone are responsible, it is up to you to take care of yourself.

SMOKING, DRINKING, AND DRUGS. Among the crazy things that most teens are tempted to try at one time or another are smoking, drinking, and drugs. You will encounter one and probably all three of these major temptations sooner or later during your teen years. And even teens who want to resist these temptations say that pressure can be strong. I won't waste time lecturing you about the dangers of these three substances, because I think most teens are intelligent enough to inform themsleves about these matters, but I do want to suggest that you use your good manners when rejecting these items. When offered any illegal or abusive substance, simply and politely say no. Do not lecture (unless they are offered by a good friend who needs your help), do not act judgmental, and above all do not make a big deal out of refusing. Just refuse, quietly and politely. If someone persists, change the subject. Or turn your refusal into a joke. When pressured to take an alcoholic drink, for example, say, "Oh, I can get enough of a high from the sugar in this soft drink." Pressured to take a cigarette, for example, say, "No thanks, I only smoke Havanas" or "I quit when I was ten." Most of the time if you do not make a moral issue out of your refusal, and you manage to treat the offer lightly so that others do not feel judged, you will not be subjected to much pressure.

FAMILY CAR. At some point during your teens, you will get a driver's license, and, if you are lucky, be permitted to use the family car. Knowing how to use the car graciously will probably result in your getting to use it more often than if you just assume that you have a right to drive it and, furthermore, do not take responsibility for your actions.

Here are some suggestions that will impress your parents with your good manners and sense of responsibility:

- Always ask permission to drive one of your parents' cars. Do not assume that you can have the car whenever you want it, but realize that it does not belong to you.
- Help keep the car clean. Washing and waxing it without being asked to do so is almost sure to impress your parents and therefore make them more inclined to let you use the car.
- If you damage the car, offer to pay for the repairs out of your allowance or by getting an extra job if necessary. Your parents may tell you that they will pay for the damages, but do not

assume that they will, and do not fail to offer.
- If you will be out later than expected in the car, call home. Parents quite rightly worry when their teens take the car for an evening. Do not do anything to add to their worries, and do what you can to alleviate them. If a call home will help put your parents' minds at ease, it is well worth the few minutes to reassure them.

Teetotaler

A teetotaler is a person who does not drink. Implied in the definition is often some degree of disapproval of those who do. A teetotaler is entitled to his or her opinion; he is not entitled to dictate the behavior of others. If you don't want to be around alcohol, decline invitations to events where it will be served. If this is too stringent for you, accept the invitation and decline the drink when it is offered.

Telephone Answering Machine

The telephone answering machine has become common today, particularly among single persons who lead such busy social lives that they are never home to answer their phones. Despite protests that these machines are impersonal, they seem to be here to stay, so the best thing to do is use them well. This means recording neither a musical nor a funny message, unless the message is devastatingly brilliant. People who call you deserve a straightforward response if a machine must stand in for you. Attempts to amuse take up too much of the caller's time. A good phone message is: "Hello, this is Jane and Jerry Jones. We are unable to come to the phone right now, but if you'll leave your name and number, one of us will call you back as soon as possible."

Also impolite is to eavesdrop on your messages, taking a call halfway through the caller's message. This may sometimes be unavoidable, but if you do pick up only after someone has identified himself, explain that you were too busy to come to the phone right away. Obviously, one purpose for having a telephone answering machine is to screen calls, but this should be done with some tact.

Telephone Manners

SEE ALSO *Business Telephone; Invitations; Pay Call.*

Telephone contact is especially important when the person on the other end knows you only through the phone, but it is also important to be polite at all times when using the telephone. Often, because we are not face-to-face with whomever we are talking to, we fail to provide the gracious little touches that do so much to make relationships run smoothly.

BEGINNING AND ENDING PHONE CALLS. Americans answer the telephone by saying "Hello" and waiting for the other person to respond. They end telephone calls by saying "Goodbye." Simply hanging up in considered too abrupt and slightly rude.

It is important when talking on the telephone never to sound abrupt because that usually translates into an unpleasant tone. You can say goodbye quickly in person with a smile on your face, but the smile is not there when you are talking on the phone.

NAMES. Unless someone knows you intimately, always give your name when calling, and preferably your complete name. It is egotistic and rude to expect someone of short acquaintance to recognize your voice. Voices do not even necessarily sound the same on the telephone as they do in person.

Never identify yourself with a title, except perhaps to a household employee. Always say, "This is Mary Snyder," never "This is Mrs. Snyder," even to someone whom you expect to call you by your surname.

It is polite always to identify yourself when calling someone's home to whomever answers the phone before asking to speak to another member of the family. If you know the person who answers, say hello briefly.

WRONG NUMBER. Always apologize when you dial a wrong number; it is rude to hang up without saying anything. If the error repeats itself, you may tell the person who answers what number you are calling with the hope that he will respond, in turn, by telling you whether you have reached the number or some other number. Never ask for the number directly. Most people are uncomfortable—justifiably so—about giving out their telephone number to a stranger.

If someone asks you what your number is, you may say, "I'm sorry, but I don't like to give my number." On the other hand, if someone has called you three times in a row, and is as frustrated as you are over this wrong number, it may be in your best interests to ask them what number they are calling or to confirm or deny whether they have reached the right number.

THREE-WAY (OR MORE) CONVERSATIONS.

Conversations where a wife (or husband) is interrupted by his partner or children are irritating and rude—and should be kept to the minimum. When you must interrupt a telephone call to speak to someone else, put your hand over the receiver. Keep in mind, however, that this does not muffle all sound, so do not say anything you would not want the caller to overhear. For example, if you and your husband are being invited out by someone whom you are not eager to socialize with, do not say, "It's the Smyths inviting us to dinner. What do you think?" That is tactless. Better is to say, "The Smyths would like us to come to dinner next Saturday. What plans, if any, do we have?" Assuming that your spouse is not keen on this invitation either, he or she can provide you with a polite but friendly reason to decline the invitation.

After an interruption, either to consult with your spouse, correct your children, or for any other reason, always apologize for the interruption. Never let a three-way conversation persist for any longer than is absolutely necessary. If your children act up or require your attention, or if anything interrupts the conversation, offer to call the person back at a more convenient time.

CHILDREN AND TELEPHONES.

The first rule regarding children and telephones is to keep them away from the phone until they are old enough to use it properly. Few adults welcome a curious little voice repeatedly asking, "Who's this?" or worse, simply not responding to requests such as, "Please, may I speak to your mommy?"

Never assume that any adult you know finds it amusing or interesting to chat with your three-year-old on the telephone. I was horrified when one friend permitted her three-year-old, an absolutely charming and poised child, to be sure, to call me at work one day. As it happened, I was in the middle of an important telephone negotiation, and could neither talk nor take the time to tell him why. I feared that if the child grew up with phone phobia, I would be responsible, but the real fault lies with his mother for permitting such a phone call to have been made in the first place.

When children are old enough to answer the family telephone, they should be taught how to do so correctly. They should be told to say "Hello" and then wait for a response. Children take pride in doing things like this nicely, and can be very handy with the telephone with just a little coaching.

SERVANTS ANSWERING THE PHONE.

When an employee answers your telephone, instruct him or her to say, "Mrs. Stanley's residence," or, if this is an egalitarian household, "The Stanley residence." No family member should answer the telephone this way, nor should a friend who answers your phone. Except for employees, the correct response is merely, "Hello."

CONVERSATION. Never be silly or obtuse when calling someone. It is rude to open a telephone call with, "Guess who?"

When calling someone to chat, always ask if your call has come at a convenient time. I have noticed that some people cannot seem to tell someone directly when they are busy. Instead, when interrupted, they will say, "I'm eating dinner, but that is okay." At my house, that is *not* okay, and if the recipient of the call is not capable of indicating that this is an awkward time to call, I think the caller should take whatever hints are offered and cut short the call.

Similarly, use some discretion about the time when calling someone. People rarely enjoy being called early in the morning or late at night. Except for an emergency, I would not call someone before work or before 10 or 11 A.M. on the weekend. The evening cutoff depends upon your taste and what you suspect the person you are calling would prefer. Some people draw the line at 9 or 9:30 P.M.; others do not call after 10 P.M. One friend told me she thinks the cutoff time for calling across America is the late-night news. She has a theory that people either go to bed when it comes on or shortly afterward, but either way, that most Americans are unavailable socially by this time of night. I tend to agree.

When calling a business, it is courteous to identify yourself to the secretary, receptionist, or switchboard operator who answers the phone.

When speaking with someone whom you do not know, for business or personal reasons, I think the conversation will be more gracious if you give your name before launching into the reason for your call, and if you ask the other person what his name is. I further suggest that you do not automatically call the other person by his or her first name, but that you call him Mr. Jones or Ms. Jones.

Finally, keep in mind that operators are people, too. Always treat them with the same courtesy with which you would treat anyone who waits on you.

Television Appearance

SEE *Public Appearance.*

Temple

SEE *Religious Services.*

Tennis

SEE *Racquet Sports.*

Theater

SEE ALSO *Business Entertaining; International Business Manners.*

Behavior at the theater is much like behavior at any other live performance. Show up on time and remain in your seat during the performance. Between acts, you are free to roam around the theater and may do so without concern that your seats will be taken. Many theaters sell drinks and refreshments between acts. These cannot be taken back to the seats as nothing could be more disturbing than a member of the audience crunching on ice or slurping a soda during the performance.

The audience usually applauds at the end of each act and at the end of the performance. Often, the first appearance of a star is also greeted with applause, as is the first viewing of the set. A particularly fine piece of acting—a monologue, for example—may generate a well-deserved burst of applause.

Toast

SEE ALSO *Anniversary Party; Wedding Reception.*

A toast, most often given at weddings and on other formal social occasions, is appropriate any time good friends are gathered and enjoying one another's company. A toast can be elaborate and well thought out or as simple as raising one's glass to the person whom one wishes to toast. The person being toasted does not drink but merely says, "Thank you," although there is some confusion about this. Here is the rule and the reason behind it: The person who is toasted does not tip his own glass because doing so would be a little like patting oneself on the back. For those awkward moments that seem to arise with alarming frequency these days when others not only do not know the rule, but also express their discomfort at the honoree's failure to raise a glass in his own honor, I have a solution. If someone is obviously upset or waiting for you to drink, grab your glass, raise it, and say, "Thank you, and here's to all of you."

People do offer toasts to one another jointly, in which case everyone does drink at once. Even the person who is not drinking can participate in a toast, using a water glass or any kind of beverage. There is no rule that says toasts must be alcoholic.

If nothing else, all languages have a toast to "health": "Skoal," "Salut," "À votre santé." In English, one simply says, "To your health."

At a formal social occasion such as a wedding or anniversary, the toasting may be orchestrated. The best man usually leads off, followed by the father of the bride and then the father of the groom.

Traditionally, men have offered toasts, but these days there is no reason that a woman—a maid of honor, sister, or mother—could not offer a toast.

Tombstone

SEE *Gravestone.*

Toothpick

Toothpicks, even those of solid gold and other precious materials, are not properly used in the company of others.

Tour Guides

Tour guides are usually well-trained specialists and it is to a traveler's advantage to pay attention to them.

If you take a tour and find that you are not interested in what the tour guide has to say, then roam away from the group slightly, so any conversations you have with your traveling companions do not detract from other tour group members' ability to listen to the tour guide.

If you do stay with the tour group, do not monopolize the tour guide with your questions; if you want in-depth knowledge, read a book or some articles. Do not play a radio or listen to a radio with earphones when the tour guide is speaking. Always thank the tour guide at the end of the tour. A gratuity may be included in the price of the tour, and tipping a tour guide is rarely obligatory. If you would like to tip, fifty cents to a dollar is acceptable for a day tour; for a tour of several days, tip five to ten dollars.

Train Travel

When traveling by train, try to travel light, as you will frequently have to carry your own luggage. If you will be sleeping in a compartment, carry an overnight bag and check the rest of your luggage.

Upon sitting down or entering a compartment, passengers usually greet one another. A passenger who settles in to watch the scenery or read a book is signaling that he or she does not wish to carry on a conversation and should be left alone. Before opening a window or pulling down a shade, it is polite to consult with a seatmate or others in the same compartment. Excuse yourself when crossing in front of someone to leave or take your seat.

When a train has full dinner service, the rules for eating are much the same as for any nice restaurant. On many trains, you must make reservations shortly after boarding.

At the appointed time, show up and wait for the porter to seat you. Tip for food service aboard a train as you would at any restaurant. You need not tip the dining car porter who functions as a headwaiter, unless he provides you with some extra service.

A sleeping car porter is tipped $1.50 or $2 a night. On a long trip, depending upon the level of service, he is tipped $1.50 per night, and the same for any special service. The tips should be given every two to three days.

Umbrella

If you are walking somewhere with a friend on a rainy day, it is kind to share your umbrella, even if this means that each of you will get a little wet. If each of you has an umbrella, you may continue to use yours separately.

It is not required but is a special kindness to have an extra umbrella or two around to give to someone who arrives at your house in clear weather and must depart in bad. The person who receives such a courtesy should make every effort to return the umbrella at the earliest opportunity.

An umbrella can be turned into a dangerous weapon or a major inconvenience if you are not careful how you wield it. Always use an umbrella with extreme awareness of those around you so that you do not accidentally poke someone. When riding on public transportation or in someone's car, keep your umbrella away from the seats so that they are not wet for the next person who has to sit on them.

Along the same line, always take care when bringing a wet umbrella into someone's home not to drip water all over everything. Leave it outside the door in an apartment building, and ask where you can put it to dry in a private house.

Unintentional Snub

Rarely these days does anyone deliberately fail to acknowledge an acquaintance. But we have all unintentionally snubbed someone because of absentmindedness, not wearing our glasses when we should, or simply not remembering a person. The cordial person returns nods and greetings from a stranger with a nod even when he cannot immediately place the person.

Unveiling

SEE *Graveside Service; Gravestone.*

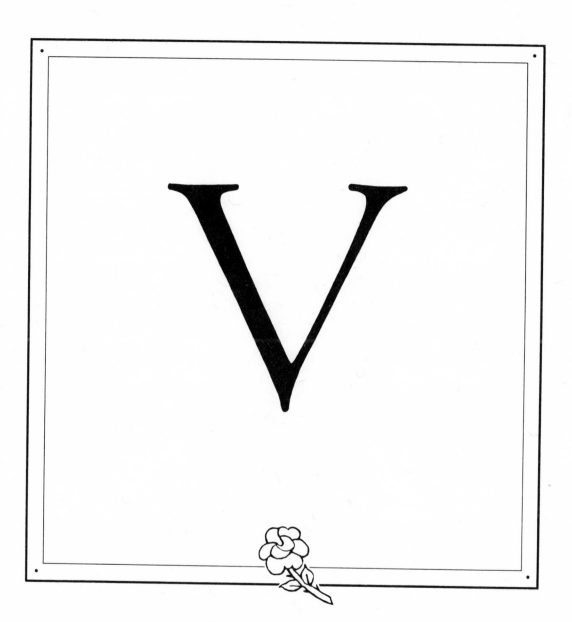

Vegetarian

SEE *Eating Habits of Guests.*

Visiting Card

SEE ALSO *Business Cards; Informals.*

In the days of formal calls, when Mrs. Wilmington used to be "at home" Wednesday mornings, and when Mrs. Smythson, Mrs. Jones, and Mrs. Carroll used to drop by on other mornings (*their* calling mornings), the latter three would leave their cards on a silver plate in the entry hall of Mrs. Wilmington's home. When someone did call on Mrs. Wilmington when she was at home, the caller's card announced her and preceded her entry into the parlor.

Even after this elaborate ritual ceased to exist, formal calls were still paid on military bases. They are even today, but visiting cards are no longer part of the ritual. Thus the visiting card has become obsolete, and few persons use them. Some married couples order them printed with their married names (provided they use the same surname). If they do not use the same surname, they are better off with separate visiting cards, since it is inappropriate and awkward-looking to print two separate and different names on one small visiting card.

Visiting cards have limited uses today, as gift enclosures, and for invitations, acceptances, and regrets. They have mostly been replaced by informals.

Another complicating factor is that since visiting cards are often put to use in ways that require that they be sent through the mail, they must meet the post office's minimum size, which is $4^{1}/_{2}$ by 3 inches. This makes them larger than the traditional visiting-card size, and I think you may as well use informals.

If you insist, after all this, a visiting card should be printed on plain white stock with black ink. It should not be panelled. For a married couple with the same surname, it should read:

Mr. and Mrs. William Gladson

For a single woman, the card should read:

> *Miss Catherine Downey*

It could read "Ms.," but if you are conservative enough to want visiting cards, you probably do not want to use the term "Ms."

Your address may be printed in the lower right-hand corner. It used to be considered indiscreet for a single woman to print her address on her visiting card, but this is a rather archaic view given that so many single women have established their own households and lead thoroughly independent lives.

Voice

A well-modulated voice is a sign of an educated person, although I am not among those who feel that all ethnic and regional accents should be ground out of a person.

I do feel that the din of our existence on this planet has become loud enough so that more noise—even in the form of the human voice—is unwelcome. All of us should take care that our voices do not boom out in public places. When talking, never speak louder than necessary for the person or persons you are with to hear you. It is possible to conduct a private conversation in public in so low a voice that those sitting around you will not be able to hear very much of it unless they make a concerted effort to eavesdrop.

Pay attention to how you sound. An excellent way to test this is to listen to a tape recording of yourself. The most attractive voices are medium-pitched. If yours is too high, too shrill, too nasal, or any of the several other qualities that can make a human voice annoying, consider taking some voice lessons, or, at minimum, check out a book on speech from the public library and practice speaking properly. The payoff will be well worth the effort.

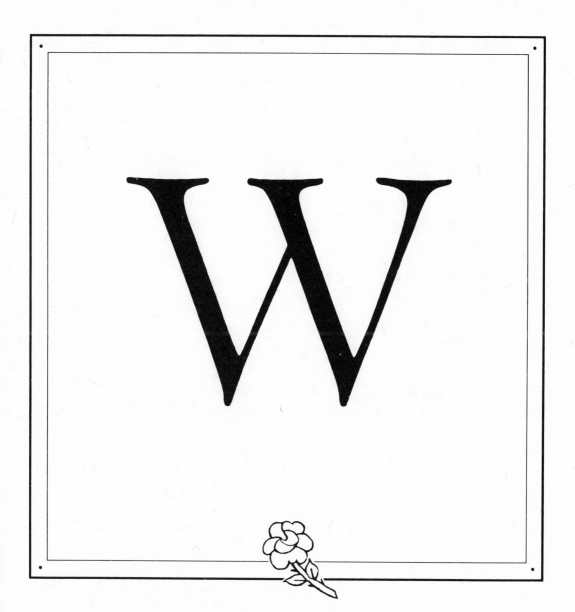

Waiter/Waitress

SEE ALSO *Restaurant Meal.*

ADDRESSING. In the United States, a waiter's attention is commanded by catching his eye or by raising a finger and nodding when he looks at you. In other countries, he may be summoned by whistling, clapping, or even yelling, all of which are totally unacceptable here. The correct form of address is "Waiter" for a man and "Waitress" or "Miss" for a woman. Do not address a waiter as "Sir." *(See also Sir and Ma'am.)*

COMPLAINING. When service is not acceptable, first complain to the waiter or waitress. If the situation is not remedied, speak to the headwaiter or the host or hostess or manager.

ORDERING. When the waiter comes to your table to take your order, either give it to him quickly or ask him to come back when you are prepared to order; don't expect a waiter to stand and wait while you study the menu. Take a clue from the waiter about the order in which he would like you to order. In fancy restaurants, the women's orders are taken first; in more casual restaurants, a waiter may prefer that people order in some kind of order, that is, by going around the table. *(See also Ordering for Your Guest.)*

PAYING AND TIPPING. When it is time to get the bill, summon the waiter and request it. A universal sign that you want the check is to move an index finger across the palm of your other hand to signify writing. The waiter will bring the check, which should be examined carefully. In better restaurants, the waiter is paid at the table; in coffee shops and cafeterias, customers may pay at the cash register. Either way, the waiter's tip should be left on the table, unless a credit card is used. A waiter should be tipped 15 percent of the total bill, 20 percent in a very good restaurant where the food and service has been excellent. In a restaurant where 20 percent is tipped, it is usually divided, with 5 percent going to the headwaiter and 15 percent to the table waiter.

When the service has been abysmal,

many diners would prefer not to give a tip but are often too timid to do so. After all, not tipping can make the customer look like a cheap boor—and it can provoke a reaction from the waiter designed to embarrass the customer. If you decide not to tip a waiter, then the best, the only, course of action is to tell him that you are not tipping him and why. It is a humbling experience to which few waiters have a response. But before you decline to tip a waiter, consider whether the problem has been his fault. It may not have been his fault if the food came out of the kitchen slowly or if there was something wrong with it when it arrived. On the other hand, if you had to ask for water three times, and the drink you received was not the drink you ordered, the waiter clearly goofed. Even these are relatively minor if annoying offenses, for which the solution may be not to return to that restaurant. Major—and far too common—offenses are arrogant or overbearing waiters, and that is definitely cause for not tipping. Put such a waiter on notice that his behavior is unacceptable and then skip the tip if the situation has not improved by the end of the meal.

Conversely, always tip something extra if a waiter has provided some extra service, or has noticed some problem before you spotted it. A waiter who says, "Oh, your fish doesn't appear to be as hot as it should be. Can I return it?" deserves a great tip.

Washing Hands

Most family members will want to wash their hands before sitting down to dinner.

Dinner guests are presumed to have arrived with clean hands, but, if necessary, they may excuse themselves before dinner to wash.

Water at Table

For formal dining, iced water is served in water goblets, which are usually the largest glasses in any set of glasses. (I say "usually" because some people have very large wineglasses.) Since few hostesses have servants, the custom today is to fill water glasses before the guests come to dinner. Glasses are refilled throughout the meal from a pitcher brought in from the kitchen. At a casual dinner, the pitcher may be put on the table.

It is acceptable to serve dinner without water, provided other beverages are served. If an individual diner needs water, he or she may request it at a quiet moment when the hostess is not busy serving other foods.

For family dining, water is often served in tall glasses, and an extra pitcher is put on the table, or the custom may be to drink no water with meals.

Wedding

SEE *Bachelor Dinner; Bridal Registry; Bride; Bridegroom; Bridesmaids' Lunch; Cancelled Wedding; Chapel Wedding; Chuppah; Civil Wedding; Double Wedding; Engagement; Formal*

WEDDING (con'd)

Wedding Invitation; Home Wedding; Informal Wedding Invitation; Military Wedding; Rectory Wedding; Remarriage of Divorced Persons; Sanctuary Wedding; Second Wedding; Wedding Announcement; Wedding Attendants; Wedding Expenses; Wedding Family Members; Wedding Flowers; Wedding Gifts; Wedding Guests; Wedding Photographer; Wedding Reception; Wedding Rehearsal; Wedding Trip.

Wedding Announcement

A wedding announcement can be sent to anyone who was not invited to the wedding. They are particularly useful since they do not obligate anyone to send a gift, but they do provide people whom you could not include on the invitation list with a small memento.

Like invitations, announcements can be issued by the bride's parents, by the bride's and groom's parents jointly, or by the couple themselves.

The announcement should be similar to the invitation—printed if the invitations were printed, engraved if the invitations were engraved, on the same or similar stock, in the same color ink. The exception is when invitations are issued in handwritten notes or by telephone and telegram; then printed announcements may be sent.

Announcements are useful when a couple have eloped or gotten married in a very quiet ceremony. An announcement should read:

Mr. and Mrs. Jacob Cohen
have the pleasure of announcing
the marriage of their daughter
Rebecca
to
David
Sunday, the tenth of December,
Nineteen hundred eighty-seven
Atlanta, Georgia

When the couple send their own announcements, they should read:

Deborah Sweazey
and
Michael Connors
have the pleasure to
announce their marriage
Friday, the first of June,
Nineteen hundred eighty-eight
New Orleans, Louisiana

Obviously, the woman's name may have changed by the time the announcements are sent, but her maiden name should still be used so persons receiving the announcement will not have to guess about the senders' identities.

Wedding Attendants

SEE ALSO *Sanctuary Wedding.*

CHOOSING ATTENDANTS. The number and kind of wedding attendants you choose will depend on how large and formal your wedding is going to be, and on how many siblings and friends you wish to honor. The larger the wedding, the greater the need for ushers, and the greater the number of ushers, the more likely you are to choose bridal attendants to pair off with them.

The bride generally chooses at least one sister and one sister of the groom, if there is one (the ones who are closest to her in age or to whom she is personally close), to be in the wedding party. If the wedding is very large, she may include more sisters and cousins. She then chooses the remainder of her attendants from among her close confidantes.

The groom chooses his attendants in the same way, asking at least one brother with whom he is close and one brother of the bride, if there is one. The rest of his honor attendants can be drawn from his pool of friends.

An invitation to be in a wedding party is an honor, one that cannot easily be declined. Even someone in mourning is expected to participate in a wedding, unless the death is so recent that attending so happy an occasion is obviously out of the question. Because an invitation to be in a wedding party cannot be turned down, a bride and groom should not ask anyone for whom the honor will pose any kind of hardship. Wedding attendants are expected to pay their way to the wedding and to pay the bill for their clothes.

In the past, brides and grooms have tended to choose people their own age as attendants, and pregnant women were excluded. Happily, these rules have broken down. If your best friend is twenty years older than you or your sister is pregnant (provided she still wants to participate) there is no reason that she cannot be in the wedding party. This is a personal decision for you and your prospective attendant to make.

Among the possibilities for honor attendants in a wedding are the following: best man, maid/matron of honor (or both, if the wedding is very large), bridesmaids, flower girl, ring bearer, and ushers.

BEST MAN. Usually the groom's brother (occasionally his father) or a very good friend, this is the attendant with the most responsibilities. A good best man assumes the groom will not be able to handle anything on his wedding day and takes responsibility for holding the bride's ring (and producing it at the right time), holding any travel tickets needed for the honeymoon, handling the groom's car, acting as head usher, paying the clergyperson and anyone else who should get a check that day, and generally masterminding the whole show from the groom's side. He stands next to the groom during the ceremony.

MAID/MATRON OF HONOR. The counterpart to the best man, a maid or matron of honor has fewer responsibilities. She holds the groom's ring and does anything she can to assist the bride on her wedding day. The maid/matron of honor stands next to the bride at the altar, takes her bouquet at the appropriate moment during the ceremony, turns back the bride's veil if necessary, and produces the ring at the right moment. The maid or matron of honor usually wears a dress that is slightly different in either design or color from that of the bridesmaids.

BRIDESMAIDS. The bridesmaids have no direct responsibilities other than to look their loveliest and be attentive to the bride. A good bridesmaid (and friend) will offer to run any errands or help out in any way during the last hectic weeks before the wedding and may offer to give the bride a shower or hold a small dinner in her honor sometime before the wedding.

JUNIOR BRIDESMAID. This is an honor accorded a young sister, cousin, or friend between the ages of eleven and fourteen or fifteen. Prepubescent is the operative word in choosing a junior bridesmaid. Girls of this tender age generally adore weddings and are especially thrilled to be honored with a role in one. If she is old enough, the junior bridesmaid can dress exactly like all the other bridesmaids; if she is still a girl (as opposed to a young woman), then she can wear a slightly younger-looking dress in the same color and general style as the bridesmaids'.

FLOWER GIRL. A girl under the age of six or seven can serve as flower girl, provided she is capable of performing under pressure. The flower girl has no real responsibilities, but she does walk in the processional and recessional (or more likely, joins her mother and father in a front pew at the end of the ceremony so she doesn't get lost in the crush at the back of the church). A

lovely, quaint touch is to have the flower girl strew flowers or rose petals as she moves down the aisle.

Sometimes a dress that coordinates with the bridesmaids' dresses can be found, and most bridal shops sell flower girls' dresses. A flower girl can also wear any pretty dress that fits in well with what the rest of the wedding party is wearing. I think flower girls look their loveliest when they are dressed as little girls rather than as miniature adults. In addition to wearing a dress that is appropriate to her age, this means wearing tights or white anklets and black or white patent maryjanes for dress shoes. If the bridesmaids wear sophisticated hats, the flower girl might wear just a few flowers in her hair or perhaps a garland of flowers; otherwise, her head covering might be a scaled-down version of theirs.

RING BEARER. A boy of six or seven can be enlisted as ring bearer, subject to the same limitations that were discussed for flower girls. If he carries the rings, they must be firmly attached to a pillow, and more often than not these days, he does not carry the rings but simply walks in the processional, perhaps paired with the flower girl.

USHERS. Ushers seat the guests at the start of the ceremony—and unseat them at the end. They also dance with any unattached women during the reception. Like the bridesmaids, they offer their services in the weeks and months before the wedding in any way they may be needed.

DRESS. The bride and groom choose the outfits of their wedding attendants. They should choose something suited to the formality (or lack of it) of the occasion and to the looks of their attendants. In a very small wedding, a bride may tell her one attendant simply to go buy a pretty dress of her choosing, but in weddings with more than one attendant, the clothes are usually coordinated and selected by the bride. The bride should try to select some style that is flattering to all her attendants. The attendants pay for their dresses and any accessories, such as gloves, hats, and shoes, so needless to say, the considerate bride keeps price in mind as she shops, and if her parents can afford to do so, they may pay for the bridesmaids' outfits.

The bridesmaids dress identically, except they may wear different shades of a color. The maid of honor usually, but not always, is distinguished from the others by wearing a different color or different dress, and/or carrying different flowers.

The dresses should complement the bridal gown, that is, they should be of similar material and design. An all-white wedding can be stunning, but it does detract, in the eyes of some, from the bride.

The bride should send color swatches to her bridesmaids as soon as possible so they can order shoes dyed to match. She may suggest jewelry she would like her attendants to wear, and she may even give, as bridesmaids' presents, lockets or earrings that she wants them to wear on the wedding day.

GROOM'S ATTENDANTS' CLOTHES. The male attendants' clothing is, for the most part, dictated by the time of day and by tradition. There has been a trend in recent years toward colored suits and shirts for men in the wedding party, but if you want a traditional wedding, you will opt for the conservative black and gray clothes that men wear on formal and semiformal occasions.

For a formal daytime wedding, men wear a gray cutaway coat, striped trousers, a gray waistcoat, a formal white shirt, a gray and black striped four-in-hand tie, gray gloves, black socks, and black plain leather shoes. For a formal evening wedding, the men wear a black tail coat, a white waistcoat, a formal white shirt, a wing collar, white bowtie, white gloves, black socks, and plain black leather shoes or patent evening pumps.

For a semiformal daytime wedding, men wear a black or dark gray sack coat, a gray waistcoat, a dressy white shirt with a four-in-hand tie, gray gloves, and black socks and shoes. For a semiformal evening wedding, men wear black tuxedoes in the winter, and they may wear a white jacket, with black pants during the summer. With either the black or white jacket, they wear a front-pleated shirt, black cummerbund, black bowtie, black socks, and plain black leather shoes.

For an informal daytime wedding, men wear a dark plain or pin-striped suit in winter and lighter-colored suit in summer. Gray and navy are preferred over black for a wedding. Alternately, in summer a white linen jacket with dark trousers or a navy or gray jacket and white trousers may be worn. For an informal evening wedding, the men wear dark suits in the winter and lighter-colored suits in the summer.

GIFTS. The bride and groom buy gifts as mementos for their attendants. The gifts should be of lasting value—jewelry, small silver boxes or frames, keychains, lighters, pens or pencils, paperweights.

Wedding Expenses

For a long time, the parents of the bride were expected to pick up all the expenses of a daughter's wedding, at least her first wedding. (They could pay for all or part of a second wedding, but were under no obligation to do so.) The groom's expenses were the bride's engagement and wedding ring; the personal flowers, that is, the bride's bouquet and the mother's and grandmother's flowers; and the wedding trip.

Times have been changing, though, and brides with careers, cohabiting couples, couples marrying for the second time, and older couples have adopted some different ways of sharing wedding expenses. It is now not unusual in some parts of the country (and among some ethnic groups) for the parents of the groom to offer to share expenses with the bride's parents, particularly when both sets of parents agree that they want a large, elaborate wedding. Couples who have been working and living on their own or together for several years often pay for their own wedding.

Paying for your own wedding, incidentally, is one way to ensure that you get the kind of wedding you want. There are many reasons for a couple to pay for their own wedding, and none of them bespeak ill relations between the couple and either set of parents. Many young two-career couples earn more than their parents do, and it makes sense for them to pay for part or all of their wedding. Add to this the couple who live several hundred miles from either set of parents, and who want to have the wedding where they live, and paying for your own wedding makes even more sense. The parents may chip in, or, if they prefer, may give the couple a reception of their own when the couple visit them. In summary, there are about as many ways to divide wedding expenses as there are couples getting married.

According to *Bride's* magazine, the average wedding costs $4,000 to $5,000. A lavish wedding can easily run $10,000 and much more, and a lovely, modest wedding could cost as little as $1,500, with careful budgeting. A home wedding is the least expensive, and the more expensive the restaurant or club, the more expensive the wedding will be.

Here is a list of the major, basic expenses of any size wedding:

Engagement ring
Wedding rings
Bride's wedding clothes
Groom's wedding clothes
Reception food and beverage costs
Invitations, announcements, and
  personal stationery
Fees—for church or synagogue,
  clergyperson, musicians
Special equipment for ceremony: aisle
  carpet runner, awning, chuppah (at
  Jewish wedding)
Reception music, church musicians if
  used
Flowers
Photographer

Minor expenses include:

> Wedding gifts exchanged by bride and groom
> Transportation to and from wedding
> Marriage license
> Gifts for attendants

Wedding expenses are typically divided as follows:

> 30 percent reception costs
> 30 percent clothes and gifts
> 12 percent miscellaneous
> 11 percent photography
> 11 percent ceremony costs
> 6 percent invitations and other stationery

These percentages will vary somewhat, of course, depending upon the kind of reception and the degree of formality of the wedding.

Wedding Family Members

MOTHER OF THE BRIDE. The mother of the bride is the official hostess at her daughter's wedding. It is on her shoulders that most of the work of planning, negotiating, and preparing the wedding falls. If the wedding is held in her hometown, while her daughter works in a nearby—or not-so-nearby—city, as is often the case today, her work is cut out for her, although admittedly this is a job that most mothers absolutely love. If the wedding is formal and large, the job of being mother of the bride can even become something of a full-time one for a while. She not only plans the wedding, but also may plan the rehearsal dinner, even if the groom's parents are paying. It is her job to ensure that her daughter gets the kind of wedding she wants, and, if her daughter is young, she is the one to soothe the inevitable ruffled feathers that occur over weddings. It is she, for example, who must tell the groom's mother that she cannot add another fifty names to her invitation list, and it is she who negotiates with the caterer . . . and the band . . . and the photographer . . . and the florist, and everyone else.

Even if the bride and groom pay for their own wedding, the mother of the bride should still act as the official hostess, especially if her daughter is young and this is her first wedding. After all, no one knows who is paying for this wedding. If her daughter is older and/or is marrying again, the mother's role as hostess may be diminished somewhat, but she should still step in to help her daughter in any way that she can.

The mother of the bride chooses her dress as soon as her daughter has selected the wedding colors so that the mother of the groom, in turn, can select her dress. Since both mothers are part of the wedding party, they may want to wear dresses in the theme colors of the wedding. Even if they do not want to dress in colors that coordinate with the wedding party, each mother will take care not to choose a dress that clashes since the mothers stand in the receiving line with the wedding party.

One other small task may be done by the bride's mother, and that is to take the initiative in establishing a relationship with the groom's family. Although the groom's mother is supposed to make the first move, by writing or calling the bride's mother, this is a little-known twist of etiquette, and an odd one at that. Many people think that since the mother of the bride is the hostess of the wedding, it is up to her to establish the first contact. If the groom's mother does not do this, either because she does not know it is her social obligation or because of shyness, then the mother of the bride should instigate their first social contact, perhaps by writing a brief note expressing her pleasure over the upcoming marriage.

FATHER OF THE BRIDE. Along with the bride's mother, the father of the bride is the host of his daughter's wedding. He is considered an official member of the wedding party since he escorts his daughter down the aisle, gives her away in some ceremonies, and may stand in the receiving line with his wife and the groom's parents. If he stands in the receiving line, he should dress in the same way as the other male members of the wedding party.

Even if he does not stand in the receiving line, the father of the bride circulates at the reception, making sure that his guests are enjoying themselves and that everything is going smoothly. Even if the couple are paying all or part of their wedding expenses themselves, the father still acts as the official host. An older couple or a couple who are remarrying may be the host and hostess of their own wedding, but a helpful father will still do some of the hosting just to help out.

The father of the bride traditionally escorts his daughter to the church, although these days she is just as likely to arrive with both her parents—or even with her husband-to-be, if they are living together before the wedding and giving the wedding themselves.

In the past, at Christian weddings, both sets of parents have tended to remain behind the scenes before the wedding, although at Jewish weddings, the parents often greet their guests and may even serve drinks and cocktail food before the wedding. More and more often today, I am seeing parents of any religion greet their guests before the ceremony. I think it is hospitable that guests, many of whom are friends and relatives who have not been seen since the last big family party, be greeted as they arrive at the church.

DIVORCED PARENTS. A touchy question that comes up frequently these days is the situation of divorced parents at their child's wedding.

Occasionally, there are bad feelings between the parents. Sometimes one parent, usually the father, has been mostly absent but shows up to play his or her role at the time of the wedding, thus angering the former partner. No solution is perfect but there are some ways to handle the problems that arise with tact.

If the bride's father has been a part of her life, and is paying for her wedding, he should give her away. If he steps back into her life after a long absence, and she would rather have an uncle or family friend who has been there all along escort her down the aisle, this is her perogative, but a woman should think seriously before denying her father this role in her big day. Her father's desire to be with her may be a sign that he badly wants to rebuild the lost relationship.

A mother who is embittered toward her ex-husband should nonetheless not stand in the way of her daughter's choice. Nor should a father who has supported and perhaps reared his children pressure a child to deny the mother her role as hostess of the wedding, even if he pays for it. If the bride has been estranged from her mother for many years, and has in effect been raised by a stepmother, then it may make more sense for her mother to be a guest and for the stepmother to be the hostess of the wedding. In short, this is a day when both parents, no matter how angry or bitter, should swallow their feelings for the sake of their child. And the final decisions regarding these touchy matters lies with the bride.

When parents are separated at the time of a child's wedding, they usually try to work together at least on the wedding day, sitting in the same pew and perhaps standing together in the receiving line.

If they cannot manage this or are divorced, the mother sits in the first pew, with her spouse or a close relative such as her mother or brother, or with an escort. The father, with his spouse, close relative, or date, sits in the second pew. Occasionally, when the father has raised the woman, this is reversed, and he sits in the first pew.

MOTHER OF THE GROOM. Although not officially a hostess, the mother of the groom is unofficially a hostess, particularly where her friends are concerned. She may circulate and pay special attention to her friends, but she cannot give any directions to the caterer or anyone else who has been hired to serve at the wedding.

The mother of the groom should consult with the bride and her mother when choosing her dress, and, if the bride requests her to do so, should choose a dress in the colors of the wedding. She stands in the receiving line with the wedding party.

FATHER OF THE GROOM. Although the groom's father has no official role, he will want to circulate among the guests, especially his friends and relatives. I encourage the father of the groom to stand in the receiving line with his wife to greet the wedding guests. If he does this, he should dress with the same degree of formality as the rest of the wedding party.

If the wedding is an evening formal affair, he should dress in formal evening wear, but if it is daytime formal or semiformal, even though the wedding party is in formal or semiformal clothes, he can still wear a dark suit if he chooses to do so.

GRANDPARENTS. They have no official role, but are of course honored guests and should be treated accordingly. This means providing a corsage for grandmothers and reserving special seats for them. Grandparents often sit behind the parents, or they may sit in the same pew with them.

OTHER IMMEDIATE FAMILY MEMBERS. Siblings, favorite aunts and uncles, and other relatives close to the bride may offer their services during the last harried weeks before the wedding. These relatives should also receive special treatment, which usually means reserved seats in pews right behind the parents.

If the bride's parents are not living, she may ask a close relative, godparent, or family friend to stand in. An uncle may escort her down the aisle, for example, or an aunt may serve as hostess.

Wedding Flowers

SEE ALSO *Wedding Expenses*.

Perhaps the single loveliest part of a wedding after the bride and her bridesmaids, wedding flowers do much to create the atmosphere at a wedding. They should be fresh and as picturesque as the family can afford, although if cost is a problem, the bride and her mother should let the florist know or should even do the flowers themselves if possible. Sometimes a friend with a talent for arranging flowers can be enlisted to offer her or his services, or flowers can be purchased from a wholesale market. A friend who is a gardener might provide flowers from his or her garden.

Although the groom pays for the bride's bouquet, the bride usually chooses her bouquet, and since it is part of her outfit, the groom does not see the flowers until the day of the wedding.

The bride's flowers can be modest and quite lovely—a single white rose or a lily, for example, or a small spray or nosegay of brightly colored flowers or—elaborate and spectacular—a cascading spray or a flower-adorned parasol. The bride's bouquet can be all white, but it need not be. A burst of color against the white wedding dress can be quite dramatic (see Figure 58).

Some brides also order flowers (wreaths are popular) for their own and their attendants' hair. This can be a charming touch, but the bride must take care to choose flowers that will not wilt over the course of several hours. Corsages must also be ordered for mothers and grandmothers, and the bride may want to order a corsage to wear with her going-away outfit. Boutonnières should be ordered for the groom and his wedding attendants.

The ways in which flowers can be used to set the stage for a wedding are endless, and the bill for decorative flowers can easily escalate into the thousands. I will not even go into some of the more elaborate ways of decorating with flowers, as any florist and enterprising bride with an unlimited budget will have no shortage of ideas. Much more difficult but entirely possible is to arrange for more modest wedding flowers, and here I do have some suggestions.

At the simplest level, two bouquets can be placed on the altar or flowers can be used to decorate candelabra, and these can then be transferred to the reception to decorate the food-service tables. Small bud vases adorning the individual tables are charming, and if done by a skilled florist will not give the appearance of skimping but rather will look like a deliberate touch of elegant understatment.

The cost of flowers can vary greatly, so estimates should be gathered from several florists before hiring one.

Wedding Gift

SEE ALSO *Bridal Registry.*

Wedding gifts are among the more expensive gifts that one gives, so they must be chosen with care. They should please both the giver and the receiver, and since the bride is setting up a household, they should take her needs into account too. When I say that wedding gifts are among the more expensive gifts that one gives, I mean only that they are more lavish than, for example, birthday gifts. I am not implying that they must be expensive. In choosing a gift, one should always spend within one's means. Giving a lavish gift that one cannot afford is embarrassing to the good friend who receives it.

It is also perfectly acceptable to give a wedding gift that one has made—an afghan,

Figure 58. Sample bridal bouquets

a ceramic pot or some other handcrafted item, a drawing or a painting—provided one's work has some level of professionalism and especially if the work has been admired by the couple getting married.

A wedding present is always given to the couple, not to an individual, even if you are acquainted with only one of the two. As a result most wedding presents are something for the home: table and bed linens, towels, dishes, flatware, glassware, small appliances, and ornamental objects are all acceptable and much-welcomed wedding gifts. Couples who have established households generally have the basics, so they may prefer more individual and unique presents: handcrafted casseroles and individual serving dishes, one-of-a-kind vases or pitchers, artwork, and wine are more likely to please them.

For a second wedding, when guets are not obligated to send anything, the present can be decidedly nontraditional: theater, ballet, or opera tickets, dinner reservations, or a subscription of some sort. Traditional wedding gifts are also given, but check first with the couple before giving them a household item that they may well own.

OBLIGATION. Anyone who receives a wedding invitation and attends the wedding is obligated to bring a wedding gift. Those who receive invitations and cannot attend may feel like sending a gift, and usually do, but are not, strictly speaking, obligated to do so.

SENDING THE GIFT. If possible, gifts should be sent before the wedding to the bride's home or the couple's shared home, if they live together. They may be delivered in person too. After the wedding, a gift may be sent to the home of the couple.

A wedding gift may be sent any time up to a year after the wedding, but if there has been a long delay, a note of explanation should accompany the gift.

Also popular is the custom of bringing wedding gifts to the wedding reception. It is now so accepted that the bride and groom should make arrangements for somone to collect the gifts at the end of the reception and keep them until they return from their honeymoon.

Among some ethnic groups, a custom also exists of giving the bride or groom envelopes of money during the reception. These envelopes of money are wedding gifts, and should be enclosed with a card or note from the giver. The bride or groom does not solicit the presents, but merely accepts them with a smile and a thank-you when they are offered.

DISPLAYING GIFTS. The custom of displaying wedding gifts prevails in many parts of the country, although it is usually only done at the bride's first wedding and in her mother's home. The gifts are usually arranged on a table that has been covered with a white cloth or in some way decorated. Gifts of similar value are displayed together. Checks are not displayed, but are acknowledged on white cards that read: "Check, Mr. and Mrs. William A. Jones." The amount is never revealed.

Finally, while not a matter of etiquette, if the gifts are displayed and the engagement has been announced in the society pages of the local newspaper, a wise precaution is to take out a floater's insurance policy on the presents. In addition, someone should be hired to guard the presents during the wedding and reception when no one is home.

THANK-YOU NOTES. Each person who sends a wedding present should receive a handwritten, thank-you note.

Some system must be devised for keeping track of the presents so that thank-you notes can be sent fairly promptly and without confusion as to who sent which gift. The preparations surrounding even the smallest wedding make it impossible to keep track of wedding gifts in one's head. I suggest using three-by-five index cards. Using the invitation list, write the name and address of each invited guest. The cards can also be used to list acceptances and regrets, but their primary purpose should be to record who sent the present, when it arrived, the store it was sent from (in case you want to return it), and a description of the present. When a thank-you note is sent, that also should be noted on the card.

In theory, the couple should send out thank-you notes as the presents arrive, particularly if the presents arrive several months or weeks before the wedding. In practice, it is a rare couple who manage to send them all out before the wedding, and an even rarer couple who manage to get them out during the last hectic weeks before the wedding, so most couples do not tackle the onerous task of writing thank-you notes until they return from their honeymoon and settle down a bit.

A thank-you note should be handwritten. Many brides have notepaper especially imprinted for the purpose. A bride must use her monogram or maiden name until she is married; thereafter, she may use her married name. This means ordering two sets of paper unless she opts not to change her name, in which case the same stationery will do before and after the wedding.

Sometimes grooms like to write some of the thank-you notes. Most do not, as a rule, but some can be gently badgered into helping out. A groom's thank-you should be written on plain stationery, either white, beige, or gray. A man never correctly uses informals.

A thank-you note should be a very personal acknowledgment. This may sound simple, but when you have received three toasters and five similar crystal vases, creativity can sink to a new low in attempting to write the third note for a toaster and the fifth note for a vase. Despite this, it will not do to thank Aunt Minnie for the "lovely vase." She must be thanked for the "stunning green pottery vase."

Another problem is thanking someone for a present that he undoubtedly finds beautiful but which offends, in a minor or a major way, your taste. Most etiquette experts advise that you try, if possible, not to lie. You need not say something is beautiful if you are quite sure it is not; say instead that it is "unusual" or "imaginative." If all else fails, though, and it is midnight and you are striving to reach your quota of ten notes a night, and you cannot think of tactful words to describe an ugly present, then lie. Say it is lovely or beautiful. After all, it is the thought behind a present that counts, and even if your Aunt Minnie's taste is diametrically opposed to yours, she tried. And she cared. And so she deserves a gracious note, even if that note does contain a white lie or two.

If the wedding is very large and so many

gifts are sent that the couple will not be able physically to write all their thank-you notes within three months, a couple may choose to send a printed formal acknowledgment of the presents. It should read:

> Mr. and Mrs. David Jones
> (or Miss Anita Williams)
> gratefully acknowledge(s)
> the receipt of your wedding gift
> and will write you a personal note
> at the earliest possible time

This never substitutes for a handwritten thank-you note; it merely buys the busy bride and groom a little time in completing this social obligation.

Wedding Guest

OBLIGATIONS TO THE BRIDE AND GROOM. As a guest at a wedding, your only obligation is to enjoy yourself. As a close friend, you may join in the toasting once it has started, and the "official" toasters have had their say. Invited guests who attend the wedding and reception are obliged to give the bride and groom a present *(see Wedding Gifts)*.

OBLIGATIONS TO WEDDING GUESTS. Out-of-town wedding guests pay for their own hotel rooms, but they can often use some help in choosing a place to stay. Mail out-of-town guests brochures from several hotels where they might stay, or if the selec-

tion is more limited, tell them what is available. Sometimes a block of rooms is reserved for wedding guests.

Out-of-town wedding guests, especially if they are family, are usually invited to the rehearsal dinner the night before the wedding.

DRESS. Those invited to a wedding are sometimes confused about what to wear. After all, the bride and groom and the wedding party are liable to be very formally dressed, even for a daytime wedding. But does this mean the wedding guests should follow suit? Not necessarily. What you as a guest wear to a wedding depends basically on the time of the wedding, not what the wedding party is wearing, and on where the wedding is held. Except for those in the wedding party, formal clothes are not properly worn before 5 or 6 P.M.

If the wedding is held during the day, women may wear anything from a tailored suit to a pretty flowered dress. If the wedding is at night, that is, after 5 or 6 P.M., guests wear dressier, evening clothes to a formal wedding. If the wedding is informal, the same kinds of clothes that are appropriate for a daytime wedding should be worn.

If the wedding takes place in a sanctuary, chapel, or clergyperson's office, this must be taken into account in choosing what to wear. It would be disrespectful to wear anything low-cut or particularly revealing. One solution is to wear a jacket or wrap of some kind that can be removed after the ceremony.

Male guests usually wear dinner jackets or dark suits to formal wedding receptions held at night, even if the wedding party is wearing white tie, unless, of course, the invitation requests black or white tie of all male guests.

At semiformal weddings, where the wedding party wears anything from dark suits to dinner jackets, the male guests usually wear dark suits.

At informal weddings, a man may wear any kind of suit, as long as it is not too casual.

Occasionally, a reception does not follow immediately after a wedding but is held later in the day. When this occurs, wedding guests should dress as they would for any other religious service. They often change into dressier clothes for an evening reception.

Wedding Guest List

SEE ALSO *Formal Wedding Invitation; Informal Wedding Invitation; Wedding Guest.*

The size of the guest list is usually a budgetary decision. If the caterer charges $50 per person, and the budget for food is $3,000, then 60 persons can be invited to the reception. Obviously these figures can be juggled: A less-expensive caterer can be found, a less expensive meal can be ordered, more of the budget can be given over to food, and so on.

If the bride's family is paying for the wedding, the guest list must be sized to suit their means. Never mind that the groom's father—or the groom himself—is rolling in money and has a thousand business associates whom he wishes to entertain at the wedding. If the bride's parents cannot afford such a lavish party, then it is not given. The fact that the groom's parents are giving the rehearsal dinner or even that they are giving the couple a generous check does not change this.

Generally the bride and her parents, after figuring out how much can be spent, decide how many persons can be invited, and they inform the groom's family, who must then tailor their list to the bride's mother's suggestion. If the couple is giving the wedding themselves, they sit down with their budget and then draw up a guest list, often after consulting with their families.

The guest list is usually divided down the middle between the two families, that is, if the bride's family gets to invite 100 people, then so does the groom's family, but some juggling may occur. If the bride's family is small compared to the groom's family, and furthermore, many of her distant cousins are not likely to travel very far to see her get married, then she might "give" a few of her guests to the groom's family—and vice versa, of course.

The groom or his mother should compile a written guest list with all the addresses of those who are to be invited and give this to the bride or her mother.

DECIDING WHOM TO INVITE. Once the size of the guest list has been determined, each family must decide whom to invite. A wedding invitation that is accepted obligates the recipient to send a present. Even if the recipient cannot attend, he or she still often wants to send a present, so there is some expense involved to the recipient of the invitation. For this reason, it is kind to invite only those persons who will really want to attend. This includes any and all relatives, although many guest lists omit distant relatives out of necessity, and a wedding with "immediate family only" is always perfectly proper and should offend no one. After family members are on the list, it is then usually expanded to close friends. After that, it gets trickier to draw the line between less close friends, acquaintances, and co-workers. Although some persons see a wedding as an occasion to pay back those who have entertained them, or worse, to get back whatever they may have spent on someone else's wedding gift, I think this is a poor reason to invite someone to a wedding. The best wedding guest lists, as far as I'm concerned, are made up of people whom you love and who love you and your spouse-to-be. Forget the obligations!

As for co-workers, it is sometimes difficult to invite some of the people with whom you work and not all of them, especially in a small office. And especially since many offices have a shower for any employee who is getting married. Even if your co-workers have given you a shower, though, you are not obligated to invite them to the wedding and/or reception.

Several possibilities exist for handling this situation tactfully. You may post a general invitation inviting them to the wedding only (if you are inviting people separately to the wedding and reception; if you had one invitation for the reception and wedding printed, this will not work). You can also invite people to both, but do so by posting a public invitation. Put a sign-up sheet beside it so those who are planning to attend can sign the sheet. (This also works well in a college dormitory or sorority or fraternity.) This kind of invitation serves two purposes. One, those who are not close to you will, one hopes, weed themselves out and decide not to attend. Two, you will at least have been saved the expense of the extra invitations. Finally, even

if your co-workers have given you a shower, you can simply not invite them to the wedding, particularly if the wedding will be held in some distant community. This should not cause any hurt feelings. Most co-workers know they will not be invited to a wedding when they decide to fête a colleague. If there are a couple of persons to whom you are especially close, you can also invite them and ask them to say nothing to those who are not invited. The latter is not the most tactful solution since it puts a slight burden on others, but it may be the only feasible one.

The clergyperson who marries you, and his or her spouse, must be sent an invitation to the wedding and reception. He or she need not be invited to the rehearsal dinner, and in many cases will decline the invitation to the reception unless you are personal friends. Those from whom you buy services—the caterer, the florist, and so on—are not invited to the wedding unless you happen also to be friends.

I am also sometimes asked whether or not one may invite one's therapist. The relationship is not at all social, yet this person not only knows you intimately but may have played an important role in bringing about the wedding. I think the therapist should be invited and allowed to beg off if he or she feels professional reasons require it. Whether he or she attends or not, receiving an invitation, which, by the way, should be addressed to him and his spouse (or her and her spouse), is a nice way to say thank you for all the support.

Another problem that arises is whether to let friends bring a date. All invitations to married couples are sent to both persons, even though you may never have met your friend's spouse, and couples who live together or who have gone together for a long time are invited together just as married couples are. It is kind to permit your unattached single friends to bring a date, particularly if there will be dancing, but not absolutely necessary if your budget just will not stretch that far. To do this, simply address the invitation to Ms. Mary Doe and Guest. A guest may not correctly ask to bring someone, and if someone does you may feel free to decline.

You may invite a couple and not invite their children, even if the children are teenagers or adults. If children are invited, their names should be listed separately on the invitation. If their names are not on the invitation, and it is addressed to the parents only, the children should not attend, nor should the parents ask the bride or groom if their children can come. Children over age eighteen should be sent their own separate invitations. If they still live at home, and you are trying to cut costs, you may include children on their parent's invitations until age twenty-one.

Finally, for those whom you regretfully cannot invite, remember that an announcement serves as a lovely memento—and obligates no one any further.

Wedding Invitation

SEE *Formal Wedding Invitation; Informal Wedding Invitation; Invitation; Wedding Announcement; Wedding Invitation Reply.*

Wedding Invitation Reply

SEE ALSO *Wedding Announcement; Formal Wedding Invitation; Informal Wedding Invitation.*

While there is no need to respond to a formal wedding announcement, an invitation always calls for a reply. The kind of reply depends upon the form of the invitation.

The fact that wedding invitations are sent out four or more weeks in advance does not give those invited three and a half weeks in which to respond. These days caterers (and anxious brides) are eager for a firm guest list as soon as possible, and your first task as a guest is to comply.

A formal invitation calls for a formal reply, either an acceptance or a regret. Write it, in your own hand, with blue or black ink, on your best stationery.

The most formal kind of acceptance you can write would read as follows:

> Mr. and Mrs. William Willig
> accept with pleasure
> the kind invitation
> of Mr. and Mrs. Bronte
> to the marriage of their daughter
> Laura Bronte
> to
> Henry Simpson
> Saturday, the tenth of August,
> at five o'clock
> St. Stephen's Church
> and afterwards at
> the Arts Club

Here is another type of acceptance, equally formal and, I think, more comfortable for many people to write:

> *Mr. and Mrs. William Willig*
> *accept with pleasure*
> *your kind invitation*
> *for*
> *Saturday, the tenth of August,*
> *at five o'clock*

A formal regret reads:

> *Mr. and Mrs. William Willig*
> *regret that they are unable to accept*
> *the kind invitation of*
> *or*
> *your kind invitation*
> *or*
> *your very kind invitation*

Since you will not be attending, there is no need to repeat the date, time, and address.

Family and very close friends, those whom you talk with nearly every day or several times a week, often feel too stiff responding to a formal invitation with a formal writen reply. These people receive invitations as mementos as much as anything since it is a given that they will be at the wedding. Members of the wedding party also need not respond to the formal wedding invitation, as they have already made plans to be there! Those who feel too close to send a formal reply can mention in a telephone call that they will, of course, be there, or can send a handwritten note, perhaps something like the following:

> *Henry,*
> *I'll be there! You know that wild horses, the plague, and a monsoon could not keep me away.*
> *Love,*
> *George*

Many brides tell me that they often find warm personal messages written on response cards when they are returned: "All best," "Looking forward to your wedding," and so on. I like this kind of spontaneity.

If you receive a nontraditional invitation, you may respond with a formal reply or with a less formal handwritten note.

When the invitation is a handwritten note, write a short note back or telephone. Usually when the invitation is issued by a handwritten note, a telephone call, or a telegram (day letter), the wedding is within a week or two. In the case of a telegram (day letter), the wedding may be scheduled within two or three days; thus, the method of issuing invitations. Whenever you receive an invitation for a wedding that is scheduled to take place shortly, it is courteous to respond as quickly as possible and by the fastest means possible.

Wedding Photography

Most people want some kind of photographic record of their wedding. For most people, this involves hiring a still photographer, and more and more people are also hiring a videotape crew to record the entire event on film with sound. Whatever kind of photography you decide you want, it is well worth the money to hire a professional photographer.

Before deciding on pictures during the ceremony itself, you must consult with the clergyperson. Some permit the entire wedding to be filmed or photographed; others will permit only a few shots during the ceremony by a still photographer; others do not permit any photographs to be taken during the ceremony. Some permit flash; others do not.

The trend today is toward permitting some photos if they are taken without disrupting the ceremony. I know of several churches that have installed their own videotaping equipment unobtrusively on the balcony. They record the wedding and then sell a videotape to the bride and groom for a more modest price than most commercial photographers charge.

Although wedding photographers have a standard repertoire of pictures they always take, they also need some guidance from you about specific pictures you would like to see taken—a shot of you with your great-aunt Minnie, you kissing your father at the altar as he gives you away, your cousins from Idaho who traveled so far for the wedding. A problem does arise because the photographer does not know all the people whose pictures are to be taken. One solution is to ask someone—a relative or close friend of the family—to work with the photographer for a half hour or so during the reception to point out who is who.

Most wedding photographers also tend to be overzealous, and a couple who like things low key should sit down with the photographer a couple of weeks before the wedding and go over the list of shots, ruling out the ones they do not want and emphasizing the ones they do want. If you want the photographer to be as unobtrusive as possible, tell him or her that. And the reverse is also true: If you want him out there aggressively recording every minute detail, tell him that, too.

Some of the standard wedding shots that you may want for your album are:

Before the ceremony
Bridesmaids helping bride get dressed
Bride in her wedding dress
Bride with her parents
Bride with honor attendant
Bride with entire wedding party
Bride leaving house with parents
    or father
Groom alone (portrait)
Groom with best man
Groom with father and mother
Groom with brothers
Groom with ushers and best man

During the ceremony
Bride arriving at church
Bride's family arriving at church
Ushers escorting grandparents to
    their seats
Usher seating groom's parents
Usher seating mother of the bride
Wedding procession: individual shots of
    each member of wedding coming
    down the aisle, bride and father at
    back of sanctuary right before
    procession, shot of bride and father

coming down the aisle, shot of
groom and ushers waiting at altar
Groom meeting bride at altar
Bride and groom exchanging vows
Bride and groom during ring ceremony
The kiss at the altar
Bride and groom coming back up aisle
Bride and groom outside church or
synagogue
Bride and groom getting into the car
Bride and groom in car waving goodbye
as they leave the church or
synagogue

*After the ceremony (before leaving for
the reception)*
Formal wedding portrait of bride and
groom
Formal portrait of entire wedding party
Formal family portraits

At the reception
Bride and groom arriving
The receiving line (several shots should
be taken since this is a good time to
photograph Great-Aunt Minnie and
all those other relatives and old
family friends)
Bride and groom mingling among guests
Buffet table
Cake
Bride and groom's first dance
Bride dancing with her father
Bride dancing with her father-in-law
Groom dancing with his mother
Groom dancing with his mother-in-law
Bride and groom cutting the cake
Bride and groom toasting one another
Bride and groom leaving reception
Table shots

The bride usually has her formal portrait
taken a few days before the wedding in the
photographer's studio or at home.

Unfortunately, about the only time to
take the other formal portraits is right after
the ceremony. No one has gotten mussed
up yet, and everyone is all together. The
only problem is that the guests like to wait
outside the church to see off the bride and
groom. They like to throw rice and follow
the wedding couple in their car, in a sort of
procession, as they drive through town to
the reception.

If the guests can be persuaded to go on to
the reception, they still cannot eat or drink
anything until they have gone through the
receiving line, so they are still waiting for
the bride and groom and other family members.

The only alternative is to take the formal
portraits immediately upon arriving at the
reception as the guests start to trickle in.
And wherever the portraits are taken, they
must be taken quickly so everyone can get
on with the festivities.

The last suggested photograph—table
shots—provide an excellent way to ensure
that you have a picture of everyone who is
at the wedding. The photographer should
be instructed to go around to every table, at
the beginning of the meal if possible, and
take a group shot. This is also a good way
to get pictures of the tables themselves,
including the centerpieces.

If you do decide to videotape the ceremony and reception, you should realize
that this will involve bright, hot lights.
Particularly if there is dancing, this can be
very uncomfortable for your guests. A solution may be to videotape a few minutes at
a time or only short segments of each event

of the day, for example, the couple at the altar, their first dance, the cutting of the cake.

Sound videotape machines are even more intrusive because they catch unsuspecting guests' conversations. Their best use is to videotape the ceremony, if the clergyperson permits this, and the "ceremonial" aspects of the reception such as the cake cutting, the first dance, the departure of the bride and groom. Photographers should not be permitted to use them to "interview" guests. Those guests who want their words on record will seek out the camera; all others should be left in peace to simply have a good time at the wedding.

Finally, even though you hire a professional photographer, it is a good idea to ask a friend or relative to take some backup shots. Similarly, if you decide to save money by letting a friend take the photographs, ask more than one person since amateurs are more prone to equipment failure than are professionals.

Wedding Reception

Most weddings are followed by a reception of some kind, whether it is an elaborate sit-down dinner in a hotel or club or a simple tea in the church parlor. The wedding need not be followed directly by the reception. Sometimes a couple gets married in the morning or afternoon, and then the reception is held later that night.

Occasionally, the reception is not held on the same day as the wedding, but is, for any number of reasons, scheduled for several days or even weeks later. A couple also may have more than one reception. One couple I know who had met at work and who lived hundreds of miles from either of the parents decided to give themselves their own wedding in the community where they had met and lived.

They gave themselves a very lovely reception attended by both sets of parents, many relatives, and their own friends; and then two weeks later they traveled 200 miles to visit her parents, who gave them another reception, to which they invited all their friends who had not been able to travel so far for the wedding. Several months later, they traveled across the country to attend a reception given by his parents for their friends.

When the reception is held later, the bride may wear her wedding dress, or she may wear another dress that is in keeping with the formality of the reception.

Obviously, the reception entails the single greatest expense, and the price may vary from three to five dollars per person for a simple church parlor reception to hundreds of dollars per person for an elaborate dinner.

BREAKFAST, BRUNCH, OR LUNCH. If the wedding is held in the morning, a breakfast or brunch is the appropriate reception. This kind of meal is usually served up to 1 P.M. in small communities, as late as 2 or 3 P.M. in large cities. There is little difference between a breakfast or brunch and a lunch except the menu. The former involves breakfast food—eggs or omelettes—and the latter does not.

BUFFET OR TEA. If a wedding is held during the early afternoon, a buffet or tea may be the most appropriate form of reception. A buffet or tea is an especially good way to entertain if your budget is tight. At minimum, you can serve finger sandwiches, and other canapés, wedding cake, and champagne or white wine (or nothing alcoholic as a rule, if the church parlor is used) can be organized. A buffet can be as elaborate as you like.

Unless the buffet is served at mealtime, a tea or light buffet usually follows a wedding held around 3 or 4 P.M.

If there are facilities to seat guests, then anything, including a full dinner, may be served. If guests must stand, then finger food or food that can be easily eaten with just a fork must be served.

DINNER. The most elaborate—and expensive—kind of wedding reception is the sit-down dinner, and certainly the sky is the limit in terms of cost and what may be served to eat and drink.

A sit-down or buffet dinner is held in the evening. The wedding is anywhere from 6 to 8 P.M., and the dinner follows.

WHERE TO HOLD THE RECEPTION. Unless a home reception is planned, it is necessary to settle on a place to hold the reception as soon as possible after you decide to get married. A reception can be held at home, in a church parlor, in a catering hall (often these are attached to synagogues), in a private club, or in a restaurant.

Certain times of the year—June, August, September, October, and December—are especially popular for weddings, and restaurant, clubs, and catering halls,

even churches and clergy, are booked, sometimes more than a year in advance.

PLANNING THE FOOD. A major consideration in deciding where to have the reception may be the kind of catering service that is available. Some places offer full catering, which means that everything—the bar, the food, the tables, table linens, and so on—will be provided and probably included in one package price. Some places, mostly those that specialize in weddings, may even provide flowers.

Other places have limited catering facilities, which may mean they will provide a room but food must be ordered from an outside supplier. Another caterer might provide everything but the wedding cake, for example.

It is a rare caterer who will provide food and no liquor since caterers make most of their money on the bar. If you do find one who will let you bring in your own liquor, this can be a good way to cut down the liquor costs, since you can buy at a case discount from a liquor store. Most caterers mark up liquor at a minimum of 100 percent.

If you plan a home wedding, if at all possible, try to hire a caterer to prepare at least some of the food. If this is not possible, prepare food in advance and freeze it. Definitely set aside some money, if only to pay neighborhood kids to serve as waiters and bartenders (if they are over eighteen years of age). The bride and her mother are not supposed to serve food on the wedding day. This is not a rule of etiquette so much as it is a matter of practicality. However much fun weddings are to plan and carry out, they are also exhausting, and the bride's mother simply will not be able to handle making all the preparations and then working the day of the wedding, too. Besides, no bride should have to lift a finger on her big day.

DECORATIONS. The sky is the limit with decorations at a wedding reception. A bride has been known to descend a garlanded staircase while a golden cage full of white doves is released from the top of the stairs to fly over her head as she floats down toward her audience. I say audience, because such extravaganzas do take on the overtones of a major Hollywood production. The cost was rumored to be more than $100,000.

I have also attended a charming home wedding where the only decorations were white curtains in front of a bay window that served as the backdrop and vases full of inexpensive (read: in season) flowers that the bride and her mother had purchased the day before wholesale and had arranged themselves. The effect was utterly charming, and the overall cost was under $200.

Most couples opt for something in between, and spend somewhere between $500 and $1,200 on decorations, mostly on flowers.

ORDER OF EVENTS. It is at the reception that people become most concerned over protocol, and, ironically, it is also at the reception where I believe protocol should be the most lenient. Some rules can be followed; others may have to be thrown out because they do not work for this particular wedding. The main thing is to avoid hurting anyone's feelings—no easy task

when two families are merged for one highly important event in their children's lives.

Photographs. The bride and groom should get to the reception as soon as they possibly can. The photographer will undoubtedly want to take a few pictures of the couple at the altar, and this should be done quickly, while their guests wait outside the church or synagogue to see them off to the reception if it is at another location. Immediately upon arriving at the reception, the photographer may need to take pictures of the wedding party. This, too, should be done quickly before the receiving line is formed.

Receiving Line. (See also Receiving Line.) The bride's parents, the groom's parents, the bride and groom, and the female members of the wedding party form a receiving line as soon as they arrive at the reception. Some wedding experts believe that only the mothers should stand in the receiving line, but I think this defeats the dual purpose of having a receiving line in the first place, which is to give the guests an opportunity to meet the parents of the bride and groom and to tell the wedding party how lovely they look. Therefore, I think fathers should definitely be included in the receiving line.

First in line are the parents of the bride, as they are the official host and hostess. Next to them are the parents of the groom, the semiofficial host and hostess. Standing next to them is the loving couple, and beside them are their lovely female attendants, with the exception of the flower girl, who is too young to understand what this is all about or to stand still for very long.

There are variations on this, as one might expect. If the bride and groom are giving themselves their own wedding, they may receive alone. An older couple or a couple at a second wedding also might receive alone. If the attendants are witnesses, i.e., there are only two attendants, they do stand in the receiving line.

If a parent is not living, the other parent does not ask a relative to stand in but simply receives alone. If neither parent is living, the bride or groom may ask a close relative to stand in and represent the family. They also may not have a stand-in; either way is perfectly correct. Of course, if the bride's mother is not living, and/or if some other relative has helped her with the wedding, that person would serve as official hostess and would stand in the receiving line.

If the parents are divorced, and standing together would be uncomfortable for either of them, the mother may stand in the receiving line while the father circulates among the guests. Sometimes, the father stands in the receiving line because he is the host, having paid for the wedding.

Toasting. At a seated meal, the toasts usually begin as soon as everyone is seated. A round of champagne may be poured for the occasion, or, if the budget is limited, wine is perfectly acceptable. At a stand-up buffet or tea, toasts may begin as soon as the guests have passed through the receiving line and have been served drinks.

The first toast at a wedding is offered by the best man. He toasts the bridal couple, and everyone except the couple raises his glass and drinks to them. The second toast is that of the groom to his bride, and the third toast is the bride's to her groom, if she chooses to make one. The father and mother of the bride and groom often toast next. After that, any good friends may also propose a toast, and after that the toasting

is liable to get out of hand and should be suspended, if only temporarily. If a sit-down dinner is served, toasting can resume for a brief time toward the end of the meal.

Seating. At minimum, a table is set aside for the bridal party at a tea or buffet, even if the other guests are not seated. At a sit-down meal, everyone is seated. The bridal party sits at one table, and the parents and grandparents generally sit at another table. Depending upon how well they know each other and local custom, there may be either two tables for the parents, one for each set, or one joint parents' table.

Arranging the seating at a wedding reception can be a tricky business in these days of reconstituted families, and the bridal couple or the bride and her mother may find they need to spend several hours on this one task. If either of the bridal couple's parents are divorced, it may not be possible to put them together at one bridal table, whether or not they have remarried. In such cases, the most tactful course of action may be to seat each parent at a table with his or her current spouse and some family and friends.

If relations between the children and the new spouses are rocky, they can be excluded, but a thoughtful couple will not make this decision lightly, as the wedding of a child is a day that a parent will want to share with the other person who is close to him or her, his or her own spouse.

Even sadder is to exclude a parent because the ex-spouses do not get along. If one parent refuses to attend the wedding unless the other parent is excluded, then the parent who is giving the reception is obviously invited, and the other parent, of his or her own volition, does not attend.

Unless the wedding is very small, there should be no reason that two sparring parents (or any two sparring relatives, for that matter) cannot successfully avoid one another for a few hours while they attend their child's wedding reception.

Seating can be left open or seats can be assigned. An alternate arrangement that is somewhere between no seating assignments and rigid seat assignments is to assign people to tables and then let them work out the seating arrangements among themselves. Only you know your family and friends well enough to know what will be most comfortable for them. Keep in mind, though, that it is often more of a kindness to seat people who do not know one another well than to let them fend for themselves.

Although husbands and wives are typically separated at dinner parties, they are seated together at weddings, first because this is often a sentimental moment for them as well as for the bride and groom, and, second, because they will want to be near one another if there is dancing.

Dancing. At some point during the reception, usually toward the end of the meal, or after everyone has gone through the receiving line if no meal is served, the bridal couple take to the dance floor for their first dance together. The couple dances a few rounds, and then the father of the bride claims the second dance with the bride. The groom dances with the mother of the bride. At some point the bride also dances with her father-in-law and the ushers and close friends and family. At a very large wedding, it simply will not be possible for her to dance with every male there, and she has the option of sitting out any dance when she becomes overtired. Apart from the cou-

ple dancing their first dance together, there need not be anything rigid about the order of the dancing. A groom, for example, might dance with his widowed or divorced mother before he dances with the bride's mother. Tact should always supplant rules in situations like this.

Cake-Cutting Ceremony. The cake is cut before dessert is served at a sit-down dinner and toward the end of the reception for a buffet or tea. The bride and groom share the first piece. The top layer of the cake is usually saved and frozen for the bride and groom to enjoy on their first wedding anniversary.

Small boxes of wedding cake or even a separately baked groom's cake used to be sent home with the guests as mementos, but these have become prohibitively expensive (the boxes as well as the cakes), and they are rarely seen these days.

Departure. Since most guests will want to see off the bride and groom, the thoughtful bridal couple do not linger too long. The only exception to this is the couple who gives their own wedding. Then they are the host and hostess, and it is the thoughtful guests who depart at a reasonable hour so they can have some time alone together. Alternately, the couple can schedule their departure like any other bridal couple and ask a friend to stand in for them, to say goodbye to departing guests. Most wedding receptions do not last more than four or five hours. If they last longer than that, several caterers reported to me, the families become cliquish, and the whole affair becomes anticlimactic.

Usually the bride retires to change into a travel outfit. This is the sign to guests that things are about to break up.

The bride's mother and her attendants or

sisters may assist her. The bride's father, and, if she is tactful, also her parents-in-law are then called in to bid her and her husband goodbye privately. The couple then head out for what is usually a rather boisterous goodbye to their guests.

The bride may throw her bouquet when she leaves to change clothes, or she may throw it when she is saying her last goodbyes. It is not, strictly speaking, in good taste for a bride to throw her wedding garter, if she wears one, but many a bride has not been slowed down by that small bit of etiquette.

The wedding couple may have been showered with rice when they left the church or synagogue, but they are often showered with it again just as they are leaving the reception.

The wedding reception usually breaks up shortly after the bridal couple leaves. Someone should have been assigned the responsibility of taking home the gifts that are brought to the reception. Gifts brought to the reception are never opened there, and they should be transported home with care, so that the cards attached to them are not lost.

ally running high by this time, particularly if the wedding is a big one, and because of this I recommend that only those actually participating in the ceremony, plus the mother of the bride, attend the actual rehearsal.

The clergyperson will direct the rehearsal in consultation with the bride and her mother. He or she has seen a lot of weddings in the sanctuary, and probably developed a pretty good sense of logistics. While the bride and her mother need not follow every suggestion made, the clergyperson will have some good ones.

Apart from the logistics of the processional and recessional, the clergyperson does dictate how the ceremony will go. If he or she wants the bridesmaids arranged on the steps of the altar that is generally where they stand.

In meetings with the clergyperson before the wedding, the couple can work out any specifics.

After the rehearsal, a dinner party is given for the wedding party, and immediate families and out-of-town guests are usually included. In some parts of the country, the parents of the groom give this party.

Wedding Rehearsal

If the wedding is large enough to warrant a rehearsal, it is usually the night before or sometimes one or two days before the wedding. The night before is actually the best time because out-of-town wedding attendants will be there.

Nerves are frayed and tensions are usu-

Wedding Trip

After the wedding, the bride and groom should schedule several days to go off somewhere by themselves. The most lavish honeymoon is an around-the-world tour, but a weekend in a quiet secluded resort will work, sometimes better than the hectic tour.

In fact, depending upon their temperaments, the wedding couple who are planning a major trip would do well to postpone it for a few days or even a few weeks so they can rest from the wedding excitement, but no couple should deny themselves a few days of honeymooning if they can possibly avoid it.

The groom is expected to pay for the wedding trip. More often than not these days it is a joint expense.

Weekend Visitors

SEE *House Party.*

West Point

SEE *Military.*

White House Invitation

Should you be fortunate enough to be invited to some event at the White House, you will be relieved to know that this is one social event where there will be little room for you to make a mistake or do anything embarrassing. You will be guided through every step of protocol that is involved. If you have any questions beforehand, call the White House Social Secretary, who will be happy to answer them. Should any questions arise during your visit, ask one of the military aides who overpopulate these functions. They are on assignment at the White House, and are quite familiar with the protocol.

A White House invitation may arrive by mail, telephone, or telegram. Its format will indicate the degree of formality, but guests always go somewhat dressed up to the President's house. Women do not wear pants, and often they wear hats and gloves to lunch. An engraved invitation to a dinner always is black tie unless the invitation specifically states white tie.

Dress for formal occasions varies somewhat with the administration, but is usually black tie for men and usually short, dressy cocktail dresses for women. Long dresses are sometimes worn, but these are not usually elaborate evening dresses. Women often do not wear gloves, although this again depends upon the current fashion. Very fancy evening dresses and long white gloves are worn to white-tie events *(see Black Tie, White Tie).*

A White House invitation must be answered promptly, within a day of its receipt, if possible. If you are out of town when a written invitation arrives, you may telephone the White House with your acceptance or regrets. Otherwise, write a formal note of acceptance or regrets as soon as possible after receiving the invitation. White House invitations are only rarely turned down, and then only for a good reason—family illness, travel outside the United States, or a wedding. The reason should be stated in the response.

> *Mr. and Mrs. Benson Greene*
> *deeply regret*
> *that owing to the wedding of their daughter*
> *they will be unable to accept*
> *the kind invitation of*
> *the President and Mrs. Adams*
> *for dinner, Friday, the sixth of June*

An acceptance would read:

> *Mr. and Mrs. Benson Greene*
> *accept with pleasure*
> *the kind invitation of*
> *the President and Mrs. Adams*
> *for dinner, Friday, the sixth of June*

Note that the title "First Lady" is not used in the reply, since it is an unofficial title.

It is a serious breach of White House etiquette not to arrive *before* the time stated on the invitation, and if you know that you are one of several hundred invited guests, you must take that into account and plan to arrive early enough so that all the guests can be admitted prior to the time stated on the invitation. Keep in mind that entering the White House grounds even with an invitation is time-consuming since you must pass through security, and since a very large number of persons may be trying to get into what is a fairly small house.

Once inside, guests remain standing until the President and the First Lady appear and have greeted all their guests. At small events, they walk around to greet their guests; at larger functions, the President and the First Lady greet their guests in a receiving line. Whichever half of a couple is more prominent and is more likely the reason they were invited to the White House goes first in the receiving line. A woman removes her glove to shake hands with the President and the First Lady. The greetings are very brief as a rule, especially if there are many guests.

An aide will sometimes prompt the President with your name or may even introduce you. If not, you say, "Mr. President, I'm Lee Smith," when you reach him in the receiving line. You may also introduce your spouse, or each of you may introduce yourselves. If you are introduced to the President or First Lady, respond simply, "Good evening [or Good day], Mr. President."

Do not linger in a receiving line unless you are detained by the President or the First Lady. Then you may converse briefly, usually responding to questions. Call the President "Sir" and address the First Lady as "Mrs. Adams." Do not call her "Ma'am."

It is best to wait for the President or the First Lady to seek you out later during the evening for further conversation, but you may approach them if you feel comfortable.

The event or evening will end when the President and the First Lady want it to, that is, when they head upstairs. Guests should not leave until they have made their exit.

Keep in mind that styles of entertaining vary with the administration. Some First Ladies like to entertain formally, while other favor casual parties. Therefore, some of the suggestions regarding dress could change. If you have any doubts, check with the White House Social Secretary or a friend who has attended functions with the same administration that has invited you.

White Lie

SEE *Lying.*

White Tie

SEE *Men's Formal Wear.*

Widow

SEE ALSO *Mourning.*

FORMS OF ADDRESS. A widow continues to use her husband's name and is known as "Mrs. John M. Smythson." Letters should be addressed to her in this manner, and she should introduce herself in this way when appropriate. If she is "Mrs. John M. Smythson, Sr.," she may continue to use this designation after her husband's death even though her son will no longer use "Jr."

REMARRIAGE. The marriage of a widow differs in some respects from that of a young, never-before-married bride. She does not wear white, nor does she wear a veil, with the possible exception of a very short veil attached to a cocktail hat. A second-time bride is never given away in marriage, although a widow may be escorted down the aisle by a son or another close male relative. She also may walk down the aisle alone. A traditional wedding shower is usually not given for a widow, primarily because she has a fully stocked household and may be merging with another fully stocked one. Prewedding parties, such as dinner parties and cocktail parties, are entirely acceptable, and the reception can follow the same format as that of any other wedding.

Both a widow and a widower may encounter opposition from their children when they remarry. This they must meet with a firm yet sympathetic touch. A frank discussion in which you clarify that you are not replacing the parent who was lost, that you have been very lonely, and that you have a right to rebuild your life should help matters, although true acceptance may take a while longer.

RINGS. A widow generally continues to wear her rings for the rest of her life or until she remarries. At the point at which a relationship becomes serious enough for her to be contemplating remarriage, she may choose to remove her wedding ring and transfer her engagement ring to her right hand. If she receives a new engagement ring, she may put her old one away, wearing it only occasionally, or she may give it to a daughter who will treasure it. A third alternative is to have the stone reset into another piece of jewelry.

Occasionally a widow, especially a young one, will choose to put away her rings as a symbol to herself that she is ready to begin a new life. This may happen long before she is thinking about remarriage to anyone specific.

SIGNATURE. A widow signs her correspondence as she has throughout her married life. In her personal correspondence, she signs "Judith Smythson"; in household and business correspondence, she may sign either "Judith Smythson," followed in parentheses by "Mrs. John M. Smythson," or simply "Mrs. John M. Smythson."

SOCIAL LIFE. A widow's social life no longer excludes her from any kind of public activities. As soon as she feels ready to resume her public and social life, she may do so. She can hope that her married friends will continue to see her, and many of them will, but there will undoubtedly be some less loving and kind souls who will view a single woman as a threat. As a result, a widow may find that she has to construct a new social life for herself, and she may find that she is more comfortable doing exactly that. Widows, widowers, and other singles often band together in clubs and tour groups, and this is often an excellent way for a widow to renew her social life.

A widow, because she has been married before, is no longer considered a blushing bride and has more leeway in the conduct of her social life than do most other women. One couple I know, a widow and widower who lost their spouses within one year of each other, had not only been lifelong friends but had often taken their annual vacations with one another and their spouses. A year after their losses, they decided to take a trip together, and they came to me for advice, worried about what their families and friends would say. I could only give my blessing and restrain from expressing my hope that something deeper would develop. Indeed, as I predicted, their behavior raised no eyebrows among their close friends.

Widower

FORMS OF ADDRESS. A widower's name and signature do not change in any way as a result of his being widowed.

REMARRIAGE. No restrictions exist on the kind of wedding a man may have whether he has been married once or five times.

RINGS. A widower may wear his wedding band for life, or he may remove it as a signal to himself that he is ready to rebuild his life.

SOCIAL LIFE. Since there are far more elderly women than men, and most widows and widowers these days are elderly, a widower may find that he is pursued socially long before he is willing to resume his social life. He must learn to say no to invitations and offers for which he is not ready, and his only explanation need be that he is not yet ready to go out again.

Wife

SEE *Family Finances; Forms of Address—Spoken; Marriage; Married Couples' Social Life.*

Wine

SEE ALSO *Apéritif.*

After decades of ignoring wine, Americans have become avid oenophiles, and our vineyards are producing wines that may be favorably compared with some of Europe's finest wines. Wine is increasingly served at dinner parties and is also becoming a favored beverage at family dinners.

WITH FOOD. The rules regarding the kinds of wines that go best with certain foods are little more than recommendations, a fact that not everyone who serves wine seems to understand. While red wine is served with red meat, and white wine is the preferred wine with fish and chicken, this guideline is more complicated than it seems (for example, what about veal? What about robust and highly seasoned chicken dishes? Or chicken dishes made with red wine?), and there are many exceptions to it. It also does not take into account individual preferences. Some people, especially dieters, may prefer white wine; others love red wine and want to drink it at every opportunity. Always feel free to follow your own instincts about which wine to serve if you have the expertise to do so; if you do not, you can follow the advice of a good wine merchant, or even the cookbook writer whose recipe you are following. Many cookbook writers mention a wine that will work well with a particular dish.

In general, red wine does complement lamb, beef, robust veal recipes, and heavily seasoned dishes. White wine complements fish, seafood, and the more delicate veal dishes, certainly those with white sauces. Poultry goes well with white wine, but it would be a crime to drink a white wine with that most famous of chicken dishes, *coq au vin*, which is prepared with a red wine. Suffice it to say that some chicken dishes do well with white; others, with red.

Only a red is strong enough to stand up to most game birds, including turkey and goose. A pasta in a white sauce may be better with a white wine, while a spicy red sauce would call for a robust red.

Contrary to popular belief, rosé and champagne are not all-purpose wines; they complement few rather than many foods, and should be served with discretion. Rosés are strong enough to stand up to only the lightest foods, and are probably best served alone. Champagne may be served as an apéritif or with dessert, but it is not, as is widely supposed, a wine that goes with everything.

There are some other things to keep in mind when planning which wines to serve: A white wine should be served before a red one, a light wine before a heavy one, a dry before a sweet one, and an inferior one before a superior one.

SERVING. Wine served at a formal or informal dinner is usually served in the bottle, and the bottle is set on the table. The exception is a very rare, old wine that has been decanted and is served from the decanter. Often white wine is served from a wine bucket, and red wine is put directly on the table. If there are enough diners, two or more bottles of wine should be opened and placed on the table at a time.

White wine should be served chilled, and red wine should be served at "room temperature," which basically means no warmer than 65 to 68 degrees F. Red wine should be uncorked at least an hour before serving so it can breathe and develop its fullest flavor. Pouring a little of the wine into a glass to empty out the "neck" of the bottle helps, too.

WINEGLASSES. Much fuss is made of the type of glasses that are proper and there are indeed differently shaped glasses for various kinds of red and white wines. But except for connoisseurs who regularly serve precious wines, most persons make do with an all-purpose wineglass, or with one white-wine glass and one red-wine glass.

A red-wine glass is the larger of the two, and the top of the glass is curved inward to protect the aroma of the wine. A white-wine glass, smaller than a red-wine glass, has a more open bowl *(see Figure 59).*

Wineglasses, along with water glasses, can be bought in matched sets, or unmatched but complementary glasses may be used. Moselle-wine glasses and dessert-wine glasses are often separate sets, and they are the only wineglasses that may properly be made of colored glass. Moselle-wine glasses have a small cup, which is often green, and a long stem.

The best wineglasses are perfectly plain ones of the very best crystal you can afford.

White-wine glasses are usually held by their stems so the holder's hands do not

Figure 59. Red-wine glass (left) and white-wine glass (right)

warm the wine, and red-wine glasses may be held by the stem or slightly higher.

IN RESTAURANTS. Increasing numbers of restaurants offer excellent wine cellars to their clientele these days. In a fine restaurant, wines are served by a wine steward, also called a *sommelier.* If you want to order wine, ask to see the wine menu and rest assured that it will arrive with the wine steward. A good wine steward is very knowledgeable, and even a so-so one knows more than most of the people he serves. Tell him what you are eating and what price range you prefer, and he will give you recommendations. Tip the wine steward 15 percent of the wine bill if he has served you personally, less if he has not.

In less fancy restaurants, wine may be chosen directly from the wine list, although the maître d'hôtel or the owner, if he or she is around, may also be knowledgeable about the wine cellar and can make suggestions.

When wine is brought to the table at a restaurant or club, it is presented first to the person who ordered it (usually the host, but the hostess if *she* is the one who knows wines). He or she checks the label to see if this is the wine that was ordered, and gives the waiter or wine steward the okay to open the wine. The wine is opened and a small amount is poured into the host's glass for him to taste and approve. After it is approved, it is poured all around, first into the women's glasses and then into the men's glasses. If it would be awkward to pour first into the women's glasses, or you prefer not to make this distinction, the waiter pours in order around the table, filling the host's glass last.

As Gifts. A bottle or two of wine makes an excellent hostess gift when you are invited to someone's house for dinner, although the hostess is under no obligation to serve wine that she receives since she will probably already have selected the wines for the meal she is cooking. A case of wine also makes an excellent present for an oenophile, and it is also an excellent wedding or anniversary gift. It is acceptable to give someone young wines that need to be put away for a few years before drinking.

Nouveau. Rapidly becoming an annual event in the United States, as it has long been in France, are the red nouveau wines that arrive in the autumn, often with much ballyhoo and correspondingly high prices in restaurants. In wine stores, these wines are relatively inexpensive, as well they should be since they are lightweight wines that are meant to be drunk right away.

Appreciation. Along with increased consumption of wine have come wine snobs. There is certainly nothing wrong with becoming knowledgeable or even avid about wines, but there is a kind of wine snobbery that is also pompous and rather silly. Exaggerated talk about a wine, particularly a wine that is good but not great, as are almost all wines that most people drink, is embarrassing anywhere except at a wine tasting, and even there, it has its limits.

In addition, only rarely will you get a bad bottle of wine in a restaurant. It may not be to your liking or exactly what you thought you were ordering, but it is rarely spoiled. The moral here, of course, is to be extremely discreet about sending back a bottle of wine, lest you merely make a fool of yourself. If a bottle of wine is truly undrinkable, call the wine steward over and quietly explain the situation to him. If he agrees with you, he will replace the wine, and even if he does not, he will often replace it.

Wine Tasting

A wine tasting is quite a pleasant way to wile away an afternoon or early evening. There is one rule about when not to schedule a wine tasting, and that is right after a heavy meal. No one wants to drink wine when he is sated with a big meal.

About five or six wines are suitable for a tasting. More than that and the palate becomes confused; fewer than that, and there is too little to compare. I recommend, as will your local wine merchant, I am fairly sure, one excellent, one mediocre, and four so-so wines to provide good balance. Since guests will drink about one or two glasses of each wine, count on about half a bottle per person. That makes twelve the ideal number to invite, although any number from six to sixteen makes for a happy wine tasting. If you invite too few people, you will not be able to taste as many wines; if you invite too many people, the wine will get lost in the party.

The only foods to serve at a wine tasting are a mild cheese and some bread. Anything spicier than this ruins the palate for the wine, but some food is needed between wines to erase the taste of the last wine.

Service is simple: Wrap the wine bottles in a towel or aluminum foil so their labels cannot be seen, and put the food out on a platter or cutting board. If you have an especially large stock of wineglasses and can offer everyone a clean glass for each wine, fine; otherwise rinse the glasses between each bottle.

The purpose of a wine tasting is to rate, discuss, and otherwise analyze the wines. Depending upon your level of competence where wine is concerned, you may feel slightly uncomfortable the first time you are invited to participate in this kind of discussion. If you feel unsure of yourself, remember you can always be a silent participant. You also need not be an expert to participate. If you like a wine or dislike it, just say so. Do not overdo it, though, if you really know little about wine. There is nothing more awkward than someone attempting to come off like an expert when he or she is not.

Women's Formal Wear—Evening

SEE ALSO *Men's Formal Wear—Evening.*

The length of gloves and kinds of fabrics used to determine how dressed up a woman was. Long, or sixteen-button, gloves were worn on the most formal occasions, when men wore white tie, and dressy fabrics such as chiffon, satin, faille, lace, and moiré were used only in evening clothes. These fabrics are still reserved for evening formal wear, but women now wear cashmere, cotton, silk, and linen evening dresses, too, when the mood suits them. Gloves may or may not be worn on any formal occasion, with the exception of the White House, where they are usually worn for all white-tie events. As you can see, the standards for

women's formal evening wear have evolved into some highly individual looks. Women even wear pants or culottes on some semiformal occasions when they are currently fashionable.

"Black-tie" clothes for women are very much tied to what is currently fashionable, and the term usually means that a woman may wear anything from a cocktail dress or dressy suit of street length to a long evening dress. Gloves may or may not be worn.

A woman may dress up more than a man on most occasions. For example, she may wear dressy evening clothes when the man wears a dark suit instead of black tie. She cannot properly dress down, however, when he is wearing white tie.

White tie, especially at the White House, calls for women to wear long evening dresses and long white gloves. Hats are never worn with evening dresses, although this does not rule out dressy hair ornaments.

For both black- and white-tie events, a woman may wear her most glittery jewels.

Evening clothes are not properly worn except at evening events. Guests at daytime weddings, for example, should wear street clothes, even though the wedding party is dressed more formally.

Women's Social Titles

SEE ALSO *Ma'am; Maiden Name; Names; Signature.*

The widely accepted social titles for women are "Mrs.," "Miss," and "Ms." These titles always appear in their abbreviated form. "Miss," which is not an abbreviation, is never written with a period.

MRS. This designation, used in colonial times by any woman of a certain age, is now used only by married women. Upon marriage a woman has the option of becoming "Mrs. John Smith," or, as some women prefer today, "Mrs. Mary Smith." A woman may also retain her maiden name, in which case she does not use "Mrs." at all.

Divorced women may use "Mrs." or "Miss" ("Ms."). A divorced woman used to become "Mrs. Jones Smith," a combination of her maiden and married names, but more often today, she prefers to become "Mrs. Mary Smith" or even to return to her maiden name, for example, "Mary Jones." A divorced woman does not keep her married name ("Mrs. John Smith") because of the confusion that would result if her ex-husband remarried.

MISS. This title designates an unmarried woman. Young girls are also addressed as "Miss Mary Jackson" in correspondence, but a girl need not be introduced as "Miss" until she is eighteen or older.

MS. This title, a product of the women's movement, has taken hold, particularly in business correspondence and in urban areas. When you do not know whether a woman is married or unmarried, a safe way to address correspondence to her is to call her "Ms. Mary Jones."

ESQUIRE. A title formerly reserved for male lawyers, back when all lawyers were men, "Esquire" is now used for male and female lawyers, despite the fact that it sounds odd. It is mostly used on professional correspondence.

M.D. A woman physician uses "M.D." just as any male doctor would. This does become confusing if she marries another doctor and uses his name, in which case correspondence to them would correctly have to be addressed to "Dr. and Dr. Jonah Devon." It is slightly less awkward if she retains her maiden name. In general, I favor less rather than more use of this title socially by women and men. Many of these awkward situations can then be avoided.

Writing Paper

SEE *Stationery.*

Yachting

SEE *Sailing, Yachting, Boating.*

Zipper

SEE *Open Fly.*

Party Checklist

Party Checklist	Service and Tax Reference			
☐ Ashtrays, lighters, matches	*Company/Name*	*Would*	*Would*	*Cost*
☐ Bartenders	*Telephone Number*	*Use*	*Not*	
☐ Candelabra, candles		*Again*	*Use*	
☐ Caterers			*Again*	
☐ Chairs, tables	Bartenders			$_____
☐ China/tableware	_____	☐	☐	
☐ Coatracks and hangers	_____	☐	☐	
☐ Crystal/glass	Caterers			$_____
☐ Decanters	_____	☐	☐	
☐ Decorations	_____	☐	☐	
☐ Entertainment	Entertainment			$_____
☐ Favors	_____	☐	☐	
☐ Finger bowls	_____	☐	☐	
☐ Flowers	Florist			$_____
☐ Food	_____	☐	☐	
☐ Games	_____	☐	☐	
☐ Invitations	Rentals			$_____
☐ Music	_____	☐	☐	
☐ Place cards	_____	☐	☐	
☐ Rentals	Valet Parking			$_____
☐ Silver/flatware	_____	☐	☐	
☐ Table linens	_____	☐	☐	
☐ Tea and coffee service	Waiters/Waitresses			$_____
☐ Trays and platters	_____	☐	☐	
☐ Valet	_____	☐	☐	
☐ Waiters/Waitresses	Other			$_____
☐ Warming plates, hot trays	_____	☐	☐	
☐ _____				
☐ _____				

Tax Notes

_____

_____

_____

Party Checklist

THEME _____ ATTIRE _____

Party Checklist	Service and Tax Reference			
	Company/Name Telephone Number	Would Use Again	Would Not Use Again	Cost
☐ Ashtrays, lighters, matches				
☐ Bartenders				
☐ Candelabra, candles				
☐ Caterers				
☐ Chairs, tables	Bartenders			$_____
☐ China/tableware	_____	☐	☐	
☐ Coatracks and hangers	_____	☐	☐	
☐ Crystal/glass	Caterers			$_____
☐ Decanters	_____	☐	☐	
☐ Decorations	_____	☐	☐	
☐ Entertainment	Entertainment			$_____
☐ Favors	_____	☐	☐	
☐ Finger bowls	_____	☐	☐	
☐ Flowers	Florist			$_____
☐ Food	_____	☐	☐	
☐ Games	_____	☐	☐	
☐ Invitations	Rentals			$_____
☐ Music	_____	☐	☐	
☐ Place cards	_____	☐	☐	
☐ Rentals	Valet Parking			$_____
☐ Silver/flatware	_____	☐	☐	
☐ Table linens	_____	☐	☐	
☐ Tea and coffee service	Waiters/Waitresses			$_____
☐ Trays and platters	_____	☐	☐	
☐ Valet	_____	☐	☐	
☐ Waiters/Waitresses	Other			$_____
☐ Warming plates, hot trays	_____	☐	☐	
☐ _____				
☐ _____				

Tax Notes

_____

_____

_____

Party Checklist

THEME _____ ATTIRE _____

Party Checklist	Service and Tax Reference			
	Company/Name *Telephone Number*	*Would Use Again*	*Would Not Use Again*	*Cost*
☐ Ashtrays, lighters, matches				
☐ Bartenders				
☐ Candelabra, candles				
☐ Caterers				
☐ Chairs, tables	Bartenders			$_____
☐ China/tableware	_____	☐	☐	
☐ Coatracks and hangers	_____	☐	☐	
☐ Crystal/glass	Caterers			$_____
☐ Decanters	_____	☐	☐	
☐ Decorations	_____	☐	☐	
☐ Entertainment	Entertainment			$_____
☐ Favors	_____	☐	☐	
☐ Finger bowls	_____	☐	☐	
☐ Flowers	Florist			$_____
☐ Food	_____	☐	☐	
☐ Games	_____	☐	☐	
☐ Invitations	Rentals			$_____
☐ Music	_____	☐	☐	
☐ Place cards	_____	☐	☐	
☐ Rentals	Valet Parking			$_____
☐ Silver/flatware	_____	☐	☐	
☐ Table linens	_____	☐	☐	
☐ Tea and coffee service	Waiters/Waitresses			$_____
☐ Trays and platters	_____	☐	☐	
☐ Valet	_____	☐	☐	
☐ Waiters/Waitresses	Other			$_____
☐ Warming plates, hot trays	_____	☐	☐	
☐ _____				
☐ _____				

Tax Notes

_____

_____

_____

Party Checklist

THEME			ATTIRE	

Party Checklist   Service and Tax Reference

Party Checklist	Company/Name Telephone Number	Would Use Again	Would Not Use Again	Cost
☐ Ashtrays, lighters, matches				
☐ Bartenders				
☐ Candelabra, candles				
☐ Caterers				
☐ Chairs, tables	Bartenders			$_____
☐ China/tableware	_____	☐	☐	
☐ Coatracks and hangers	_____	☐	☐	
☐ Crystal/glass	Caterers			$_____
☐ Decanters	_____	☐	☐	
☐ Decorations	_____	☐	☐	
☐ Entertainment	Entertainment			$_____
☐ Favors	_____	☐	☐	
☐ Finger bowls	_____	☐	☐	
☐ Flowers	Florist			$_____
☐ Food	_____	☐	☐	
☐ Games	_____	☐	☐	
☐ Invitations	Rentals			$_____
☐ Music	_____	☐	☐	
☐ Place cards	_____	☐	☐	
☐ Rentals	Valet Parking			$_____
☐ Silver/flatware	_____	☐	☐	
☐ Table linens	_____	☐	☐	
☐ Tea and coffee service	Waiters/Waitresses			$_____
☐ Trays and platters	_____	☐	☐	
☐ Valet	_____	☐	☐	
☐ Waiters/Waitresses	Other			$_____
☐ Warming plates, hot trays	_____	☐	☐	
☐ _____				
☐ _____				

Tax Notes

_____

_____

_____

Easy Checklist for the Bar

THE BASIC BAR

Vodka (2 quarts)
Scotch (2 quarts)
Gin (2 fifths)
Bourbon (1 fifth)
Blended whiskey (1 fifth)
Rum (1 fifth)

Dry vermouth (1 fifth)
Sweet vermouth (1 fifth)
Campari (2 fifths)
Dubonnet (2 fifths)

White wine (3 bottles)
Mineral water (2 large
bottles)

THE COMPLETE BAR

Vodka (2 quarts domestic;
1 fifth imported)
Scotch (2 quarts blended;
1 fifth single malt)
Gin (1 quart domestic; 1
fifth imported)
Bourbon (1 quart)
Tennessee sour mash (1
fifth)
Blended whiskey (1 fifth
American; 1 fifth
Canadian)

Rum (1 fifth Puerto Rican
light; 1 fifth Puerto
Rican golden; 1 fifth
Jamaican dark)
Tequila (1 fifth)
Pernod (1 fifth)
Lillet (1 fifth)
Dubonnet (1 fifth)
Punt É Mes (1 fifth)
Dry vermouth (1 fifth)
Sweet vermouth (2 fifths)

Campari (1 fifth)
White wine (6 bottles
varietal)
Red wine (2 bottles fine
claret)
Champagne (1 bottle
French; 1 bottle
California)
Beer (2 six-packs German
or Dutch)
Creme de Cassis (1 small
bottle)
Mineral water (6 bottles)

BAR EQUIPMENT CHECKLIST

- [ ] Bar cloth, table tray
- [ ] Beverages
- [ ] Bottle caps
- [ ] Bottle opener
- [ ] Coasters
- [ ] Cocktail shakers
- [ ] Cocktail napkins
- [ ] Corkscrew
- [ ] Ice
- [ ] Ice bucket and tongs
- [ ] Jiggers

- [ ] Lemon squeezer
- [ ] Long-handled spoon
- [ ] Mixers
- [ ] Paring knife
- [ ] Strainer
- [ ] Water pitcher, carafes
- [ ] Wine and champagne
  coolers

Garnishes for Drinks:
- [ ] Lemons
- [ ] Oranges

- [ ] Cherries
- [ ] Olives
- [ ] Onions

Glassware:
- [ ] Wineglasses
- [ ] Highballs
- [ ] Old-fashioneds
- [ ] Brandy snifters
- [ ] Goblets
- [ ] Champagnes
- [ ] Cordials

Wine Chart

BEFORE DINNER

Dry sherry	Dubonnet	Light sauterne
Madeira	Vermouth	Champagne

DURING THE MEAL

White wines before red
Dry wines before sweet
Light wines before heavy
Young wines before old
Oysters or Clams:
  Chablis
  Rhine
  Moselle
  Dry champagne
Melon:
  Medium sherry
  Sweet sauterne
  Madeira
Soup:
  Light dry sherry
  White burgundy
  Graves
  Beaujolais
Fish:
  Moselle
  Chablis
  Rhine
  White burgundy
  Sauvignon blanc
  Soave
Entrées:
  Light claret
  Chianti
  Light red burgundy
  Cabernet sauvignon
  Saint-Emilion

Roasts:
  Still or sparkling
  burgundy
  Rich red claret
  Zinfandel
  Chianti
Game:
  Wild duck—burgundy
  Rabbit—claret or
  burgundy
  Grouse—burgundy
  Partridge—claret
  Venison—burgundy
  Pheasant—claret or
  burgundy
  Quail—champagne
  Hare—burgundy
  Woodcock—burgundy
Poultry:
  Chicken—champagne
  or chenin blanc
  Turkey—claret or
  medium burgundy
  Duck—Rhine wine or
  burgundy
  Goose—burgundy or
  champagne
  Squab—champagne or
  sauterne
Steaks and chops:
  Claret
  Burgundy
  Dry champagne

Ham:
  Claret
  Champagne
Spaghetti:
  Claret
  Chianti
  Valpolicella
Salad:
  No wine
Cheese:
  Mild cheeses—claret or
  burgundy
  Stronger cheeses—port,
  sherry, madeira, or
  tokay
Dessert:
  Sweet champagne
  Sweet sauterne
  Port
  Madeira
  Muscatel

AFTER DINNER

Brandy	Marsala	Port
Cognac	Madeira	Angelica
Liqueurs	Tokay	

Host and Hostess Dinner Party Record

DATE: _____

GUESTS: _____

_____

_____

_____

WINE SERVED AND COMMENTS: _____

_____

FOOD SERVED AND COMMENTS: _____

_____

_____

_____

DATE: _____

GUESTS: _____

_____

_____

_____

WINE SERVED AND COMMENTS: _____

_____

FOOD SERVED AND COMMENTS: _____

_____

_____

_____

Host and Hostess Dinner Party Record

DATE: _____

GUESTS: _____
_____
_____
_____

WINE SERVED AND COMMENTS: _____
_____

FOOD SERVED AND COMMENTS: _____
_____
_____
_____

DATE: _____

GUESTS: _____
_____
_____
_____

WINE SERVED AND COMMENTS: _____
_____

FOOD SERVED AND COMMENTS: _____
_____
_____
_____

Host and Hostess Dinner Party Record

DATE: _____

GUESTS: _____
_____
_____
_____

WINE SERVED AND COMMENTS: _____
_____

FOOD SERVED AND COMMENTS: _____
_____
_____
_____

DATE: _____

GUESTS: _____
_____
_____
_____

WINE SERVED AND COMMENTS: _____
_____

FOOD SERVED AND COMMENTS: _____
_____
_____
_____

Host and Hostess Dinner Party Record

DATE: _____

GUESTS: _____
_____
_____
_____

WINE SERVED AND COMMENTS: _____
_____

FOOD SERVED AND COMMENTS: _____
_____
_____
_____

DATE: _____

GUESTS: _____
_____
_____
_____

WINE SERVED AND COMMENTS: _____
_____

FOOD SERVED AND COMMENTS: _____
_____
_____
_____